MARKETING DECISIONS UNDER UNCERTAINTY

INTERNATIONAL SERIES
IN QUANTITATIVE MARKETING

Editor:

Jehoshua Eliashberg
The Wharton School
University of Pennsylvania
Philadelphia, Pennsylvania, U.S.A.

Other books in the series:

MARKETING DECISIONS UNDER UNCERTAINTY

DUNG NGUYEN
University of Pittsburgh

KLUWER ACADEMIC PUBLISHERS
Boston/Dordrecht/London

Distributors for North America:
Kluwer Academic Publishers
101 Philip Drive
Assinippi Park
Norwell, Massachusetts 02061 USA

Distributors for all other countries:
Kluwer Academic Publishers Group
Distribution Centre
Post Office Box 322
3300 AH Dordrecht, THE NETHERLANDS

Library of Congress Cataloging-in-Publication Data

A C.I.P. Catalogue record for this book is available from the Library of Congress.

Printed on acid-free paper.

Printed in the United States of America
JK

To
Chau and Quynh Thanh

CONTENTS

PREFACE

Remarkable advance in quantitative marketing research in the last two decades, incorporating applied microeconomic theories, operations research and management applications, has brought the field of marketing alongside with finance, accounting and production to within an executive's reach for a sophisticated toolbox for decision-making in an increasingly competitive and complex business environment. A quick look at *Marketing*, a recently published book edited by Eliashberg and Lilien would indicate even to the casual reader the extent of such methodological progress made by marketing scholars. Even in such an impressive and nearly exhaustive collection of topics, with the notable exception pointed out by the editors of applications of the scanner data, and in spite of the reference to it, an important omission is related to the issues of marketing decisions under conditions of uncertainty. It is fairly obvious to the marketing executive and academician alike to recognize the important role uncertainty plays in marketing decisions such as pricing, promotion, advertising, sales force management, and others.

The major purpose of this study is to address certain major marketing decision variables within the general context of an uncertain environment. While there have been significant progresses in analyzing marketing behaviors in a stochastic environment, the sources scatter among different management and marketing journals; and to the extent that these issues are addressed at all, they have aimed mainly at each separate, specific topic at a time. Thus, our effort to bring these studies together in the same framework should facilitate our in-depth analysis of these important phenomena. My approach here will not only allow a useful synthesis but will also identify and explore issues which have remained open for further research.

While the theory of consumer choice has been significantly enriched with stochastic generalizations, it will not be a central theme in this work. Instead, it is the decisions of the firms which form the basic framework in our inquiry. First, I shall start by focusing on a number of major marketing decisions facing the firm; each particular marketing activity is analyzed in isolation from others. These issues include the analysis of pricing decisions, advertising, sales promotion, and salesforce compensation and management. Second, I then identify and study a number of topics in which the driving force is the potential interaction among the firm's marketing efforts. Included in the subjects considered are the marketing mix problem, the more recent work on the joint production-marketing decision-making and the multiple-product firms. I will choose to address these interactive activities within a number of contexts: market shares analyses, the production-inventory-marketing framework, the diffusion processes, and issues of competition. Finally, I will conclude by specifically examining certain dynamic characterizations of the firm's decision process on the basis of an experimentation-adaptive control problem and reporting a sample of some limited empirical work on the subject.

While this book is written mainly with marketing, applied economics graduate students and researchers in mind, I am also aware that marketing executives are keenly interested in applying sophisticated mathematical techniques to their marketing decisions and strategies. Further, even when certain models have not been developed to the extent that a complete implementation is feasible, the insights obtained from theoretical analyses can often complement the executive's decision-making which may be based on other approaches as well as his own judgement. With that as a motivational background, I will attempt to develop the models and the arguments with an emphasis on intuition and interpretations instead of dwelling on the very technicality of the various mathematical derivations. Consequently, it is hoped that the book will serve as a reference for academicians as well as a handbook for practical decision makers.

While I have tried to at least refer to the available literature relevant to our current study and of which I am aware, the book is not intended to represent a literature survey in the usual sense of the word. Rather, to a large extent, it reflects my own interpretation and emphasis on topics which I have done original research in, and which are, I believe, particularly important and relevant from a managerial point of view.

From my perspective, only when one is deeply engaged in doing extensive research for a project of this sort can one begin to truly sense the heavy intellectual debt accumulated over the years to one's teachers, colleagues, and other researchers in the field. I should like to take this opportunity to particularly acknowledge with profound gratitude the intellectual influence of Professor Jose Encarnacion during the formative years of my academic development. I am most fortunate to be able to work on this project under the editorship of Professor Jehoshua Eliashberg of Wharton School who offers encouragement and helpful comments on an earlier draft of the book for which I am very thankful. To the two reviewers who thoroughly read and commented on an earlier version of the manuscript, I am indebted to them indeed. Further, I am very grateful to Julie Kaczynski who, as Kluwer's Acquisition Editor, has offered professional guidance and encouragement throughout various stages of the project's development. Finally, I wish to thank the Institute for Operations Research and the Management Sciences (INFORMS); Elsevier Science Inc.; the University of Chicago Press; and the editors of the *American Journal of Agricultural Economics* and *Southern Economic Journal* for their kind permissions to reprint with modifications some of my papers published originally in their journals.

Pittsburgh, Pennsylvania

GLOSSARY OF SYMBOLS

Indices
I, II,... brand I, II, ..., N
i, j the i, j-th brand, the i, j-th firm, etc.
$-i$ other firms in the industry, except firm i
k index of the decision variables in the marketing mix
$t=1,2,...,T$ time index

Parameters
$\alpha, \beta, \gamma, \nu$ coefficients in sales response functions, etc.
a, b demand coefficients; other deterministic parameters; estimates of α, β, etc.
c constant average, marginal production cost
d constant parameter, usually associated with cost function

Variables
A advertising budget; also attraction
B low-productivity workers
$c(.)$ average production cost function
$C(.)$ cost function
D depth of discount ($D=r-s$); industry's total attraction, $D \equiv \sum_{j=1}^{n} A_j$
DIS discount percentage
$E(.)$ expectations operator
$f(.)$ demand function, sales response function
FC fixed cost
$g(.)$ inverse demand function
G goodwill; high-productivity workers
h effort
$h(.)$ implicit demand function, sales response function
H hours
I investment
J Hessian matrix
k competitive price-reaction elasticity
L salesforce
m marketing activity, usually referring to advertising
M industry's marketing budget, $M = \sum_{j=1}^{n} m_j$
MC marginal cost
MCI multiplicative competitive interaction models
MNL multinomial logistic models

n	number of competitors; also length of a sales cycle
N	number of brands; also number of consumers
p	unit product price
$\bar{p}$	average price
q_i	firm i's sales
Q	industry sales
Q_t	cumulative sales
r	the Pratt-Arrow index of risk aversion; discount rate; regular price
R	conjectural variation
s	market share; sales price
S	market size
T	matrix transposition operator
TR	total revenue
$U(.)$	utility function
V	value of firm; objective of the firm
w	selling cost per salesperson
W	selling cost
$\mathbf{x}$	vector of the firm's marketing variables
y	a random variable; also production when different from quantity demanded
z	Wiener process
γ	product quality index
δ	depreciation rate
∂	partial differentiation operator
ε	(absolute value of) own price elasticity of demand
ε_i	sales elasticity with respect to decision variable i
ζ	random sales, demand
η	cross-price elasticity, other elasticity concepts
θ	index of consumer deal-proneness; heterogeneous salesforce, etc.
κ	rate of culling
λ	shadow price
μ	mean
ξ	random error term
π	probability
Π	profit
ρ	discount factor
σ^2	population variance
$\varphi(.)$	density function
$\Phi(.)$	cumulative distribution function
ψ	vector of relevant information
Ω	variance-covariance matrix

Part I

BACKGROUND AND COMPONENTS OF THE MARKETING MIX

1

INTRODUCTION

The main purpose of this introductory chapter is two-fold, first to give an overview of the major issues addressed in the book, on a chapter by chapter basis, and second, to set up some of the basic analytical framework which we will often refer to throughout the book. We will find it useful to devote a technical-oriented section on the discrete stochastic dynamic programming method which underlines the solution approach we use in several contexts examined in the book as well. As we seek to follow a rather uniform notation, the materials presented in this chapter should familiarize the reader from the very beginning with some of the frequently used notation employed throughout the book.

One of the more fundamental assumptions in most analyses in management sciences and social sciences in general is that decision makers possess perfect knowledge about the environment in which they operate. This assumption has been seriously challenged in various studies which take into account the fact that managerial strategies are typically formulated within an uncertain world. Not unlike the introduction of time dimension which has transformed management, economics and finance into sciences with important dynamic characterizations, incorporating uncertainty and risk-taking attitude allows one to understand countless observed phenomena and social behaviors otherwise unexplainable. Within management science, the field of finance has benefited greatly from the development of economics of uncertainty. On the other hand, while stochasticity has played a crucial role in recent advances in theories of consumer behavior and choice (Lilien, Kotler, and Moorthy [1992], Chapter 2), the impact of uncertainty on the firm's marketing decisions has not been addressed systematically in the literature. In this regard, it may also be helpful to use the classification scheme proposed by Eliashberg and

Chatterjee[1985] who distinguish structural stochasticity from parameter stochasticity. It is the latter category which is of direct concern to us in most of this work. Thus, while uncertainty can arise in different forms and from different sources, we will typically capture its presence by specifying certain random sales response functions related to the firm's various marketing activities such as pricing, producing, advertising, price promotion, and personal selling.   In different contexts of competition and planning horizon, we will examine how and if market uncertainty and the firm's attitude toward risk would affect the firm's marketing and other managerial strategies. We first turn to an overview and organization of the materials to be analyzed in the book.

1 OVERVIEW

In what follows in this chapter, we will present the standard marketing mix model with some of their well-known properties which have been obtained and analyzed in a deterministic framework. Our motivation here is, to a large extent, to present the firm's various marketing and other relevant decision variables in a common theoretical framework with a uniform notation to set up the background for our investigation of the impact of various conditions of market uncertainty. We do so in a calculated effort to integrate and in many instances explore the potential interactions among these different marketing variables. An important example of course is the well-known marketing mix problem which is quite unique in the field of marketing, started out with the famous Dorfman-Steiner model [1954]. Another example would be the joint output production and marketing decision process by work done recently by Eliashberg and Steinberg [1993]. Also, the effect of the salesforce operating within the firm's integrating decision framework has largely been neglected.

Chapter 2, entitled Pricing Under Uncertainty, specifically addresses situations in which pricing decisions represent the major marketing activity. There the role of pricing is isolated so that the impact of demand uncertainty and risk-taking behavior can be seen more clearly in a number of different contexts such as dynamics and multiple-product firms. While we seek to analyze the firm's pricing decision in isolation, we will nevertheless make every effort to at least point to the direction where price and other decision variables may interact. Thus, we will also address the implications for the different modes of pricing vs. producing decision-making under random demand.

Chapter 3, Advertising Under Uncertainty, focuses exclusively on the issue of optimal advertising under conditions of uncertainty. The main advantage of such an isolated consideration is once again to allow us to get more clear-cut results and hence managerial implications can be seen in a more direct fashion. However, since we will have covered the pricing decision in Chapter 1, we will be in a better position to make additional assessments on the potential interactions among certain marketing variables. We will, as usual, consider first the static framework and then extend it to an intertemporal framework where dynamic considerations are explicitly taken into account. Further, we will then address the optimal advertising decision making within the context of a multi-product, multi-brand firm.

Chapter 4, Price Promotions, addresses a special issue in the general topic of pricing which represents a very common marketing activity. Unlike the advertising literature, the academic literature on sales promotion has a more modest history. However, its importance in both marketing practice as well as in academic research has been realized more fully in recent years. As in much of the literature, we will highlight the role of heterogeneity in consumer information in affecting the firm's optimal pricing policy. While there are different forms of sales promotion, we will only emphasize the issue of price discount for consumers, leaving aside other promotional issues like trade promotions and retailer promotions for further studies.

Chapter 5, Salesforce Size, Compensation and Labor Heterogeneity, examines again the salesforce issues separately from the firm's other marketing mix variables. We will find it necessary to address the issue from both the static and the dynamic perspective of the firm. It should also be noted that the literature dealing with an unknown environment typically concentrates on agency problems in which the agent's efforts are not known and observed by the firm's manager. Since this particular topic has been examined in a number of readily available surveys, we will only be very brief in our analysis in this chapter. On the other hand, one particular item which is essential in the firm's salesforce operations and yet hardly addressed in the marketing literature is concerned with the issue of labor quality and its relation to pay. For the labor market, labor quality is basically uncertain; thus it is natural for us to develop this particular theme in this chapter.

Chapter 6, Market Share and Diffusion Models, represents specific contexts within which different marketing activities jointly operate. Regarding market share models, there exists a variety of formulations, among the most well-known is a class of the multiplicative competitive interaction models (MCI) with both empirical and normative implications. Since the strategic and equilibrium implications for empirically popular multinomial logistic models (MNL) have not been available, we will address this type of models in some detail here. We then report a number of studies which examine the stochastic extensions of well-known diffusion models and in doing so, the effects of uncertainty on the firm's diffusion processes and its managerial implications will be considered.

Chapter 7, Marketing, Inventory and Production Decisions, considers efforts to modify the traditional operations research approach to production and inventory modelling in order to take into account the firm's marketing functions. Of particular interest for us here, of course, is the treatment of demand uncertainty as well as other forms of randomness within the firm's operating environments. We will examine both the short-run considerations with the explicit role of inventory when appropriate as well as the long-run analysis where capital investment plays an essential role. In each of these scenarios, we will pay particular attention to the way the firm's pricing interacts with other production and investment activities.

Chapter 8, Competitive Marketing Strategies, concentrates on the treatment of the firm's decisions in a competitive environment subject to demand and other sources of uncertainty. The chapter addresses competitive issues which we will have intentionally left aside as we consider different components of the marketing mix in the earlier chapters. The analysis is mainly based on equilibrium concepts formalized in game theoretic modelling; even though we will also examine partial equilibrium approaches where a particular firm's marketing decision is made on the basis of the chosen decisions of the other firms in the market. For convenience, we will organize our presentation on the basis of the different major marketing decision variables such as pricing, advertising and production.

Chapter 9, Adaptive Behavior, Experimentation and Some Empirical Results, specifically addresses approaches to operationalize some of the theoretical development to deal with the general subject of marketing decision-making under uncertainty. Of particular interest in our presentation is the notion that the firm experiments in order to learn more about certain parameters of the sales response function. We will also report a number of simulation and econometric exercises in which aspects of uncertainty in the sales response are explicitly present. As such, we will not dwell on time-series studies which mainly focus on data analyses and on empirical decision models which typically use simulations methods.

Chapter 10, Concluding Notes, ends the book with a brief summary and general topical suggestions for future research.

2 A GENERAL DETERMINISTIC, STATIC FRAMEWORK

We report here perhaps a most integrative theoretical structure within the context of a normative, deterministic, static framework that triggers a very large literature in research in marketing, both theoretical and empirical. The Dorfman-Steiner paper, published originally in 1954, builds the foundation for what has become known as the marketing mix models. Other highly successful integrative analyses fall under the general approach called decision models which are not of immediate interest to us in this work. We are here thus more concerned with the normative implications of the various models of marketing decisions.

We consider a general static framework in which the sales response function is assumed to have the following form:

$$q = f(p, m, \gamma, L) \tag{1.1}$$

where q denotes the quantity sold, p the product price, m represents the extent of the marketing activity exemplified specifically by advertising spending, γ represents certain index of product quality, and L denotes the level of the salesforce.

We typically use the notation $f(.)$ to designate a demand function or a sales response function specified with the various arguments or marketing choices. As usual, we will assume that the quantity sold varies inversely with respect to the product price and that advertising, product quality and selling efforts all positively affect the firm's sales. While further assumptions regarding the second partial derivatives of q with respect to each of the arguments on the right hand side of the preceding demand specification can be made here, we will need to do so only within certain specific contexts later so that their significance can be seen more clearly.

The firm's objective function is to maximize the one-period profit Π defined to be:

$$\Pi = [p - c(\gamma)]q - m - wL - FC$$
$$= [p - c(\gamma)][f(p, m, \gamma, L)] - m - wL - FC$$

(1.2)

where $c(\gamma)$ denotes the *average* cost function, w the selling cost per salesperson, and FC represents the firm's fixed cost.

We should make a number of remarks here regarding the firm's cost specification. For the most part, since we will be mainly concerned with marketing aspects of the firm decision, we will typically assume *constant* average and thus marginal production or acquisition cost. Here, the presence of the product quality dimension dictates that a variable average cost be assumed. Clearly, it is most reasonable to assume that higher quality requires higher cost. With respect to the cost of marketing efforts, more specifically advertising spending, we will very often assume the monetary value for this variable, thus sidestep from important implications of the issue of diminishing returns in advertising. Only when this particular issue arises and we specifically address it, the variable m will enter both as the cost of advertising and a determinant of the sales equation. Getting back to the firm's maximization in (1.2), the first-order conditions for optimality can then be determined as follows:

$$\frac{\partial \Pi}{\partial p} = 0 \implies q + (p - c)\frac{\partial q}{\partial p} = 0 \tag{1.3}$$

$$\frac{\partial \Pi}{\partial m} = 0 \implies (p - c)\frac{\partial q}{\partial m} = 1 \tag{1.4}$$

$$\frac{\partial \Pi}{\partial L} = 0 \implies (p - c)\frac{\partial q}{\partial L} = w \tag{1.5}$$

$$\frac{\partial \Pi}{\partial \gamma} = 0 \implies (p - c)\frac{\partial q}{\partial \gamma} = q\frac{\partial c(\gamma)}{\partial \gamma} \tag{1.6}$$

where partial derivatives are expressed by the operator ∂ as usual.

Clearly, managerial implications can be immediately given. Eq. (1.3) is the familiar requirement that marginal revenue be equal to marginal cost; eq. (1.4) represents the condition that a one-dollar advertising expenditure be equal to its contribution to the firm's net profit at the margin; eq. (1.5) simply requires that the salesforce will increase until the marginal salesperson yields net profit exactly equal to his or her compensation. Eq. (1.6) indicates that the quality be chosen so that its marginal net profit justifies its marginal cost.

Further, the preceding conditions can be expressed in terms of various notions of elasticity as follows:

$$\varepsilon = \frac{pq}{m}\varepsilon_m = \frac{pq}{wL}\varepsilon_L = \frac{p}{\gamma\frac{\partial c(\gamma)}{\partial \gamma}}\varepsilon_\gamma \qquad (1.7)$$

where ε denotes absolute value of the own price elasticity of demand, ε_i represents sales elasticity with respect to the decision variable i; $i = m, L, \gamma$ for advertising, salesforce size, and quality, respectively.

As a side remark on the notation, we will use ε_i for demand elasticities with respect to various choice variables and typically use η to denote other notions of elasticities.

While we have formulated this general problem in terms of the four decision variables of price, advertising, quality and salesforce, it can be easily seen that similar results can be obtained for different sets of decision variables. In particular, the presence of the expenditure for distribution can be incorporated with slight and obvious modifications of the model's specifications. The resulting elasticity conditions summarized in (1.7) can be written as:

$$\varepsilon = \frac{pq}{m}\varepsilon_m = \frac{pq}{wL}\varepsilon_L = \frac{p}{\gamma\frac{\partial c(\gamma)}{\partial \gamma}}\varepsilon_\gamma = \frac{pq}{D}\varepsilon_D \qquad (1.7a)$$

where the new notation is obvious with D representing the distribution spending.

Depending on contexts, we invariably work with different subsets of the preceding marketing and other decision variables. For instance, in Chapter 5 we will present a model by Jagpal and Brick [1982] who use a valuation approach in finance literature to assess the potential impact of uncertainty on the basis of this marketing mix model. In addition, within a deterministic framework, the above conditions have been extended by Lambin, Naert, and Bultez [1975] and Hanssens [1980] for the case of a competitive market structure, a subject we will address in Chapter 8.

3 A STOCHASTIC FRAMEWORK: STATICS

As we begin to set up the model in order to examine the impact of uncertainty and the firm's risk-taking behavior, it will be important to modify the objective function as well as the specifications for the firm's sales response functions. For simplicity of presentation we will presently work with a simplest form of demand specification where price is the only decision variable. In other word, one can generally write the random demand function in the following implicit form (see Leland [1972], among others):

$$h(q,\mathbf{x},\xi)=0 \qquad (1.8)$$

where $\mathbf{x}\equiv\{x_1,x_2,...,x_k\}$ denotes the vector of the firm's k decision variables, e.g., $\mathbf{x}\equiv\{p,m,D\}$, and ξ is a random disturbance term with known density function $\varphi(\xi)$.

More specifically, assuming that for a given set of marketing mix $\mathbf{x}$, the conditional density of sales can be specified as $\varphi(q|\mathbf{x})$, and assume further the von Neumann-Morgenstern utility function $U(\Pi)$, the firm's objective is to maximize its expected utility of profits defined to be:

$$E\{U[\Pi(q)]|\mathbf{x}\} = \int U\{\Pi(q)\}\varphi(q|\mathbf{x})dq$$
$$= \int U[pq-C(q)-FC]\varphi(q|\mathbf{x})dq \qquad (1.9)$$

where $C(q)$ denotes the known variable cost function and FC the firm's fixed cost.

We will typically consider a problem such as above where the implicit demand is expressed as a sales response function to a single marketing variable or certain combinations of the firm's marketing mix. The clear exception is when the production choice constitutes a part of its decision process. In the latter cases, one would express the implicit demand in form of an inverse demand equation. In this chapter, we will present the analysis in terms of the sales response specification.

We should also note that the utility function is generally non-linear and hence it would include the risk-neutral firm (with a linear utility function) as a special case. As usual, we assume positive marginal utility everywhere with increasing (constant, decreasing) marginal utility for the risk-preferred (risk-neutral, risk-averse) firm. Symbolically, we assume that:

$$U'(\Pi) = \partial U(\Pi)/\partial\Pi > 0 \qquad (1.10a)$$

$$\text{and} \quad U''(\Pi) = \partial^2 U(\Pi)/\partial\Pi^2 \begin{bmatrix} >0 \text{ for risk preference} \\ =0 \text{ for risk neutrality} \\ <0 \text{ for risk aversion} \end{bmatrix}. \qquad (1.10b)$$

It should be noted that in those situations where there are more than one decision makers in the firm, it may not be possible to represent the firm's behavior by a single well-behaved utility function. This difficulty was first formally shown in Arrow's famous Impossibility Theorem [1963] regarding the existence of a social welfare function for a group of individuals. There exists a large literature on this subject of social choice after the publication of Arrow's work. However, it should be pointed out that there are numerous successful attempts in the literature to show that it is possible to transform individuals' utility functions into a social welfare function if certain "reasonable" conditions are satisfied. See, for instance, Keeney and Kirkwood [1975], Bailey [1979], and Eliashberg and Winkler [1981]. Also, empirical justifications to the use of cardinal utility functions are given in Swalm [1966].

Further, we typically assume positive marginal cost in the variable cost function, i.e., $\partial C(q)/\partial q = C'(q) > 0$; the shape of the marginal cost will be specified in each particular context.

Under appropriate assumptions regarding the third-order and higher-order moments, the expected utility expression in (1.9) can be approximated by a Taylor's series expansion about $E(\Pi)$ as

$$E[U(\Pi)] = U[E(\Pi)] + \frac{1}{2}U''E(\Pi - E\Pi)^2$$

where, for notational simplicity, we have suppressed the sales variable q in the firm's profit function as well as the conditional operator.

With a typical decision variable x, the first-order conditions for optimality can be expressed as

$$\{U' + \frac{1}{2}[E(\Pi - E\Pi)^2]U'''\}\frac{\partial E(\Pi)}{\partial x}$$

$$= -\frac{1}{2}U''[\frac{dE(\Pi - E\Pi)^2}{dx}]$$

which, upon assuming a quadratic utility function, i.e., $U''' = 0$, would become

$$\frac{\partial E(\Pi)}{\partial x} = -\frac{1}{2}(\frac{U''}{U'})[\frac{dE(\Pi - E\Pi)^2}{dx}].$$

Noting that one can define an index of risk aversion $r = -U''/U'$ following the Pratt-Arrow definition (Pratt [1964]; Arrow [1965]), let us rewrite the preceding condition as

$$\frac{\partial E(\Pi)}{\partial x} = \frac{1}{2}r[\frac{dE(\Pi - E\Pi)^2}{dx}]$$

based on which the assessment of the impact of risk-taking attitude and uncertainty in the sales response function can be made.

Detailed analysis of earlier development of the static stochastic framework can be found in Horowitz [1970].

4 A STOCHASTIC FRAMEWORK: DYNAMICS

4.1 Preliminaries

First, for ease of reference, let us record here the relationship between the static and the dynamic specifications within the deterministic framework. Further, to simplify the presentation, we will assume in the following analysis that price is the only decision variable which affects the demand facing the firm. Thus, for a one-period demand function under certainty, the standard specification can be written in the implicit form:

$$h(p,q)=0 \qquad (1.11)$$

where the usual assumption of a well-behaved demand curve would involve an inverse relationship between p and q.

A static extension of this equation to a multi-period demand function under certainty would be:

$$h(p_t,q_t)=0 \qquad (1.12)$$

where again, p_t and q_t are known with certainty for any period t; $t = 1,2, ...,T$ where $T \geq 2$.

Correspondingly, one might postulate that a multi-period random demand function is of the following form:

$$h(p_t,q_t,\xi_t)=0 \qquad (1.13)$$

where the ξ_t's are random disturbances with known densities, $t = 1,2,...,T$.

Clearly, the preceding random demand specification may not be the most general one as we can still extend it further in a number of ways. There exist several important dynamic versions of this specification. We will note with special interest two particular ones here. The first is the dynamic advertising model of Nerlove and Arrow [1962] (recall that we use price variable only for presentation purposes) and the second is the diffusions process of the Bass type [1969]. However, we will treat these types of models in certain contexts later. Here, our comments will address other scenarios where dynamic characterizations can arise. To that end, let us suppose that the implicit form of a multi-period random demand can be written as follows:

$$h(\beta, \psi^{t-1}, p_t, q_t, \xi_t) = 0 \tag{1.14}$$

where ξ_t's are random disturbances whose densities depend on an unknown parameter λ, β represents a time-invariant unknown parameter of the response function, and ψ^{t-1} is a vector of information which can be defined in our framework as:

$$\psi^{t-1} \equiv \{p_0, p_1, \ldots, p_{t-1}; q_0, q_1, \ldots, q_{t-1}\} \equiv \{p^{t-1}, q^{t-1}\} \tag{1.15}$$

where $p^{t-1} = \{p_0, p_1, \ldots, p_{t-1}\}$; and $q^{t-1} = \{q_0, q_1, \ldots, q_{t-1}\}$.

A number of comments on eq. (1.14) are in order:

(*i*) When the parameter β is completely known, and the density function of ξ_t is subjectively known (and so is λ), eq. (1.14) represents an extension of eq. (1.13) in the following sense. The presence of the term ψ^{t-1} implies that the relation between price level and quantity demanded is not static. From the view-point of a price-setting firm, for example, in addition to the current price level, sales in previous periods may have some effects on current sales as well. A simple example for such a situation can be given as:

$$h(q_t, q_{t-1}, p_t, \xi_t) = 0. \tag{1.14a}$$

It seems that a complete specification for the demand equation is subject to empirical considerations rather than a purely theoretical assumption. For full generality, we will be using the demand function described in eq. (1.14) in our discussion which follows.

(*ii*) When all lagged variables are absent in eq. (1.14) while the value of β is known with certainty, eq. (1.14) represents another extension of (1.13). The resulting demand function would be interesting in our framework of an adaptive environment since the monopolist, facing an unknown parameter λ, may be capable of learning more about the density functions of ξ_t's through time. Under this situation, the model thus generated would allow for the revision of the firm's expectations based on information which is accumulated through time. A standard treatment of this learning possibility would involve the assumption of a Bayesian expectation revision scheme a detailed description of which will be presented within different contexts in the book. (See, for example, Raiffa and Schlaifer [1963] and DeGroot [1970]).

(*iii*)   If we assume that the random disturbance terms ξ_t's possess known probability density functions while the value of β is unknown, we are dealing with another interesting case of adaptive behavior for the monopolistic firm. When the value of β is not known, it is necessary to express explicitly the argument β as in eq. (1.14). In line with our interest in the assumption of the firm's adaptive behavior, the monopolist is supposed to attempt to learn more about the true value of β through time. In a simple case of a single parameter β (that is, β is a scalar instead of a vector), one can interpret the preceding notion of learning about β as an experimentation. To put it more clearly, the firm would be involved in some kind of experimentation in order to gain more information about the true value of β. Again, a Bayesian approach will be used to analyze this problem. A full description of this method applied specifically to certain contexts, in particular those contained in Chapter 9 will be presented when appropriate.

In the following presentation, we will work with the demand equation implied in item (i) above. That is, we will assume a complete absence of learning and experimentation on the part of the firm. The dynamic characteristic of our problem as compared to static models such as Baron [1971] and Leland [1972] arises because of the presence of the lagged variables in the demand specification.

On the other hand, other demand functions as implied in items (ii) and (iii) are subjects for discussion in the various chapters which follow. Since it is possible for the firm to learn about some unknown parameters in the demand equation, we will also analyze the issues of value of information, cost of information in those models throughout the book.

4.2 The Monopolistic Firm's Maximization Problem

With a known discount factor, let us assume that the firm's objective is to maximize the expected value of the discounted sum of utilities $U(\Pi_t)$ over the planning horizon T, conditional on the initial information vector ψ°:

$$\text{Max. } E[\sum_{t=1}^{T} \rho^t U(\Pi_t) | \psi^0] \qquad (1.16)$$

where E denotes the expectation operator, ρ the firm's discount factor, and the profit function Π_t in period t is defined as:

$$\Pi_t = p_t q_t - C(q_t) - FC \qquad (1.2a)$$

where, as before, $C(q_t)$ is the known variable cost function and FC is the fixed cost. We also assume that T is finite and that $T \geq 2$.

Clearly, the utility function shown in eq. (1.16) is of an additive separable type. This characteristic of the utility function will enable us to make use of the dynamic programming technique in solving our maximization problem.

For simplicity of exposition, in this chapter we will work with a variant of the random demand function shown in eq. (1.14) as follows:

$$q_t = f(p_t, \psi^{t-1}, \xi_t) \qquad (1.14b)$$

where it will be recalled that the random disturbances ξ_t's possess known probability density functions.

It should be clear that equations (1.16), (1.2a), and (1.14b) constitute our intertemporal optimization problem which may involve finding either optimal levels of quantity produced or price levels set. It is important to note here that under certainty, the price-setting strategy and the quantity-setting strategy are equivalent for a monopolist. The reason is that the demand function of the form $p_t = f(q_t)$ is assumed to have the monotonic transformation property; hence one would have $q_t = f^{-1}(p_t) = g(p_t)$ where f^{-1} is the inverse function of f, assuming its existence; the function $g(.)$ typically denotes inverse demand specifications. In this case, one is free to work with either p_t or q_t as the decision variable without changing the conclusion.

Under the stochastic specification of the demand function of the form shown in (1.14b), however, one has to distinguish between the price-setting strategy and the quantity-setting strategy since it has been shown in the literature that the choice of the decision variable is capable of producing different final results. See, for example, Leland and Baron. We will encounter this particular issue again in the competitive framework of Chapter 8. We have mentioned above that only the price-setting case is discussed in the present chapter while the quantity-setting case will be analyzed in later chapters.

Thus, for a firm which uses the price-setting strategy, its optimization problem can be summarized as

$$\text{Max. } E\{\textstyle\sum_{t=1}^{T} \rho^t U[\Pi_t(p_t, q_t)] \,|\, \psi^0\} \tag{1.16a}$$
$$\{p_t\}_{t=1}^{T}$$

$$\text{Subject to } \Pi_t = p_t q_t - C(q_t) - FC \tag{1.2a}$$

$$\text{and } q_t = f(p_t, \psi^{t-1}, \xi_t). \tag{1.14b}$$

In any period t within the planning horizon, the monopolist is assumed to make a decision about the product price p_t before the realization of the disturbance term ξ_t. Then, after a level p_t is determined, the firm will be able to observe the corresponding sales level which is ultimately realized depending upon the behavior of the random term ξ_t. The chosen price and its corresponding observed sales level will then become new elements in the firm's vector of information which will be used for the next period's decision problem.

The preceding problem in (1.16a) can be solved by the standard method of stochastic dynamic programming an exposition of the basic steps of which will be shown in the following discussion. Our presentation is based on Aoki [1967] and Chow [1975]. As is usual for a dynamic programming algorithm, one would start with the last-period maximization problem.

Suppose that the decision maker who is at the end of period (T-1), or the beginning of the last period T, wants to find an optimal value of p_T to :

$$\text{Max.} \quad E\{U[\Pi_t(p_T, q_T)] | \psi^{T-1}\} \qquad (1.17)$$
$$\{p_T\}$$

where it is recalled that ψ^{T-1} denotes a vector consisting of all relevant information observed up to, but not including, the last period T.

By definition, we have:

$$E\{U[\Pi_t(p_T, q_T)] | \psi^{T-1}\} = \int \int U[\Pi_t(p_T, q_T)] \varphi(p_T, q_T | \psi^{T-1}) dp_T dq_T \qquad (1.18)$$

where $\varphi(p_T, q_T | \psi^{T-1})$ is the joint probability density function of random variables p_T and q_T conditional on information available at T-1, namely ψ^{T-1}. Although the joint density $\varphi(p_T, q_T | \psi^{T-1})$ is not generally given *a priori*, we will show how this density can be generated with certain given conditions.

To do this, we first note that:

$$\varphi(p_T, q_T | \psi^{T-1}) = \varphi_1(p_T | \psi^{T-1}) \cdot \varphi_2(q_T | \psi^{T-1}, p_T) \qquad (1.19)$$

where $\varphi_1(.|.)$ is the conditional density of p_T given ψ^{T-1}, and $\varphi_2(.|.)$ is the conditional density of q_T given ψ^{T-1} and p_T. The equality in (1.19) follows directly from the definition of conditional probability densities. Two comments concerning the relationship in (1.19) are in order.

(*i*) The first expression on the right-hand side of (1.19) refers to the conditional density of p_T given the information available up to period T-1. Since our maximization problem is that for a monopolist, it is reasonable to assume that the firm wishes to make a definite decision regarding the price level to be charged. That is, the probability density function $\varphi_1(p_T | \psi^{T-1})$ is assumed to concentrate at point p_T which thus has the probability of one. In other words, assuming that a solution to the maximization problem in (1.17) exists and that it is unique, then for a given vector ψ^{T-1}, there is only one value of p_T which maximizes the expression in (1.17). Since our present problem involves the determination of an optimal price p_T instead of an optimal specification of the conditional density of p_T, we are in effect dealing with a so-called non-randomized control problem. We have already mentioned that this assumption seems reasonable because our maximizer is a monopolist. When the firm is of an oligopolistic type, for instance, it makes sense to argue that the firm will not reveal and then stick to the chosen price in view of the competition within the market system. Under this circumstance, the firm may behave like a player in the context of game theory. Our maximization problem will then be of a randomized control type in which the firm will attempt to obtain an optimal density function of p_T for a given information vector ψ^{T-1}. In our present discussion, only the case of a monopolist is analyzed.

(*ii*) On the other hand, the second conditional density on the right-hand side of (1.19) can be calculated with certain given specifications in our problem formulation. Recall that our demand function is of the form $q_T = f(p_T, \psi^{T-1}, \xi_T)$ given in eq. (1.14b), and note also that the density function of ξ_T is assumed known. Hence, in principle, one would be able to obtain the conditional density $\varphi_2(q_T | \psi^{T-1}, p_T)$. We will be able to perform some of these calculations in our discussion in the present and next chapters.

With the preceding comments, our last-period optimization problem in (1.17) can now be written as

$$\text{Max. } \Gamma_T = E\{U[\Pi_T(p_T, q_T)] | \psi^{T-1}\} \tag{1.17a}$$

$$= \int U[\Pi_T(q_T)] \varphi_2(q_T | \psi^{T-1}, p_T) dq_T$$

$$= E\{U[\Pi_T(q_T)] | \psi^{T-1}, p_T\}$$

where we have written $U[(\Pi_T(p_T, q_T)]$ as $U[(\Pi_T(q_T)]$ for notational simplicity.

We note in the above development that the joint density function of p_T and q_T in effect degenerates to a conditional density function of q_T given p_T. To simplify the notation further, we will drop the subscript 2 in the density $\varphi_2(q_T | \psi^{T-1}, p_T)$ in the following presentation.

Accordingly, for our non-randomized control problem, optimal p_T^* is defined to be a price level which maximizes Γ_T defined in eq. (1.17a). It can be shown that under the assumption of a strictly concave utility function, which characterizes the firm's risk-averse behavior, there exists such a price level p_T^* which is also unique. See Leland [1972].

As p_T^* is obtained, one can calculate in principle the maximum value of $E\{U[\Pi_T(q_T)] | \psi^{T-1}, p_T\}$ in eq. (1.17a), which will be denoted as V_T^*.

We consider now the last two stages of our stochastic dynamic programming problem. With the discount rate ρ, the monopolistic firm's decision maker seeks an optimal price path in order to:

$$\text{Max. } V_{T-1} = E\{U[\Pi_{T-1}(p_{T-1}, q_{T-1})] + \rho U[\Pi_T(p_T, q_T)] | \psi^{T-2}\} \tag{1.20}$$
$$\{p_{T-1}, p_T\}$$

Subject to the appropriate forms of eqs. (1.2a) and (1.14b).

This problem can be shown to be quite similar to the last-period optimization problem discussed above. To see this, consider each element of V_{T-1} as follows.

The first element of V_{T-1}, using our argument of non-randomized control, yields:

$$E\{U[\Pi_{T-1}(p_{T-1}, q_{T-1})] | \psi^{T-2}\} = \int U[\Pi_{T-1}(q_{T-1})] \varphi(q_{T-1} | \psi^{T-2}, p_{T-1}) dq_{T-1} \tag{1.20a}$$

$$= E\{U[\Pi_{T-1}(q_{T-1})] | \psi^{T-2}, p_{T-1}\} = \Gamma_{T-1}$$

using the previous notation implied in eq. (1.17a).

For the second element of V_{T-1} in eq. (1.20), we write:

$$E\{\rho U[\Pi_T(p_T,q_T)]\,|\,\psi^{T-2}\} = \rho E\{U[\Pi_T(p_T,q_T)]\,|\,\psi^{T-2}\}$$

$$\quad (1.20b)$$

$$= \rho E\Big(E\{U[\Pi_T(p_T,q_T)]\,|\,\psi^{T-1}\}\,|\,\psi^{T-2}\Big)$$

where the last equality follows by employing the principle of iterated expectations, and by noting that:

$$\psi^{T-2} \equiv \{p^{T-2},q^{T-2}\} \subset \{p^{T-1},q^{T-1}\} \equiv \psi^{T-1}.$$

Combining the results in (1.20a) and (1.20b), we are able to write the firm's maximization objective as:

$$\text{Max. } V_{T-1} = E\{U[\Pi_{T-1}(p_{T-1},q_{T-1})] + \rho U[\Pi_T(p_T,q_T)]\,|\,\psi^{T-2}\}$$
$$\{p_{T-1},p_T\}$$

$$= \Gamma_{T-1} + \rho E\Big(E\{U[\Pi_T(p_T,q_T)]\,|\,\psi^{T-1}\}\,|\,\psi^{T-2}\Big). \qquad (1.21)$$

Now, from the famous principle of optimality a la Bellman (see Bellman [1957]), the preceding equation becomes:

$$\text{Max. } V_{T-1} = \Gamma_{T-1} + \rho E[V_T^*\,|\,\psi^{T-2}]$$

where it is recalled that

$$V_T^* = E\{U[\Pi_T(p_T^*,q_T)]\,|\,\psi^{T-1}\} = E\{U[\Pi_T(q_T)]\,|\,\psi^{T-1},p_T^*\}$$

with p_T^* being the optimal price level for the last-period problem.

To simplify (1.21) further, consider its second term:

$$\rho E[V_T^*\,|\,\psi^{T-2}] = \rho E[V_T^*(p_{T-1},q_{T-1})\,|\,\psi^{T-2}]$$

$$= \rho \int \int V_T^*(p_{T-1},q_{T-1})\varphi(p_{T-1}\,|\,\psi^{T-2})\varphi(q_{T-1}\,|\,\psi^{T-2},p_{T-1})dq_{T-1}dp_{T-1}$$

$$= \rho \int V_T^*(q_{T-1})\varphi(q_{T-1}\,|\,\psi^{T-2},p_{T-1})dq_{T-1}$$

where we have written the explicit form for the function V_T^* which depends on the previous period's information, p_{T-1} and q_{T-1}. The second equality of the preceding equation follows directly from the definition of conditional density, and the last equality is obtained by noting once again that $\varphi(p_{T-1}\,|\,\psi^{T-2})$ takes the value of one.

Thus, eq. (1.21) can now be written as:

$$\text{Max.} \; V_{T-1} = \Gamma_{T-1} + \rho \int V_T^*(q_{T-1}) \varphi(q_{T-1} | \psi^{T-2}, p_{T-1}) dq_{T-1} \qquad (1.21a)$$
$$\{p_{t-1}\}$$

$$= \int \{U[\Pi_{T-1}(q_{T-1})] + \rho V_T^*(q_{T-1})\} \varphi(q_{T-1} | \psi^{T-2}, p_{T-1}) dq_{T-1}$$

$$= E\Big(\{U[\Pi_{T-1}(q_{T-1})] + \rho V_T^*(q_{T-1})\} | \psi^{T-2}, p_{T-1}\Big).$$

One will quickly recognize the similarity between the maximization problem in eq. (1.21a) and that in eq. (1.17a). The optimal price which maximizes V_{T-1} defined in (1.21a) will be accordingly denoted by p_{T-1}^*. It should be noted that for the case of risk aversion, a strictly concave utility function assures the existence and uniqueness of an optimal price p_t^* in each separate period. Thus, a unique value of p_{t-1} can be found to maximize the expected value of $U[\Pi_{T-1}(q_{T-1})]$ conditional on ψ^{T-2} and p_{T-1}. However, one can not be so sure about the existence and uniqueness of value of p_{T-1} which maximizes the whole expression appearing at the end of eq. (1.21a), namely:

$$E\Big(\{U[\Pi_{T-1}(q_{T-1})] + \rho V_T^*(q_{T-1})\} | \psi^{T-2}, p_{T-1}\Big).$$

While it appears possible to establish conditions under which such an optimum can be found, the exercise would seem to be of purely mathematical interest. To confine the present discussion to a managerial context, we will simply assume that an interior solution to the problem in (1.21a) does exist and that the solution is unique. However, the interested reader may want to consult Denardo [1967] for a discussion on the existence of optimal policies for this type of dynamic programming models.

Our results concerning the optimal path of pricing decisions can now be readily extended for a more general situation of the last τ-period problem. For $\tau = T$, the problem is solved in its entirety.

The general form of our optimization problem is

$$\text{Max.} \; E\{\textstyle\sum_{t=1}^{T} \rho^t U[\Pi_t(p_t, q_t)] | \psi^0\} \qquad (1.22)$$
$$\{p_t\}_{t=1}^{T}$$

$$\text{Subject to} \quad \Pi_t = p_t q_t - C(q_t) - FC$$

$$\text{and} \quad q_t = f(p_t, \psi^{t-1}, \xi_t) \;, \text{ for } t=1,2,...,T.$$

For a general last τ-period problem, we consider the situation at the end of period $(T-\tau)$ of the monopolistic firm which wants to

$$\text{Max. } V_{T-\tau+1} = E[U(\Pi_{T-\tau+1}) + \rho U(\Pi_{T-\tau+2}) + \ldots + \rho^{\tau-1}U(\Pi_T)\,|\,\psi^{T-\tau}].$$

To simplify the notation, we define a new subscript as $s = (T-\tau+1)$. The preceding problem then becomes:

$$\text{Max. } V_s = E\left\{\sum_{t=s}^{T} \rho^{t-s} U[\Pi_t(p_t, q_t)]\,|\,\psi^{s-1}\right\} \qquad (1.23)$$
$$\{p_s\}$$

where $s = 1,2,\ldots,T$ since $\tau = 1,2,\ldots,T$.

It can be readily shown, by the same method used to obtain eq. (1.21a), that one can write, for $s = 1,2,\ldots,T$:

$$\text{Max. } V_s = \Gamma_s + \rho \int V_{s+1}^*(q_s)\varphi(q_s\,|\,\psi^{s-1},p_s)dq_s$$
$$\{p_s\}$$

$$\text{where } \Gamma_s = \int U[\Pi_s(q_s)]\varphi(q_s\,|\,\psi^{s-1},p_s)dq_s$$

$$V_{s+1}^*(q_s) = \text{Max. } V_{s+1}$$
$$\{p_{s+1}\}$$

and $V_{T+1}^*(q_T) = 0$ since T is the final period of the planning horizon.

Again, for ease of interpretation to be discussed in different contexts later on, it is useful to rewrite one of the above relations as:

$$V_s = \int \{U[\Pi_s(q_s)] + \rho V_{s+1}^*(q_s)\}\varphi(q_s\,|\,\psi^{s-1},p_s)dq_s. \qquad (1.24)$$

We have thus completed the derivation of a solution algorithm to the imperfectly competitive firm's maximization problem, using the standard technique of stochastic dynamic programming. We will be using this solution approach in a number of different models in which we will be able to offer more specific economic as well as marketing implications.

5 CONCLUDING REMARKS

This chapter summarizes the general direction with which we will present the results analyzed throughout the book. It allows us to draw a general outline of how various aspects of different issues of marketing activities are related to each other as well as how they even interact within the same framework. We further set out the mathematical approaches we will most likely utilize throughout. In particular we present the simplified quadratic utility formulation which, in spite of its well-known theoretical drawback, has the significant empirical advantage with its implementability which we think is of utmost importance to the marketing professionals. We also present a discrete stochastic dynamic programming approach which will allow us to examine a number of dynamic marketing decision problems. We have chosen to skip the continuous stochastic dynamic approach here since there exists excellent texts within the management literature such as Tapiero [1990].

REFERENCES

AOKI, M., 1967, *Optimization of Stochastic Systems*, Academic, New York.

ARROW, Kenneth J., 1963, *Social Choice and Individual Values*, 2nd Ed., Wiley, New York.

ARROW, Kenneth J., 1965, *Some Aspects of the Theory of Risk Bearing*, Helsinki: Jahnssonin-Saatio.

BAILEY, Martin J., 1979, "The Possibility of Rational Social Choice in an Economy," *Journal of Political Economy*, Vol. 87, pp. 37-56.

BARON, David P., 1971, "Demand Uncertainty in Imperfect Competition," *International Economic Review*, Vol. 12 , pp. 196-208.

BASS, Frank M., 1969, "A New Product Growth Model for Consumer Durables," *Management Science*, Vol. 15, pp. 215-227.

BELLMAN, Richard, 1957, *Dynamic Programming*, Princeton University Press, Princeton, N. J.

CHOW, Gregory, 1975, *Analysis and Control of Dynamic Economic Systems*, Wiley and Sons, Inc., New York.

DEGROOT, Morris H., 1970, *Optimal Statistical Decisions*, McGraw-Hill, Inc., New York.

DENARDO, E. V., 1967, "Contraction Mappings in The Theory Underlying Dynamic Programming," *SIAM Review*, Vol. 9, pp. 165-177.

DORFMAN, R., and P. O. STEINER, 1954, "Optimal Advertising and Optimal Quality," *American Economic Review*, Vol. 64, pp. 826-836.

ELIASHBERG, Jehoshua, and Rabikar CHATTERJEE, 1985, "Stochastic Issues in Innovation Diffusion Models," in *Models for Innovation Diffusion*, Vijay MAHAJAN, and R. A. PETERSON (eds.), Sage, California, pp. 151-199.

ELIASHBERG, J., and R. STEINBERG, 1993, "Marketing-Production Joint Decision-Making," in Jehoshua ELIASHBERG, and Gary L. LILIEN (eds.), *Marketing*, Handbooks in Operations Research and Management Science, Vol. 5, pp. 827-880, Elsevier Science Publishers.

ELIASHBERG, Jehoshua, and Robert L. WINKLER, 1981, "Risk Sharing and Group Decision-Making," *Management Science*, Vol. 27, pp. 1221-1235.

HANSSENS, Dominique M., 1980, "Market Response, Competitive Behavior, and Time Series Analysis," *Journal of Marketing Research*, Vol. 27, pp. 470-485.

HOROWITZ, Ira, 1970, *Decision Making and the Theory of the Firm*, Holt, Rinehart and Winston, Inc.

JAGPAL, H. S., and I. E. BRICK, 1982, "The Marketing Mix Decision Under Uncertainty," *Marketing Science*, pp. 79-92.

KEENEY, R. L., and C. W. KIRKWOOD, 1975, "Group Decision Making Using Cardinal Social Welfare Functions," *Management Science*, Vol. 22 , pp. 430-437.

LAMBIN, Jean-Jacques, Philippe A. NAERT, and Alain BULTEZ, 1975, "Optimal Marketing Behavior in Oligopoly," *European Economic Review*, Vol. 6, pp. 105-128.

LELAND, Hayne, 1972, "Theory of the Firm Facing Uncertain Demand," *American Economic Review*, Vol. 62, pp. 278-291.

LILIEN, Gary L., Philip KOTLER, and K. Sridhar MOORTHY, 1992, *Marketing Models*, Prentice-Hall, Englewood Cliffs, NJ.

NERLOVE, Marc, and Kenneth J. ARROW, 1962, "Optimal Advertising Policy Under Dynamic Conditions," *Economica*, Vol. 39, pp. 129-142.

PRATT, John W., 1964, "Risk Aversion in the Small and in the Large," *Econometrica*, Vol. 2, pp. 122-136.

RAIFFA, Howard, and R. SCHLAIFER, 1961, *Applied Statistical Decision Theory*, Harvard University Press, Cambridge, MA.

SWALM, R. O., 1966, "Utility Theory — Insights into Risk Taking," *Harvard Business Rev.*, Vol. 44, pp. 123-136.

TAPIERO, Charles S., 1990, *Applied Stochastic Models and Control in Management*, 2nd impression, Elsevier Science Publishers, The Netherlands.

2

PRICING UNDER UNCERTAINTY

1 OVERVIEW

This chapter specifically addresses situations in which marketing activities are dominated mainly by pricing decisions. Here, we will try to isolate the role of pricing in order to examine at length the impact of demand uncertainty and risk-taking attitude of the firm on this essential component of the firm's marketing mix. It is well-known that marketing mix represents a central approach in understanding marketing phenomena and strategic decision-making for the firm under deterministic scenarios. Ideally, one would want to examine the interactions among these marketing variables under general conditions of demand uncertainty and in this respect, our present work seeks to partially respond to that challenge. However, as will be seen throughout the book, even for decision variables in isolation, it can often be difficult to assess the impact of uncertainty, especially when elements such as dynamics and multiple-products are involved. It would therefore be most helpful for us to proceed with models as simple as we can in order to gradually gain insight into these complex marketing phenomena. Thus, for example, while marketing scholars and practitioners would rightly regard price discount as part of the firm's pricing decisions, we will consider this important tool within the context of the firm's sales promotional activities, in a separate chapter below.

In the next section, we set up the basic problem involving a single-product firm which has monopoly power and which operates within a static, single-period time horizon. There we will analyze how random demand would have an impact on the well-known rule for optimal pricing under deterministic conditions. In the process we will also examine how the firm's attitude towards risk as reflected through the specification of the utility function would have an important impact on its pricing strategy. In that section, we will next explore the implications of a joint decision involving not only pricing but also production or acquisition decisions. Further, we shall show how the formal equivalence between pricing and producing decisions within a deterministic framework will no longer be valid once we allow for the existence of randomness in demand. Section 3 considers the pricing strategy for firms which produce a set of multiple products or a line of products under conditions of demand uncertainty. We shall attempt to address the impact of taxation on the firm's pricing with a view towards introducing additional public policy issues to the existing marketing literature. We will then begin in Section 4 an investigation of the dynamic pricing first under conditions of certainty and then under demand uncertainty. We shall again indicate how the simple optimal pricing rule under static and deterministic conditions have to be modified to accommodate elements of dynamics as well as randomness in the sales response functions. Further dynamic analyses will be performed in Section 5 in which we indicate the general intertemporal nature of the firm's dynamic pricing strategy in its efforts to maximize its utility of profits. We will report there certain results on a particular dynamic learning process involving experimentation while leaving a more thorough exploration of this particular topic to Chapter 9 of the book.

2 SINGLE-PRODUCT PRICING: STATIC ANALYSIS

In this section, we record the results for price-setting firms which have certain monopoly power. Our focus here will be on single-product firms and only the one-period static decision-making will be assumed in this section. Dynamic consider-ations will be examined in a subsequent section in this chapter; multiple-product analyses in another section and the impact of competition will be considered in Chapter 8. The major emphasis in this section will be to look at the effects of uncertainty on the firm's pricing decisions and in examining those effects we will analyze the impact of risk-taking behavior as well.

2.1 The Pricing Firm

Linear Utility
Within the framework of a one-period decision-making for the firm, let us assume that the random demand function facing the firm takes the following implicit form:

$$h(p,q,\xi) = 0 \qquad\qquad (2.1)$$

where p denotes the unit price of the product, q the quantity demanded, and ξ is a random variable, assumed to have probability density $d\Phi(\xi)$.

To signify the nature of the price-setting process applicable to the firm under consideration, let us write the random demand function as:

$$q = f(p, \xi). \tag{2.1a}$$

Facing the preceding demand, the (random) profit function can be expressed as follows:

$$\Pi = pq(p, \xi) - C[q(p, \xi)] - FC \tag{2.2}$$

where $C[q(p, \xi)]$ denotes the firm's cost function, and FC represents fixed cost.

The first-order condition for an optimal solution to the preceding problem can be seen as:

$$E[q + p\frac{\partial q}{\partial p} - C'\frac{\partial q}{\partial p}] = 0 \tag{2.3}$$

where $C' = \partial C[q(p, \xi)]/\partial q$, representing the marginal cost, and E denotes the expectations operator.

Baron [1971] argues that under the assumption of linear utility (risk-neutral), a price-setting strategy amounts to choosing a price and satisfying whatever the quantity demanded at that price, following the conditional density function $\varphi(q|p)$ with the resulting expected demand $\mu_q = E(q|p) = \int q\varphi(q|p)dq$ and variance $\sigma^2_q = E[q - E(q|p)]^2 = \int [q - E(q|p)]^2 \varphi(q|p)dq$. Note that we are assuming that inventory does not play any role here. We will address this particular issue of production and inventory decision, together with the firm's pricing strategies in a more complete treatment in Chapter 7 and will shortly present a simplified version of these types of model in a subsequent sub-section in this chapter.

Under these specifications, the objective function of maximizing the expected value of the random profit in (2.2) can be expressed as:

$$E(\Pi) = \int [pq - C(q)]\varphi(q|p)dq - FC = pE(q|p) - E[C(q)|p] - FC. \tag{2.2a}$$

The first-order condition for optimality can then be written as:

$$\frac{dE(\Pi)}{dp} = E(q|p) + p\frac{dE(q|p)}{dp} - \frac{dE[C(q)|p]}{dp} = 0 \tag{2.3a}$$

and the second-order condition can simply be thought as the requirement that the expected profit function must be strictly concave, $[\partial^2 E(\Pi)/\partial p^2] < 0$.

The first two components on the right-hand side of the expression (2.3a) constitute the marginal expected quantity (demanded), whereas the last component is interpreted as the marginal expected output (produced). We note that while the second component contains a price figure p, the whole term represents a quantity figure. To see this, note that $[\partial E(q|p)/\partial p]$ is a change in expected quantity with respect to a change in price level. Multiplying this with a given level of price would produce a corresponding level of output. Thus the necessary condition can be interpreted as the equality of marginal expected quantity demanded and marginal expected output to be produced.

In order to compare the preceding condition in (2.3a) to the deterministic counterpart, a useful way is to define what can be called as a certainty-equivalent solution; that is we assume the firm is making the decisions as if the demand function is known with certainty which takes on the value of the demand mean $E(q|p)$. The optimal condition is then simply:

$$\frac{d\overline{\Pi}}{dp} = E(q|p) + p\frac{dE(q|p)}{dp} - \frac{dC[E(q|p)]}{dp} = 0 \qquad (2.3b)$$

which immediately yields the result that, for risk-neutral firms, any divergence between the price under uncertainty and the certainty-equivalent conditions is due to the specification of the cost function.

For the case of constant marginal cost c, the optimality condition in the preceding expression becomes:

$$E(q|p) + p\frac{\partial E(q|p)}{\partial p} = c\frac{\partial E(q|p)}{\partial p} \qquad (2.3c)$$

which is actually the condition for the certainty-equivalent solution where q takes on its expected value; the condition being the equality of the marginal revenue, expressed in terms of a price change, and the marginal cost.

Thus, in this scenario a risk-neutral firm would set a price under random demand at the same level with that under equivalent deterministic conditions with the resulting expected profit being equal to the firm's deterministic profit.

In several retailing markets where costs of acquisition of goods rather than production costs constitute major outlays, the assumption of a *constant* average variable cost is a very reasonable one. In this situation, it is simple to show that the expected cost is approximated, by a Taylor's expansion, by the cost of the expected demand; i.e., $E[C(q|p)] \approx C[E(q|p)]$. For a general cost function, the comparison can be seen to depend on the concavity of the cost function, via Jensen's inequality.

For a specific example, consider a Taylor's expansion about demand mean $E(q|p)$ of the firm's expected cost function, ignoring moments higher than second order:

$$E[C(q)] = C[E(q|p)] + \frac{1}{2}\int [q - E(q|p)]^2 \frac{\partial^2 C(q)}{\partial q^2}\varphi(q|p)dq \qquad (2.4)$$

which, by comparing the previous two equations (2.3b) and (2.3c), would lead us to the condition that:

$$\frac{dE(\Pi|\bar{p})}{dp} - \frac{d\bar{\Pi}}{dp}E(q|\bar{p}) = -\frac{1}{2}\frac{d}{dp}\left[\int [q-E(q|\bar{p})]^2\frac{\partial^2 C(q)}{\partial q^2}\varphi(q|\bar{p})dq\right]$$ (2.5)

where $\bar{p}$ denotes the certainty-equivalent optimal price.

Given that the second-order condition is satisfied, that is the derivative of the expected profit with respect to price is a decreasing function of price, the difference between optimal prices under the two conditions depends on the sign of the expression on the right-hand side of (2.5). Baron [1971] shows that for a quadratic cost function, there would be no differences in optimal prices even though the expected profits would be different from the certainty-equivalent profits.

Further we can also express the optimal pricing condition in terms of price elasticity of demand as defined for the standard deterministic formulation. Thus, it may be useful to record the well-known deterministic pricing rule for a monopolistic firm. The basic marginal revenue marginal cost equality can be written as follows:

$$p^* = [\frac{\varepsilon}{\varepsilon-1}]MC$$ (2.6)

where MC represents the firm's marginal cost and ε denotes the *absolute* value of the price elasticity of demand.

This expression represents the basic optimal pricing rule under the assumption of a static decision process (one-period) as well as static cost configuration (no learning/experience effect). Demand specifications will eventually dictate the exact rule: e.g., linear specification, constant elasticity, attraction specification etc. (see Simon [1989]). As an empirical note, we record that estimates for price elasticity of demand ε have been found to be 1.76 (Tellis [1988]), and 2.6 for closely substitutable brands (Ehrenberg [1995]).

Non-linear Utility
Now, for non-linear utility, the firm's objective is to maximize its expected utility of profits defined in eq. (2.2).

In general, the first-order condition is:

$$E\{U'(\Pi)[q(p,\xi) + p\frac{\partial q(p,\xi)}{\partial p} - C'\frac{\partial q(p,\xi)}{\partial p}]\} = 0$$ (2.7)

where U' denotes the first derivative of utility with respect to the expected profits.

In order to contrast the optimal price under random demand and that under certainty, Leland [1972] makes use of the following notion of the certainty demand curve equivalent to the random demand: the demand curve which would result if the firm knew quantity would equal its expected value with certainty for all p levels, that is:

$$q = E(q|p) = g(p).$$

As our earlier analyses suggest, if the marginal cost is not constant, the risk-neutral firm's optimal price in comparison to that under certainty-equivalent conditions, depends on the shape of the marginal cost curves. Under the common and reasonable assumption of constant marginal cost and under the additional assumption of a specific case of demand which is additively separable in p and ξ, Leland obtains the result that risk aversion will lead to a lower price in comparison to risk-neutral firm's price.

Using the conditional density function $\varphi(q|p)$ as we specified earlier in the previous sub-section, the objective function for a firm which has non-linear utility is:

$$\begin{aligned} E\{U[\Pi(q)]|p\} &= \int U[\Pi(q)]\varphi(q|p)dq \\ &= \int U[pq - C(q)]\varphi(q|p)dq. \end{aligned} \tag{2.8}$$

The necessary and sufficient conditions for an optimal solution to the above problem can be shown respectively as:

$$\begin{aligned} & E\{U'(\Pi).[\frac{\partial(pq)}{\partial p} - C'(q)(\frac{\partial q}{\partial p})]|p\} \\ & = E\{U'(\Pi).[f(p,\xi) + p\frac{\partial q(p,\xi)}{\partial p} - C'(q)\frac{\partial q(p,\xi)}{\partial p}]|p\} = 0 \end{aligned} \tag{2.9}$$

$$\text{and} \quad E\{U'(\Pi).\frac{\partial^2\Pi}{\partial p^2} + U''(\Pi).[\frac{\partial\Pi}{\partial p}]^2|p\} < 0. \tag{2.10}$$

There is no standard economic interpretation for the necessary condition in (2.9) for the reason that within the deterministic theory of the firm, the conventional treatment would involve a quantity choice instead of a price decision; and thus the optimal condition just requires the equality between the marginal revenue and the marginal cost. Our economic interpretation follows that earlier proposed by Baron for the case of a linear utility function.

The condition in (2.9) can therefore be interpreted in a similar manner with some obvious modifications. Specifically, we can state that the condition requires the equality between the expected adjusted marginal quantity demanded (*EAMQD*) and the expected adjusted marginal output produced (*EAMOP*). The qualifier "adjusted" refers to the presence of the term $U'(\Pi)$ representing the non-constant marginal utility of profits. While this notion of *EAMQD* and *EAMOP* is by no means conventional, we are using it for the sake of presentational convenience.

The sufficient condition in (2.10) requires that the first derivative of the expected utility of profit $E[U'(\Pi)]$ be a decreasing function of p. More specifically, for a risk-averse firm, $U'(\Pi) > 0$ and $U''(\Pi) < 0$, the profit function must be concave in the argument p. On the other hand, under the assumption of risk neutrality, the second-order condition in (2.10) is satisfied when $(\partial^2\Pi/\partial p^2) < 0$; i.e., the profit function Π should be strictly concave in p. In any event, we will assume throughout the analysis that the sufficient condition for optimality is satisfied.

2.2 The Joint Pricing-Producing Firm

The previous sub-section addresses the pricing decision in isolation with the view towards obtaining as simple as possible decision rules in the firm's effort to maximize its expected economic profits. While there exist several scenarios in which the firm's product acquisitions would have been made at any point in time, thus leaving pricing decisions the major responsibility for the managers, it is equally likely in real life that a significant number of situations arise where the firm has to make joint decisions involving pricing and product acquisitions. We shall explore the production/acquisition decisions in further details in Chapter 7 in the framework of an inventory problem structure. Yet, in the mean time we will need to highlight certain features of this important joint decision process in this sub-section.

The theoretical structure has been associated mainly with Mills [1961] and analyzed in Horowitz [1970] so we will be fairly brief here. Let us assume that the firm is faced with a linear cost function with average cost c and the demand function for a perishable good of the following form:

$$q = f(p,\xi) \equiv f(p) + \xi \qquad (2.11)$$

where ξ denotes the random term with zero mean.

In this model with potential unsatisfied demand implications, a basic assumption here is that an output level, say, q^*, is decided upon before the realization of the random term in the uncertain demand function for a chosen level of price. Hence, once a chosen price is made, the realized output q may be smaller or higher than q^*; in the former case the demand will of course be satisfied, in the latter case, some demand will not be satisfied. Here we are presenting a simplified version to see if additional implications can be derived in comparison with the standard price-setting scenarios analyzed in the previous sub-section. Defining q^* as the predetermined output level in a given period of time, then the firm's expected profits can be defined as:

$$E(\Pi|p) = \int_0^{q^*} pq\varphi(q|p)dq + \int_{q^*}^{\infty} pq^*\varphi(q|p)dq - C(q^*) \qquad (2.12)$$

from which the first-order conditions with respect to price and quantity can be expressed respectively as:

$$E(q|p^*)+p^*\frac{\partial E(q|p^*)}{\partial p^*}=\int_{q^*}^{\infty}[(q-q^*)+p^*\frac{\partial f(q|p^*)}{\partial p^*}]\varphi(q|p^*)dq \qquad (2.13)$$

$$\text{and}\quad p^*[1-\Phi(q^*|p^*)]=\frac{\partial C(q^*)}{\partial q^*} \qquad (2.14)$$

where $\Phi(q|p^*)$ is the *cumulative* distribution function of demand and p^* denotes optimally chosen price.

Note that, due to the additivity of the random term in the above demand function, the first of the preceding conditions can be written as:

$$E(q|p^*)+p^*\frac{\partial E(q|p^*)}{\partial p^*}$$
$$=p^*\frac{\partial E(q|p^*)}{\partial p^*}[1-\Phi(q^*|p^*)]+\int_{q^*}^{\infty}(q-q^*)\varphi(q|p^*)dq. \qquad (2.13a)$$

Let us now interpret the economic significance and marketing implications of these conditions. To obtain the jointly optimal producing and pricing decisions, we immediately replace the second of the conditions into the preceding expression in (2.13a) to yield:

$$E(q|p^*)+p^*\frac{\partial E(q|p^*)}{\partial p^*}-\frac{\partial C(q^*)}{\partial q^*}\frac{\partial E(q|p^*)}{\partial p^*}$$
$$=\int_{q^*}^{\infty}(q-q^*)\varphi(q|p^*)dq. \qquad (2.15)$$

We have earlier analyzed how the deterministic optimal pricing rule involves setting the equality of marginal revenue and marginal cost as summarized in eq. (2.6) and the necessary modifications for risk-neutral optimal pricing under random demand as exemplified in eq. (2.3a). In contrast, the necessary condition here can simply be written as:

$$[MR-MC]\frac{\partial E(q|p^*)}{\partial p^*}=\int_{q^*}^{\infty}(q-q^*)\varphi(q|p^*)dq>0 \qquad (2.16)$$

where *MR* and *MC* denote, respectively, the firm's marginal revenue and marginal cost; and where we have noted specifically that the expression on the right-hand side of the equality is positive.

Noting further that the expected demand function is sloping downward, the preceding condition simply means that the output and the price should be chosen jointly so that it typically involves setting price lower than the usual case where output can be produced to satisfy any demand given that the firm has chosen a price for its product. This is so since the second-order condition, which we did not state, implies that the marginal revenue must be declining. The expression appearing on the right-hand side of (2.16) denotes the expected shortage of supply; that is the quantity expected to be unsatisfied given that a particular production level has been decided upon. Thus the implication for deviations from the normal rule of optimal pricing is the tendency to charge a little lower price to reduce the economic loss due to this foregone opportunity of unsatisfied demand. We will notice that the same result will appear again in the context of inventory-related problems in Chapter 7, especially when there are costs associated with the potential cost of losing customers whose demand were not met by the firm.

It may be of interest to note the following special case when the firm's cost function consists mainly of the acquisitions costs; it is thus essentially characterized as a linear function. In this situation, we have a simplified objective function as:

$$E(\Pi|p) = \int_0^{q^0} (p-c)q\varphi(q\,|p)dq + \int_{q^0}^{\infty} (p-c)q^0\varphi(q\,|p)dq \qquad (2.12a)$$

where we again denote the density function of demand conditional on a chosen price as $\varphi(q\,|p)$ which can be seen to follow directly from an assumed known density function of ξ.

The first expression on the right-hand side of the preceding relation refers to the expected profits received when demand, conditional on the firm's chosen price, falls short of the predetermined output q^0; and the second expression refers to that received when demand turns out to be larger than the fixed quantity presently available.

Under the assumption of non-linearity in utility, no clear-cut results can be obtained in general. However it should be mentioned here that if the demand curve is additively separable in p and ξ and that marginal cost is non-decreasing, then it can be shown that for quadratic utility functions, a small increase in risk aversion will lead the firm to reduce both the price and output (Horowitz [1970]).

2.3 Pricing vs. Producing Firms

The authors of previous studies on the subject of the monopolistic firm's decision under uncertainty did not repeat themselves when they considered both quantity-setting and price-setting strategies in a common theoretical framework. Leland [1972] has discussed at considerable length different assumptions regarding various behavioral modes of the representative firm in his article. He also illustrated by a simple example the important implications which are due to different choices of behavioral mode by the firm. We are here mainly concerned with the distinction between quantity and price level as the relevant decision variable. Examples can be easily found to demonstrate the fact that depending on circumstances, one or both of those decision variables (quantity or price) are relevant.

In the world of deterministic demand, it is well-known that pricing and production decisions would lead to the identical optimal rule involving equality between marginal revenue and marginal cost. This is so since a deterministic demand function fully characterizes one variable with the choice of the other. Thus, the existence of the inverse function of the demand equation $p_t = f(q_t)$ would assure us the operational equivalence between producing and pricing strategies under certainty. On the other hand, it has been shown that, with a random demand specification, different results are obtained depending on whether price or quantity is the decision variable that the firm makes. Both pricing and producing strategies are analyzed under separate assumptions concerning the linearity of a Von Neumann-Morgenstern utility function. In order to facilitate theoretical analyses, Baron [1971] uses the hypothesis that quantity and price variables are jointly normally distributed. This assumption was taken in part because in his book, Sengupta [1967] had argued strongly in its favor. When a fixed quantity q is offered to the market, the price p that consumers pay is a random variable with the conditional density $\varphi(p|q)$. When a fixed price p is charged, the quantity demanded q is a random variable with the conditional density $\varphi(q|p)$. At a small risk of possible confusion, note the way we use the identical function $\varphi(.\,|\,.)$ to generically denote the different conditional density functions for both p and q. Under the linear utility assumption, the problem for the firm which follows the producing strategy is to choose an output level in order to maximize the expected value of profits:

$$E(\Pi|q) = \int [pq - C(q)]\varphi(p|q)dp \qquad (2.17)$$

where $\varphi(p|q)$ is subjectively known to the firm.

The first-order condition for an optimal solution to the problem defined in eq. (2.17) is:

$$E(p|q) + q\frac{\partial E(p|q)}{\partial q} = \frac{\partial C(q)}{\partial q} \qquad (2.18)$$

which, as usual, can be interpreted as the equality between the marginal expected revenue and the marginal cost.

Consequently, in defining deterministic conditions as scenarios in which the firm behaves as if demand equals its mean, it follows that maximizing expected profit under random demand yields the same output level as that under certainty-equivalent conditions.

Under the assumption of non-linear utility function, the optimization problem becomes:

$$Max.\ E[U(\Pi)|q] = \int U[pq-C(q)]\varphi(p|q)dp. \qquad (2.19)$$

The first-order condition for an optimal solution to the problem in (2.19) can then be derived accordingly. However, due to an interest in comparing the results between the linear and non-linear utility assumptions, let us write eq. (2.19) as a Taylor's expansion about the expected profit $E(\Pi)$ as:

$$E[U(\Pi)|q] = U[E(\Pi|q)] + \frac{1}{2}\int [\Pi - E(\Pi|q)]^2 U'' \varphi(p|q)dp \qquad (2.19a)$$

where primes denote appropriate partial derivatives.

Upon taking first derivatives of (2.19a) and making use of the first-order condition for the linear-utility case, the following conclusion concerning the difference in optimal outputs between the non-linear utility case and the linear utility case is obtained: for a strictly concave and quadratic utility function, the optimal output is smaller than that obtained from a linear utility function, provided that the conditional density $\varphi(p|q)$ is normal (Baron [1971]. Furthermore, under the same condition, as risk aversion increases, the optimal output would decline.

The important question of the impact of uncertainty on the optimal output under the assumption of a more general random demand equation was addressed formally in Leland [1972]. Recall the following implicit random demand function postulated in eq. (2.1):

$$h(p,q,\xi) = 0 \qquad (2.1)$$

where ξ is the random disturbance term with a *known* probability density $\varphi(\xi)$, and the demand function $h(p,q,\xi)$ is assumed to be continuous, twice differentiable.

Further, let us record here the principle of increasing uncertainty which states that as total expected revenue increases, the "riskiness" (dispersion of the distribution) of total revenue will increase. We will discuss both situations, one in which the firm wants to find an optimal output level (quantity-setting or producing strategy), another to find an optimal price level (price-setting or pricing strategy). The results derived from these different assumptions will be illustrated by an example taken from Leland.

For the producing strategy case, the optimization problem facing the monopolist is of the following form:

$$\text{Max. } E\{U[\Pi(q)]\} \qquad (2.20)$$
$$\{q\}$$

$$\text{subject to } \quad p = g(q,\xi) \qquad (2.1b)$$

$$\text{and } \quad \Pi(q) = pq - C(q) - FC \qquad (2.2b)$$

where the notation is familiar, except that the implicit form of the demand function $h(p,q,\xi)=0$ in (2.1) is now written as $p=g(q,\xi)$ where it is assumed that $(\partial p/\partial q) < 0$; and $(\partial p/\partial \xi) > 0$.

The first-order condition for optimality to the preceding problem can be easily shown to be:

$$E[\frac{\partial U}{\partial \Pi}\frac{\partial \Pi}{\partial q}] = E\{U'(\Pi)[\frac{\partial(pq)}{\partial q} - C'(q)]\} = 0 \qquad (2.21)$$

which can be expressed alternatively as:

$$E\{U'(\Pi).[MR - MC]\} = 0. \qquad (2.21a)$$

The second-order conditions are assumed to be satisfied throughout. In order to analyze the impact of uncertainty on optimal output, it is necessary to find a suitable notion of the certainty demand schedule compatible with the random demand equation. The following notion of such a certainty demand schedule was suggested by Leland. The expected price certainty demand is defined to be one which, for all levels of q, would result if the firm knew price would equal its expected value with certainty. This definition certainty-equivalent demand curve, coupled with the principle of increasing uncertainty, enabled Leland to obtain a result concerning the impact of uncertainty on output. We summarize that result in the following theorem.

Theorem 2.1. (Leland [1972]) *For the quantity-setting risk-averse monopolist, the principle of increasing uncertainty implies that the optimal output under uncertainty would be smaller than that under certainty.*

This represents an extension of a similar result due to Sandmo [1971], among others, who examined the perfectly competitive case. The result exemplified in the preceding theorem will be modified as our present study will indicate. A corollary of the preceding theorem is the result that demand uncertainty would not have any impact on the risk-neutral firm's optimal output and that risk preference would induce the firm to choose a larger output level when faced with increasing uncertainty.

The maximization problem for the price-setting monopolist can be carried out in a similar fashion. Of course, the quantity to be produced by the firm is no longer the relevant decision variable. It was noted earlier that the quantity-setting problem and price-setting problem are not completely symmetrical in the sense that one would solve the latter just by interchanging p for q and vice versa in the preceding analysis. This is due to the presence of the cost function which is assumed to be a function of output q. It has been demonstrated that, while examining the effect of uncertainty on optimal output, the specification of the cost function, in addition to the firm's attitude towards risk, is crucial. This characteristic is in contrast with that for the quantity-setting case where only the risk-taking behavior of the firm plays the crucial role. Due to the preceding reasons, a definite comparison between optimal output obtained under uncertainty and that under certainty for a price-setting monopolist can not be made in general. That is, a result parallel to that in Theorem 2.1 can not be established for the case in which the imperfectly competitive firm wants to choose the pricing strategy. It should be of interest, however, to record here some of the results for certain important special cases. When marginal costs are constant as we will very often assume in this work, there would be no divergence of a risk-neutral firm's pricing decision under random demand from that chosen under certainty. On the other hand, assuming that the random demand function is additively separable in price p and in the error term ξ, as we do very often as well, a risk-averse firm tends to charge a price lower than that set by a risk-neutral firm, provided that marginal costs are non-decreasing. As we mention, in several contexts relevant to marketing decision-making, marginal costs are typically constant; thus the preceding result that risk aversion induces a price-setting firm to lower its price with a resulting increase in expected sales is in direct contrast with the result reported earlier that a quantity-setting firm with an identical attitude towards risk would choose to reduce sales in view of demand uncertainty. The following simple example illustrates such an asymmetry between a price-setting and a quantity-setting monopolist facing a random demand equation. Suppose that the firm is faced with the following maximization problem:

$$\text{Max. } U(\Pi) = \log(\Pi).$$

The implicit demand function is:

$$h(p,q,\xi) = 2 - p - q + \xi = 0$$

where ξ has the distribution: $Pr(\xi=1/3) = Pr(\xi=-1/3) = 1/2$.

Assuming further the deterministic cost function of the form $C(q) = q$, it can be readily shown that:

(i) Under certainty, optimal values for p and q are: $p^*=3/2$, and $q^*=1/2$.

(ii) Under uncertainty, the quantity-setting monopolist would choose $q^*=[(9-\sqrt{17})/12]<1/2$ with the expected price higher than 3/2.

(iii) Under uncertainty, the price-setting monopolist would choose $p^*=[(21-\sqrt{17})/12]<3/2$ and expect to produce at a level higher than 1/2.

From these results, it is observed that under demand uncertainty, the quantity-setting monopolist behaves more monopolistically while the price-setting monopolistic firm behaves less monopolistically.

It should be of interest to note that the asymmetry between pricing and producing strategies under uncertainty will be analyzed further within the context of competition among firms, a subject we will address in Chapter 8.

3 MULTIPLE-PRODUCT PRICING

The theory of multiple-product pricing has a long and useful tradition in both economics and marketing literature as evidenced by the extensive surveys in Monroe [1990] and Rao [1993]. The notion of a product line defined as a set of demand-interdependent products produced and sold by a firm represents an important concept in any firm's strategy formulation (see, for instance, Saghafi [1988] which contains many references.) A closely related pricing method of optimal bundling has also received a great deal of attention more recently (Adams and Yellen [1976], Schmalensee [1984], and Venkatesh and Mahajan [forthcoming]).

It is of interest to record here the formula for optimal pricing for a product line under certainty; it is derived in Reibstein and Gatignon [1984].

Consider the following demand function for brand i:

$$q_i = f_i(p_1, p_2, \ldots, p_N); \quad i = 1, 2, \ldots, N$$

where p_i is the unit price of the i-th brand, q_i is the quantity demanded for the i-th brand.

Assuming further the firm's variable cost function is known and is of the form $C(q_1, q_2, \ldots, q_N)$ and denoting the fixed cost as FC, the firm's objective is to maximize the profit function:

$$\Pi = \sum_{i=1}^{N} p_i q_i - C(q_1, q_2, \ldots, q_N) - FC.$$

It has been shown that the first-order conditions can be expressed in the following form in terms of various price elasticities:

$$p_i^* = \frac{\varepsilon_i}{\varepsilon_i - 1} MC_i - \sum_{j=1, j\neq i}^{N} \left(\frac{\varepsilon_{ji}}{1 + \varepsilon_i}\right) \frac{q_j(p_j - MC_j)}{q_i}; \quad i,j = 1, 2, \ldots, N \qquad (2.22)$$

where ε_i denotes the i-th brand's own price elasticity, ε_{ji} the cross price elasticity of the j-th brand's sales with respect to a change in the price of brand i.

We should note that the preceding expressions for the product prices are themselves not closed-form solutions. And yet, useful managerial and marketing implications can be seen. For further discussion on this regard, see Simon [1989] for instance. Clearly, the preceding pricing rule immediately reduces to the deterministic pricing rule in (2.6) for the single-product case.

However, the issue of potential impact of demand uncertainty on the firm's pricing decision within a multiple-product context has remained largely unexplored. This is the focus of our analysis in this section. We shall first set up the basic theoretical structure, then explore the consequence of demand uncertainty and the firm's attitude towards risk.

For these purposes, consider a price-setting monopolistic firm which produces N distinct products. The sales response function for the i-th product is assumed to be:

$$q_i = f_i(p_1, p_2, ..., p_N, \xi_i); \quad i = 1, 2, ..., N$$

where ξ_i represents the random term.

We further specify that $E(q_i | p_1, p_2, ..., p_N) = h(p_1, p_2, ..., p_N)$ and denote the conditional variance-covariance matrix of output as $\Omega \equiv [\sigma_{ij}]$; $i,j = 1, 2, ..., N$.

For the risk-neutral firm, the objective is to set unit prices of its products so that to:

$$\text{Max. } E[\sum_{i=1}^{N} p_i q_i - C(q_1, q_2, ..., q_N)] - FC \tag{2.24}$$

where E is the expectations operator, and note also that quantities demanded are functions of prices of all products.

The first-order conditions can be written in general as:

$$E(q_i | \mathbf{p}) + \sum_{i=1}^{N} p_i [\frac{\partial E(q_i | \mathbf{p})}{\partial p_i}] = \sum_{j=1}^{N} [\frac{\partial C(q_1, q_2, ..., q_N)}{\partial q_j} \frac{\partial E(q_j | \mathbf{p})}{\partial p_i}] \tag{2.25}$$

for $i = 1, 2, ..., N$ and where we denote $\mathbf{p} \equiv \{p_1, p_2, ..., p_N\}$.

These conditions can be expressed using price elasticity formulae in the same fashion used in presenting the deterministic results. Further, in this regard, it may be of interest to note that Simon ([1989], pp.244-245) discusses cases involving loss leader scenarios and dynamic elasticities and conditions.

For many practical problems in retailing, it is reasonable to assume that acquisition costs are linear, we thus have:

$$E(\Pi | \mathbf{p}) = \sum_{i=1}^{N} (p_i - c_i) E[q_i | \mathbf{p}] - FC. \tag{2.24a}$$

More generally, when the utility function is non-linear, the objective of the firm is modified to be

$$E[U(\Pi) | \mathbf{p}] = \int \int ... \int \{U[\sum_{i=1}^{N} (p_i - c_i) q_i - FC]\}. \tag{2.26}$$
$$\varphi(q_1, q_2, ..., q_N | \mathbf{p}) dq_1, dq_2, ..., dq_N$$

where $\varphi(q_1, q_2, ..., q_N | \mathbf{p})$ is the conditional joint density of sales.

Upon linearizing the utility function, the first-order conditions for optimality to the preceding problem can be shown to be:

$$\{U' + \frac{1}{2}[\sum_{i=1}^{N}\sum_{j=1}^{N}\sigma_{ij}(p_i-c_i)(p_j-c_j)]U'''\}[\frac{\partial E(\Pi)}{\partial p_i}] = -[\sum_{j=1}^{N}\sigma_{ij}(p_j-c_j)]U''; \quad i = 1, 2, \ldots, N$$

which can be written in matrix notation as:

$$\frac{\partial E(\Pi)}{\partial \mathbf{p}} = -\frac{U''}{U' + \frac{1}{2}(\mathbf{p}-\mathbf{c})^{\mathrm{T}}\Omega(\mathbf{p}-\mathbf{c})U'''}\Omega(\mathbf{p}-\mathbf{c})$$

where $\mathbf{c} \equiv \{c_1, c_2, \ldots, c_N\}$ and, with superscript T denotes transposition,

$$\frac{\partial E(\Pi)}{\partial \mathbf{p}} = \{\frac{\partial E(\Pi)}{\partial p_1} \quad \frac{\partial E(\Pi)}{\partial p_2} \quad \cdots \quad \frac{\partial E(\Pi)}{\partial p_N}\}^{\mathrm{T}}.$$

Applying the approach in Chapter 1, for a quadratic utility function, the first-order condition will be modified to be:

$$\frac{\partial E(\Pi)}{\partial p_i} = \frac{r}{2}\frac{d[E(\Pi-E\Pi)^2]}{dp_i}$$

where it is recalled that r is positive for a risk-averse firm and r is negative for risk preference, and where

$$\frac{d[E(\Pi-E\Pi)^2]}{dp_i} = 2\sum_{i=1}^{N}(p_i-c_i)\sigma_i^2.$$

The preceding necessary condition would enable us to assess the change in expected profits with respect to a change in a particular product's price as well as that of a related product. Let us rewrite the condition in matrix notation as:

$$\frac{\partial E(\Pi)}{\partial \mathbf{p}} = r\Omega(\mathbf{p}-\mathbf{c}). \tag{2.27}$$

The second-order condition can be shown to be:

$$[\mathbf{J}-r\Omega] \text{ is negative definite} \tag{2.28}$$

where $\mathbf{J}$ is the Hessian matrix of the expected-profit function with respect to $\mathbf{p}$. As usual, we assume that $\mathbf{J}$ is negative definite.

Since Ω is positive definite, the second-order condition in (2.28) is seen satisfied for the risk-averse firm (r is positive). For the risk-preferred firm, we specify below a sufficient condition for an optimal solution to the problem in (2.26).

Lemma 2.1. *For the risk-preferred firm, the solution which satisfies* (2.27) *is optimal if the maximum eigenvalue of* **J** *is smaller than the maximum eigenvalue of* $(-r\Omega)$.

In order to prove Lemma 2.1, we use the following result:

Lemma 2.2. (Weyl's Inequalities) *Let* $\mathbf{V} = \mathbf{J}\text{-}r\Omega$, *where* **V**, **J**, *and* $(-r\Omega)$ *are* $(N{\times}N)$ *symmetric matrices. Then*

$$\lambda_i(\mathbf{V}) \le \lambda_i(\mathbf{J}) + \lambda_{max}(-r\Omega); \quad i=1,2,...,N$$

where $\lambda_i(\mathbf{V})$, $\lambda_i(\mathbf{J})$ *are the i-th eigenvalues of* **V** *and* **J**, *respectively, and* λ_{max} $(r\text{-}\Omega)$ *is the largest eigenvalue of* $(-r\Omega)$.

Proof. See Franklin [1968], for instance.

Proof of Lemma 2.1. From Lemma 2.2, we note that if $[\lambda_i(\mathbf{J}) + \lambda_{max}(-r\Omega)]$ is negative for all i, all eigenvalues of **V** would be negative, which would in turn imply that the second-order condition is satisfied. We further note that **J** is negative definite; hence if $[\lambda_{max}(\mathbf{J}) + \lambda_{max}(-r\Omega)] < 0$, it follows that $[\lambda_i(\mathbf{J}) + \lambda_{max}(-r\Omega)] < 0$ for all i.
$Q.E.D.$

Throughout the analysis that follows, we will assume that the second-order condition in (2.28) is satisfied. That is $(\mathbf{J}\text{-}r\Omega)$ is a negative definite matrix. The result we obtain in Lemma 2.1 appears to improve that given in Dhrymes' paper ([1964], Corollary 2) in which he stated that his result is somewhat incomplete (p. 651).

In general, differentiating the expression in (2.27) with respect to r yields:

$$\frac{\partial^2 E(\Pi)}{\partial \mathbf{p}^2}(\frac{\partial \mathbf{p}}{\partial r}) - \Omega(\mathbf{p}-\mathbf{c}) - r\Omega(\frac{\partial \mathbf{p}}{\partial r}) = 0.$$

$$\text{Or} \quad (\mathbf{J}-r\Omega)\frac{\partial \mathbf{p}}{\partial r} = \Omega(\mathbf{p}-\mathbf{c}) \tag{2.29}$$

from which the impact of risk-taking attitude on the firm's prices can be assessed.

One particularly noteworthy implication of the preceding result is that the clear-cut impact of risk aversion in this scenario of constant marginal cost for the single product firm which has been obtained may no longer hold. This can be seen as follows. For the single product firm, the preceding condition is

$$[\frac{\partial^2 E(\Pi)}{\partial p^2} - r\sigma^2]\frac{\partial p}{\partial r} = \sigma^2(p-c)$$

where the second-order condition requirement dictates that the term in the squared bracket is negative, yielding the necessary result that risk aversion tends to induce firms to reduce its price (compared with the result in the previous section). On the other hand, the multi-product condition is

$$\frac{\partial \mathbf{p}}{\partial r} = (\mathbf{J} - r\Omega)^{-1}\Omega(\mathbf{p} - \mathbf{c}) \tag{2.30}$$

which indicates that in general, one cannot obtain unambiguous results on the impact of risk aversion on the firm's prices for its individual products.

One can also examine the effect of increase in uncertainty exemplified by an increase in the variance-covariance of sales on the firm's pricing decision. Differentiating the first order condition in (2.27) with respect to elements of the variance covariance matrix of sales yields the following expression:

$$\frac{\partial \mathbf{p}}{\partial \sigma_{ij}} = r(\mathbf{J} - r\Omega)^{-1}\mathbf{M}_{ij}(\mathbf{p} - \mathbf{c}) \tag{2.31}$$

where $\mathbf{M}_{ij}$ represents a symmetric matrix which contains ones in the (i,j) cell and zeroes in all others.

Once again, it is straight-forward to note that for risk-averse single-product firms, increasing uncertainty leads to lower price, confirming the results we report in the previous section. The multi-product firms are faced with a more difficult pricing rule as the interactions among the sales of its various products will have to be first sorted out and evaluated.

Finally, we will address briefly the potential impact of certain forms of taxation on the firm's pricing decision. Consider in particular the impact of an excise tax. The firm's profit function becomes:

$$\Pi = \sum_{i=1}^{N} (p_i - c_i - t_i)q_i - FC \tag{2.32}$$

where t_i denotes the excise tax on the i-th product.

Following the preceding development and denoting $\mathbf{t} \equiv \{t_1, t_2, ..., t_N\}$, the optimal conditions are written as:

$$\frac{\partial E(\Pi)}{\partial \mathbf{p}} = r\Omega(\mathbf{p} - \mathbf{c} - \mathbf{t}) \tag{2.33}$$

which yields:

$$(\mathbf{J} - r\Omega)\frac{\partial \mathbf{p}}{\partial t_i} = -r\Omega\mathbf{i}; \quad i = 1, 2, ..., N \tag{2.34}$$

where $\mathbf{i}_i$ denotes an $N \times 1$ column vector which contains all zero entries except the i-th element which is unity.

Our earlier comments apply here as well. For the single-product firm, the result is more clear-cut. Any increase in an excise tax would likely lead to an increase in the firm's price. The presence of such a tax on multiple-product firms would be harder to evaluate. Thus, for example

$$(\mathbf{J} - r\Omega)\frac{\partial p_j}{\partial t_j} = -r\sigma_j^2; \ j = 1, 2, ..., N \tag{2.35}$$

from which an unambiguous impact of the excise tax on the product's own price may not in general be obtained.

Our discussion of the multi-product pricing decision may be naturally connected to some analysis in the literature on store price image. In a different context in a subsequent chapter below on price promotion, we will conceptually address this notion of store price images (e.g., Simon [1989], pp.243ff) in an effort to explain the potential equilibrium in scenarios where price differences among the stores may exist even when consumers learn.

Further, the reader may want to consult Nagle and Holden [1995, pp.237ff] for a discussion on practical approaches to pricing substitute and complementary products within a multi-product framework.

4 OPTIMAL PRICING IN A DYNAMIC CONTEXT

The last two sections analyze the firm's pricing strategy within a static decision framework. To reflect the more realistic nature of the way firms actually operate, one would need to address the theoretically more challenging issue of dynamic characterizations of pricing decisions. We will begin with a model by Kalish [1983] who considers a dynamic pricing structure under deterministic conditions. We will then report the results for a stochastic version obtained recently by Raman and Chatterjee [1995] in a subsequent sub-section.

4.1 Deterministic

Since the model has been analyzed in several marketing texts and research monographs, we will be very brief here. Our major interest is to set up the basic theoretical structure based on which the stochastic extensions can be highlighted. For these purposes, assume that the deterministic sales function has the following form:

$$\frac{dQ_t}{dt} \equiv q_t = f(Q_t, p_t) \tag{2.36}$$

where Q_t denotes cumulative sales.

The existence of the cumulative sales as a determinant of current sale has a celebrated tradition in the marketing literature. We will explore further the implications of this type of sales specification in Chapter 6 where diffusion models will be analyzed. We should note simply here that the presence of the cumulative sales in (2.36) signifies the involvement of both the diffusion and the saturation effects on current demand.

Suppose further that the unit cost is a function of cumulative sales, denoted as $c'(Q_t)$ where it is assumed that $c'(Q_t) \leq 0$ in order to reflect the potential positive learning effect on production cost. Denoting the discount rate as r, the firm's objective function is:

$$\text{Max.} \int_0^\infty e^{-rt}\Pi(p_t, Q_t)dt \equiv \int_0^\infty e^{-rt}[p_t - c(Q_t)]q_t dt \tag{2.37}$$

Subject to (2.36) and the initial condition $Q_{t=0} = Q_0$.

Defining the Hamiltonian as:

$$H = e^{-rt}[\Pi(p,Q) + \lambda f(p,Q)] \equiv e^{-rt}[p - c(Q) + \lambda].f(p,Q) \tag{2.38}$$

from which the solutions are partially characterized as:

$$\frac{d\lambda}{dt} = r\lambda - \frac{\partial H}{\partial Q} = r\lambda - [p - c(Q) + \lambda]f_Q + c'(Q)f(p,Q) \tag{2.39}$$

where $f_Q = \partial f(p,Q)/\partial Q$.

The standard economic interpretation of the preceding result is that the marginal profits and capital gain due to output accumulation combined must be equal to the opportunity cost facing the firm.

Further, an optimal value of price can be determined as:

$$\frac{\partial H}{\partial p} = 0 \Rightarrow p^* = c(Q) - \lambda - \frac{f(p,Q)}{f_p} \tag{2.40}$$

where $f_p = \partial f(p,Q)/\partial p$.

In terms of elasticities, the preceding condition can be expressed in the following form:

$$p^* = \frac{\varepsilon}{\varepsilon - 1}[c(Q) - \lambda] \tag{2.41}$$

which may be suggestive to relate to the static optimal pricing rule we recorded earlier in (2.6).

In doing so, we note that in essence the dynamic nature of the pricing rule can be summarized by the presence of the term λ in (2.41).

The second-order condition can be written, evaluated at p^*, as:

$$[2-\frac{f_{pp}f(.)}{f_p^2}]\geq 0 \qquad (2.42)$$

where we use the short hand expression $f(.)\equiv f(p,Q)$.

On the basis of (2.40), one also obtains:

$$\frac{dp}{dt}=c'(Q)\frac{dQ}{dt}-\frac{d\lambda}{dt}-\frac{d}{dt}[\frac{f(.)}{f_p}]$$

which, upon using (2.39) and noting that $(dQ/dt)=q=f(p,Q)$, and that

$$\frac{d}{dt}[\frac{f(.)}{f_p}]=[1-\frac{f(.)f_{pp}}{f_p^2}]\frac{dp}{dt}+[\frac{f_Q}{f_p}-\frac{f(.)f_{pQ}}{f_p^2}]f(.),$$

yields the following expression:

$$[2-\frac{f_{pp}f(.)}{f_p^2}]\frac{dp}{dt}= -r\lambda-\frac{2f(.)f_Q}{f_p}+\frac{f_{pQ}f^2(.)}{f_p^2} \qquad (2.43)$$

where again appropriate partial derivatives and cross derivatives are denoted with relevant subscripts.

Noting the second-order condition, an important implication of the preceding condition is that the time path of optimal prices is characterized by the relative forces represented by the terms on the right-hand side. Clearly, for certain specific model formulation concerning the diffusion process and the experience curve specifications, the preceding expression can be assessed in a more definite fashion. The reader will find other interpretations and specific results in Kalish's paper most interesting and insightful. We should note that a dynamic formulation allows us to understand important practical pricing schemes such as skim pricing, sequentially skimming and penetration pricing, detailed descriptions and interpretations of which can be found in Nagle and Holden [1995]. In this regard, we should also mention a pioneering paper by Jeuland and Dolan [1982] on dynamic pricing of a new product the demand of which is subject to a diffusion process and its production costs are changing with the firm's accumulated output. Our immediate purpose here, however, is to present the stochastic extension of the preceding theoretical framework by Raman and Chatterjee [1995] to which we now turn.

4.2 Stochastics

The stochastic version is formulated by assuming that the cumulative sales follows a Brownian motion of the form::

$$dQ=f(Q_t,p_t)dt+\sigma(Q_t)dz \qquad (2.44)$$

where dz represents the increment of a Wiener (Brownian) process z.

For a risk-neutral monopolistic firm, the objective function can be defined to be the expected discounted stream of profits subject to the preceding stochastic sales equation. We thus write:

$$\text{Max. } E\int_0^\infty e^{-rt}\Pi(p_t,Q_t)dt = E\int_0^\infty e^{-rt}[p_t-c(Q_t)]dQ_t \qquad (2.45)$$

where, as before, $c(Q_t)$ is the unit cost which is assumed to depend on cumulative sales to reflect the potential learning effects.

The method of solution to the preceding problem involves an application of the stochastic optimal control technique with continuous time. We have provided in Chapter 1 an exposition of the fundamental steps for the discrete-time stochastic dynamic programming approach. For the present problem, the general approach of decomposition following Bellman's Principle of Optimality remains the same. The major departure from the solution approach to the discrete formulation is the fact that the stochastic process in (2.44) is continuous in time but is not differentiable. And since one would need to differentiate functions of this stochastic process in order to apply the dynamic programming technique, an application of Ito's Lemma becomes essential. Because the technical details of this mathematical technique is generally accessible, we will not present it here. Instead, to get some intuition and in addition, as we will see another application of this technique in the dynamic, stochastic formulation of optimal advertising pioneered by Tapiero [1990] to be presented in the next chapter, it may be helpful to develop a few crucial steps of the solution concept here. To that end, let us write the Bellman equation in the following form:

$$V_t(Q_t) = \underset{\{p_t\}}{\text{Max.}} \; \{\Pi_t(p_t,Q_t) + [1/(1+r)]E[V_{t+1}(Q_{t+1})|\psi^t]\}$$

which resembles the recursive solution algorithm in (1.24) with appropriate modifications in notation and where ρ denotes the discount *factor*, thus $\rho=1/(1+r)$, and as before, ψ^t denotes the vector of available information up to time t.

Due to the fact that our present problem has an infinite time horizon, a technical implication is that the preceding equation is *itself* time independent; consequently, it can be written as

$$V(Q,t) = \underset{\{p\}}{\text{Max.}} \; \{\Pi(p,Q,t)\Delta t+[1/(1+r\Delta t)]E[V(Q',t+\Delta t)|p,Q]\}$$

where the time variable t is shown explicitly to indicate that the *value* of V depends on t as the cumulative sales Q depends on time, Δt denotes the length of each time interval, and Q' is the cumulative sales at time $t+\Delta t$.

Denoting $\Delta V(Q,t)=V(Q',t+\Delta t)-V(Q,t)$, the previous relation yields:

$$rV(Q,t)\Delta t = \underset{\{p\}}{\text{Max.}} \; \{\Pi(p,Q,t)\Delta t(1+r\Delta t)+E[\Delta V(Q,t)|p,Q]\}$$

which upon dividing both sides by Δt, then letting it approach zero, yields:

$$rV(Q,t) = \text{Max.} \{\Pi(p,Q,t) + (1/dt)E[dV(Q,t)|p,Q]\}.$$
$$\{p\}$$

In general, if the sales response function in (2.44) and thus the firm's profit function are explicitly time-dependent, applying Ito's Lemma to the function $V(Q,t)$ enables us to write the preceding expression as:

$$rV(Q,t) = \text{Max.} \{\Pi(p,Q,t) + V_t(Q,t) + f(p,Q,t)V_Q(Q,t) + (1/2)\sigma^2(p,Q,t)V_{QQ}(Q,t)\}$$
$$\{p\}$$

where the subscripts denote appropriate partial derivatives.

For the case considered by Raman and Chatterjee, the sales response specification does not depend explicit on the time variable, and in addition recall that we are dealing with the case of infinite planning horizon, this expression is further reduced to:

$$rV(Q) = \text{Max.} \{\Pi(p,Q) + f(p,Q)V_Q(Q) + (1/2)\sigma^2(Q)V_{QQ}(Q)\}. \qquad (2.46)$$
$$\{p\}$$

The first-order condition for an optimal price, assuming its existence, can be shown to be:

$$p^{**} = c(Q) - \frac{f(p,Q)}{f_p(p,Q)} - V_Q(Q) \qquad (2.47)$$

which can be expressed in terms of price elasticity as:

$$p^{**} = \frac{\varepsilon}{\varepsilon - 1}[c(Q) - \lambda]. \qquad (2.48)$$

Once again, we can compare the preceding results with those obtained earlier for the monopolistic and deterministic rule as well as those for the Kalish dynamic case. It should be noted that, unlike the deterministic case, the shadow price λ in (2.48) is itself a stochastic process.

Important implications of the model can be seen by examining the time path of the firm's prices over the horizon. That is, one is interested in the stochastic characterization of the firm's pricing decision. Raman and Chatterjee show that such a characterization can be expressed in its expected value, involving the change in price with respect to the cumulative output, and depends on a deterministic component and a stochastic component. The deterministic counterpart is in Kalish as we recorded earlier with corresponding economic and managerial interpretations there. The (sign of) the stochastic part can be decomposed in the following way:

$$\sigma^2[-\frac{(f/f_p)_{QQ}}{2} + \frac{c_{QQ}}{2} + \frac{\lambda_Q\sigma_Q}{\sigma}]. \qquad (2.49)$$

Interpretations can be given as follows: The first term within the brackets in the preceding expression is related to demand since it is dependent on the sales equation specification. Interesting cases where this term is zero include well-tested specification of static sales equations, multiplicatively separable and the so-called simple price-timing model for durables. The second term involves the cost effect, exhibiting the effect of learning as we recall the assumption of the dependence of unit cost on cumulative sales. The third term concerns a particular nature of the randomness such that its effect would be zero if variance is constant.

More specific results are derived by the authors for certain sales response functions, one is based on the static linear demand, the other, the price-timing model for durables in which sales is proportional to the remaining market potential. Assuming linear demand specification for the sales equation and a linear cost of learning, they show that the firm's optimal time path is linear and decline in cumulative sales for reasonable parameters of the system. Further, demand uncertainty, which is defined to be either constant, linearly decreasing, or linearly increasing in cumulative sales has distinct effects on the price path. While constant demand uncertainty has no effect whatsoever, decreasing (increasing) uncertainty tends to raise (lower) the price path everywhere without affecting its slope.

For the price-timing model, the sales specification is

$$f(p,Q) = \alpha[S(p) - Q] = \alpha(S - \beta p - Q) \tag{2.50}$$

where market potential is denoted as S (as in Size), consistently used throughout the book, which is assumed to be linear in the product price.

Assuming again linear learning on the cost side, the authors obtain the result that the optimal time path is linear and declining in cumulative sales. On the other hand, while constant demand uncertainty has no effect on the firm's optimal price path, decreasing demand uncertainty tends to lower, not raise, the price everywhere without changing the slope of the path. It is of interest to note the direct contrast of this result with that reported for the linear demand model above.

To conclude this sub-section, we should note another effort to model dynamic pricing under random demand by Chen and Jain [1992] who characterize demand uncertainty by a Poisson process, which would be most appropriate for sudden, discrete shocks in demand.

5 DYNAMICS: OTHER DEVELOPMENT

The dynamics of the firm's pricing decision in the contexts discussed in the previous section are driven by the presence of the cumulative sales in both the sales response function and in the cost function. We now examine dynamic aspects of the firm's optimization problem on the basis of the motivations outlined in Chapter 1. In particular, the presence of both the carry-over effect and the learning or experimentation effects will be assumed in this section. To a large extent, the method of analysis follows very closely that presented in the previous chapter. We will therefore ignore some of the steps in the course of our discussion whenever the issues are thought to be sufficiently clear.

As usual, we will first discuss the problem formulation and the solution to the problem. We will then perform a comparison between our own results with those obtained earlier in the literature.

5.1 The Problem Formulation and Its Solution

Let us first recall from Chapter 1 the implicit multi-period random demand function of the form:

$$h(p_t, q_t, \psi^{-1}, \xi_t) = 0 \qquad (2.51)$$

which can be written in the following explicit form:

$$q_t = f(p_t, \psi^{-1}, \xi_t) \qquad (2.52)$$

where for expositional simplicity it is assumed that the random disturbance terms ξ_t's possess known density functions. We will further assume in (2.52) that the random term ξ_t is stochastically independent of the price level p_t.

The maximization problem for the price-setting monopolistic firm will then be formulated as follows:

$$\text{Max.} \quad E\{\sum_{t=1}^{T} \rho^t U[\Pi_t(q_t)] \,|\, \psi^{-1}, p_t\} \qquad (2.53)$$
$$\{p_t\}_{t=1}^{T}$$

$$\text{subject to} \quad \Pi_t = p_t q_t - C(q_t) - FC \qquad (2.54)$$

$$\text{and (2.52) for } t=1,2,...,T.$$

We observe that the utility function is of an additive separable type with the specification of each single-period utility function being the same.

Applying the standard technique of stochastic dynamic programming as we did in the previous chapter will enable us to reproduce the algorithm to the problem in (2.53) as follows:

$$\text{Max.} \quad V_t = \Gamma_t + \rho \int V_{t+1}^*(q_t) \varphi(q_t \,|\, \psi^{-1}, p_t) dq_t \qquad (2.56)$$
$$\{p_t\}_{t-1}^{T}$$

$$\text{where} \quad \Gamma_t = \int U[\Pi_t(q_t)] \varphi(q_t \,|\, \psi^{-1}, p_t) dq_t$$

$$V_{t+1}^*(q_t) = \text{Max.} \quad V_{t+1} \text{ and } V_{T+1}^*(q_T) = 0.$$
$$\{p_{t+1}\}$$

One would recognize that since price level is the *ex ante* decision variable, the expectations appearing in eq. (2.53) are taken with respect to the conditional density $\varphi(q_t|\psi^{t-1},p_t)$. This density function is obtainable due to our assumption of known density for the random disturbance term ξ_t in the demand equation (2.52). Hence our problem is well-defined and the solution can, in principle, be found.

5.2 Optimal Price Level and the Analysis

We seek to combine in a single framework the three different situations: the deterministic model, the one-period stochastic model, and the extended intertemporal stochastic model with its dynamic characteristics. Since our present task would involve an extension of one-period models under uncertainty, it will be helpful for us to first show that these models are special cases of our dynamic model. After that, we will indicate in which ways the results from conventional deterministic models as well as those obtained in the literature should be modified if the firm is assumed to operate in a multi-period planning horizon where either the demand function is itself dynamic or learning is assumed to take place in the firm's decision process.

To obtain the one-period model from the algorithm in (2.56), let $T = 1$. We then have:

$$\underset{\{p_1\}}{\text{Max.}} \ V_1 = \int U[\Pi_1(q_1)]\varphi(q_1|p_1)dq_1 = E[U(\Pi_1)|p_1] \qquad (2.56a)$$

$$\text{where} \quad \Pi_1 = p_1 q_1 - C(q_1) - FC$$

$$\text{and} \quad q_1 = f(p_1,\xi_1)$$

which is precisely the single-period problem defined earlier in this chapter.

Of course, (2.56a) is obtained by noting that the information vector ψ^0 becomes irrelevant in a one-period problem, and that the terminal condition implies that $V_2=0$.

We are now in a position to examine the effect of our extension to a multi-period framework of the firm's decision problem. At the beginning of the first period, the dynamic programming algorithm in (2.56) enables one to write the maximization problem as:

$$\underset{\{p_1\}}{\text{Max.}} \ V_1 = \int \{U[\Pi_1(q_1)] + \rho V_2^*(q_1)\}\varphi(q_1|\psi^0,p_1)dq_1 \qquad (2.56b)$$

$$= E[U(\Pi_1)|\psi^0,p_1] + \rho E(V_2^*|\psi^0,p_1).$$

It would be most convenient to assume in the preceding relation that the planning horizon consists of two periods; i.e., $T=2$; hence $V_3^*=0$. Then it should be clear that the maximization problem in (2.56b) differs from that of (2.56a) because of the term $E[V_2^*|\psi^0,p_1]$. The first-order condition for the maximization problem in (2.56b) is:

$$\frac{\partial V_1}{\partial p_1} = E\left[U'(\Pi_1)[\frac{\partial(p_1 q_1)}{\partial p_1} - C'(q_1)\frac{\partial q_1}{\partial p_1}]|\psi^0,p_1\right] + \rho E[\frac{\partial V_2^*}{\partial p_1}|\psi^0,p_1] = 0.$$

$$\text{Or } E\left[U'(\Pi_1)[\frac{\partial(p_1 q_1)}{\partial p_1} - C'(q_1)\frac{\partial q_1}{\partial p_1}]|\psi^0,p_1\right] = -\rho E[\frac{\partial V_2^*}{\partial p_1}|\psi^0,p_1]. \quad (2.57)$$

The value of p_1 which satisfies the condition in (2.56b) is called the intertemporal optimal price, denoted by p_1^{**}. Similarly, the one-period optimal price is that level which satisfies the condition in maximizing (2.56a) above, denoted by p_1^*. It is clear that a comparison between p_1^{**} and p_1^* can be made depending on the behavior of the expression $E[(\partial V_2^*/\partial p_1)|\psi^0,p_1]$.

The following theorem summarizes a qualitative comparison between the two optimal prices.

Theorem 2.2.   *For a price-setting monopolistic firm, the intertemporal optimal price p_1^{**} is greater (equal, smaller) than the one-period optimal price p_1^* if the expression $E[V_2^*|\psi^0,p_1]$ is an increasing (a constant, decreasing) function of p_1 for each vector ψ^0.*

Remark 2.1.   As we have argued in the introductory chapter, when elements of learning are present explicitly in the formulation as the sales response function contains unknown parameters, even a static demand specification would still result in certain dynamic characteristics for the firm's decision problem. In this case, it is possible to interpret the result summarized in Theorem 2.2 as the effect of learning on the optimal price level.

We may find it useful to make use of a diagram to illustrate the necessary condition in (2.57) as well as the result in Theorem 2.2. In *Figure* 2.1 below, quantity and price are still shown in the conventional coordinate system. The two relevant curves are the expected adjusted marginal quantity demand (*EAMQD*) and the expected adjusted marginal output produced (*EAMOP*). The second-order condition would dictate that the *EAMQD* curve is downward-sloping and the *EAMOP* curve is upward-sloping, both with respect to the quantity axis. The reader will recognize its correspondence with the well-behaved situation in the conventional deterministic theory. With the assumption that $E[(\partial V_2^*/\partial p_1)|\psi^0,p_1]>0$, the right-hand side of eq. (2.57) is negative; hence *EAMQD* < *EAMOP*; which on the basis of *Figure* 2.1, would result in a higher p_1^{**} compared to p_1^* at which *EAMQD=EAMOP*. Of course, other cases can be shown in a similar fashion.

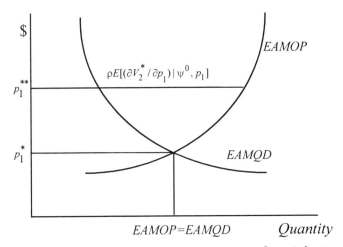

Figure 2.1 depiction:

$$EAMOP$$

$$\rho E[(\partial V_2^* / \partial p_1)|\psi^0, p_1]$$

$$p_1^{**}$$

$$p_1^*$$

$$EAMQD$$

$$EAMOP=EAMQD \qquad Quantity$$

Figure 2.1 *Intertemporal Optimal Price* $E[(\partial V_2^*/\partial p_1)|\psi^0, p_1]>0$

We have thus just completed a comparison between the one-period price decision and the multi-period price decision for a monopolistic firm. It will be emphasized again that under the assumption of uncertainty and that of learning about the unknown slope of a linear demand equation, the preceding analysis could be interpreted as the impact of learning on the firm's decision about the optimal price level. The single-period price level is myopic in the sense that no learning takes place whereas the intertemporal price decision would involve certain learning capabilities on the part of the firm in its search for a higher level of the total discounted expected utility.

Our next task naturally calls for an incorporation into the analysis the price level which would result under the conditions of uncertainty. In his one-period static model, Leland [1972] extensively explored the effect of uncertainty on optimal price. The results contained in his analysis for the price-setting case suggested that one can not obtain a clear-cut conclusion regarding the impact of uncertainty on price level. For a risk-averse price-setting firm, for example, Leland demonstrated that the effect of risk aversion on price depends upon the change in uncertainty of profit in response to a change in price. However, the sign of the change in uncertainty of profit with respect to a price change is indeterminate, in spite of the principle of increasing uncertainty. This fact represents a significant divergence from the quantity-setting case where the impact of uncertainty on output can be unambiguously determined via the principle of increasing uncertainty. Leland noted that while the shape of the cost curve has no role in determining the effect of uncertainty on output in the quantity-setting case, it is crucial in the analysis for the price-setting case. For our present purposes, it will be noted here that the only cases in which Leland was able to obtain specific results are those under the assumption of risk neutrality. Further, this is also the assumption under which Baron [1971] arrived at certain conclusions about the comparison between optimal output price determined under certainty and that under uncertainty. Specifically, we summarize their result as follows: *Assuming that marginal cost is constant, the presence of uncertainty does not affect the optimal price level for the price-setting risk neutral monopolistic firm.*

One can readily observe that this result does not hold for the firm which seeks to maximize the discounted sum of utilities of profits. To see this, we note that for a linear utility function, the necessary condition in (2.57) becomes

$$E\{[\frac{\partial(p_1 q_1)}{\partial p_1} - C'(q_1)\frac{\partial q_1}{\partial p_1}]|\psi^0,p_1\}\underset{\geq}{\overset{\leq}{}}0$$

$$\text{for } E[\frac{\partial V_2^*}{\partial p_1}|\psi^0,p_1]\underset{\leq}{\overset{\geq}{}}0.$$

This condition implies that while the one-period uncertainty effect may be zero for a risk-neutral firm, the intertemporal (dynamic) effect on current price as exhibited in the behavior of $E[(\partial V_2^*/\partial p_1)|\psi^0,p_1]$ would still be operative. The combined impact of these two effects will ultimately result in a divergence between the optimal price under uncertainty and that under deterministic conditions.

If we assume that the random demand function contains an unknown parameter, and that the firm wishes to learn about the true value of that parameter; then the preceding condition could be interpreted differently. In this situation, we may state that a risk-neutral monopolist who is engaged in learning about the unknown parameter of the demand curve might set a price which may be higher, equal to, or smaller than the optimal certainty-equivalent price level.

Several other qualitative statements can be made in a similar manner when the marginal cost is no longer constant. The intertemporal dimension of the present study can then be incorporated in a straightforward way into the various results obtained by Leland and Baron. We will not carry out these exercises any further because they do not seem to yield any additional insights of our present interest.

5.3 A Learning Process

While we will address the process of learning through experimentation in more detail in Chapter 9, it would be appropriate to explore this aspect within the firm's pricing strategy. In particular, we now examine explicitly the process in which the firm attempts to learn more about the true value of the unknown parameter β of the demand function. There have been several attempts in the literature to deal with the problem of ignorance about price and/or demand conditions. Among the earlier studies, Clower [1959] describes some adjustment mechanisms to reconcile the monopolist's conjectured prices and output with those which are ultimately realized. Tisdell [1968], in commenting on the Hicksian deterministic production theory, also notes that output choices beyond the current period should be contingent on changes of information and learning. In different contexts, the notion of learning has been addressed more recently by Cohen and Levinthal [1994] on the firm's investment in its absorptive capacity and Thompson and Horowitz [1993] on the firm's acquisition of perishable goods. One way to improve the firm's knowledge about market conditions is to devote resources to market research in order to reduce price or demand uncertainty (see Manning [1979] and Paroush [1981]).

On the other hand, the following model, which is based on Nguyen [1984], is motivated by the notion that the monopolist learns more about β through experimentation. Basically, the firm chooses a particular price level to charge and then observes the resulting demand which would clear the market. This realized demand would become a new element in the set of information available to the monopolist based on which he revises his expectation about the unknown parameter β. On the basis of the demand function, it can be shown that an application of Bayes' rule enables us to write (see Raiffa and Schlaifer [1961] and Zellner [1971])

$$\varphi(\beta \mid q^{\,t}) \propto \varphi_1(\beta \mid q^{\,t-1}) \cdot \varphi_2(q_t \mid \beta, q^{\,t-1}) \qquad (2.58)$$

where $\propto$ represents the proportionality factor.

To initiate the recursive relationships in the preceding relation, one would need to assume an initial prior $\varphi_0(\beta)$ reflecting the firm's initial beliefs about β. The resulting density $\varphi(\beta \mid q^t)$ in (2.58), couple with the obtainable density $\varphi(q_t \mid \beta, \psi^{t-1}, p_t)$, would enable us to calculate the expressions required in the solution algorithm (2.56). We shall give an illustrative example below.

Using the resulting calculations in (2.58), it would be possible for us to make a qualitative comparison between the optimal one-period price and the optimal intertemporal price in a manner similar to that discussed in the previous sub-sections. However, under the assumption that the demand curve contains an unknown parameter β, and that the monopolist is a Bayesian and so is implicitly assumed to learn about that parameter through experimentation, we will offer a further economic interpretation concerning the optimal decision of the firm under random demand. To do so, we note the following points. First, to isolate the effect of learning, let us consider a variant of (2.52) such as

$$q_t = f(\beta, p_t, \xi_t)$$

which contains explicitly an unknown parameter β. The above demand function is static in the sense that lagged output variables do not appear in the demand equation.

Second, for such a static demand function it can be readily shown that in the complete absence of learning about β, the multiperiod problem represents a sequence of one-period problems. Thus, under a static demand specification, one-period results are equivalent to those obtained under a nonlearning multiperiod model. Third, we can therefore interpret the one-period optimal price p_1^* as *price in the first period for the multiperiod model in the nonlearning case*. Finally, when the planning horizon consists of more than two periods, the optimal intertemporal price p_1^{**} can be interpreted as *price in the first period for the multiperiod model in the learning case*.

We will now introduce some additional definitions as follows:

Definition 2.1. Viewed from the first period of the whole planning horizon, the firm's expected cost of learning in terms of foregone utility is defined to be:

$$E[U(\Pi_1)|\psi^0, p_1^*] - E[U(\Pi_1)|\psi^0, p_1^{**}].$$

Remark 2.2. If demand is static, and if the firm chooses not to be involved in learning, it would consider maximizing only its current period's expected utility. The firm would then charge the price p_1^*. However, the firm decides to charge p_1^{**} in an attempt to maximize its discounted expected utilities for the whole planning horizon. In effect, p_1^{**} is chosen because learning takes place in the decision process about the firm's price. Compared to p_1^*, the decision in the current period to charge p_1^{**} would be nonoptimal concerning period 1 utility and thus it would involve a certain kind of cost in terms of lost utility. Since the difference between p_1^* and p_1^{**} is due entirely to whether or not learning is present, we may term such a cost as the cost of learning. Clearly, the expected cost of learning is nonnegative as p_1^* maximizes $V_1 = E[U(\Pi_1)|\psi^0, p_1]$. In the absence of learning, $p_1^* = p_1^{**}$; hence the expected cost of learning is identically zero.

Definition 2.2. Viewed from the first period of the whole planning horizon, the firm's expected benefit of learning is defined to be

$$E[V_2^*|\psi^0, p_1^{**}] - E[V_2^*|\psi^0, p_1^*].$$

Remark 2.3. After paying the expected cost of learning to gain knowledge on a certain type of information, the firm expects to obtain as a reward an increase in utilities in future periods. The decision to price at p_1^{**} instead of p_1^* is expected to give rise to such a reward. Once again, since the difference between p_1^* and p_1^{**} is due entirely to whether or not learning takes place, that reward is defined as the firm's expected benefit of learning. When learning is absent, there is no difference between $E[V_2^*|\psi^0, p_1^{**}]$ and $E[V_2^*|\psi^0, p_1^*]$; hence the expected benefit of learning is zero.

On the basis of the preceding definitions, the solution of our dynamic programming problem implies that the expected benefit of learning as a result of the first period experimentation is nonnegative and is at least equal to the expected cost of learning.

In order to see clearly the intertemporal nature of the firm's maximization problem even in the presence of a static demand equation, provided that learning takes place, let us perform some calculations for the following problem:

$$\text{Max.} \quad E[\textstyle\sum_{t=1}^{2} \rho' \Pi_t | \psi^0]$$

$$\text{where} \quad \Pi_t = p_t q_t - C(q_t) - FC$$

$$q_t = a - \beta p_t + \xi_t$$

$$\text{and} \quad C(q_t) = c q_t; \ t = 1,2$$

in which β is an unknown parameter whose subjective distribution will be specified shortly and ξ_t is normally and independently distributed with mean zero and known variance σ_ξ^2.

As for β, let us assume that for the given initial vector of information ψ^0, β is normally distributed with mean m_1 and variance v_1. Once the information in period 1 is obtained, i.e., when ψ^1 is given, the density of β conditional on ψ^1 can be generated using Bayes' formula as discussed earlier, namely

$$\varphi(\beta | \psi^1) \propto \varphi_1(\beta | \psi^0) \cdot \varphi_2(q_1 | \beta, \psi^0, p_1).$$

From the given demand function and our assumption about $\varphi_1(\beta | \psi^0)$, it is possible to show that

$$\varphi(\beta | \psi^1) \propto \exp[-(1/2v_2)(\beta - m_2)^2]$$

$$\text{where} \quad m_2 = [\frac{m_1}{v_1} - \frac{(q_1 - a)p_1}{\sigma_\xi^2}][\frac{1}{v_1} + \frac{p_1^2}{\sigma_\xi^2}]^{-1}$$

$$\text{and} \quad v_2 = [\frac{\sigma_\xi^2 \cdot v_1}{p_1^2}][\frac{\sigma_\xi^2}{p_1^2} + v_1]^{-1}. \tag{2.59}$$

Applying the solution algorithm in (2.56), we see that the last-period problem is to maximize

$$V_2 = E[\Pi_2(q_2) | \psi^1, p_2] = E\{p_2[a - \beta p_2 + \xi_2] - c[a - \beta p_2 + \xi_2] | \psi^1, p_2\}$$

where the expectation is taken with respect to the information in the first period ψ^1.

Since ξ_2 has a zero mean and the posterior distribution of β is normal with mean m_2 given in (2.59), we write

$$V_2 = -ca + (a + cm_2)p_2 - m_2p_2^2.$$

The optimal p_2^* is obtained by setting

$$\frac{\partial V_2}{\partial p_2} = (a + cm_2) - 2m_2p_2 = 0$$

which yields $p_2^* = \dfrac{a + cm_2}{2m_2}$.

Hence, $V_2^* = \dfrac{(a - cm_2)^2}{4m_2}$.

The preceding expression clearly indicates the nature of intertemporality of the present model. We note that V_2^* is a function of m_2 which, through (2.59), is in turn a function of p_1. It can be readily verified that as V_2^* is a decreasing function of m_2 which is in turn decreasing in p_1, V_2^* is an increasing function of p_1. From the result in Theorem 2.2, it follows that the intertemporal optimal price (learning policy) p_1^{**} is higher than the one-period optimal price (multiperiod nonlearning policy) p_1^*.

6 CONCLUDING REMARKS

In this chapter we have explored a number of topics related to the firm's pricing decisions under conditions of uncertainty. We first set up the basic static problem facing the firm, seeking the divergence if any in the pricing rules under separate scenarios of known and deterministic demand and under random demand. By looking at both the case of linear utility and non-linear utility, we also examine the impact of the firm's attitude towards risk on how its pricing decisions may have to be modified. We first analyzed these issues in a simplest possible world where there exists only one firm and thus the effect of competition is for the moment ignored. We also started out with a case where the only decision variable is pricing, then addressed the issues of joint pricing-acquisition or producing decisions. On a different dimension, we initially examined the single-product firm then devoted a section on how the firm's optimal pricing be dictated within a context of multiple products or product line decisions under random demand. Finally, we also indicated how an extension of a longer time horizon within this context of random sales would have significant implications for the firm's dynamic pricing strategy.

As we have mentioned repeatedly, each and every one of these rich features will be attempted in later chapters so that we will address the competition issues, the joint decision with output and inventory, the diffusions process etc. In the meantime we should also mention a number of related efforts in the literature which are some way related to the research on pricing we report in this chapter in addressing the general issue of decision under uncertainty for relevant marketing problems. In particular, we should mention the literature on competitive bidding surveyed in Monroe [1990], and examined in Samuelson [1986]. We should also refer to the behavior-based pricing involving comparative shopping and search for the lowest price and reference pricing, a topic which we will partially address in Chapter 4 on price discount and coupon promotions.

To conclude this chapter, it should be noted that the second part of the book will attempt to somehow present the pricing decision within a more integrating framework. Thus not only pricing but also other variables such as personnel decisions, advertising, investment and inventory decisions may have to be made simultaneously. However, before our attempt to do so, we will turn to another key decision variable for particular emphasis in the next chapter: advertising.

REFERENCES

ADAMS, W. J., and Janet L. YELLEN, 1976, "Commodity Bundling and the Burden of Monopoly," *Quarterly Journal of Economics*, Vol. 90, pp. 475-498.

BARON, David P., 1971, "Demand Uncertainty in Imperfect Competition," *International Economic Review*, Vol. 12 , pp. 196-208.

CHEN, Y. M., and D. C. JAIN, 1992, "Dynamic Monopoly Pricing under a Poisson-Type Uncertain Demand," *Journal of Business*, Vol. 65, pp. 593-614.

CLOWER, Robert W., 1959, "Some Theory of An Ignorant Monopolist," *Economic Journal*, Vol. 69, pp. 705-716.

COHEN, Wesley M., and Daniel A. LEVINTHAL, 1994, "Fortune Favors the Prepared Firm," *Management Science*, Vol. 40, No. 2, pp. 227-251.

DHRYMES, Phoebus J., 1964, "On the Theory of the Monopolistic Multi-product Firm under Uncertainty," *International Economic Review*, Vol. 5 , pp. 239-257.

EHRENBERG, A. S. C., 1995, "Empirical Generalizations, Theory, and Method," *Marketing Science*, Vol. 14, pp. G20-G28.

FRANKLIN, Joel N., 1968, *Matrix Theory*, Prentice-Hall, Inc., NJ.

HOROWITZ, Ira, 1970, *Decision Making and the Theory of the Firm*, Holt, Rinehart and Winston, Inc.

JEULAND, Abel P., and Robert J. DOLAN, 1982, "An Aspect of New Product Planning: Dynamic Pricing," in A. A. ZOLTNERS (ed.), *Marketing Planning Models*, pp. 1-21, TIMS Studies in the Management Sciences, Vol. 18, North-Holland, NY.

KALISH, Shlomo, 1983, "Monopolist Pricing With Dynamic Demand and Production Cost," *Marketing Science*, Vol. 2 , pp. 135-159.

LELAND, Hayne, 1972, "Theory of the Firm Facing Uncertain Demand," *American Economic Review*, Vol. 62, pp. 278-291.

MANNING, R., 1979, "Market Research by a Monopolist: A Bayesian Analysis," *Economica*, Vol. 46, pp. 301-306.

MILLS, Edwin S., 1961, *Price, Output and Inventory Policy*, John Wiley and Sons, NY.

MONROE, K. B., 1990, *Pricing: Making Profitable Decisions*, 2nd edition, McGraw-Hill, New York.

NAGLE, Thomas T., and Reed K. HOLDEN, 1995, *The Strategy and Tactics of Pricing*, 2nd edition, Prentice-Hall, Englewood Cliffs, NJ.

NGUYEN, Dung, 1984, The Monopolistic Firm, Random Demand, and Bayesian Learning," *Operations Research*, Vol. 32, pp. 1038-1051.

PAROUSH, J., 1981, "Market Research as Self Protection of a Competitive Firm under Price Uncertainty," *International Economic Review*, Vol. 22, pp. 365-376.

RAIFFA, Howard, and R. SCHLAIFER, 1961, *Applied Statistical Decision Theory*, Harvard University Press, Cambridge, MA.

RAMAN, Kalyan, and Rabikar CHATTERJEE, 1995, "Optimal Monopolist Pricing Under Demand Uncertainty in Dynamic Markets," *Management Science*, Vol. 41, No. 1, pp. 144-162.

RAO, Vithala R., 1993, "Pricing Models in Marketing," in Jehoshua ELIASHBERG, and Gary L. LILIEN (eds.), *Marketing*, Handbooks in Operations Research and Management Science, Vol. 5, pp. 517-552, Elsevier Science Publishers, Amsterdam, The Netherlands.

REIBSTEIN, D. J., and H. GATIGNON, 1984, "Optimal Product Line Pricing: The Influences of Elasticities and Cross-Elasticities," *Journal of Marketing Research*, Vol. 21, pp. 259-267.

SAGHAFI, Massoud M., 1988, "Optimal Pricing to Maximize Profits and Achieve Market-Share Targets for Single-Product and Multiproduct Companies," in T. DEVINNEY (ed.), *Issues in Pricing: Theory and Research,* pp. 239-253, Lexington Books, Lexington, MA.

SAMUELSON, William, 1986, "Bidding for Contracts," *Management Science*, Vol. 32, pp. 1533-1550.

SANDMO, A., 1971, "On the Theory of the Competitive Firm under Price Uncertainty," *American Economic Review*, Vol. 61, pp. 65-73.

SCHMALENSEE, Richard A., 1984, "Gaussian Demand and Commodity Bundling," *Journal of Business*, Vol. 57, pp. S211-S230.

SENGUPTA, S. Sankar, 1967, *Operations Research in Seller's Competition*, John Wiley and Sons, NY.

SIMON, Herman, 1989, *Price Management*, Elsevier, North Holland.

TAPIERO, Charles S., 1990, *Applied Stochastic Models and Control in Management*, 2nd impression, Elsevier Science Publishers, The Netherlands.

TELLIS, G. J., 1988, "The Price Elasticity of Selective Demand: A Meta-Analysis of Econometric Models of Sales," *Journal of Marketing Research*, Vol. 25, pp. 331-342.

THOMPSON, Patrick, and Ira HOROWITZ, 1993, "Experimentation and Optimal Output Decisions: the Cooperative Versus the Entrepreneurial Firm," *Management Science*, Vol. 39, No. 1, pp. 46-53.

TISDELL, C. A., 1968, *The Theory of Price Uncertainty, Production and Profit*, Princeton University Press, Princeton, NJ.

VENKATESH, R., and Vijay MAHAJAN, *forthcoming*, "A Probabilistic Approach to Pricing a Bundle of Products or Services," *Journal of Marketing Research.*

ZELLNER, Arnold, 1971, *An Introduction to Bayesian Inference in Econometrics*, John Wiley and Sons, NY.

3

ADVERTISING

1 OVERVIEW

As we have concentrated in the previous chapter on the pricing decision by the marketing manager in fulfilling the firm's objective, we will now examine the impact of demand uncertainty as well as other forms of randomness on the firm's advertising activities. The importance of this particular marketing activity has been stressed in the literature; what we want to focus here is the notion that in many real world situations, the effect of marketing efforts on the performance of the firm such as sales and profits is rarely known, if ever, with certainty. We will present a number of different and important contexts in which we shall analyze the way uncertainty would modify the marketing decisions. Broadly, we shall first be concerned with the usual static, one-period optimization problem where the firm's short-run objective is emphasized. In this context, the role of advertising is to basically shore up sales which can then translate into profitability. Thus, in the next section, a basic model is formulated and the nature of uncertainty specified. There we shall examine the implications for a joint decision involving advertising, pricing, and production or acquisition. We will also look at the optimal advertising decision in conjunction with the firm's pricing strategies. In Section 3, we shall examine the implications for a multi-brand environment in which a firm is typically concerned with the joint performance of several brands of products it produces. Next, Section 4 considers the dynamic problem in which advertising also plays the role of building a capital stock of goodwill in the long run. The stochastic formulation is presented immediately after the deterministic model so that the impact of uncertainty can be clearly assessed. The last section provides a summary of the results obtained in this chapter.

2 SINGLE-PRODUCT ADVERTISING: STATIC MODELS

2.1 Background

The vast literature on aggregate advertising models as exemplified in a survey by Little [1979] appears to concentrate mainly on deterministic advertising response functions whether they are static or dynamic. However, results obtained from the literature on the firm's behavior under uncertainty cast serious doubts about validity of various conclusions regarding the firm's optimal output/pricing decisions which are traditionally derived from assumptions of a deterministic world. As we have presented in the previous chapter, in general, decision rules (output/price) derived from the traditional theory of the firm under deterministic conditions should be modified in the presence of uncertainty in the sales response to the firm's decisions. Within this framework of behavior of the firm under uncertainty, the impact of the firm's attitude toward risk is also extensively explored in the literature. Since uncertainty has been shown to have important implications for the firm's output/price decisions, it is of interest to examine its possible effects on the firm's advertising activities. This represents the major purpose in this section. The material developed in this and the next sub-section is based on Nguyen [1985].

We consider here the static one-period model while postponing dynamic multi-period formulations to subsequent analyses, some will be addressed in this chapter, some in Chapter 9. Our concern is to examine the potential impact of uncertainty in scenarios in which sales response to advertising expenditures is subject to random fluctuations.   To focus on the role of advertising, we assume that unit prices are fully controlled by the firm; they are thus assumed known with certainty by the decision makers. In general, we assume that the firm's attitude toward risk can be represented by a non-linear utility function of the von Neumann-Morgenstern type. The objective of the firm is to maximize the expected value of the discounted sum of utilities derived from profits over the planning horizon. Finally, we assume that the source of uncertainty is associated with the advertising response function which relates the amount of advertising expenditures to the corresponding sales level. For the static one-period model considered in this section, it is assumed that the response function is subject to random disturbances while other parameters are known with certainty. On the other hand, in the dynamic multi-period model presented in Chapter 9, we will assume that, in addition to a random disturbance term, the response function contains an unknown parameter the true value of which the firm wishes to learn about. We will formulate this model as a stochastic dynamic programming problem the solution of which involves a Bayesian revising scheme concerning the firm's expectations about the unknown parameter of the response function. Additional assumptions concerning the cost function, the more specific form of the sales-advertising response function, etc. will be spelled out whenever appropriate.

2.2 A Basic Theoretical Structure

In this section, we examine the firm's optimal advertising decision when the response function contains a random term. Since the firm wishes to maximize the expected value of utility of profits in each period, the objective function can be written as:

$$\text{Max.} \quad E[U(\Pi)] \tag{3.1}$$

$$\text{where } \Pi = pq - C(q) - m - FC \tag{3.2}$$

$$\text{and } q = f(m) + \xi \tag{3.3}$$

where equation (3.2) defines the profit function and (3.3) represents the sales response function to advertisement.

In the preceding problem, E is the expectations operator; $U(\Pi)$ is the von Neumann-Morgenstern utility function with positive marginal utility everywhere, and with decreasing (constant) marginal utility for the risk-averse (risk-neutral) firm; p is the unit price; q is the units of sales; $C(q)$ is the known (manufacturing) cost function excluding advertising expenditures with its properties to be specified shortly; m is the advertising budget; FC is the firm's fixed costs; and the additive random term ξ possesses a known density function $\varphi(\xi)$ with mean zero and known variance. Two comments on the model's specifications are in order:

(*i*) For the sake of certain degree of generality, we assume in this section that the response function in (3.3) exhibits a positive marginal response of sales to advertisement at a non-increasing rate; i.e. $f'(m)>0$, and $f''(m)\leq0$. This theoretical form of the response function is empirically supported on the basis of various work (see Little [1979], for instance). As our discussion in the introductory chapter indicates, one would ideally wish to include many marketing variables such as price, advertising and personal selling in the sales response function as in the marketing mix framework. For a general nonlinear utility function, such a demand specification would be more difficult to deal with under the assumption of uncertainty. As a first step, we assume throughout this section that sales depends only on advertising via the specified sales response function in (3.3). For a particular class of products such as cigarettes, soft drinks, etc. in which price competition is dominated by non-price competition, the sales equation used in the following analysis can be reasonably justified as a first approximation. In this regard, we should also note that carry-over effects of advertising are assumed away. It is done here mainly for expositional simplicity as its inclusion would not affect the following analysis in any substantive way. The reader may want to consult Givon and Horsky [1990] for a recent treatment of the carry-over effect.

(*ii*) In the interest of realism, we will typically assume that the marginal manufacturing cost is positive and non-increasing over the relevant output range. While the more common assumption on the firm's cost structure is that both average cost and marginal cost curves are of U-shape, empirical findings tend to support the hypothesis that marginal cost is generally declining or constant (see Walters [1963] for a summary of empirical results). We will thus, for most of the ensuing discussion, develop the analysis on the basis of the assumption that $C'(q)=[\partial C(q)/\partial q]>0$, and $C''(q)=[\partial^2 C(q)/\partial S^2]\le 0$. We should, however, note the constrained capacity problem in connection with the production process with its implications for increasing marginal costs as the firm approaches its production capacity. Consequently, we will report the results for the case of increasing marginal cost as well.

The first-order and second-order conditions for optimality for the problem in eq.(3.1) are given respectively as:

$$E[U'(\Pi)\frac{\partial \Pi}{\partial m}] = E\{U'(\Pi)[pf'(m) - C'(q)f'(m) - 1]\} = 0 \qquad (3.4)$$

$$\text{and}\quad E[U''(\Pi).(\frac{\partial \Pi}{\partial m})^2 + U'(\Pi).\frac{\partial^2 \Pi}{\partial m^2}] < 0. \qquad (3.5)$$

We should address briefly the second-order condition (3.5) here. The inequality in (3.5) holds if the whole expression inside the brackets is negative. To examine the sign of this expression, let us rewrite (3.5) in a more complete form:

$$E\{U''(\Pi)[pf'(m) - C'(q)f'(m) - 1]^2 + U'(\Pi)[\{p - C'(q)\}f''(m)$$
$$- \{f'(m)\}^2 C''(q)]\} < 0. \qquad (3.5a)$$

We note that the expression $U''(\Pi)[pf'(m) - C'(q)f'(m) - 1]^2$ is negative for risk aversion and is zero for risk neutrality; that

$$\{U'(\Pi)[p - C'(q)]f''(m)\} \le 0; \text{ and that } \{-U'(\Pi)[f'(m)]^2 C''(q)\} \gtrless 0 \text{ for } C''(q) \lessgtr 0.$$

Since the preceding expressions have opposite signs, their relative strengths determine whether or not the second-order condition in (3.5) is satisfied. In particular, if $C''(q)\ge 0$, the assumption of risk aversion would be sufficient to satisfy condition (3.5). However, if $C''(q)<0$, condition (3.5) may require either that the firm is sufficiently risk-averse, or that $f''(m)$ is sufficiently negative, or both in such a way that the whole expression inside the expectation operator $E[.]$ in (3.5a) is negative. In view of our earlier assumptions regarding the utility function and the response function, it is reasonable for us to assume in the following analysis that the second-order condition is satisfied.

Let us try to interpret the condition in (3.4). The easiest way to interpret this necessary condition is to start with a deterministic model for a risk-neutral firm. For such a firm, the counterpart to eq. (3.4) can be written as:

$$pf'(m) = C'(q)f'(m) + 1. \tag{3.6}$$

The term on the left-hand side indicates the additional (marginal) revenue as a result of a one-dollar increase in the advertising budget. The first term on the right-hand side of (3.6) measures the additional (marginal) manufacturing cost (excluding advertising) as a result of a one dollar increase in the advertising budget. The condition thus simply requires that the sum of the marginal manufacturing cost and the one dollar increase in advertising be equal to the marginal revenue generated as a result of this marketing activity.

An economic interpretation for (3.4) is parallel to that for (3.6) with an obvious modification for the presence of the marginal utility term in the condition. Further, since the response function is not known with certainty, one can only calculate the expected values for marginal cost and marginal revenue.

We will now examine the effect of uncertainty in the response function on the firm's advertising decisions by comparing the advertising level under random response function to that under a certainty-equivalent condition. A common procedure in economics literature to define a certainty-equivalent random variable is to assume that the decision maker behaves as if he knew with certainty that random variable would equal its mean. (see Theil [1957]). To prove *Theorem* 3.1 below, we first prove the following:

Lemma 3.1. *Assume that the marginal manufacturing cost $C'(q)$ is linear in the sales level, then: $E[(\partial \Pi(\bar{m}, \xi)/\partial m] = 0$ where $\bar{m}$ satisfies $[\partial \Pi(\bar{m}, 0)/\partial m] = 0$.*

Proof. We first note that the random profit function depends on m and the disturbance term ξ. We define a certainty-equivalent response function by setting $\xi = 0$, i.e. we assume that the firm behaves as if it knew with certainty the sales level would be equal to its expected value. The value $\bar{m}$ defines the certainty-equivalent (deterministic) solution. That is, we define $\bar{m}$ such that:

$$\frac{\partial \Pi(\bar{m}, 0)}{\partial m} = pf'(\bar{m}) - C'[f(\bar{m})]f'(\bar{m}) - 1 = 0. \tag{3.7}$$

Now consider: $E[\dfrac{\partial \Pi(m, \xi)}{\partial m}] = pf'(m) - E[C'(q)]f'(m) - 1$

$$= pf'(m) - C'[E(q)]f'(m) - 1 = pf'(m) - C'[f(m)]f'(m) - 1 \tag{3.8}$$

where we note that the second equality follows since $C'(q)$ is linear. From eqs. (3.7) and (3.8), it follows that $E[\partial \Pi(\bar{m}, \xi)/\partial m] = 0$.

Q.E.D.

We now state and prove the following:

Theorem 3.1. *For the risk-averse firm, if the marginal manufacturing cost is a decreasing (increasing) function of the sales level then the firm's optimal advertising expenditure under random sales response is less (more) than that under deterministic conditions. For the risk-neutral firm, the optimal advertising under certainty will be identical to that under random demand. Further, if the marginal manufacturing cost is constant, uncertainty in the sales response function does not have any impact on the firm's advertising decisions.*

Proof. We first prove the case in which the marginal manufacturing cost is a decreasing function of sales level, i.e., $C''(q) < 0$.

Let us denote the optimal advertising level under a random response function as m^*, i.e., m^* satisfies

$$E\{U'[\Pi(m^*,\xi)].\frac{\partial\Pi(m^*,\xi)}{\partial m}\} = 0. \tag{3.9}$$

Now, from the profit function, we have

$$\frac{\partial^2\Pi}{\partial m\partial\xi} = -g'(m).C''(q).\frac{\partial q}{\partial\xi} > 0 \tag{3.10}$$

since $C''(q) < 0$ and $g'(m) > 0$.

It then follows that

$$[\frac{\partial\Pi(m,\xi)}{\partial m}]\underset{<}{\overset{>}{\lessgtr}}[\frac{\partial\Pi(m,0)}{\partial m}] \text{ for } \xi\underset{<}{\overset{>}{\gtrless}}0. \tag{3.11}$$

Further, note that $(\partial U'(\Pi)/\partial\xi) = U''(\Pi).(\partial\Pi/\partial\xi) \leq 0$ for $U''(\Pi) \leq 0$ since $(\partial\Pi/\partial\xi) = p - C'(q) > 0$. We then have: For $\xi\underset{<}{\overset{>}{\gtrless}}0$,

$$U'[\Pi(m,\xi)]\underset{>}{\overset{<}{\lessgtr}}(=)U'[\Pi(m,0)] \text{ when } U''(\Pi) < (=)0. \tag{3.12}$$

From (3.11) and (3.12), let us write:

$$\{[U'[\Pi(m,0)] - U'[\Pi(m,\xi)]\}[\frac{\partial\Pi(m,0)}{\partial m} - \frac{\partial\Pi(m,\xi)}{\partial m}] \leq 0 \text{ when } U''(\Pi) \leq 0.$$

Upon evaluating the preceding expressions at $\bar{m}$, we have:

$$-\frac{\partial\Pi(\bar{m},\xi)}{\partial m}\{U'[\Pi(\bar{m},0)] - U'[\Pi(\bar{m},\xi)]\} \leq 0 \text{ when } U''(\Pi) \leq 0.$$

Upon taking expectations with respect to $f(\xi)$ and applying Lemma 3.1, the preceding relations become:

$$E\{U'[\Pi(\bar{m},\xi)].\frac{\partial\Pi(\bar{m},\xi)}{\partial m}\} \leq 0 \text{ when } U''(\Pi) \leq 0. \tag{3.13}$$

Since the second-order condition in (3.5) requires that the partial derivative of $E[U'(\Pi).\{\partial\Pi/\partial m\}]$ with respect to m is negative, a comparison between eqs. (3.9) and (3.13) gives us the desired result: $m^* \leq \bar{m}$ when $U''(\Pi)\leq0$.

For $C''(q) > 0$, following identical steps would lead to the result that $m^* \geq \bar{m}$ when $U''(\Pi)\leq0$. For a constant marginal cost function, $C''(q) = 0$, hence the expression in eq. (3.10) is zero. It follows that:

$$E\{U'[\Pi(\bar{m},\xi)].\frac{\partial\Pi(\bar{m},\xi)}{\partial m}\} =0$$

which, in comparison to (3.9), implies that: $m^* = \bar{m}$.

Q.E.D.

Economic implications of the preceding theorem can be immediately seen. Our result shows that the firm's attitude toward risk plays a crucial role in determining the optimal level of advertisement. The risk-neutral firm, facing a random response function, would behave as if it was confronted with a certainty-equivalent(deterministic) response function. For the risk-averse firm, the effect of uncertainty in the response function on the firm's advertising spending depends upon the cost structure the firm is faced with. For the case of decreasing marginal manufacturing cost, uncertainty in the sales response function would result in a reduction in the firm's advertising budget. On the other hand, if the cost structure is such that marginal cost is an increasing function of output, the firm's optimal level of advertisement under random sales response is higher than that under certainty-equivalent conditions.

2.3 The Joint Production-Advertising Model

Unlike the basic model in the previous sub-section where advertising is the sole decision variable, we consider below a model, due to Horowitz [1971], in which in addition to the advertising expenditure, the firm has also to make a decision on production level before the realization of the random term. Consider the demand function of the form:

$$q = f(p,m) + \xi \qquad (3.14)$$

which is of course related to the previous sales response function in (3.3).

Even though it is exogenously given here, the explicit presence of the price variable p in (3.14) reminds us that price can potentially be an important decision variable in this context, a feature we will explore in the next sub-section. In the mean time, the problem facing the firm is to choose jointly an optimal output level, denoted as q^* in advance of actual q which is determined by the product price and the company's advertising activities in order to maximize expected utility of profits. To see clearly the implications of demand uncertainty, it will be assumed that there would be no inventory, a simplifying assumption which will be relaxed in our analysis in Chapter 7. Further, we will also be assuming constant marginal cost with the consequent expected profits functions defined as follows:

$$\Pi_1 = pq - C(q^*) - m - FC \quad \text{for} \quad q \leq q^*$$

$$\text{and} \quad \Pi_2 = pq^* - C(q^*) - m - FC \quad \text{for} \quad q > q^*. \tag{3.15}$$

Hence the firm's objective function is:

$$\text{Max.} \quad E[U(\Pi)] = \int_0^{\xi^*} U(\Pi_1)\varphi(\xi)d\xi + U(\Pi_2)\int_{\xi^*}^{\infty}\varphi(\xi)d\xi$$

where $\xi^* = q^* - f(p,m)$.

The first-order conditions involve setting both $\partial E[U(\Pi)]/\partial q$ and $\partial E[U(\Pi)]/\partial m$ equal zero. The first condition yields the result that risk-averse firms produce less for any given level of marketing activity, a result which is basically standard in the quantity-setting case. To show this result, first note that the expected marginal utility of profits is defined to be:

$$E[\frac{\partial U(\Pi)}{\partial \Pi}] \equiv E[U'(\Pi)] = \int_0^{\xi^*} U'(\Pi_1)\varphi(\xi)d\xi + U'(\Pi_2)\int_{\xi^*}^{\infty}\varphi(\xi)d\xi$$

where $U'(\Pi_1) = \partial U(\Pi_1)/\partial \Pi$, $U'(\Pi_2) = \partial U(\Pi_2)/\partial \Pi$.

The first-order condition can be written as:

$$\frac{\partial E[U(\Pi)]}{\partial q^*} = 0 \Rightarrow \alpha_U p \int_{\xi^*}^{\infty}\varphi(\xi)d\xi = C'$$

$$\text{where} \quad \alpha_U \equiv \frac{U'(\Pi_2)}{E[U'(\Pi)]}. \tag{3.16}$$

In the preceding relation, the left-hand side represents risk-adjusted expected marginal revenue (since the price is fixed and given, and $\int_{\xi^*}^{\infty}\varphi(\xi)d\xi$ represents the probability that the product, once acquired or produced, will be sold). The easiest way to interpret the preceding condition is to note that α_U exhibits the firm's risk-taking behavior; with the value of unity for risk neutrality and the value less than unity for risk aversion. The left-hand side in the equality condition in (3.16) represents risk-adjusted expected marginal revenue, being required to be equal to known marginal cost $C'(q^*)$ on the right-hand side. Thus, for risk neutrality, the condition in (3.16) becomes $p\int_{\xi^*}^{\infty}\varphi(\xi)d\xi = C'(q^*)$, which simply implies that the expected marginal revenue equals the firm's constant marginal cost. For risk aversion, α_U is less than 1, the condition implies that the firm should choose an output level so that the expected revenue (due to expected demand) exceeds the marginal cost; which in turn implies that the risk-averse firms select smaller output to begin with due to the second-order condition which dictates that the marginal revenue must be declining for the truly optimal output to emerge.

On the other hand, regarding the advertising decision variable, the necessary condition can be shown to yield:

$$p\frac{\partial f(p,m)}{\partial m}[1-\alpha_U\int_{\xi*}^{\infty}\varphi(\xi)d\xi]=1 \qquad (3.17)$$

where α_U is defined previously.

Clearly, for risk neutrality, $\alpha_U=1$, the preceding expression becomes:

$$p\frac{\partial f(p,m)}{\partial m}[1-\int_{\xi*}^{\infty}\varphi(\xi)d\xi]=p\frac{\partial f(p,m)}{\partial m}[\Phi(\xi*)]=1 \qquad (3.17a)$$

where $\Phi(\xi*)\equiv\int_{0}^{\xi*}\varphi(\xi)d\xi$.

The preceding result simply states that for a chosen output level, the additional dollar spent on advertising should only be justified if it yields an identical expected marginal revenue. Note that we assume here a linear cost of advertising and note also that in the decision range, it is assumed once again that marginal productivity of advertising with respect to sales is positive but diminishing as the advertising expenditure increases.

For risk aversion, $\alpha<1$, it follows that for any given output level that was chosen by the firm, the expression $(p)[\partial f(p,m)/\partial m]$ is necessarily smaller in order to satisfy the equality required by (3.17a). This, coupled with the fact that the sales response function exhibits positive but diminishing marginal contribution by marketing spending, yields the result that optimal advertising is larger for a risk-averse firm in comparison to that of a risk-neutral firm. The result for the risk-preferred firm can be seen in the opposite; but we will not report it here. While Horowitz emphasizes the qualifications of this result on the basis of his assumption that both advertising and the output are chosen *jointly*, it appears that the implications for the impact of risk-taking attitude on advertising decisions in the context of this model may have been misunderstood by other writers.

To fully understand this result, note that the firm has chosen an output level to produce, taking into account the potential role of advertising in inducing consumers to buy whatever the amount produced. Since there is no salvage value and there is no penalty to under supply, a risk-neutral firm will select the output and advertising level so that the expected revenue equal production cost and at the same time the expected revenue generated from advertising equal advertising cost. Now, the risk-averse firm, on the one hand, tends to choose a lower output level, but for any output level chosen, the advertising will be larger than the risk-neutral choice in order to assume that the produced amount is going to be sold. Since both decisions are being made jointly, there is no clear-cut results regarding the advertising levels between the two types of risk-taking firms.

It should also be of interest to note that combining (3.16) and (3.17), it follows immediately that:

$$[p-C'(q*)]\frac{\partial f(p,m)}{\partial m}=1. \tag{3.18}$$

Of course, the result can be made more general to reflect the nonlinear cost of advertising or it can be a little more specific for the constant marginal cost which is assumed with considerable regularity in this work and elsewhere in marketing literature.

2.4 The Joint Pricing-Advertising Problem

For the price-setting firm, then the problem is to find p and m to maximize the expected utility of profits:

$$\text{Max.}\quad E[U(\Pi)]=\int_0^\infty U(\Pi)\varphi(\xi)d\xi$$

where the profit function is now simply defined as:

$$\Pi=pf(p,m)-C(q)-m-FC.$$

Once again, the first-order conditions amount to setting both $\{\partial E[U(\Pi)/\partial q\}$ and $\{\partial E[U(\Pi)/\partial m\}$ equal zero. The first yields the result that whether risk-averse firms charge a lower or higher price depends crucially on the firm's cost characterization, and the second can be shown to yield:

$$\frac{\partial f(p,m)}{\partial m}\equiv\frac{\partial E(q)}{\partial m}=\frac{E[U'(\Pi)]}{\int_0^\infty U'(\Pi)[p-C'(q)]\varphi(\xi)d\xi} \tag{3.19}$$

where $U'(\Pi)\equiv[\partial U(\Pi)/\partial\Pi]$.

For risk neutrality, $E[U'(\Pi)]=U'(\Pi)$, it would follow from the preceding expression that

$$[p-C'(q)]\frac{\partial f(p,m)}{\partial m}=[p-C'(q)]\frac{\partial E(q)}{\partial m}=1 \tag{3.18a}$$

which, while identical to (3.18), is derived from a completely different set of assumption; hence numbered differently to avoid confusion.

The condition again simply means that the expected marginal revenue generated from advertising, net of production cost, equals to the advertising cost which is unity.

For risk aversion, $E[U'(\Pi)]<U'(\Pi)$, it follows from (3.19) that at any given price level, the marginal productivity of advertising expressed as the expression $[\partial f(p,m)/\partial m]$ is smaller, resulting in a larger advertising level. It is interesting to

compare this result to the results previously obtained and summarized in Theorem 3.1 which states that the firm's risk-taking attitude has no impact on the firm decisions when the marginal cost is constant. The reason for this seemingly contrary results can be spelled out as follows. Previously, the price is fixed by the market, there it was shown that the additivity of the random disturbance would simply induce the firm to behave as in a certainty-equivalent fashion. Now, this part of the argument remains the same, except that the firm is also deciding on the price which is lower for the risk-averse firm; lower price tends to increase sales; hence the increased advertising is a direct result of this expected increase in demand.

The most important distinction here in comparison to the previous result is that both price and advertising decisions are to be made jointly. Thus, for a chosen price level, risk-averse firms tend to advertise more. However, since risk-averse firms want to lower their prices to begin with, there is no way to tell whether risk-averse firms in fact advertise less or more than the decisions made by the risk-neutral firms.

It is of interest to note that on the basis of (3.19), a number of implications can be seen. For a determined output level, as in the previous sub-section, and a given price, the optimal advertising implied by (3.19) allows us to write

$$[p - C'(q^*)] \frac{\partial f(p,m)}{\partial m} = 1 \tag{3.18b}$$

which is again identical to (3.18), but due to a different interpretation.

On the one hand, note that regardless of risk-taking behavior, provided that the price is determined exogenously and that marginal cost is constant we would also obtain an identical result which indicates clearly that, uncertainty of the additive type assumed in the present analysis has no impact on the firm's advertising decision as the firm behaves in a certainty-equivalent manner by acting on the basis of the expected value of the random sales.

On the other hand, in a truly simultaneous decision-making involving both pricing and marketing activities, both conditions have to be satisfied at the same time, hence (3.18a) does not in general hold. To assess the impact of demand uncertainty in this framework of joint decision, one would need to explicitly explore both conditions. Dehez and Jacquemin [1975] extended this particular interpretation implied by the Horowitz analysis.

In particular, it can be shown that the optimization problem facing the firm subject to similar constraints, with a constant marginal cost denoted as c, yields the following first-order conditions:

$$(p - c) \frac{\partial E(q)}{\partial p} + E(q) = -\frac{E[U'(\Pi)\xi]}{E[U'(\Pi)]} \tag{3.20}$$

$$\text{and } (p - c) \frac{\partial E(q)}{\partial m} = 1$$

from which it follows that the introduction of uncertainty leaves the optimal pricing policy of the risk-neutral firm *unchanged*. By the same token, the firm's marketing decisions will also be similar.

For risk-averse firms, it can be shown that

$$\frac{\partial E[U(\Pi|p^*,m^*)]}{\partial p} < \frac{\partial E[U(\Pi|p_r,m_r)]}{\partial p} = 0$$

$$\text{and } \frac{\partial E[U(\Pi|p^*,m^*)]}{\partial m} = \frac{\partial E[U(\Pi|p_r,m_r)]}{\partial m} = 0$$

where the asterisk denotes the risk-neutral solution and the subscript r denotes the risk-averse solution.

The result can be summarized as follows. Assuming that the second-order conditions are satisfied and as before, using an upper bar to denote the certainty-equivalent solution, it can then be shown that $p_r < p^* = \bar{p}$; i.e., risk-averse firm reduces its price. On the other hand $m_r > m^* = \bar{m}$ when $\{\partial^2 E[U(\Pi)]/\partial p\partial m < 0\}$ and $m_r < m^* = \bar{m}$ when $\{\partial^2 E[U(\Pi)]/\partial p\partial m > 0\}$. Then it is shown that whether the risk-averse firm advertises less or more depends on the nature of the movement of advertising and the price changes. In particular, the result is that the risk-averse firm advertises more if advertising is of a defensive type in the sense that as price is cut, advertising goes up. This appears to be driven by the same force which operates behind the joint price-quantity setting in the Baron-Leland framework we discussed in the previous chapter. We should note a different but related empirical observation that an increase in non-price advertising tends to lead to lower price sensitivity (see, e.g., Kaul and Wittink [1995]).

3 MULTI-BRAND ADVERTISING

3.1 Background

This section examines theoretical implications for the firm's advertising decisions under conditions of random sales response to advertising within the context of multibrand competition. The competitive environment that we assume here is characterized not only by interactions among different companies within a given industry but also by interactions among different brands produced by a single company. Since advertising plays an important role in promoting product differentiation, it is most appropriate to address the issue of advertising in a multibrand multicompany framework. A theoretical model is formulated to enable us to examine the effect of uncertainty in the sales-advertising relations and that of the firm's attitude toward risk on its advertising allocation decisions. We will assess the theoretical results by estimating an econometric model in the Lanchester warfare tradition using cigarette data. The empirical exercise will be reported in Chapter 9 of the book.

Theoretical and empirical studies on the optimal advertising issue have mostly concentrated on single-product/single-brand cases. In particular, the impact of uncertainty on advertising decisions for single-product firms has been examined extensively in the literature (e.g., see Monahan [1983]; Nguyen [1985]). These studies show generally that deterministic decision rules should be modified under the assumption of random demand. The large body of economics literature on the general subject of economic decisions under conditions of risk and uncertainty has also dealt almost exclusively with single-product firms (see the survey paper by McCall [1971], for instance). However, two papers on the theory of the monopolistic multiproduct firm under random demand (Dhrymes [1964]; and Blair and Heggestad [1977]) offer some economic insights that are absent in the one-product case. For example, the standard result that a higher degree of risk aversion leads to a smaller output may not apply to the multiproduct firm because of stochastic interactions among different products of the firm. Since the model in this section deals with a multibrand environment in which interactions are crucial, one of our major objectives is to examine the possible effect of attitude toward risk and the effect of the random sales response function on the multibrand firm's advertising budgets. It turns out that only under fairly restrictive conditions regarding random sales response specifications, cost structure, and the firm's utility function can one determine the direction of the impact of uncertainty and risk behavior on advertising.

The next sub-section formulates a theoretical model for a multibrand firm that wishes to maximize its expected utility of profits by allocating its advertising budgets to its various brands, subject to random sales responses to advertising. We then examine the impact of the firm's attitude toward risk and that of uncertainty in the response functions on its advertising decisions. The results we report in this section are based on Nguyen [1987].

3.2 The Theoretical Model

In this subsection, we formulate the firm's expected utility maximization problem in which the decision variables are the firm's advertising levels in its different brands. We then derive necessary and sufficient conditions for an interior solution to the problem.

Assume that a particular company produces N brands whose sales levels follow the following sales response functions:

$$q_i = g_i(Lq_i, m_1, m_2, ..., m_N, m_{i0}, \xi_i); \ i = 1, 2, ..., N, \qquad (3.21)$$

where q_i is the level of sales of brand i, Lq_i is the one-period lagged level of q_i, m_i

represents the advertising level of the i-th brand, m_{i0} refers to the advertising level of all the remaining brands in the industry, and ξ_i is a random term.

The sales response function in (3.21) represents an extension to the standard response function in the literature. As usual, lagged sales level is included as an independent variable in order to take into account the carry-over effect. To incorporate into the model potential interactions among different brands within a single company as well as those among different companies, we include all the m_i's; $i = 1,2,...,N$, as well as m_{i0} in the set of explanatory variables. We will report in Chapter 9 that a linear form of (3.21) is empirically supported on the basis of data on cigarettes. We further specify that

$$E(q_i|\psi_i) = h_i(\psi_i),$$

where E is the expectation operator and for convenience we denote $\psi_i \equiv (Lq_i, m_1, m_2,..., m_N, m_{i0})$. The conditional variance-covariance matrix of sales of the N brands is denoted as

$$\Omega \equiv [\sigma_{ij}]; \ i,j = 1,2,...,N.$$

Next, we assume that the firm's total cost (C), excluding advertising expenditures, is represented by the following quadratic cost function:

$$C = \mathbf{c}^T\mathbf{q} + \frac{1}{2}\mathbf{q}^T\mathbf{Dq} \tag{3.22}$$

where $\mathbf{c}^T = \{c_1,c_2,...,c_N\}$; $\mathbf{q}^T = \{q_1,q_2...,q_N\}$; $\mathbf{D} = [d_{ij}]$; $i,j = 1,...,N$, and as before, the superscript T denotes transposition.

It follows that $MC_i = \partial C/\partial q_i = c_i + d_{ii}q_i + \sum_{j=1,j\neq i}^{N} d_{ij}q_j$, where MC_i is the marginal cost of producing one extra unit of brand i. Thus it can be seen that c_i represents the constant for the marginal cost function, $d_{ii} = \partial^2 C/\partial q_i^2$, and $d_{ij} = \partial^2 C/\partial q_i \partial q_j$.

For a nonlinear utility function, the objective of the firm is to

$$\text{Max. } E[U(\Pi)|\psi]$$

$$= \int \int ... \int [U(\sum_{i=1}^{N} p_i q_i - C - \sum_{i=1}^{N} m_i)] \varphi(q_1,q_2,...,q_N|\psi)dq_1 dq_2...dq_N, \tag{3.23}$$

where, for convenience, we define $\psi \equiv \{\psi_1, \psi_2,...,\psi_N\}$ and where $\varphi(q_1,q_2,...,q_N|\psi)$ is the conditional joint density of sales.

Again, with linearized utility, the first-order conditions for optimality to (3.23) can be shown to be

$$\{U' + \frac{1}{2}[E(\Pi - E\Pi)^2]U'''\}\frac{\partial E(\Pi)}{\partial m_i}$$

$$= -\frac{1}{2}U''[\frac{dE(\Pi - E\Pi)^2}{dm_i}]; \quad i=1,2,\ldots,N \tag{3.24}$$

where $E(\Pi - E\Pi)^2 = \sum\limits_{i=1}^{N}\sum\limits_{j=1}^{N} p_i p_j \sigma_{ij} + E(C - EC)^2 - 2E[(C - EC)\sum\limits_{i=1}^{N} p_i \xi_i].$

The model can be greatly simplified without much sacrifice by working with a quadratic utility function, in which case, eq. (3.24) becomes

$$\frac{\partial E(\Pi)}{\partial m_i} = \frac{r}{2}[\frac{dE(\Pi - E\Pi)^2}{dm_i}] \tag{3.25}$$

which requires that the marginal contribution of advertising on the i-th brand to the firm's overall expected profits must be equated against its contribution to the variance of the firm's profits, subject to the firm's attitude toward risk.

It turns out that, for the sales response function of the general form in (3.21), it is virtually impossible to derive simple and interpretable results implicitly contained in (3.25). We therefore work with a linear form of (3.21) in the remaining analysis. It should be noted again that the available empirical results lend support to such a linear form of the sales response function to advertising. Let us write, therefore,

$$q_i = h_i + \xi_i \tag{3.21a}$$

where $h_i = \sum\limits_{j=1}^{N} \gamma_{ij} m_j + \alpha_i Lq_i + \gamma_{i0} m_{i0}$ in which γ_{ij}'s, α_i, and γ_{i0} are linear coefficients.

The matrix form of (3.21a) is

$$\mathbf{S} = \mathbf{h} + \mathbf{U}$$
$$= \mathbf{\Gamma m} + \alpha \mathbf{Lq} + \gamma_0 \mathbf{m}_0 + \mathbf{U} \tag{3.26}$$

where $\mathbf{\Gamma}$ is the $N \times N$ coefficient matrix, $\mathbf{\Gamma} = [\gamma_{ij}]$; $\alpha = \text{diag}\{\alpha_1, \alpha_2, \ldots, \alpha_N\}$; $\mathbf{m}^T = \{m_1, m_2, \ldots, m_N\}$; $\mathbf{Lq}^T = \{Lq_1, Lq_2, \ldots, Lq_N\}$; $\gamma_0 = \text{diag}\{\gamma_{10}, \gamma_{20}, \ldots, \gamma_{N0}\}$; $\mathbf{m}_0^T = \{m_{10}, m_{20}, \ldots, m_{N0}\}$; $\mathbf{U}^T = \{\xi_1, \xi_2, \ldots, \xi_N\}$; and $\mathbf{h}^T = \{h_1, h_2, \ldots, h_N\}$.

To calculate $dE(\Pi - E\Pi)^2/d\mathbf{m}$, we proceed as follows. First, note that the profit function is $\Pi = \mathbf{p}^T \mathbf{q} - C - \mathbf{e}^T \mathbf{m}$, where $\mathbf{p}^T = \{p_1, p_2, \ldots, p_N\}$ and $\mathbf{e}^T = \{1, 1, \ldots, 1\}$. One thus has

$$E(\Pi) = \mathbf{p}^T E(\mathbf{q}) - E(C) - \mathbf{e}^T \mathbf{m}$$

based on which one obtains

$$E[\Pi - E(\Pi)]^2 = \mathbf{p}^T \Omega \mathbf{p} + E[C - E(C)][C - E(C)]^T - 2E(\mathbf{p}^T \mathbf{U}[C - E(C)]^T) \tag{3.27}$$

where $E(C) = \mathbf{c}^T E(\mathbf{q}) + \frac{1}{2} E(\mathbf{q}^T D \mathbf{q}) = \mathbf{c}^T \mathbf{h} + \frac{1}{2} \mathbf{h}^T D \mathbf{h} + \frac{1}{2} E(\mathbf{U}^T D \mathbf{U}).$

Straightforward calculation yields

$$E[C-E(C)][C-E(C)]^T$$

$$=(\mathbf{h}^T\mathbf{D}^T\mathbf{\Omega}\mathbf{D}\mathbf{h}+\mathbf{h}^T\mathbf{D}^T\mathbf{\Omega}\mathbf{c})+\text{ terms not involving }\mathbf{h}.$$

(3.28)

Also, $E(\mathbf{p}^T\mathbf{U}[C-E(C)]^T)=\mathbf{c}^T\mathbf{\Omega}\mathbf{p}+1/2\mathbf{h}^T\mathbf{D}^T\mathbf{\Omega}\mathbf{p}+$ terms not involving $\mathbf{h}$. From (3.28) and (3.29), rewrite (3.27) as

$$E[\Pi-E(\Pi)]^2=\mathbf{h}^T\mathbf{D}^T\mathbf{\Omega}\mathbf{D}\mathbf{h}+\mathbf{h}^T\mathbf{D}^T\mathbf{\Omega}[\mathbf{c}-\mathbf{p}]+\text{ terms not involving }\mathbf{h}.$$

Note that in (3.26), $\mathbf{h}=\mathbf{\Gamma}\mathbf{m}+\alpha\mathbf{L}\mathbf{q}+\gamma_0\mathbf{m}_0$. Note also that we will calculate $dE(\Pi-E\Pi)^2/d\mathbf{m}$ in (3.30), and the relation in (3.29) can be simplified further as

$$E[\Pi-E(\Pi)]^2=[\mathbf{m}^T\mathbf{\Gamma}^T\mathbf{D}^T\mathbf{\Omega}\mathbf{D}\mathbf{\Gamma}\mathbf{m}+2\mathbf{m}^T\mathbf{\Gamma}^T\mathbf{D}^T\mathbf{\Omega}\mathbf{D}(\alpha\mathbf{L}\mathbf{q}+\gamma_0\mathbf{m}_0)$$

$$+\mathbf{m}^T\mathbf{\Gamma}^T\mathbf{D}^T\mathbf{\Omega}(\mathbf{c}-\mathbf{p})]+\text{ terms not involving }\mathbf{m}$$

based on which it follows that

$$\frac{dE(\Pi-E\Pi)^2}{d\mathbf{m}}=2\mathbf{\Gamma}^T\mathbf{D}^T\mathbf{\Omega}\mathbf{D}\mathbf{\Gamma}\mathbf{m}$$

$$+\mathbf{\Gamma}^T\mathbf{D}^T\mathbf{\Omega}[2\mathbf{D}(\alpha\mathbf{L}\mathbf{q}+\gamma_0\mathbf{m}_0)+(\mathbf{c}-\mathbf{p})]$$

(3.30)

which indicates the impact of advertising on the variance of the firm's profits. One can now rewrite the first-order condition as

$$\frac{\partial E(\Pi)}{\partial\mathbf{m}}-r\mathbf{\Gamma}^T\mathbf{D}^T\mathbf{\Omega}\mathbf{D}\mathbf{\Gamma}\mathbf{m}$$

$$-r\mathbf{\Gamma}^T\mathbf{D}^T\mathbf{\Omega}[\mathbf{D}(\alpha\mathbf{L}\mathbf{q}+\gamma_0\mathbf{m}_0)+\frac{1}{2}(\mathbf{c}-\mathbf{p})]=0$$

(3.31)

where r is positive for a risk-averse firm and r is negative for risk preference. The second-order condition is that

$$\frac{\partial^2 E(\Pi)}{\partial\mathbf{m}^2}-r\mathbf{\Gamma}^T\mathbf{D}^T\mathbf{\Omega}\mathbf{D}\mathbf{\Gamma}$$

(3.32)

be negative definite.

For the risk-averse firm (i.e., $r>0$), a sufficient condition to satisfy (3.32) is that $[\partial^2 E(\Pi)/\partial m^2]$ be negative definite since $\mathbf{\Omega}$ is positive definite. The assumption of negative definiteness of $[\partial^2 E(\Pi)/\partial m^2]$ is a standard one in economics literature which implies declining expected marginal profits. Thus the second-order condition in (3.32) is satisfied for the risk-averse firm.

For $r < 0$, one cannot be assured that (3.32) is satisfied. We have obtained theoretical conditions for (3.32) to be satisfied for $r < 0$; it was summarized by Lemma 2.1 in Chapter 2. It appears, however, that risk preference represents purely an academic exercise without much empirical support.

3.3 Theoretical Analysis: Effect of Risk Aversion

We now examine the effects of risk aversion and of the random sales response function on the firm's advertising budgets for its various brands. Let us first consider the impact of risk aversion.

Differentiating (3.31) with respect to r, one has, after rearranging terms,

$$[\Gamma^T J \Gamma - r \Gamma^T D^T \Omega D \Gamma] \frac{\partial m}{\partial r} = \Gamma^T D^T \Omega D \Gamma m$$

$$+ \Gamma^T D^T \Omega [D(\alpha L q + \gamma_0 m_0) + \frac{1}{2}(c - p)]$$

(3.33)

where we define $J = [\partial^2 E(\Pi)/\partial h_i \partial h_j]$ and it is recalled that $h_i = E(q_i)$. It is not readily possible to determine the sign of the column vector ($\partial m/\partial r$) on the basis of (3.33). To do so, we need a number of conditions regarding the matrices D, Γ, and Ω. Since we will often refer to these conditions later, let us specify them here together with their justifications.

1. *Structural complementarity.* This condition simply refers to the nonnegative effects of advertising on various brands of a company on the sales levels of that company's brands. Formally, this condition specifies that Γ is a nonnegative matrix; that is, all of its elements are nonnegative. We specify that the (i,i) element of Γ, namely, γ_{ii}, $i=1,2,...,N$, be positive since $\gamma_{ii} = \partial q_i/\partial m_i$ represents the partial effect of a one-unit change in advertising on brand i on its own brand's sales level. Further, we specify that $\gamma_{ij} \geq 0$ for $i \neq j$ since $\gamma_{ij} = \partial q_i/\partial m_j$, which represents the partial effect of a one-unit change in advertising on brand j on the sales level of brand i of the *same* firm. This condition of structural complementarity has been empirically tested using the cigarette data.

2. *Nondeclining cost function.* This condition specifies that $d_{ij} \geq 0$ where $d_{ij} = \partial^2 C/\partial q_i \partial q_j; i,j=1,2,...,N$. Although empirical results in the literature have indicated otherwise, the standard second-order condition for optimality for the single-product firm's profit maximization problem is that the marginal cost is increasing. The condition that $d_{ij} \geq 0$ is not therefore completely out of line with the traditional assumption regarding cost structure. Also, this condition implies that all joint economies of scale are exhausted, and it may be of interest to relate this condition to the notion of economies of scope introduced in Baumol, Panzar, and Willig [1982].

3. *Stochastic complementarity.* While the diagonal elements of Ω are all positive, we further specify the condition that all off-diagonal elements of Ω be nonnegative. This condition states that sales in a particular company's various brands are not negatively correlated with each other. Again, this condition is subject to empirical testing on the basis of the cigarette data.

Having specified the preceding conditions, let us now consider (3.33). The column vector on its right-hand side contains elements that are all positive. This fact follows directly from equation (3.31), where $r > 0$ for risk-averse firms and where $[\partial E(\Pi)/\partial \mathbf{m}]$ is positive (the standard assumption of positive marginal expected profits). Thus we write (3.33) as

$$\frac{\partial \mathbf{m}}{\partial r} = [\mathbf{\Gamma}^T \mathbf{J} \mathbf{\Gamma} - r\mathbf{\Gamma}^T \mathbf{D}^T \mathbf{\Omega} \mathbf{D} \mathbf{\Gamma}]^{-1}\mathbf{K} \qquad (3.33a)$$

where $\mathbf{K}$ is defined accordingly, and we just showed that $\mathbf{K} > 0$.

We will now be able to state and prove the following result regarding the impact of the firm's risk behavior on its advertising decisions, that is, the sign of $(\partial \mathbf{m}/\partial r)$ in (3.33a):

Theorem 3.2. *For the risk-averse firm, given that the "structural complementarity" condition, the "nondeclining cost function" condition, and the "stochastic complementarity" condition are satisfied, then the higher the degree of risk aversion, the lower the advertising budgets for all brands if $\mathbf{J}_{ij} > r(\mathbf{D}^T \mathbf{\Omega} \mathbf{D})_{ij}$, where the subscript (i,j) denotes the (i,j) element of each matrix for $i \neq j$.*

Proof. Let us consider the matrix $-[\mathbf{\Gamma}^T \mathbf{J} \mathbf{\Gamma} - r\mathbf{\Gamma}^T \mathbf{D}^T \mathbf{\Omega} \mathbf{D} \mathbf{\Gamma}]$. For $r > 0$, this matrix is positive definite since the second-order condition in (3.32) is satisfied. Now if all three conditions 1, 2, and 3 hold, the matrix $r\mathbf{\Gamma}^T \mathbf{D}^T \mathbf{\Omega} \mathbf{D} \mathbf{\Gamma}$ contains all nonnegative elements. Recalling that $\mathbf{J}$ is negative definite, it then follows that all *diagonal* elements of $[\mathbf{\Gamma}^T \mathbf{J} \mathbf{\Gamma} - r\mathbf{\Gamma}^T \mathbf{D}^T \mathbf{\Omega} \mathbf{D} \mathbf{\Gamma}]$ are negative. Further, if $\mathbf{J}_{ij} > r(\mathbf{D}^T \mathbf{\Omega} \mathbf{D})_{ij}$, then all off-diagonal elements of $[\mathbf{\Gamma}^T \mathbf{J} \mathbf{\Gamma} - r\mathbf{\Gamma}^T \mathbf{D}^T \mathbf{\Omega} \mathbf{D} \mathbf{\Gamma}]$ are positive. Taking all these together, the matrix $-[\mathbf{\Gamma}^T \mathbf{J} \mathbf{\Gamma} - r\mathbf{\Gamma}^T \mathbf{D}^T \mathbf{\Omega} \mathbf{D} \mathbf{\Gamma}]$ has a special sign pattern that all diagonal elements are positive while all off-diagonal elements are negative. Due to this sign pattern, one can always find a scalar λ and a *positive* matrix $\mathbf{H}$ such that $-[\mathbf{\Gamma}^T \mathbf{J} \mathbf{\Gamma} - r\mathbf{\Gamma}^T \mathbf{D}^T \mathbf{\Omega} \mathbf{D} \mathbf{\Gamma}] = [\lambda \mathbf{I} - \mathbf{H}]$. Now, using a well-known result in positive (Perron-Frobenius) matrix enables one to see that $(\lambda \mathbf{I} - \mathbf{H})^{-1}$ is nonnegative if and only if $\lambda > \lambda_{max}(\mathbf{H})$, where $\lambda_{max}(\mathbf{H})$ denotes the Perron-Frobenius eigenvalue of $\mathbf{H}$. However, it is clearly seen that λ is indeed greater than $\lambda_{max}(\mathbf{H})$ due to the fact that $[\lambda \mathbf{I} - \mathbf{H}]$ is positive definite; that is, all eigenvalues of $[\lambda \mathbf{I} - \mathbf{H}]$ should be positive. Thus, the inverse matrix $-[\mathbf{\Gamma}^T \mathbf{J} \mathbf{\Gamma} - r\mathbf{\Gamma}^T \mathbf{D}^T \mathbf{\Omega} \mathbf{D} \mathbf{\Gamma}]^{-1}$ is positive, which then implies that $[\mathbf{\Gamma}^T \mathbf{J} \mathbf{\Gamma} - r\mathbf{\Gamma}^T \mathbf{D}^T \mathbf{\Omega} \mathbf{D} \mathbf{\Gamma}]^{-1}$ is negative. Now, putting this result back into (3.33a), bearing in mind that $\mathbf{K} > 0$, would complete the proof for the stated result that $[\partial \mathbf{m}/\partial r]$ is negative.

Q.E.D.

One possible implication of the preceding result is that, if those stated (sufficient but not necessary) conditions are not satisfied, it *may* be the case that, as the firm becomes more risk averse, it *increases* its advertising budgets for some brands with the expectation that corresponding levels of sales will increase. This conclusion is in contrast with a more conventional result in the single-product models that risk aversion induces a *decrease* in advertising, which results in a lower expected sales level (see, e.g., Nguyen [1985]). One can directly derive this conventional result by analyzing a special case of equation (3.33). For the one-brand company, equation (3.33) in effect implies that

$$(-)[\frac{\partial m}{\partial r}] = (+) \tag{3.33b}$$

where $(-)$ and $(+)$ denote, respectively, a negative and a positive expression. The result implied by (3.33b) is that $(\partial m / \partial r) < 0$ unambiguously.

For the multibrand firm, the theoretical result we obtained above would also enable one to compare the advertising levels for risk-averse and risk-neutral firms. In the context of this model, risk neutrality can be viewed as the limit of risk aversion as the degree of risk aversion becomes smaller. Our result would then imply that the risk-averse firm's advertising budgets for all brands are lower than those chosen by the risk-neutral firm if $J_{ij} > r(\mathbf{D}^T \mathbf{\Omega} \mathbf{D})_{ij}$, and if conditions 1, 2, and 3 are all satisfied. A sub-section in Chapter 9 will offer empirical perspectives on some of these conditions.

3.4 Effect of Random Sales Responses to Advertising

Differentiating equation (3.31) with respect to σ_{ij} yields

$$[\mathbf{\Gamma}^T \mathbf{J}\mathbf{\Gamma} - r\mathbf{\Gamma}^T \mathbf{D}^T \mathbf{\Omega} \mathbf{D}\mathbf{\Gamma}]\frac{\partial m}{\partial \sigma_{ij}} = r\mathbf{\Gamma}^T \mathbf{D}^T \mathbf{M}_{ij} \mathbf{D}\mathbf{\Gamma}\mathbf{m}$$
$$+ r\mathbf{\Gamma}^T \mathbf{D}^T \mathbf{M}_{ij}[\mathbf{D}(\alpha \mathbf{Lq} + \gamma_0 \mathbf{m}_0) + \frac{1}{2}(\mathbf{c} - \mathbf{p})] \tag{3.34}$$

where $\mathbf{M}_{ij}$ denotes an $N \times N$ symmetric matrix whose (i,j)th or (j,i)th elements are unity and the remaining elements are zeros.

We earlier showed that the right-hand side of (3.33) is positive for a risk-averse firm. It then follows that the right-hand side of (3.34) is also positive for a risk-averse firm ($r > 0$); hence the sign of $(\partial m / \partial \sigma_{ij})$ depends on $[\mathbf{\Gamma}^T \mathbf{J}\mathbf{\Gamma} - r\mathbf{\Gamma}^T \mathbf{D}^T \mathbf{\Omega} \mathbf{D}\mathbf{\Gamma}]^{-1}$. We further demonstrated in the proof of Theorem 3.2 that, if the "structural complementarity" condition, the "nondeclining cost" condition, and the "stochastic complementarity" condition hold, and if $J_{ij} > r(\mathbf{D}^T \mathbf{\Omega} \mathbf{D})_{ij}$ for $i \neq j$, then the inverse matrix $[\mathbf{\Gamma}^T \mathbf{J}\mathbf{\Gamma} - r\mathbf{\Gamma}^T \mathbf{D}^T \mathbf{\Omega} \mathbf{D}\mathbf{\Gamma}]^{-1}$ for the risk-averse firm contains all negative elements. Under these conditions, the column vector $(\partial m / \partial \sigma_{ij})$ is negative; that is, a change in the covariance among any (different) pair of sales values would induce a change in each brand's advertising expenditure in the opposite direction.

The effect of a change in variance of sales on advertising can be similarly derived. This special case of (3.34) is

$$[\boldsymbol{\Gamma}^T\mathbf{J}\boldsymbol{\Gamma} - r\boldsymbol{\Gamma}^T\mathbf{D}^T\boldsymbol{\Omega}\mathbf{D}\boldsymbol{\Gamma}]\frac{\partial \mathbf{m}}{\partial \sigma_{ii}} = r\boldsymbol{\Gamma}^T\mathbf{D}^T\mathbf{M}_{ii}\mathbf{D}\boldsymbol{\Gamma}\mathbf{m}$$

$$+ r\boldsymbol{\Gamma}^T\mathbf{D}^T\mathbf{M}_{ii}[\mathbf{D}(\alpha\mathbf{Lq} + \gamma_0\mathbf{m}_0) + \frac{1}{2}(\mathbf{c}-\mathbf{p})]$$

(3.35)

where $\mathbf{M}_{ii}$ is an $N\times N$ symmetric matrix that contains all zero elements with the only exception of the (i,i)th diagonal element, which is unity.

It is seen that the conditions that are sufficient to assure that $(\partial \mathbf{m}/\partial \sigma_{ij})$ is negative are sufficient to yield a negative column vector $(\partial \mathbf{m}/\partial \sigma_{ii})$. Of particular interest is the potential result that, as the variance of sales of a particular brand increases, the company *may* attempt to increase that brand's sales level by increasing its advertising budget. This potential result contrasts with the conventional analysis of the firm's behavior under uncertainty (see, e.g., McCall [1971]), by which an increase in the demand randomness induces a decline in the firm's output level. This conventional result for the one-brand firm can be directly verified in the current framework. For the one-brand firm, (3.35) becomes

$$(-)[\frac{\partial m}{\partial \sigma^2}] = (+)$$

(3.35a)

where, as before, $(-)$ and $(+)$ designate a negative and a positive expression, respectively. Clearly, (3.35a) implies that $\partial m/\partial \sigma^2$ is negative.

Getting back to the more general framework of the multibrand firm, let us examine a special case in which not only the production processes among the firm's various brands are independent of each other but so are the "structural" relationships between advertising and sales. Formally, we wish to examine the effect of a change in sales variances σ_{ii}'s on various brands' advertising budgets for the special case in which both matrices $\boldsymbol{\Gamma}$ and $\mathbf{D}$ are diagonal. Let us rewrite (3.35) as

$$\frac{\partial \mathbf{m}}{\partial \sigma_{ii}} = r\mathbf{Q}^{-1}\boldsymbol{\Gamma}^T\mathbf{D}^T\mathbf{M}_{ii}\mathbf{B}$$

(3.36)

where, for notational convenience, we denote $\mathbf{Q} = [\boldsymbol{\Gamma}^T\mathbf{J}\boldsymbol{\Gamma} - r\boldsymbol{\Gamma}^T\mathbf{D}^T\boldsymbol{\Omega}\mathbf{D}\boldsymbol{\Gamma}]$ and $\mathbf{B} = \mathbf{D}\boldsymbol{\Gamma}\mathbf{m} + \mathbf{D}(\alpha\mathbf{Lq} + \gamma_0\mathbf{m}_0) + \frac{1}{2}(\mathbf{c}-\mathbf{p})$.

Note that, when matrices $\boldsymbol{\Gamma}$ and $\mathbf{D}$ are diagonal, the resulting diagonal matrix $\boldsymbol{\Gamma}^T\mathbf{D}^T\mathbf{M}_{ii}$ contains all zero elements except the (i,i)th element in its diagonal. Therefore, the matrix $\mathbf{Q}^{-1}\boldsymbol{\Gamma}^T\mathbf{D}^T\mathbf{M}_{ii}$ on the right-hand side of (3.36) has only one nonzero column, namely, the i-th column. It would then follow that

$$\frac{\partial \mathbf{m}_i}{\partial \sigma_{ii}} = r\mathbf{Q}^{ii}\mathbf{B}_i$$

(3.37)

where the subscript i denotes the i-th element of a column vector and $\mathbf{Q}^{ii}$ denotes the (i,i)th element of the inverse matrix $\mathbf{Q}^{-1}$.

Since it can be easily seen that $\mathbf{B}_i$ is positive, the sign of $(\partial \mathbf{m}_i/\partial \sigma_{ii})$ is identical to that of $\mathbf{Q}^{ii}$ for the risk-averse firm $(r > 0)$. Our task is to determine the sign of $\mathbf{Q}^{ii}$. Since $\mathbf{Q}$ is negative definite, it can be readily shown that $\mathbf{Q}^{ii}$ is negative for all i. To see this, one has:

$$\mathbf{Q}^{-1} = \frac{adj\ \mathbf{Q}}{|\mathbf{Q}|}$$

$$\text{or} \quad diag\{\mathbf{Q}^{-1}\} = \frac{diag\{adj\ \mathbf{Q}\}}{|\mathbf{Q}|} \tag{3.38}$$

where $diag\{adj\ \mathbf{Q}\} = \{|\mathbf{Q}_{11}|, |\mathbf{Q}_{22}|,..., |\mathbf{Q}_{NN}|\}$, in which $|\mathbf{Q}_{ii}|$ represents the cofactor of the (i,i)th element of $\mathbf{Q}$.

Now if N is even, then $|\mathbf{Q}|>0$ and $|\mathbf{Q}_{ii}|<0$ for all i since $\mathbf{Q}_{ii}$ is of order $(N-1)$, which is odd. So from (3.38), all elements of $diag\{\mathbf{Q}^{-1}\}$ are negative. If N is odd, $|\mathbf{Q}|<0$ and $|\mathbf{Q}_{ii}|>0$, again due to the fact that $\mathbf{Q}$ is negative definite. Hence from (3.38), all elements of $diag\{\mathbf{Q}^{-1}\}$ are again negative.

Thus (3.37) tells us that $(\partial \mathbf{m}_i/\partial \sigma_{ii})$ is negative for all i for the risk-averse firm. In other words, as the sales variance in a particular brand changes, the advertising expenditure for that brand would change in the opposite direction when the firm is risk averse.

4 DYNAMICS

Advertising is intrinsically a dynamic process. While this fact has been recognized perhaps very early as a marketing concept, an important formalization has been based on the Nerlove-Arrow [1962] paper. For ease of reference and as an aid to intuition, we shall first summarize the major point of the dynamic structure before presenting the stochastic extension of this framework. Other contexts in which dynamic advertising plays a natural role include the Vidale-Wolfe diffusions model as well as relevant extensions of the Bass diffusion process. We will address with some details certain aspects of the Bass model in Chapter 6 and will mention briefly the basic specification of the Vidale-Wolfe model in the next sub-section. On the other hand, it is the Nerlove-Arrow model which represents the central focus in our dynamic treatment here. In doing so, we benefit greatly from the survey by Sethi [1977], with the follow-up in Feichtinger, Hartl, and Sethi [1994]. The major results on stochastic analysis of dynamic advertising activities have been obtained by and reported in Tapiero [1990].

4.1 A Deterministic Formulation

Consider the following advertising capital stock of Goodwill at time t, denoted as G_t, being generated by the simple process:

$$\frac{dG}{dt} = m_t - \delta G_t \quad ; \quad G_{t=0} \equiv G_0 \tag{3.39}$$

where m_t represents advertising effort and δ denotes the rate of depreciation of goodwill, that is, the rate of forgetting.

For simplicity, we assume linear cost of advertising; that is the firm's advertising effort is measured by actual monetary spending, not by its effectiveness as in an earlier paper by Gould [1970] or in a more recent study by Fershtman, Mahajan and Muller [1990], for instance. The specification is dynamic and is similar to the capital accumulation process analyzed in economics literature.

Assume further that the sales response equation is

$$q_t = f(p_t, G_t). \tag{3.40}$$

Assuming constant average cost excluding the advertising expenditure, denoted as c as before, the optimization problem facing the firm is to choose price and advertising levels to maximize the following objective function of discounted sum of profits with r as the discount rate:

$$\text{Max. } V = \int_0^\infty e^{-rt}[\Pi(p_t, G_t)]dt \tag{3.41}$$

$$\equiv \int_0^\infty e^{-rt}[(p_t - c_t)q_t - m_t - FC]dt.$$

It can be shown that the solution amounts to, on the one hand, the standard deterministic form of the optimal pricing rule $p^* = [\varepsilon/(\varepsilon-1)]c$ which we already analyzed in Chapter 2. On the other hand, the optimal advertising level can be determined by defining H as the current-value Hamiltonian, as follows:

$$H = \Pi(G) + \lambda(m - \delta G). \tag{3.42}$$

It is well-known that the solution involves the dual variable λ, reflecting the shadow price of advertising, to follow:

$$\frac{d\lambda}{dt} = r\lambda - \frac{\partial H}{\partial G} = (r+\delta)\lambda - \frac{\partial \Pi}{\partial G} \tag{3.43}$$

with the condition that $\lim_{t \to \infty} e^{-rt}\lambda_t = 0$.

The relation in (3.43) has an important economic interpretation that the marginal instantaneous profits and capital gain due to advertising in equilibrium must be equal to the opportunity cost of the advertising as an investment good. Other economic interpretations of these results are sufficiently well-known so we will be very brief. In particular, the implicit solution for an optimal goodwill stock can be written as:

$$\varepsilon[(r+\delta)\lambda - \frac{d\lambda}{dt}]G^* = \varepsilon_G p^* q \qquad (3.44)$$

where ε_G denotes the goodwill elasticity of demand, $\varepsilon_G = (\partial q/\partial G)(G/q)$ and as before, ε denotes the price elasticity of demand.

It is of interest to look at the optimal long-run stationary equilibrium of goodwill, denoted as G_*; that is, we evaluate G^* at its dual price, which can be seen to be unity due to our assumption of linear cost of advertising, and at the point where $d\lambda/dt = 0$ in the long run. The result is:

$$\varepsilon(r+\delta)G_* = \varepsilon_G p^* q. \qquad (3.44a)$$

4.2 Stochastic Formulation

A Stochastic Optimal Control Approach

The important and pioneering work by Tapiero [1978] remains the major reference on this approach to stochasticity in dynamic advertising. A number of applications of the continuous time stochastic control problem to various marketing and other management issues is addressed in his book [1990]. Our presentation here is based on this approach. In this section, we concentrate on the stochastic optimal control approach to the Nerlove-Arrow goodwill model, leaving the random walk formulation involving a birth-death process for Chapter 6 on diffusion processes.

The stochastic version is formulated by assuming that increment in goodwill in a given interval of time, dG, consists of a deterministic component, $g(G,m)dt$, and a stochastic component, represented by $\sigma(G,m)dz$ where z is a Weiner process. That is, it is assumed that the accumulated goodwill stock follows a Brownian motion of the form:

$$dG = g(G,m)dt + \sigma(G,m)dz \qquad (3.45)$$

where dz represents the increment of a Wiener process z.

For a monopolistic firm, the objective function can be defined to be the expected discounted stream of utilities of profits subject to the preceding sales equation. We thus write:

$$\text{Max. } V = E \int_0^\infty e^{-rt} \Pi(G_t, m_t) dt \qquad (3.41a)$$

where, upon assuming that the price is given exogenously to concentrate only on the advertising diffusion process, we explicitly denote $\Pi(G, m)$ as a function of both G and m and which represents the expected value of the same objective function in (3.25).

Recall the steps involved in addressing the stochastic, dynamic pricing problem we detailed in the Chapter 2, the Bellman equation can be written as:

$$rV(G,t) = \text{Max.} \ [\Pi(G,m,t) + \frac{E(dV)}{dt}].$$

The standard interpretation of the preceding relation is that the return on asset on the left-hand side should equal the profit flow which is the dividend and the expected capital gain on the right-hand side. Upon noting that the specification in (3.45) is independent of the time variable, an application of Ito's Lemma would yield:

$$rV(G) = \text{Max.} \ [\Pi(G,m)\} + V_G g(G,m) + \frac{1}{2} V_{GG} \sigma^2(G,m)] \qquad (3.46)$$

where the subscripts denote derivatives.

One way to interpret (3.46) is to understand the meaning of each of its elements: $[dV/dG] \equiv V_G$ represents the shadow price of sales which we will denote as λ; and $V_{GG} \equiv [d^2V/dG^2]$ thus represents the change in the shadow price as a result of a change in sales; i.e., $[d\lambda/dG]$. The dynamic programming algorithm allows the interpretation that the Hamiltonian $H = \Pi + \lambda g(G,m) + (1/2)(d\lambda/dG)\sigma^2(G,m)$ in effect decomposes the firm's objective through time; that is single-period optimization problems can be seen to be related to the intertemporal problem.

The reader will immediately recognize the technical similarity of this solution approach to the dynamic pricing problem we presented in Chapter 2, Sub-section 4.2. As typical for these types of formulation, it is in general extremely difficult to obtain analytical solution to the preceding problem. For specific sales response function, consider a version of the Nerlove-Arrow model which represents a stochastic version of the deterministic specification in (3.39) as follows:

$$dG = [m - \delta G(m)]dt + \sigma(G,m,)dz \qquad (3.45a)$$

where again z is a Weiner process, a stochastic process with independently distributed normal random variables with zero mean and unit variance.

Tapiero shows that $\sigma(G,m,t)$ for the preceding process can be approximated by a Taylor's series expansion to yield a linearized solution

$$\sigma^2(G,m) \approx m + \delta G(m). \qquad (3.47)$$

Consequently, the stochastic problem for the Nerlove-Arrow model is:

$$\text{Max.} \ V = E \int_0^\infty e^{-rt} [\Pi(G,m)]dt$$

subject to $dG = [m - \delta G(m)]dt + [m + \delta G(m)]^{1/2} dz.$

The Bellman equation to this problem can be obtained by a direct application of (3.46). The stochastic equation describing the dynamics for the shadow price equation is:

$$d\lambda = -[\frac{dH}{dG}]dt + \frac{\partial\lambda}{\partial G}\sigma dz \qquad (3.48)$$

where H is the Hamiltonian defined above.

However, the computation of the preceding solution may be very difficult. It turns out that an application of Bismut's stochastic maximum principle [1973] — a stochastic counterpart of the Pontryagin's deterministic maximum principle — which intuitively represents a stochastic version of the duality concept in optimal control problems, enables one to gain important insights to the solution to the firm's optimization problem in (3.41a). The current-value Hamiltonian is:

$$H = \Pi(G,m) + \lambda(m - \delta G) + v\sigma(G,m) \qquad (3.49)$$

which represents the stochastic counterpart of the previous deterministic Hamiltonian. The current-value dual variable λ follows:

$$d\lambda = (r\lambda - \frac{\partial H}{\partial G})dt + vdz + dI \qquad (3.50)$$

$$= [(r+\delta)\lambda - \frac{\partial\Pi}{\partial G} - v\frac{\partial\sigma}{\partial G}]dt + vdz + dI. \qquad (3.51)$$

The additional terms are due to the presence of the stochastic elements in the state equation with the following interpretations: $-v_t$ reflects the cost involving the risk factor at time t; with a positive value of v to reflect risk-taking behavior and a negative value risk-aversion. On the other hand, I represents some notion of information in association with the uncertain dynamic process in the goodwill accumulation.

The first-order condition for an interior optimum is

$$\frac{\partial H}{\partial m} = 0 \Rightarrow \lambda + v\frac{\partial\sigma}{\partial m} = 1 \qquad (3.52)$$

where $\partial\sigma/\partial m = 1/2\sigma$ due to the approximation in (3.47).

Note that in the deterministic case, a first-order condition for an interior solution for an optimal level of advertising, on the basis of (3.42) can be seen as:

$$\lambda = 1 \qquad (3.52a)$$

which of course equates the marginal profit of advertising to its cost, assumed to be unity due to our simplifying assumption of linear advertising cost; the non-linear case can easily be represented by some functions of m.

The effect of uncertainty on the optimal advertising condition can be accounted for by the term $\nu(\partial\sigma/\partial m)$. Noting that for risk aversion, ν is negative; to satisfy (3.52) given that the expected marginal profits must be declining to have a truly optimal advertising policy, it should be the case that advertising level be chosen at a level less than the deterministic counterpart. This represents a fundamental result of this dynamic analysis.

A particularly insightful observation is that under a certain approximation procedure, it is possible to derive a certainty-equivalent solution so that the problem becomes essentially a deterministic optimal-control problem. More specifically, if θ is defined as

$$\theta = \frac{-\nu}{2\lambda\sigma} \quad \text{where} \quad 0 \leq \theta \leq 1 \quad \text{for} \quad \nu < 0$$

where we note that ν is negative for risk aversion, then the certainty-equivalent solution can simply be obtained by dealing with the problem defined earlier in (3.41) except that the discount rate now, instead of r, is $(r+\delta\theta)$. Consequently, the certainty-equivalent counterpart of the solution in eq. (3.44) and eq. (3.44a) can be written accordingly as:

$$\varepsilon[(r+\delta+\delta\theta)\lambda - \frac{d\lambda}{dt}]G^* = \varepsilon_{cp}p^*q$$

(3.44b)

$$\text{and} \quad \varepsilon(r+\delta+\delta\theta)G_* = \varepsilon_{cp}p^*q$$

from which it easily follows that everything else being the same, risk aversion with the effective increase in the discount rate to account for uncertainty, leads to smaller advertising activities in order to satisfy (3.44b).

It may be of interest also to report here Tapiero's stochastic formulation of the Vidale-Wolfe model [1957], a deterministic version of which can be expressed as:

$$\frac{dQ_t}{dt} \equiv q_t = -\delta Q_t + \alpha m_t(S-Q_t)$$

where δ, in this context denotes the rate at which sales spontaneously erode, S denotes saturation sales level, similar to the market Size, Q_t the cumulative sales up to time t, and α a coefficient reflecting the constant response coefficient to advertising.

A stochastic version of the Vidale-Wolfe diffusion model is:

$$dQ = [-\delta Q + \alpha m(S-Q)]dt + \sigma(Q,m,t)dz$$

where as before, dz is the increment of a Wiener process.

It can be shown that $\sigma(G,m,t)$ for the preceding process can be given by a mean variance approximation as:

$$\sigma^2(Q,m,t) \approx \delta Q + \alpha m(S-Q).$$

Consequently, the stochastic equation representing the Vidale-Wolfe model is

$$dQ = [-\delta Q + \alpha m(S - Q)]dt + [\delta Q + \alpha m(S - Q)]^{1/2}dz$$

on the basis of which normative analysis may be performed.

We further note that on the basis of the stochastic version of the Nerlove-Arrow goodwill accumulation model, implications for the ratio rule in setting the firm's advertising spending have been analyzed by Raman [1990].

Additive Random Sales

We now consider a dynamic extension to the previous model of stochastic, static advertising (Dehez-Jacquemin [1975], Horowitz [1970], and see Section 2.4 above). We noted that Tapiero concluded that his results on the impact of risk-taking behavior is confirmed by the Dehez-Jacquemin analysis but contradicts that of Horowitz. It appears, however, that this may not exactly be the case due to a misinterpretation of the Horowitz results. Further, when considered in conjunction with the joint price-producing decisions, the results seem to be very consistent. This fact is in itself actually quite remarkable due to the differences in the various approaches used in the way stochastic elements are formulated. Let us record the basic features of the dynamic model here. Assume that

$$q_t = f(p_t, m_t, G_t) + \xi_t$$

where G_t represents the stock of goodwill, assumed to be governed by:

$$\frac{dG_t}{dt} = m_t - \delta G_t$$

where δ represents the constant rate of depreciation in goodwill.

The objective of the firm is, as usual

$$\text{Max.} \quad V_t = \int_0^\infty e^{-rt} E[U(\Pi_t)]dt.$$

The Hamiltonian is:

$$H_t = e^{-rt}\{E[U(\Pi_t)] + \lambda_t \frac{dG}{dt}\} = e^{-rt}\{E[U(\Pi_t)] + \lambda_t(m_t - \delta G_t)\}$$

which yields the following first-order conditions:

$$(p-c)\frac{\partial E(q)}{\partial p} + E(q) = -\frac{E[U'(\Pi)\xi]}{E[U'(\Pi)]}$$

$$(p-c)\frac{\partial E(q)}{\partial m} = 1 - \frac{\lambda}{E[U'(\Pi)]}$$

$$\frac{d\lambda}{dt} = (r + \delta)\lambda - (p - c)\frac{\partial E(q)}{\partial G} E[U'(\Pi)]$$

$$\text{and } \frac{dG}{dt} = m - \delta G.$$

The results can be summarized as follows. Referring to (3.20), the first of these conditions show that both static and dynamic conditions are the same. For risk-averse firms, in both static and dynamic setting, price is lower under risk aversion since at the optimal price level, current expected marginal revenue should be greater than marginal cost. Regardless of the firm's attitude toward risk, the current expected marginal revenue generated by advertising is less than the marginal cost, an optimal condition which implies that the optimal level of advertising expenditures is higher under dynamic than under static conditions provided that goodwill has a positive economic value.

It is also of interest to note the following result regarding the pricing decision. Regardless of risk-taking attitude, the optimal price is higher under dynamic than under static conditions if $\{\partial^2 E[U(\Pi)]/\partial p \partial m > 0\}$. This offers additional insights into the firm's optimal pricing under uncertainty which we considered earlier in Chapter 2 on pricing.

5 CONCLUSIONS

We have explored in this chapter elements of advertising decisions in dealing with markets where firms have certain monopoly power. In the framework of a one-period static model, we first analyzed the impact of a random response function on the firm's advertising level, assuming that while product price is predetermined, the sales response to advertisement is subject to random fluctuations. In this model, we showed that, for constant product price, the impact of uncertainty in sales response to advertising on the risk-averse firm's promotional spending depends on the cost structure facing the firm. If the marginal manufacturing cost is a decreasing (increasing) function of sales, the firm's optimal advertising expenditure under random sales response is less (more) than that under deterministic conditions. We then further analyzed the managerial implications of joint decisions involving both advertising strategy and production as well as the joint pricing-advertising decision.

We next examined the impact of uncertainty in the sales response to advertising on the firm's advertising decisions when the firm produces several brands of its product. The theoretical analysis indicates that, in contrast to the single-brand case, the effect of risk-taking attitude and that of the random sales response function on the firm's advertising budgets for its various brands are quite difficult to evaluate. Only with fairly restrictive specifications regarding the utility function, cost structure, sales-advertising relationships, and the structure of error terms are we able to determine sufficient conditions under which risk aversion leads to a reduction in advertising for all brands, with the expectation that the resulting sales levels are also reduced. Similar conditions must also hold if we are to be able to determine that, as variance of sales and covariance of sales among any pair of brands change, the company's advertising budgets of all brands change in the opposite direction. Finally, we studied the firm's advertising behavior when its planning horizon is extended to more than one-period. There we concentrated on the analysis of a stochastic version of the Nerlove-Arrow goodwill model in order to examine the impact of uncertainty on the firm's dynamic advertising decisions.

A fairly consistent result seems to be that despite the various approaches with which uncertainty is introduced into the system at hand, risk aversion appears to induce firms to reduce their marketing activities. Clearly, the fundamental reason for this result appears to be due to the fact that advertising positively affect sales; and it has been established firmly in the literature that risk aversion tends to reduce output level; consequently when firms are faced with advertising decisions alone in the context of non-price competition for instance, they would find it optimal to reduce advertising spending. We will see that this basic result will be challenged in the course of our analysis in the subsequent chapters of the book. Specifically, within the framework of the multiperiod model, we will explore the possibility that the firm is able to experiment in order to gain more information about the true value of the unknown linear parameter of a quadratic sales response function. This important subject will be left to Chapter 9. Another important element which we have not considered is the nature of competition among firms within certain industries. We shall explore this topic in Chapter 8. We should also point out that while we have tried to include in this chapter certain degrees of interactions among advertising decision, pricing and production, further efforts along this line within a competitive framework will be examined further, in particular popular models of market share in Chapter 6.

REFERENCES

BAUMOL, William J., J.C. PANZAR, and Robert D. WILLIG, 1982, *Contestable Markets and the Theory of Industry Structure*, San Diego, CA: Harcourt Brace Jovanovich.

BISMUT, J. M., 1973, "Conjugate Convex Functions in Optimal Stochastic Control," *Journal of Mathematical Analysis and Applications*, Vol. 44, pp. 384-404.

BLAIR, R. D., and A.A. HEGGESTAD, 1977, "Impact of Uncertainty Upon the Multiproduct Firm," *Southern Economic Journal*, Vol. 44, pp. 136-142.

DEHEZ, Pierre and Alex JACQUEMIN, 1975, "A Note On Advertising Policy Under Uncertainty and Dynamic Conditions," *The Journal of Industrial Economics*, Vol. 24, No. 1, pp. 73-79.

DHRYMES, Phoebus J., 1964, "On the Theory of the Monopolistic Multi-product Firm under Uncertainty," *International Economic Review*, Vol. 5 , pp. 239-257.

FEICHTINGER, Gustav, Richard F. HARTL, and Suresh P. SETHI, 1994, "Dynamic Optimal Control Models in Advertising: Recent Developments," *Management Science*, Vol. 40, No. 2, pp. 195-226.

FERSHTMAN, Chaim, Vijay MAHAJAN, and Eitan MULLER, 1990, "Market Share Pioneering Advantage: A Theoretical Approach," *Management Science*, Vol. 36, pp. 900-918.

GIVON, M., and D. HORSKY, 1990, "Untangling the Effects of Purchase Reinforcement and Advertising Carryover," *Marketing Science*, Vol. 9, pp. 171-187.

GOULD, John P., 1970, "Diffusion Processes and Optimal Advertising Policy," in Edmund S. PHELPS et al., *Microeconomic Foundations of Employment and Inflation Theory*, W. W. Norton & Company, Inc., NY.

HOROWITZ, Ira, 1970, "A Note on Optimal Advertising and Uncertainty," *Journal of Industrial Economics*, Vol.18 pp. 151-160.

KAUL, Anil, and Dick R. WITTINK, 1995, "Empirical Generalizations About the Impact of Advertising on Price Sensitivity and Price," *Marketing Science*, Vol. 14, pp. G151-G160.

LITTLE, John D. C., 1979, "Aggregate Advertising Models: The State of the Art," *Operations Research*, Vol. 27, pp. 629-667.

McCALL, J. J., 1971, "Probabilistic Microeconomics," *Bell Journal Economics and Management Science*, Vol. 2, pp. 403-433.

MONAHAN, G. E., 1983, "Optimal Advertising With Stochastic Demand," *Management Science*, Vol. 29, pp. 106-117.

NERLOVE, Marc, and Kenneth J. ARROW, 1962, "Optimal Advertising Policy Under Dynamic Conditions," *Economica*, Vol. 39, pp. 129-142.

NGUYEN, D., 1985, "An Analysis of Optimal Advertising Under Uncertainty," *Management Science*, Vol.31, pp. 622-633.

NGUYEN, Dung, 1987, "Advertising, Random Sales Response and Brand Competition: Some Theoretical and Econometric Implications," *Journal of Business*, Vol. 60, No. 2, pp. 259-279.

RAMAN, Kalyan, 1990, "Stochastically Optimal Advertising Policies under Dynamic Conditions: The Ratio Rule," *Optimal Control Applications and Methods*, Vol. 11, pp. 283-288.

SETHI, Suresh P., 1977, "Dynamic Optimal Control Models in Advertising: A Survey," *Siam Review*, Vol. 19, pp. 685-725.

TAPIERO, Charles S., 1978, "Optimum Advertising and Goodwill Under Uncertainty," *Operations Research*, Vol. 26, pp. 450-463.

TAPIERO, Charles S., 1990, *Applied Stochastic Models and Control in Management*, 2nd impression, Elsevier Science Publishers, The Netherlands.

THEIL, H., 1957, "A Note on Certainty Equivalence in Dynamic Planning," *Econometrica*, Vol. 25, pp. 346-349.

VIDALE, M. L., and WOLFE, H. B., 1957, "An Operations Research Study of Sales Response to Advertising," *Operations Research*, Vol. 5, pp. 370-381.

WALTERS, A. A., 1963, "Production and Cost Functions," *Econometrica*, Vol. 31, pp. 1-66.

4

PRICE PROMOTIONS

1 OVERVIEW

In this chapter, we will explore the general issue of promotional price discounts, particularly consumer price discounts. That we consider this pricing practice in a chapter separately from the firm's pricing decisions discussed in Chapter 2 reflects the importance marketing practitioners and scholars alike attach to these common marketing phenomena. While different forms of price discounting practice have been observed; including trade discount, producers discount, large quantity discounts, etc., we will be mainly concerned here with consumer discount such as temporary reduction in price and couponing phenomenon. By and large, the phenomenon has been analyzed using a number of economic motivations, ranging from inventory-related explanations, price discrimination, and others. This pricing practice has been analyzed within the monopolistic context as well as in competitive market structure under certainty.

To a large extent, most of the economics-based models of price discount are based on the notion that the potential consumers are not completely informed about attributes of certain products. Firms typically seek to exploit the heterogeneity of the buying population regarding information on prices in order to discriminate them by charging different prices to different segments of consumers. The analytical approach, formulation as well as specific motivations for these models differ significantly. However, many of these models essentially highlight the role with which consumer information heterogeneity plays in the firm's optimal pricing process. The challenge to managers is that while they are aware of the fact that consumers typically differ in the extent of information on prices and product quality and that they may differ in tastes and preferences as well as income and wealth, it is virtually impossible to identify them with perfect information. Research efforts have been made to address this fundamental problem and their results have been reported in various surveys on the economic models of price discount (see, e.g., Blattberg and Neslin [1990] and Rao [1993]). Other detailed presentations and analyses of these models are also reported in the textbook by Lilien, Kotler and Moorthy [1992]. Due to the relatively easy access to these surveys, we shall not report these well-known models here. Instead, we shall concentrate on a number of models in this topic which reflect our own interest in this area of research. The main feature of the models we analyze in this chapter is that firms are exercising some form of price discrimination to enhance profits. The basis for price discrimination is that of imperfect information regarding consumers. This represents the general notion of uncertainty with which we are concerned in this work. In this context, uncertainty is understood broadly to include situations where the firm is not able to identify consumers with certain characteristics which help them to discriminate against certain segments as in the textbook price discrimination analysis. Instead, different sorting mechanisms need to be used if the firm is to be able to practice price discrimination successfully.

In the next section, we will analyze a simple model to explain the price discount decisions for firms with monopoly power. In Section 3, we offer an informal discussion on a monopolistically competitive equilibrium on the basis of which some empirical evidence of this type of price promotion can be given. We then address a stochastic version of a cyclic pricing model on the basis of the deterministic formulation by Conlisk, Gerstner, and Sobel [1984] in Section 4. We continue with an application of the price discrimination model to an industrial organization phenomenon called resale price maintenance with some empirical results in Section 5. Section 6 proposes a model to examine the observed phenomenon that even when the consumers learn, price differentials among competing firms may exist in equilibrium. This chapter ends with some conclusions in Section 7.

2 THE MONOPOLISTIC FIRM'S PRICE DISCOUNT DECISIONS

2.1 The Basic Model

In this sub-section, we spell out the basic assumptions regarding the consumers' decision processes and the seller's optimization problem.

The problem can be posed as follows: An individual or a household is faced with the decision either to purchase a product at a full price or go through a process of getting a deal, e.g., waiting for a sale; searching for, collecting and redeeming a coupon, etc. so that he or she can purchase the product at a discount price. Among other considerations, the potential buyer takes into account the monetary savings as a result of the deal as well as the cost of getting the deal. Clearly, monetary savings are to be determined by the seller whom we assume to have some price-setting monopoly power. Further, we will assume that the buyer's costs of getting a deal depend not only on his/her demographic and other characteristics but also on the seller's chosen relative frequency with which deals are offered. In short, the buyer's decision regarding the mode of purchasing the product directly depends on the seller's pricing and deals frequency variables. On the other hand, given its cost structure, the monopolistic firm has to take into account the potential buyer's decision processes in formulating its profit-maximizing objective function. The firm should decide on a full price to charge for its product, on whether it should offer deals from time to time and if so at what discount price and how frequent.

The model so formulated exhibits basic characteristics of a price discrimination model. The seller charges different prices to different groups of consumers for the same product. The text-book case of price discrimination of course involves the difference in price elasticities of demand among different segments of consumers. Issues of price discrimination have been extensively studied in the literature from various points of view. Among earlier studies on this subject in economics literature are those related to the optimal taxation (Mirrlees [1971]), non-linear pricing (Stiglitz [1977]), intertemporal price discrimination (Stokey [1979], and Conlisk, Gerstner and Sobel [1984]), and informational price discrimination (Pratt, Wise, and Zeckhauser [1979], Salop [1977] and Varian [1980]). Earlier marketing applications of the price discrimination model include those by Frank and Massy [1965], Monroe and Della Bitta [1978], Blattberg, Buesing, Peacock, and Sen [1978] and Jeuland and Narashimhan [1985]. The book by Blattberg and Neslin [1990] provides an extensive review of the literature.

First, the problem facing potential consumers. When the need for a particular (frequently purchased) product arises, a consumer can obtain the product either at a regular price or at a discount price by "getting a deal" if feasible. The consumer may of course decide not to purchase the product at all. Getting a deal, however, is not costless to the consumer since it involves time-consuming search, collecting, storage, and waiting, etc. The basic problem for the consumer is therefore to compare the potential monetary savings as a result of the deal to the opportunity cost of getting that deal. In what follows, we will assume that while the potential savings are known with certainty, each consumer's opportunity cost is subject to elements of randomness. This is so since a consumer would not know exactly when a deal is offered by the seller. Consequently, the relevant representation of a consumer's cost is an expected cost function of getting a deal which we now specify.

We assume that potential consumers differ in their "deal-proneness" toward purchasing the product. The issue of identifying the "deal-prone" segment has been addressed by several theoretical and empirical studies in the literature (see the literature cited above). For our present purposes, deal-proneness refers to the likelihood that a consumer will go through a dealing process in purchasing a product. Using this definition, we shall use a parameter θ to characterize a potential consumer according to his/her deal-proneness. In the literature, variables which may affect θ include education level, wage level, employment status, and other demographic variables, etc., either separately or as a combination of all these. We shall show later that in addition to this traditional representation, deal proneness will also be affected by both the depth of discount and the deal frequency. We specify that $\theta \in [0,\theta^H]$ where θ^H stands for the highest value of θ. It is convenient to define θ so that a higher value of θ corresponds to a lesser degree of deal-proneness. That is, a more deal-prone consumer is characterized by a lower θ-level. We assume that a consumer's degree of deal-proneness is related to his/her expected cost of getting a deal as specified below.

Another variable in the expected cost function is the relative frequency of deals. Let π be the probability that the product can be obtained at the discount (**Sales**) price s, and r be the full (**Regular**) price. The expected price Ep of the product is defined simply as:

$$Ep = \pi s + (1-\pi)r. \tag{4.1}$$

We will often refer to π as relative frequency of deals and let us note that π is implicitly chosen by the seller (as we will explain later), that π is constant over time, and that π is known to all potential consumers. It may be instructive for us to interpret the expected price Ep to represent what has been known in marketing literature as the reference price. By implications, eq.(4.1) indicates that as frequency of deals increases the (expected) reference price is lower, an established empirical observation in the literature (see, e.g., Kalwani and Yim [1992] and Blattberg, Briesch, and Fox [1995]).

In summary, the expected cost of getting a deal is specified to be:

$$EC = C(\theta, Ep) \tag{4.2}$$

where $C_\theta = \partial EC / \partial \theta > 0$ and $C_{Ep} = \partial EC / \partial Ep > 0$ and where ∂ denotes the partial derivative of expected cost with respect to the relevant argument.

Let us note that we have specified EC as a function of Ep instead of π mainly for mathematical convenience and ease of economic interpretations later. For given r and s, the value of Ep is uniquely determined once π is chosen. It is the seller's chosen π which affects the consumer's expected cost of getting a deal as indicated in (4.2).

It is of interest to justify the signs of the two partial derivatives C_θ and C_{Ep}. For a given π the cost of getting a deal for the higher θ-type consumers is higher than that for their lower θ-type counterparts (recalling that a higher value of θ corresponds to a lesser degree of deal-proneness). If θ reflects the educational level of the consumer, for example, positive C_θ implies that higher educated consumers are faced with higher cost of getting a deal, mainly due to higher opportunity costs in engaging in such activities. For a particular θ-type consumer, the less frequent deals are offered (lower π), the higher the expected cost of getting a deal. (As an example, expected search costs for coupons are higher when coupons are available less frequently). Since a lower π results in a higher Ep, it follows that as Ep increases, so does the expected cost of getting a deal, i.e. $C_{Ep} > 0$.

The decision rule for a potential consumer of type θ is as follows:

$$\left\{ \begin{array}{l} \text{If } EC(\theta,Ep) \geq (r\text{-}s), \text{ then purchase the product at the full price } r. \\ \text{Otherwise, purchase only through a deal.} \end{array} \right.$$

The preceding decision rule states that for given levels of Ep and $(r\text{-}s)$, consumers of a type higher than or equal to certain critical level of θ, say θ^*, would purchase the product at the full price r. The critical level of θ is defined to be: $EC(\theta^*,Ep) = (r\text{-}s)$ which yields the following relationship:

$$\theta^* = g(Ep,D) \tag{4.3}$$

where we define $D = (r\text{-}s)$ and where $\partial\theta^*/\partial Ep = \theta^*_{Ep} < 0$, and $\partial\theta^*/\partial D => < 0$.

Clearly, D denotes the depth of the discount. The relation in (4.3) can be verified by noting that for a particular reference price level Ep, consumers of a type higher than certain critical level of θ, i.e. θ^*, would purchase the product at regular price. However, suppose that the reference price Ep declines as a result of an increase in the relative frequency of deals (π), the critical level θ^* must increase. This is so since a higher π would reduce the consumer's expected cost of getting a deal (e.g. less search costs); hence it would "require" a higher critical level of θ (e.g. education) for the consumer to buy the product at the regular price. Put it differently, as deals become more frequent, the reference price is thus adjusted downward, some consumers who would otherwise purchase the product at regular price may now become deal-prone and thus choose to buy the product at a discount price.

It is important to recognize the manner in which the critical deal-proneness parameter θ^* is determined in our model. In contrast to the implications of traditional models in marketing literature in which deal-prone segments are exogenously defined largely by demographic variables, we show here how both the depth of discount D and the reference price Ep endogenously determine the critical cut-off point of deal-proneness.

Let us now specify the demand function for the product at the regular price as:

$$D^r = h(\theta,\theta^*,D) \tag{4.4}$$

where the superscript r is used in D^r to emphasize that only demand for the product at the regular price is accounted for. While there are no *a priori* reasons to specify the signs of the partial derivatives of D' with respect to θ and to θ^*, it is reasonable to assume that

$$h_D = \partial h / \partial D < 0 \qquad (4.4a)$$

which simply states that as the depth of discount D increases, everything else being equal, more people would tend to go through the process of getting a deal; hence demand for the product at the regular price should be lower.

Combining (4.3) with (4.4) enables us to write the demand function for the product at the regular price as:

$$D' = h[\theta, g(Ep, D), D] \qquad (4.5)$$

which would yield the total output to be sold at regular price as: $R = \int_{\theta^*}^{\theta''} h[\theta, g(Ep, D), D] d\theta.$ We have thus far derived and described the demand function facing the seller. We have assumed implicitly that the seller has information on the consumers' expected cost of getting a deal and the distribution of θ; hence the demand function (4.5) is known to the seller. We now specify other relations which the seller should take into account in his profit maximization problem. One is a specification of the largest potential market for the product which we assume to take the form:

$$M = M(s) \qquad (4.6)$$

where $M'(s) < 0$, which is nothing but a familiar downward-sloping demand schedule for that product.

Another is a cost function which we assume to be:

$$C = \Phi[M(s)] \qquad (4.7)$$

where for later reference, average cost is denoted as $c(s) \equiv \Phi[M(s)]/M(s)$.

2.2 Theoretical Analysis

In this sub-section, we analyze the seller's profit maximization problem. The decisions facing the seller can be made within the framework of a simple uncon-strained optimization problem in which the three choice variables are the relative frequency of deals (π), the regular price (r), and the discount price (s) as a result of the deal. One should note that the behavior of potential consumers has been taken into consideration via the derived demand equation in (4.5). The firm's problem is:

$$\text{Max. } \Pi = TR - C$$

$$= r \int_{\theta^*}^{\theta''} h[\theta, g(Ep, D), D] d\theta + s\{M(s) - \int_{\theta^*}^{\theta''} h[\theta, g(Ep, D), D] d\theta\} - \Phi[M(s)]$$

$$= (r - s) \int_{\theta^*}^{\theta''} h[\theta, g(Ep, D), D] d\theta + sM(s) - \Phi[M(s)]. \qquad (4.8)$$

In the above problem, the total quantity sold is M which consists of the quantity sold at regular price $R = \int_{\theta*}^{\theta''} h[\theta, g(Ep,D),D]d\theta$ and the quantity sold at the discount price $S = M - R$. The first-order conditions are:

$$\frac{\partial\Pi}{\partial r} = (r-s)\int_{\theta*}^{\theta''}(h_{\theta*}\cdot\theta_r^* + h_D)d\theta + \int_{\theta*}^{\theta''}h[g(\theta,Ep,D),D]d\theta = 0 \quad (4.9)$$

$$\frac{\partial\Pi}{\partial s} = (r-s)\int_{\theta*}^{\theta''}(h_{\theta*}\cdot\theta_s^* - h_D)d\theta - \int_{\theta*}^{\theta''}h[g(\theta,Ep,D),D]d\theta$$
$$+ [s-\Phi']M'(s) + M(s) = 0 \quad (4.10)$$

and $\quad \frac{\partial\Pi}{\partial\pi} = \frac{\partial\Pi}{\partial\theta*}\frac{\partial\theta*}{\partial Ep}\frac{\partial Ep}{\partial\pi} = -(r-s)^2\int_{\theta*}^{\theta''}(h_{\theta*}\cdot\theta_{Ep}^*)d\theta = 0 \quad (4.11)$

where $h_{\theta*} = \partial h/\partial\theta*$, $\theta_r^* = \partial\theta*/\partial r$, $h_D = \partial h/\partial D$, $\theta_s^* = \partial\theta*/\partial s$, $\theta_{Ep}^* = \partial\theta*/\partial Ep$, and the primes denote derivatives.

Conditions in (4.9) and (4.10) yield

$$(r-s)\int_{\theta*}^{\theta''}(h_{\theta*}[\theta_r^* + \theta_s^*])d\theta + [s-\Phi']M'(s) + M(s) = 0. \quad (4.12)$$

Let us explore possible economic and managerial implications of the preceding conditions. We will first consider the possibility of an optimal single-price policy and then that of the two-price (regular and discount) policy.

Case 1: *The Single-Price Solution*

From (4.12), it follows that the condition $r = s$ represents a possible solution to the seller's problem. It states that it may be optimal for the seller not to offer any deals to consumers. Thus the best pricing policy to the seller is to charge a uniform price s to all potential consumers. This is shown formally as follows.

From (4.12), it can be seen that if $\int_{\theta*}^{\theta''}(h_{\theta*}\cdot\theta_{Ep}^*)d\theta \neq 0$, then $(r-s)=0$ represents the only possible solution to the seller's problem. Returning to the objective function in (4.8), the problem becomes:

$$\text{Max. } \Pi = sM(s) - \Phi[M(s)] \quad (4.8a)$$

which is the standard textbook case of single pricing for the firm.

The necessary condition is:

$$\frac{\partial\Pi}{\partial s} = (s-\Phi')M'(s) + M(s) = 0 \quad (4.10a)$$

which represents the equality of marginal revenue and marginal cost, with reference to price s, instead of output M.

This condition can also be verified by noting that if $r = s$, the condition in (4.10) simply reduces to (4.10a). Intuitively, the optimal single price scenario would arise as follows. When the firm offers its product at a discount price, a number of customers who would have purchased the product at the regular price would now get it at a discount. This represents a loss in the firm's revenue. On the other hand, lowering price through discount programs would lead to revenue gain due to additional sale to customers who would not otherwise be buying the product. In this particular scenario, the revenue loss outweighs the gain; hence the one-price policy would be optimal. The preceding analysis can also accommodate the additional impact of a declining average cost function.

Case 2: The Two-Price Solution

For the two-price policy (regular price and discount price) to be optimal, it is necessary from (4.11) that

$$\int_{\theta*}^{\theta''} h_{\theta*}[\theta,g(Ep,D),D]d\theta=0 \tag{4.13}$$

where we have written the function $h_{\theta*}$ with its explicit arguments and we note also that θ_{Fp}^* does not depend on θ and it is generally assumed that $\theta_{Fp}^* \neq 0$.

Taking into account (4.13) and noting further from (4.12) that both θ_r^* and θ_s^* are not dependent on θ, equation (4.13) is further reduced to:

$$[s-\Phi']M'(s)+M(s)=0 \tag{4.14}$$

which is identical to the condition for the single-price case reported in (4.10).

Due to the preceding two conditions, both necessary conditions in (4.9) and (4.10) result in:

$$(r-s)\int_{\theta*}^{\theta''} h_D[\theta,g(Ep,D),D]d\theta+\int_{\theta*}^{\theta''} h[\theta,g(Ep,D),D]d\theta=0. \tag{4.15}$$

Conditions (4.13), (4.14), and (4.15) constitute the optimal two-price solution. Since (4.14) does not depend on two decision variables r and $\theta*$, the optimal level of the discount price (s) can be first obtained independently on the basis of (4.14). As we mentioned above, s would be identical to the firm's optimal price had the single price policy been the only optimal solution. We should also note that

$$(r-s)=\frac{-\int_{\theta*}^{\theta''} h[\theta,g(Ep,D),D]d\theta}{\int_{\theta*}^{\theta''} h_D[\theta,g(Ep,D),D]d\theta} > 0$$

since $h_D[\theta,g(Ep,D),D]<0$ on the basis of our earlier assumption in (4.4a).

Optimal values of r and θ^* (which in turn, implies optimal relative frequency of deals) can be theoretically obtained by solving (4.13) and (4.15) simultaneously, provided that the second-order conditions for an interior solution are satisfied. Upon taking into account the first-order conditions, the sufficient conditions for optimality can be expressed as:

$$\frac{\partial^2\Pi}{\partial r^2}=(r-s)\int_{\theta*}^{\theta''}[(\theta_r^*)^2h_{\theta*\theta*}+2\theta_r^*h_{D\theta*}+h_{DD}]d\theta+2\int_{\theta*}^{\theta''}h_D d\theta < 0$$

$$\frac{\partial^2\Pi}{\partial\pi^2}=(r-s)^3\int_{\theta*}^{\theta''}[(\theta_{Ep}^*)^2h_{\theta*\theta*}]d\theta<0$$

$$\text{and} \quad \frac{\partial^2\Pi}{\partial r^2}\cdot\frac{\partial^2\Pi}{\partial\pi^2} > \left[\frac{\partial^2\Pi}{\partial r\partial\pi}\right]^2$$

$$\text{where} \quad \frac{\partial^2\Pi}{\partial r\partial\pi}=\frac{\partial^2\Pi}{\partial\pi\partial r}=$$

$$-(r-s)^3\theta_{Ep}^*\int_{\theta*}^{\theta''}\{h_{\theta*\theta*}[\theta_{Ep}^*(1-\pi)+\theta_D^*]+h_{D\theta*}\}d\theta.$$

It should be noted that conditions in (4.13) and (4.15) in general represent a non-linear system of two equations for which analytical solutions are not in general available. We shall therefore use a diagram to summarize the solution as follows.

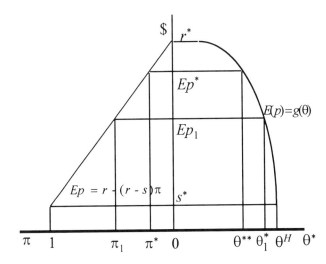

Figure 4.1 *The Optimal Two-Price Solution*

On the right panel of *Figure* 4.1 is a relation between Ep and θ^* for an optimally chosen level of s and for a certain value of r. This relation has been shown to be negative in our discussion following eq. (4.3); hence the curve representing it is downward-sloping. Further, the reference price $Ep = \pi s + (1-\pi)r$ is represented as a function of π on the left panel of the diagram. Note again that r and θ^* are determined simultaneously; thus the diagram represents only the final state of the whole process. At r^* and θ^{**} in the diagram, which denotes, respectively, optimal value of the regular price and that of the critical deal-proneness parameter, both conditions (4.13) and (4.15) are satisfied while s^* satisfies condition (4.14). Corresponding to θ^{**} is the optimal reference price Ep^* in the diagram which is seen clearly to imply an optimal relative frequency of deals denoted as π^*.

The diagram clearly indicates that the optimal degree of deal proneness depends not only on the basic demographic variables summarized by the θ parameter but also on the reference price Ep^* which is in turn affected by the firm's relative frequency of deals as well as the depth of discount. Thus, for a given depth of discount, an increase in π from π^* to π_1 in the diagram, for instance, would lead to a decline in the reference price to Ep_1 which in turn determines the new critical deal-proneness at θ_1^*. Customers whose θ-values are between θ^{**} and θ_1^* in the diagram, who previously would have bought the product at the regular price, would now purchase the product at the discount price as the result of an increase in the deals frequency.

Further economic interpretations of conditions (4.13) and (4.15) can be obtained as follows. For a given level of θ^* and that of s^* which is determined independently in (4.14), the demand function for the product at the regular price can in effect be written as:

$$\int_{\theta*}^{\theta''} h[\theta,g(Ep,D),D]d\theta \equiv R(r).$$

Hence, $\int_{\theta*}^{\theta''} h_D[\theta,g(Ep,D),D]d\theta = \partial R(r)/\partial r = R'(r)$. Condition (4.15) can therefore be simplified to read:

$$(r-s)R'(r)+R(r)=0. \qquad (4.16)$$

Equation (4.16) represents the necessary condition in order to maximize an objective function equals to $(r-s)R(r)$, using r as the decision variable. Now recall that, for the two-price policy, the firm's total revenue is $TR = rR + s[M(s) - R] = (r-s)R + sM(s)$. It has been shown that an optimal level of the discount price s^* can be chosen in the same way an optimal single price would have been chosen. Thus the objective function $(r-s)R(r)$ simply represents the additional revenue the seller would obtain as a result of its pricing policies. To the extent that the two-price policy is optimal, this would be the increase in the firm's total revenue due to its ability to increase sales through promotional efforts.

3   MONOPOLISTICALLY COMPETITIVE EQUILIBRIUM AND SOME EMPIRICAL EVIDENCE

3.1 Industry Equilibrium

Our discussion in this sub-section concerning a monopolistically competitive equilibrium is motivated mainly for the purpose of empirical implementation. It should be regarded as highly heuristic even though we will argue that it appears to reflect rather closely elements of actual retail markets.

Suppose that there are n stores which sell an identical product to a given market. We shall follow the Salop and Stiglitz strategy [1977] in deriving market equilibrium: that is, a potential equilibrium is first proposed, then the next step is to check whether that potential equilibrium indeed qualifies as an actual equilibrium. In what follows, we consider a possible equilibrium configuration in which all n stores charge identical regular prices r during the "non-sale" period, and all charge identical sales price s during the "sale" period. To make notations for each store consistent with those used above for the monopolistic firm, let us denote total market demand as $n.M$ which includes quantities sold at both regular and sales prices. Clearly, M consists of the quantity sold at the regular price, denoted previously as R, and that sold at the sales price, denoted as S. Since all stores are identical, each individual store's total quantity sold is broken down as:

$$M=R+S.$$

Since the representative store's profit is: $\Pi=(r-s)R+(s-c)M$, and industry equilibrium requires that economic profits be zero for all stores, the following relation must hold for the representative firm:

$$(r-c)R+(s-c)S=0.$$

One should also note that since all stores are assumed to charge the sales price at almost the same time (this assumption appears reasonable when we observe that on holiday occasions such as Labor Day, Memorial Day, Thanksgiving, etc., all retail stores offer price discounts), potential customers do not involve in search activities. While the assumption of search plays an important role in many studies on the subject of price dispersion, it is assumed away in the present model in order to concentrate more on other aspects of consumer behavior as analyzed earlier.

Would the preceding equilibrium configuration be an actual equilibrium? To see this, let us ask the question that, at the proposed equilibrium, would a "deviant" store increase its profits by either reducing or increasing its sales price? Given that all other stores' sales prices are known, the deviant store *may* find it profitable in the short-run to lower its sales price to gain more customers which in turn would imply lower average costs. However, other stores would follow the deviant store's lower sales price strategy in order to regain their market shares. Thus, the industry as a whole would now set the sales price at a lower level as compared to that in the original market equilibrium. This would, however, result in negative profits for every store due to the fact that in the original industry equilibrium, economic profits are zero and that the original equilibrium was attained via optimal policies concerning the determination of the sales price. Thus, the potential deviant store would not wish to lower its sales price from the proposed equilibrium price in anticipation of possible unpleasant consequences of its action even though that action might prove to be profitable in the short-run.

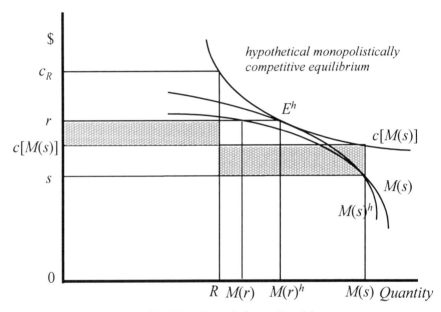

Figure 4.2 *Two-Price Industry Equilibrium*

On the other hand, would it be profitable for the deviant store to either offer a higher sales price or not to engage in any price promotional activities? The analysis is summarized in *Figure* 4.2 where the proposed market equilibrium is shown with the demand function $M(s)$, regular price r, sales price s, average cost c, total volume sold $M(s)$ broken down into R sold at the regular price and $S=M(s)-R$ sold at the sales price. Since this scenario represents a potential market equilibrium, economic profits are zero; hence the two marked areas in the diagram should be equal. Further, this scenario indicates that the two-price (sales and regular) strategy is superior to the single-price (not shown in the diagram) policy. Now if the deviant store decides to offer a sales price higher than all other stores' sales price s, it follows that it can not sell any amount of its product at the sales price during the sales period. The potential deviant store can only sell an amount equal to R at the regular price r, but it is faced with an average cost c_R which is higher than the unit price r. The fact that at quantity R, the corresponding average cost is *necessarily* higher than the regular price r will be demonstrated shortly below. We note now that the preceding configuration represents an economic loss to the deviant store. Clearly the same conclusion would be obtained should the deviant store decide *not* to offer its product at the sales price in any time periods. It is important to note that the average cost function necessarily lies above the demand curve. This follows immediately by observing that if there exists an output range in which price is higher than the corresponding average cost, the store would have made a profit by simply selling an amount within that output range (through an appropriate single price). However, since the initial proposed market equilibrium both implies that economic profits are zero and that the two-price scheme is superior, such an output range would not exist.

In short, the proposed market equilibrium qualifies as an actual equilibrium. With the preceding heuristic argument for the monopolistically competitive equilibrium, we shall now offer some empirical evidence to support the theoretical model presented in the previous section.

3.2 Empirical implications

One of the key variables in the theoretical model is the seller's chosen frequency of deals. While we do not have data on this variable, it appears that a particular implication of the model indirectly related to the deals frequency may be subjected to empirical testing. Using the profit function defined earlier, the seller's profits can be seen as:

$$\Pi = (r-s)R + (s-c)M \qquad (4.8b)$$

which follows by recalling that $R = \int_{\theta*}^{\theta''} h[\theta, g(Ep, D), D] d\theta$ and that c represents the average cost.

Upon noting that the total quantity sold M consists of the quantity sold at the full price (denoted as R) and that sold at the discount price (denoted as S), i.e., $M = R + S$, the profit function for the seller can be rewritten as:

$$\Pi = (r-c)R + (s-c)S. \qquad (4.17)$$

Defining $DIS = (r-s)/r = 1 - (s/r)$, the preceding equation becomes:

$$DIS = [1 - \frac{c}{r}][\frac{R+S}{S}] - \frac{1}{r}[\frac{\Pi}{S}]. \qquad (4.18)$$

If all the variables in this equation are measured without errors, it would be just an accounting identity whether the firm is maximizing its profit or not. However as the observed values of S and R are realizations of certain pricing policies of the firm, the equation represents a basis for a testable hypothesis related to the optimality of the firm's behavior. Thus, we are dealing in effect with a statistical relation such as:

$$DIS = \alpha + \beta X + \xi \qquad (4.19)$$

where the random term is assumed to satisfy all standard assumptions in the classical linear regression model and where $\alpha = -(1/r)(\Pi/S)$, $\beta = 1 - (c/r)$, and $X = (R+S)/S$.

The preceding equation represents certain features of the theoretical model as can be seen as follows. Recall that the seller's optimal solution involves the simultaneous determination of the full price r and the relative frequency of deal π since the discount price s is chosen independently. The dependent variable DIS in (4.18) reflects the extent to which the full price r is determined. On the other hand, while data on π are not available, the impact of π can be partially realized through the composition of the total quantity sold M, namely, R — the quantity sold at the full price and S — that sold at the discount price. The dependent variable DIS in (4.18) is defined to be the percentage discount (divided by 100), i.e., the data which are often advertised in newspapers and other media as 25% off or 40% off, etc. The explanatory variable is $X = (R+S)/S$ which is nothing but the *reciprocal* of the ratio of the quantity sold at the discount price to the *total* quantity sold by the seller (at the discount price *and* at the full price combined). For estimation purposes, one helpful feature of this variable is that one would only need to know the ratio $(R+S)/S$ without requiring specific values of R and S separately.

Our model's theoretical construction requires that $c<r$ which implies that $[1-(c/r)] = \beta$ is positive. That is, one of the theoretical implications of the present model is that as the ratio $S/(R+S)$ increases (i.e., as X decreases), the percentage discount DIS declines. It appears at first glance that this represents a test of the slope of the demand function. However, it is important to realize that this particular implication is in *direct contrast* with that of a downward-sloping demand function. With appropriate modifications in interpreting DIS, S, and s, a negative-sloped demand function would have implied that as the ratio $S/(R+S)$ increases (i.e. as X decreases), the value of DIS increases. We shall therefore view that obtaining a statistically positive estimate for the coefficient $\beta = [1-(c/r)]$ would be consistent with the theoretical model.

Let us now make a few comments regarding the data used in our empirical exercise. The National Retail Merchants Association publishes annually its *MOR* (*Merchandising and Operating Results*) for various department stores. Goods sold by those stores are classified into nine major categories, namely Adult Female Apparel; Adult Female Accessories; Adult Male Apparel and Furnishings; Infant Boys' and Girls' Clothing and Accessories; Personal Needs and Smallwares; Hobby,

Recreation, and Transportation; Home Furnishings: Furniture and Decorative Accessories; Home Furnishings: Appliances and Utility Equipment; and Food, Beverages, Tobacco and Home Goods. Each line of product contains information on, among other things, monthly markdowns (percentages of price discount) and ratios of monthly volume sold with respect to total (yearly) volume sold. A quick look at those data reveals that the markdowns in the month of January each year represent by far the largest discount as compared to other months. We have, therefore chosen the markdown in January as the proxy for variable DIS in estimating (4.18). On the other hand, data for the independent variable $X=(R+S)/S$ are those corresponding to the month of January each year. As mentioned earlier, the MOR of the National Retail Merchants Association reports data on $S/(R+S)$; i.e. the ratio of the January volume to the yearly volume sold. Thus while explicit data for R and S are not given, data for the ratio $X=(R+S)/S$ can be obtained directly from MOR.

 Table 4.1 presents the $OLSQ$ estimations of (4.18) for each of the nine categories mentioned earlier in two years, 1968 and 1969. Overall, the estimates for the coefficient $\beta=[1-(c/r)]$ are statistically greater than zero for the majority of cases reported in the table. In the few cases in which the estimates are negative, they are not statistically significant; hence they are not statistically different from zero. The estimates for the constant term which represents $-(1/r)(\Pi/S)$ in fitting (4.18) have mixed signs. As can be seen from the table, several estimated intercepts are either not statistically different from zero or statistically greater than zero, and quite a few are statistically smaller than zero. It would appear that the preceding estimates of the slope β tend to be consistent with the theoretical specification in (4.18) as we had argued earlier. That is, we have found the interesting result that the higher the ratio of the quantity sold at discount prices to the total quantity sold, the lower the seller's discount percentages; a result which appears to offer empirical support to the theoretical model we propose here.

4 A STOCHASTIC CYCLIC PRICING MODEL

In the previous section, the basic motivation for sales activities undertaken by the firm is based on the firm's effort to discriminate the heterogeneous buying population through some kind of sorting device. The device here is of course the frequency of sales. Due to the fact that sales activities are not certain phenomena, rather they occur only in a probability sense allow the firm to charge higher prices (regular prices) to people who, given the wealth and/or the need/taste, would be willing to pay at that price and charge lower prices (sales prices) for the remaining segment of the population. Intuitively, if sales events are deterministic in the sense that the buying population is aware in advance of the forthcoming price reduction, the optimal solution would involve a reduction of price over time to reflect the decline in the cost of waiting as the sales dates are approaching. Assuming that there exists a unit

Table 4.1 *Empirical Implications of the Two-Price Equilibrium*

Dependent Variable: *DIS*

Product Group Code	Product Description	Year	Number of Observs.	Constant Term	$(R+S)/S$ Independent Variable	F-Statistics
1000	Adult Female Apparel	1969	91	.198 (6.74)	.006 (4.08)	16.67
		1968	64	.348 (7.36)	-.003 (-1.16)	1.35
2000	Adult Female Accessories	1969	59	-.125 (-2.27)	.018 (5.64)	31.82
		1968	38	-.142 (-1.70)	.019 (4.26)	18.11
3000	Adult Female Apparel Accessories	1969	35	.118 (.99)	.006 (.94)	.88
		1968	22	.500 (3.61)	-.011 (-1.49)	2.20
4000	Infant Boy's & Girl's Clothing & Accessories	1969	82	.129 (2.55)	.007 (3.10)	9.59
		1968	34	.333 (1.63)	.001 (.13)	.017
5000	Personal Needs & Smallwares	1969	49	-.020 (-.27)	.008 (2.10)	4.41
		1968	37	-.134 (-1.91)	.015 (4.09)	16.75
6000	Hobby Recreation Transportation	1969	11	-.342 (-3.46)	.022 (6.66)	44.37
		1968	10	-.182 (-1.08)	.016 (2.62)	6.86
7000	Home Furnishings: Furniture & Decorative Accessories	1969	54	.029 (.80)	.006 (2.64)	6.99
		1968	35	-.003 (-.07)	.009 (3.47)	12.04
8000	Home Furnishings: Appliances & Utility Equipment	1969	30	-.030 (-.84)	.007 (3.89)	15.10
		1968	17	.068 (3.64)	.002 (2.92)	8.51
9000	Food, Beverages, Tobacco & House Goods & Others NEC	1969	25	.099 (3.30)	-.001 (-.70)	.50
		1968	13	.11 (4.90)	-.003 (-1.76)	3.11

Note: Figures in parentheses are *t*-statistics

cohort of consumers for a particular product, Stokey [1979] analyzes the resulting implications for the firm's practice of intertemporal price discrimination. On the other hand, when there exist different cohorts of consumers, it has been shown by Conlisk, Gerstner and Sobel [1984] that the monopolist may find it optimal to choose a cyclic pricing behavior.

Our analysis in this section is motivated by the Conlisk-Gerstner-Sobel formulation. These authors assume that in each new cohort of consumers which enters the market for possible purchase of a non resalable durable product, there are two types of consumers which are characterized by their high or low willingness to pay for the product. Under the assumption of perfect consumer information, they then show that the optimal strategy for the monopolistic seller is to follow a cyclic pricing pattern. Within each cycle, the optimal pricing pattern involves a declining sequence of prices designed in such a way that consumers of the high reservation price type buy the product immediately on entering the market. Further, there may exist an equilibrium length for each cycle which ends at the time period when the monopolist charges the low reservation price to sell to the accumulated group of the low type consumers.

One important characteristic of the preceding strategy is that the monopolist's pricing decisions are deterministic which in turn reinforce the previously assumed notion of perfect information on the part of consumers. In this regard, the following casual observations have motivated us to look into the problem from a different perspective:

(*i*) The product under consideration in their study is *not* seasonal; this is due to the assumption that each cohort of consumers in each period is the same. Thus the traditionally observed sales phenomenon each January after the Holiday Season, for instance, would not fit well with this type model assumed by Conlisk, Gerstner and Sobel. For unseasonal products, it would appear that stores hold sales in a rather unpredictable fashion, thus consumer information is likely to be imperfect.

(*ii*) It is hard to think of examples which exhibit the cyclic behavior suggested by the Conlisk-Gerstner-Sobel pricing strategy. We can easily observe declining pricing patterns for novelty products such as Rubik's cubes, seasonal products in clearance sales such as summer clothes as fall approaches, or "year-end model" products such as automobiles as the new models arrive, etc. However, the prices in those examples, while declining, are *not* cyclic. The cyclic pricing is more likely to be associated with the two-price behavior, namely, the regular price vs. the sale price; i.e. stores charge regular prices most of the time, then occasionally offer the product at a lower sale price for a limited period, then raise the price back to the regular price again in a cyclic fashion.

The preceding observations are given here mainly to motivate our further analysis of the Conlisk-Gerstner-Sobel problem. We shall attempt to show in this section that within the Conlisk-Gerstner-Sobel theoretical framework, there exists another pricing strategy which may prove to be superior to the deterministic cyclic pricing proposed in the Conlisk-Gerstner-Sobel paper.

In order to see clearly the extent of our stochastic extension, let us briefly report here the basic theoretical structure and the main result of the Conlisk-Gerstner-Sobel model. The monopolistic firm, facing constant and conveniently assumed to be zero unit cost, is assumed to choose a price in each discrete time period to maximize its discounted profits with the discount factor ρ where $0 < \rho < 1$. The demand is characterized on the basis of the assumption that in each period, N consumers enter the market for the infinitely durable good. Of each of these cohorts of consumers, there are two types: the "high"-type consumer who has a reservation price for the product calculated as $V_1 = b_1/(1 - \beta)$ where b_1 represents his monetary valuation of the product per period and β his discount factor; and the "low"-type consumer whose reservation price is calculated similarly to be $V_2 = b_2/(1 - \beta)$. It is clear from the designation of the consumer types that $b_1 > b_2 > 0$. Assume further that the fraction of the high type in each cohort is constant, denoted by α.

With the preceding assumptions, the authors show the following result: In equilibrium, the monopolistic firm's optimal pricing policy is characterized by the following cyclic patterns:

$$p_j = (1 - \beta^{n-j})V_1 + \beta^{n-j}V_2 \text{ for } j = 1, 2, \ldots n$$

where n denotes the length of the cycle.

The preceding result indicates that within each cycle, the prices chosen by the monopolistic firm fall steadily until $j = n$ when $p_n = V_2$. The lowest price p_n is interpreted to be the sales price offered by the firm. As we have argued earlier, in spite of its interesting theoretical implications, most actual marketing price promotional schemes do not seem to fit with such a description of pricing patterns. Consequently, we are motivated here to consider a stochastic version of this type of model with the aim to provide a rationale for a two-price policy frequently observed in the real market situation. It is best to summarize the result here first, to be followed by its detailed justifications and interpretations.

Theorem 4.1. *The optimal pricing strategy for the monopolist under examination can be characterized as follows:*
(*i*) *A single regular price, optimally chosen, is charged for all time periods in each cycle except the sales period in which a lower sales price, set at the low reservation price, is charged.*
(*ii*) *The number of "sales" events follows a Poisson distribution with the mean to be optimally chosen.*

Remark 4.1. As usual, the sales period marks the end of each cycle. The following cycle starts as soon as the firm charges the regular price again. Using a well-known result in mathematical statistics (see Feller [1971], for instance), let us note that the length of the time interval between successive sales events has an exponential distribution provided that the number of sales events is Poisson. Thus the length of each cycle (between successive sales events) under the strategy specified in the theorem is exponentially distributed with a constant mean, denoted by τ. Further, analyses surrounding the so-called "waiting time paradox" suggest that regardless of the epoch of its entry into the market, the expected waiting (for a sale) time for each cohort of consumers would be τ.

Proof of Theorem 4.1. Using an argument similar to that in the Conlisk-Gerstner-Sobel paper, the monopolist would set the following set of prices to induce the high-type consumers to purchase the product upon entering the market:

$$V_1 - p_j \geq \beta^{\tau-1}(V_1 - p_\tau) \; ; \; j=1,2,..;\tau-1 \tag{4.20}$$

which would yield the upper bounds for the p_j's as:

$$p_1 = p_2 = ... = p_{\tau-1} \leq (1-\beta^{\tau-1})V_1 + \beta^{\tau-1}p_\tau. \tag{4.21}$$

Clearly $p_\tau = V_2$ and all other p_j's are identical. For consistency with the notations used in the previous sections, we denote $p_\tau = V_2$ as s which is the sales price and the remaining p_j's as r which is the regular price. In short, the optimum regular price is:

$$r = (1-\beta^{\tau-1})V_1 + \beta^{\tau-1}s \tag{4.22}$$

in which an optimal τ is yet to be determined.

The objective of the monopolist is to maximize the expected discounted sum of an indefinite sequence of profits:

$$\text{Max. } \phi(\tau,\infty) = \phi(\tau,1)[1+\rho^\tau+\rho^{2\tau}+...] = \frac{\phi(\tau,1)}{1-\rho^\tau} \tag{4.23}$$

where $\phi(\tau,1) = \rho^{\tau-1}Ns[\alpha+\tau(1-\alpha)] + \alpha Nr \sum_{i=1}^{\tau-1} \rho^{i-1}$ in which $\phi(\tau,1)$ defines the expected profits generated in each cycle, discounted to the beginning of the cycle.

Using (4.22), and assuming that $\rho=\beta$, and setting $N=1$ without loss of generality, eq. (4.23) can be written as:

$$\text{Max. } \phi(\tau,\infty) = \frac{1}{(1-\rho^\tau)}[\rho^{\tau-1}\psi(\tau) + \frac{\alpha V_1}{(1-\rho)}] \tag{4.23a}$$

where we will later find it convenient to define:

$$\psi(\tau) = (1-\alpha)s\tau + \frac{(V_1-s)\alpha\rho^{\tau-1}}{(1-\rho)} - [2\alpha(V_1-s)+s\alpha\rho] \tag{4.24}$$

where it can be readily verified here that $\partial^2\psi(\tau)/\partial\tau^2 > 0$.

The first-order condition for optimality in (4.23a) can be shown to be:

$$\frac{\partial \psi(\tau^*)}{\partial \tau} = \frac{-\ln\rho\psi(\tau^*)}{(1-\rho^{\tau^*})} - \frac{\alpha\rho\ln\rho V_1}{(1-\rho)(1-\rho^{\tau^*})} \tag{4.25}$$

where the asterisk denotes optimal value of τ, and *ln* denotes natural logarithm. The second-order condition can be derived as:

$$\frac{\partial^2 \psi(\tau^*)}{\partial \tau^2} < -\ln\rho \frac{\partial \psi(\tau^*)}{\partial \tau}. \tag{4.26}$$

Economic interpretations of these conditions will be given in a remark below. We now need to show that the preceding solution yields higher expected discounted profits in comparison to the discounted profits obtained from the Conlisk-Gerstner-Sobel deterministic strategy. For purposes of comparison, let us write Conlisk, Gerstner and Sobel's maximum profits as:

$$\Pi(n^*) = \frac{1}{(1-\rho^{n^*})}[\rho^{n^*-1}n^*(1-\alpha)p_n + \alpha\sum_{i=1}^{n^*}\rho^{i-1}p_i] \tag{4.27}$$

where $p_n = s = V_2$; $p_1 > p_2 > ... > p_{n-1} > p_n$; $p_1^* = (1-\rho^{n^*-1})V_1 + \rho^{n^*-1}V_2$; n^* denotes the optimum cycle length obtained in their study, and note also that $\partial p_i/\partial n > 0$.

On the other hand, our maximum profits are:

$$\phi(\tau^*, \infty) = \frac{1}{1-\rho^{\tau^*}}[\rho^{\tau^*-1}s[\alpha + \tau^*(1-\alpha)] + \alpha r\sum_{i=1}^{\tau^*-1}\rho^{i-1} \tag{4.28}$$

where $r^* = (1-\rho^{\tau^*-1})V_1 + \rho^{\tau^*-1}V_2$.

Clearly, τ^* can be greater than, equal to, or smaller than n^*. For $n^* \leq \tau^*$, it follows that a comparison between (4.27) and (4.28) would yield the result that $\Pi(n^*) < \phi(\tau^*, \infty)$. For the case in which $n^* > \tau^*$, we have $\Pi(n^*) < \phi(n^*, \infty) < \phi(\tau^*, \infty)$ where the first inequality follows from comparing (4.27) and (4.28) and the second inequality is due to the fact that τ^* maximizes $\phi(\tau, \infty)$. In short, we have: $\Pi(n^*) < \phi(\tau^*, \infty)$.

Q.E.D.

Remark 4.2. The results contained in the preceding theorem can be most easily interpreted for the simple case in which the monopolist considers only one cycle for his product. This could arise in a context where the firm considers introducing a new model at the end of the cycle, for instance. The maximization problem facing the firm is:

$$\text{Max. } \phi(\tau, 1) = [\frac{\alpha V_1}{(1-\rho)}] + \rho^{\tau-1}\psi(\tau) \tag{4.29}$$

where number 1 in $\phi(\tau, 1)$ denotes the one-cycle horizon.

The first and second-order conditions can be written simply as:

$$\frac{\partial\psi(\tau^{**})}{\partial\tau} = -\ln\rho\psi(\tau^{**}) \qquad (4.25a)$$

$$\text{and } \frac{\partial^2\psi(\tau^{**})}{\partial\tau^2} < -\ln\rho\frac{\partial\psi(\tau^{**})}{\partial\tau} \qquad (4.26a)$$

where the double asterisks denote the optimal value of τ in maximizing (4.29).

The economic interpretation of the necessary condition in (4.25a) can be given here. First, it is helpful to think of the objective function (4.29) as total expected profits which consist of two components: the first is $[\alpha V_1/(1-\rho)]$ which represents the expected discounted profits if the monopolist simply charges the single price V_1 to sell to the high reservation price consumers; the second component, $[\rho^{\tau-1}\psi(\tau)]$, represents the expected discounted profits to the firm due to the sales strategy with periodic sales at every τ periods. For convenience we shall refer to the first component as "base" profits and the second the "strategic" profits. Now if the sales strategy proves to be more profitable, then one would need to look at the strategic profits to find out the optimal expected cycle length. The left hand side of (4.25a) simply represents the marginal strategic profits by delaying the expected cycle length by one period and the right hand side of (4.25a) represents the foregone interest earned on strategic profits by delaying one period. To see this, note that $(-\ln\rho)$ can be simply converted to the implicit interest rate r where $r = -\ln\rho$ when we define $\rho^\tau = e^{-r\tau}$. The first-order condition simply requires that at the optimal expected cycle length, marginal strategic profits be equal to the foregone interest on strategic profits.

Remark 4.3. Since $\ln\rho < 0$, optimality conditions for both the single-cycle and the indefinite-cycle cases require that $\partial\psi(\tau)/\partial\tau$ be positive at the chosen cycle length. Thus the relevant portion of the $\psi(\tau)$ curve is increasing in τ and so is that of the $-\ln\rho\psi(\tau)$ curve. Also, recall that $\partial^2\psi(\tau)/\partial\tau^2$ is positive for all τ; hence the $\partial\psi(\tau)/\partial\tau$ curve is increasing throughout. The optimal expected cycle length is then determined by the intersection of the $\partial\psi(\tau)/\partial\tau$ curve and the $-\ln\rho\psi(\tau)$ curve which are both upward-sloping. The second-order condition further requires that the $\partial\psi(\tau)/\partial\tau$ curve intersects the $-\ln\rho\psi(\tau)$ curve from above at the optimal cycle length. Bearing this in mind with the help of the diagram, a comparison between the single-cycle optimal expected cycle length and the indefinite-cycle optimal expected cycle length can be made. From the right-hand side of (4.25), it is noted that $-\ln\rho\psi(\tau)/(1-\rho^\tau)$ is greater than $-\ln\rho\psi(\tau)$ since $0 < \rho < 1$ and that $-\alpha\rho\ln\rho V_1/[(1-\rho)(1-\rho^\tau)]$ is positive. Hence, together with the second-order condition, a comparison between (4.25a) and (4.25) shows unambiguously that $\tau^* < \tau^{**}$; i.e., as the horizon becomes indefinite, the optimal expected cycle length becomes shorter. This is illustrated in *Figure* 4.3.

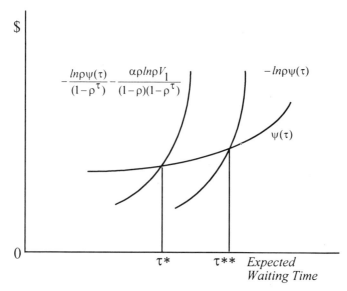

Figure 4.3 *Effects of Planning Horizon on Optimal Expected Cycle Length*

The economic interpretation we give in Remark 4.2 can be extended to the indefinite-cycle case as follows. From the right hand side of (4.25), as the expected cycle length is extended by one period, there are two negative effects on the firm's expected strategic profits: the first is the foregone interests earned on an indefinite stream of strategic profits indicated by $-\ln\rho\psi$ (τ) which would yield the discounted foregone interests on strategic profits equal to $[-\ln\rho\psi(\tau)/(1-\rho^\tau)]$; the second is the foregone interests earned on an indefinite stream of base profits $[-\ln \rho\alpha\rho V_1/(1-\rho)]$ which would yield the discounted foregone interests on base profits equal to $[-\ln\rho\alpha\rho V_1/(1-\rho^\tau)]$. Thus, the condition in (4.25) requires that the expected cycle length is optimal when the marginal strategic profits equals to the sum of discounted foregone interests earned on future base profits and future strategic profits as a result of the firm's sales strategy.

Remark 4.4. A possible objection to the preceding analysis can be raised on the basis of the well-known issue of dynamic time consistency in this type of problem. It can be readily shown, however, that by a simple introduction of a reputation effect and/or the possibility of learning by consumers, the preceding solutions would be dynamically optimal. For example, under reasonable assumptions, it can be shown that the sufficient statistic reflecting the store's true value of the sales cycle is simply the mean of its observed sales cycles over time. The optimal solution characterized in Theorem 4.1 will therefore be reinforced if the penalty imposed on deviations from its mean is sufficiently large.

In concluding this section, we should also note here that the deterministic cyclic pricing has been extended to take into account of the competitive reactions in an oligopolistic market in Sobel [1984]. The model assumes that in such a market, there exist two types of consumers who make up the total buying population which is normalized at unity. One is of the high-type, at the fraction α, who values a particular product at $\$V_1$ with zero discount factor which reflects the high search cost both spatially as well as temporally; and the other is the low-type consumer, at the fraction $(1-\alpha)$, who values the same product at $\$V_2$, with the discount factor of ρ. Clearly it is assumed implicitly that $V_1 > V_2 > 0$. Assume further that the firms are faced with zero, constant cost per product unit for simplicity and assume in addition that for the i-th store, the proportion α_i/α who values the product at V_1 would buy upon entering the market. One theoretical implication of the model which is of particular interest here is the result that there exists a symmetric equilibrium in simple strategies, defined to represent a pricing strategy that depends only on the number of the high-type and the low-type consumers. Further, such an equilibrium is characterized by a pricing strategy involving the high prices charged by all stores for a number of periods after the sale; then any store will have a sale with a positive probability. The sales price is offered in order to induce the purchase by the consumers who have low reservation prices. This pricing strategy is again based on certain notion of price discrimination.

5 RESALE PRICE MAINTENANCE

In the preceding two sections we have analyzed a number of different approaches in using price discrimination to enhance a firm's economic profits. The model on price discount is developed with the presumption that the firm would have to set both the regular price and the sales price and in addition, for a continuous spectrum of heterogeneous buying population, the firm also seeks to find an optimal frequency of sales. In the stochastic cyclic model, there exist two types of consumers, one has a high-reservation price and the other a low-reservation price and the firm may find it optimal to offer the higher regular prices for the entering cohort of consumers and then, with an optimally chosen level of regularity (probability), to offer the product at the sales price to capture the accumulated low-reservation price consumers. In both of these types of price discount, there is only one type of store as we assume firms have monopoly power. The consumers are sorted so that different prices can be charged by the same store. On the other hand, in view of imperfect consumer information of the competing firms' product and prices, there have also been efforts to examine market structure involving the coexistence of two different types of firms, one investing in information and consequently charges a higher price and the other not doing so and then charges a lower price. This is the subject of this section and in the process we will also show how a policy application of the price discount can be seen in the context of uncertainty in product and pricing. Since the interactions between marketing analysis and public policy-oriented issues can potentially be very important and yet remained largely neglected, we will devote some length here for this application.

In this regard, we base our analysis on a paper by Mathewson and Winter [1983] who address the issue of Resale Price Maintenance (*RPM*) in the context of imperfect consumer information. Their model enables them to draw several important implications regarding price dispersion, the welfare effects of *RPM* and consequently policy issues surrounding the legal aspect of *RPM*. In our view, the notion of a pre-*RPM* two-price industry equilibrium (the monopoly price charged by informing stores and the wholesale price charged by discount stores) represents a useful framework to study the impact of *RPM*. However, Mathewson and Winter then examine exclusively the post-*RPM* single-price industry equilibrium where the discount stores disappear and the remaining informing stores charge a single price which is lower than the pre-*RPM* monopoly price. For the case of administered prices, it would of course be necessary that the post-*RPM* price be identical across all remaining stores, provided that the monopolistic wholesale manufacturer chooses to adopt such a *RPM* policy. For the case of price floor, the authors' exclusive focus on the post-*RPM* single-price equilibrium represents an unfortunate choice since it would appear from casual empirical observations that even after the price floor is imposed, the post-*RPM* two-price equilibrium continues to prevail in most, if not all, retail markets. As a result, policy implications derived from their analysis would appear to be less relevant for the public debate on the issue of *RPM* and its legal implications. Our current exercise attempts to address this particular problem of their model, and in doing so, we will first offer some comments on their result that administered pricing improves the monopolistic manufacturer's profits; we then analyze the post-*RPM* two-price equilibrium using a slightly modified version of their model; and finally we will reinterpret some empirical findings obtained from a rather out-of-date yet still the most comprehensive available, for our current purposes, survey conducted for the Druggist's Research Bureau in 1940.

5.1 Comments On The Administered Price Model

Mathewson and Winter [1983] consider the following maximization problem facing the pre-*RPM* monopolistic manufacturer:

$$\text{Max. } \Pi(p_w) \equiv nM(n).[\lambda d(p_m) + (1-\lambda) d(p_w)] [p_w - 1] \qquad (4.30)$$

where Π denotes profits, $nM(n)$ the total number of visitors of n informing stores, $d(p)$ the average demand of informed consumers, λ the proportion of high search cost customers, p_w the product's wholesale price, p_m the monopoly price, and for convenience, the firm's unit production cost is set at unity.

In the pre-*RPM* equilibrium, the non-informing stores charge p_w and thus earn zero economic profits; and the informing stores charge p_m and the number of informing stores satisfies the zero-profit condition:

$$\lambda nM(n).d(p_m).(p_m - p_w) - nI = 0 \qquad (4.31)$$

where I represents the fixed monetary information cost.

It is then demonstrated that by simply imposing *RPM* in form of an optimally set administered price $\hat{p}$, the manufacturer would obtain the optimal profits as if it were a vertically-integrated firm. The manufacturer's problem is:

$$\text{Max. } \hat{\Pi}(\hat{p},\hat{n}) \equiv \hat{n}M(\hat{n}).d(\hat{p})(\hat{p}-1) - \hat{n}I \qquad (4.32)$$

where the "hats" denote post-*RPM* values of respective variables.

On the basis of these relations, the authors then claim that it is always the case that administered pricing increases the manufacturer's profit. That is, maximum value of $\hat{\Pi}$ defined in (4.32) is always greater than the maximum value of Π defined in (4.30). The obvious implication of this result is that the wholesale manufacturer would choose to implement *RPM* due to the profit incentives.

It does not appear that this particular result is valid in general. We will presently show that the reverse may be true; and our result could well explain the fact that we rarely observe the administered pricing strategy: the more common form of *RPM* being the price floor practice as indicated in Scherer and Ross [1990]. Let us show this result.

From (4.30), let us write:

$$\Pi = nM(n)[\lambda d(p_m) + (1-\lambda)d(p_w)][p_w - p_m + p_m - 1]. \qquad (4.30a)$$

Taking into account the constraint in (4.31), eq. (4.30a)) becomes:

$$\Pi = p_m nM(n)\lambda d(p_m) + p_w nM(n)(1-\lambda)d(p_w)$$
$$-nM(n)[\lambda d(p_m) + (1-\lambda)d(p_w)] - nI \qquad (4.30b)$$

which is exactly the maximization problem facing a hypothetical vertically integrated monopolistic manufacturer which engages in some form of price discrimination. The discriminating monopolist would charge a higher monopoly price p_m to the "high" search cost customers and a lower wholesale price p_w to the "low" search cost customers. This problem is thus similar to that faced by the noisy monopolist who uses some kind of sorting device to distinguish lower and higher search cost consumers as analyzed in Salop [1977] and, with appropriate modifications in interpretation, the price discount model discussed in Section 2 above.

Thus, at issue is whether or not our hypothetical vertically integrated monopolistic manufacturer would choose to engage in price discrimination. A comparison between (4.32) and (4.30b) would enable the monopolist to answer this question. Unlike the text book case of price discrimination where the firm is faced with two completely segmented thus independent markets for its product; and where price discrimination is always profitable, this is *not* necessarily the case in our current problem since demands for the product from the informing stores and the uninforming discount stores are interdependent. It can be seen that whether or not price discrimination is profitable would depend on several parameters of the model such as λ, n, and the average demand function $d(p)$. The following diagram should prove helpful in capturing the preceding point.

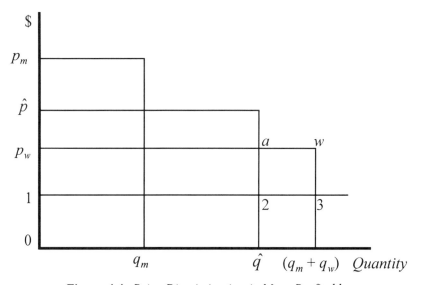

Figure 4.4 *Price Discrimination is More Profitable*

Figure 4.4 illustrates a particular scenario for the monopolistic manufacturer. For notational convenience, let us define $q_m = nM(n)\lambda d(p_m)$, $q_w = nM(n)(1-\lambda)d(p_w)$, and $\hat{q} = \hat{n}M(\hat{n})d(\hat{p})$. The discriminating monopolist sells q_m at price p_m and sells q_w at p_w. The total quantity is of course $q_m + q_w$ as denoted in the diagram. With the average production cost set at unity, the profit obtained by the manufacturer is represented by the rectangular area marked by $1p_w w3$ in the diagram, as can be seen directly from eq. (4.30). It can also be graphically verified that the same area measures the identical profit defined in eq. (4.30b) by noting that $nI = q_m(p_m-p_w)$, due to the zero-profit condition in (4.31). On the other hand, if the manufacturer considers the imposition of an administered price level $\hat{p}$, the resulting quantity would be $\hat{q}$ and the resulting profit can be represented by the area $1p_wa2$ in the diagram. Again, we note that the zero-profit condition is satisfied so that $\hat{n}I = \hat{q}(\hat{p}-p_w)$. It can be clearly seen that price discrimination is profitable if (q_m+q_w) is greater than $\hat{q}$. In other words, the monopolistic manufacturer would choose the administered pricing strategy only if $\hat{q}$ is greater than $q_m + q_w$. The fact that one rarely observes administered pricing in reality may indicate that this particular condition is *not* satisfied. Further, it is a natural result of the typical downward-sloping demand schedule.

5.2 The Post-*RPM* Two-Price Equilibrium

On the basis of the analysis in the preceding sub-section, we note that a pre-*RPM* two-price equilibrium may be attained when the manufacturer sets the wholesale price at p_w; the discount retailers then sell the product at p_w, making zero economic profit; and the informing stores then sell at p_m which is higher than p_w by an amount equal to the information cost, also making zero economic profit. Let us now suppose that the manufacturer chooses to impose *RPM* in the form of price floors. The only interesting case which arises is when the price floor p_f is higher than the pre-*RPM* discount stores' retail price p_w. As Mathewson and Winter argue, if p_f is sufficiently close to p_m, then the discount stores will disappear and the informing stores would reduce their retail prices to p_f, resulting in a single equilibrium in the post-*RPM* configuration. However, if p_f is not sufficiently high, a post-*RPM* two-price equilibrium may exist. This is the case which we think empirically most interesting but is unfortunately left out in their analysis. One apparent problem of this scenario is that the imposition of a price floor would not result in a stable equilibrium since while informing stores would earn zero profits, the discount stores are "forced" to earn positive economic profits (p_f is always higher than p_w). We find this configuration hard to justify.

As an alternative, let us consider the assumption that the price floor p_f is set at the level of p_w. Without *RPM*, we thus implicitly assume that the discount retailers set a price lower than p_w, namely p_ℓ. The weakness of this assumption is that the discount stores suffer economic loss by selling the particular product under consideration. However, we can offer some justifications for this assumption: (*i*) in our view, it is preferable to the assumption that $p_f > p_w$ since the discount stores are forced to earn positive profits in the presence of *RPM* while the informing stores earn zero profits; (*ii*) it has some casual empirical support in form of the well-known loss leader phenomenon; and (*iii*) discount stores normally carry several products so that economic loss in one product may not be inconsistent with overall zero profit conditions since positive economic profits may be made in other products to sufficiently compensate for its economic loss. In Section 5 of this chapter, we will advance the implications in (*ii*) and (*iii*) a little further. We should note here that the argument we present in this section regarding the impact of *RPM* would not significantly depend on our preceding assumption. We now introduce an additional assumption to our model.

Instead of a fixed parameter, the proportion λ of high-cost search consumers is a function of the difference Δp in high and low prices. That is, we assume that $\lambda = \lambda(\Delta p)$ where $\lambda'(\Delta p) < 0$; the higher the price difference the smaller the retained proportion of the informed consumers. Our assumption is in line with the implicit result in search theory (see Salop [1977], for instance.) A customer chooses to be informed if expected benefits of being informed are not less than expected cost of information. A change in price difference Δp would result in a change in expected benefits of information, hence λ would also have to change.

Our problem can be stated as follows. In the absence of *RPM*, given that the discount stores charge the price p_ℓ, the monopolistically competitive informing stores would set p_h in order to:

$$\text{Max.} \quad \phi = (p_h - p_w)\lambda(\Delta p_h)M(n)d(p_h) - I \tag{4.33}$$

where $\Delta p_h = p_h - p_\ell$ and n is so that the zero-profit condition is satisfied.

The first-order condition is:

$$(p_h - p_w)[\lambda(\Delta p_h)d'(p_h) + d(p_h)\lambda'(\Delta p_h)] + \lambda(\Delta p_h)d(p_h) = 0. \tag{4.34}$$

On the other hand, upon the implementation of *RPM* in form of the price floor $p_f \equiv p_w$, the informing stores would set p_m in order to:

$$\text{Max.} \quad \hat{\phi} = (p_m - p_w)\lambda(\Delta p_m)M(\hat{n})d(p_m) - I \tag{4.33a}$$

where $\Delta p_m = p_m - p_w$ and $\hat{n}$ is so that the zero-profit condition is again satisfied.

The first-order condition is:

$$(p_m - p_w)[\lambda(\Delta p_m)d'(p_m) + d(p_m)\lambda'(\Delta p_m)] + \lambda(\Delta p_m)d(p_m) = 0. \tag{4.34a}$$

A number of interesting observations can be seen by comparing (4.34) and (4.34*a*). If λ is assumed fixed, then (4.34) and (4.34*a*) yield the result that $p_m \equiv p_h$. That is, whether the discount stores decide to charge p_ℓ or p_w would not affect the price charged by the informing stores, the information level, the maximum (zero) profits of the informing stores, and the maximum profits of the monopolistic manufacturer. Suppose that the discount stores charge p_ℓ, then the net effect is an economic loss in the discount stores which is transferred to the low-search cost customers in form of gain in consumers' surplus. There is no economic reason for the manufacturer to seek a *RPM* imposition in form of a price floor at p_w.

However, when we adopt the assumption that λ is a function of Δp, then upon inspecting (4.34) and (4.34a), we will conclude that p_m may be higher, equal to, or lower than p_h. The possibility that p_h equals to p_m represents merely a cutting-line case and thus is not interesting. Both possibilities that p_h is higher than p_m or p_h is lower than p_m are strictly theoretical and would crucially depend on the specification of the function $\lambda(\Delta p)$, among other things.

To summarize, if we view that prior to a *RPM* imposition, the discount stores charge p_ℓ and the informing stores charge p_h then after *RPM* is implemented (p_w is charged by the discount stores), the informing stores would find it optimal to charge p_m either higher or lower than p_h. For instance, facing a higher p_w in the discount stores, the marginal consumers who would otherwise leave the informing stores may no longer find the price reduction in the discount stores sufficiently attractive; hence the informing stores might decide to reduce their price from p_h to a lower level p_m in order to retain these marginal consumers. The economic argument in the opposite direction could also be given. As p_ℓ is raised to p_w, the informing stores may choose to raise their price accordingly since they could retain the same proportion of buyers and in the process earn higher per-unit profits. As we mention earlier, the direction of the change in p_h is basically an empirical question. The next section offers some interesting empirical observations to this issue.

Within the preceding theoretical framework, it is very difficult to derive welfare implications of *RPM*. Consider the impact of *RPM* on the product's average price, for example. The pre-*RPM* average price is:

$$\bar{p} = \frac{p_h \lambda(\Delta p_h) d(p_h) + p_\ell [1 - \lambda(\Delta p_h)] d(p_\ell)}{\lambda(\Delta p_h) d(p_h) + [1 - \lambda(\Delta p_h)] d(p_\ell)} \tag{4.35a}$$

and the post-*RPM* average price is:

$$\hat{p} = \frac{p_m \lambda(\Delta p_m) d(p_m) + p_w [1 - \lambda(\Delta p_m)] d(p_w)}{\lambda(\Delta p_m) d(p_m) + [1 - \lambda(\Delta p_m)] d(p_w)}. \tag{4.35b}$$

Once again, a comparison between $\bar{p}$ and $\hat{p}$ can only be settled on the basis of empirical observations. The next section also offers some empirical result for calculations similar to (4.35a) and (4.35b).

Our preceding analysis also offers a rationale for the monopolistic manufacturer to be interested in implementing *RPM*. By imposing a price floor at p_w, the manufacturer would induce the informing stores to charge p_m and provide information worth $\hbar I$. As we had shown earlier, the resulting profit would then be equivalent to that obtained from the hypothetical vertically-integrated firm which exercises price discrimination. Thus, *RPM* is bound to result in an increase in the manufacturer's profits; hence it would be an economically logical reason for the firm to implement such a policy. This particular result is of course very similar to a result shown earlier by Mathewson and Winter. The crucial difference is that we work with a post-*RPM* two-price equilibrium while they concentrated on a post-*RPM* one-price equilibrium.

5.3 Some Empirical Evidence

Despite considerable empirical efforts in the literature, the impact of *RPM* on the product's average price has not been conclusively evaluated. Frankel [1955], after surveying much of the empirical literature available at the time, registers his frustration by stating that further empirical efforts on this issue should prove useless. Here, we attempt to reinterpret some empirical findings obtained by the Druggists' Research Bureau in a most comprehensive survey conducted in 1940, after forty-four states had approved Fair Trade contracts (*RPM*). While these findings were carefully reported in the Bureau's study, our interpretation in view of the preceding theoretical model should offer some additional useful insights.

Table 4.2 is reproduced from Ostlund and Vickland's study ([1940], Table 3, page 12). The table is self-explanatory to a large extent. For our current purposes, chain stores correspond to our definition of non-informing discount stores since they engage frequently in price reduction through special sales (Ostlund and Vickland, p. 32) and their pricing strategy is directly subjected to *RPM*. On the other hand, "independent" stores appear to correspond to our notion of informing stores. This is so since independent stores, especially the smaller ones, rely heavily on personal services, sales force, product's information, product display to introduce and then persuade potential customers to buy the product at their stores. Thus, if one were to adopt the preceding categorization, the data contained in *Table* 4.2 reveal some interesting observations. First, before Fair Trade, the weighted average prices charged by the chain stores are lower than the minimum contract price to be imposed by *RPM*. On the contrary, the weighted average prices charged by independent stores are, with some minor exceptions, higher than the minimum contract price to be imposed by *RPM*. Second, as a result of the Fair Trade Laws, the 1939's weighted average prices in the chain stores are virtually identical to the *RPM*-imposed minimum prices. On the other hand, the post-*RPM* prices charged by independent stores indicate that they are higher than the minimum contract prices. This configuration does lend support to the notion of a post-*RPM* two-price equilibrium. Thirdly and most importantly, as chain stores increase their prices due to *RPM*, independent stores *reduce* their prices accordingly, again with some minor exceptions. This empirical finding is particularly interesting in our framework since the model presented in the preceding section does allow this possibility to arise. Using our earlier notation, we could argue here that the informing (independent) stores would find it optimal to reduce their higher price p_h to a lower level p_m in order to compete against the discount (chain) stores whose prices are now higher because of the *RPM* imposition. Fourth, since the prices charged by the chain stores and independent stores move in opposite directions, the net change in the overall average prices would

Table 4.2 Retail Price Indices of Fifty Leading Drug Store Items Before and After Distribution under Fair Trade Contract for Chains and Various Sizes of Independents by City-Size Groups

(Weighted Average List Price = 100)

Drug Store Type And Size	All City-Size Groups			By City-Size Groups											
				Under 10,000			10,000 to 100,000			100,000 to 1,000,000			1,000,000 and Over		
	Before Fair Trade	1939	Change	Before Fair Trade	1939	Change	Before Fair Trade	1939	Change	Before Fair Trade	1939	Change	Before Fair Trade	1939	Change
Independents By Store-Size Groups**															
1. Under $10,000	93.1	90.6	-2.5	98.0	95.4	-2.6	93.9	88.3	-5.6	90.0	87.2	-2.8	85.5	85.3	-0.2
2. $10,000-$19,999	92.7	89.3	-3.4	96.9	93.0	-3.9	92.6	87.8	-4.8	90.7	87.1	-3.6	84.8	84.9	+0.1
3. $20,000-$29,999	91.7	88.2	-3.5	96.0	91.4	-4.6	91.2	87.0	-4.2	88.9	86.2	-2.7	83.7	84.3	+0.6
4. $30,000-$49,999	90.6	87.3	-3.3	95.2	90.0	-5.2	90.1	86.4	-3.7	87.9	85.7	-2.2	82.8	84.4	+1.6
5. $50,000 and Up	85.8	85.4	-0.4	92.3	87.8	-4.5	87.8	85.6	-2.2	83.5	84.9	+1.4	81.2	84.4	+3.2
Chains	78.6	83.5	+4.9	80.5	83.7	+3.2	78.6	83.4	+4.8	78.8	83.7	+4.9	77.9	83.2	+5.3
All Drug Stores	87.9	87.0	-0.9	95.6	91.7	-3.9	87.4	85.9	-1.5	84.6	85.2	+0.6	81.7	84.2	+2.5

Note: The Weighted Average Minimum Contract Price = 83.3
*The Price Index is the percentage of the Weighted Average Price of 50 items to the Weighted Average List Price times 100.
**Store Size classification is based on Annual Volume.

Source: Table 3, Ostlund and Vickland [1939].

depend on relative strengths of these two opposite forces. Thus the impact of *RPM* on the overall average price is generally ambiguous and is subject to empirical interpretations. Incidentally, the data contained in Table 4.2 indicate that in comparison to the pre-*RPM* average price, the post-*RPM* (1939) average price declined by about 1% when counting all drug stores for all city-size groups. This represents perhaps the most important empirical finding of the Druggists' Research Bureau survey, from the point of view of consumer welfare.

5.4 Summary

The Mathewson-Winter model of pre-*RPM* two-price equilibrium in the context of imperfect consumer information provides a useful framework to study the impact of *RPM*. Their analysis concentrates on a post-*RPM* single-price equilibrium for both cases of administered prices and price floors.

In this section, we explore the possible impact of *RPM* using their basic theoretical framework with some slight modifications. In particular, we address the issue for the case of post-*RPM* two-price equilibrium, a case which appears to prevail in several actual retail markets. We show that when *RPM* is imposed in the form of price floors, the discount stores will of course raise their price to meet this constraint and the informing stores may find it optimal to either increase or reduce their prices. As a result, any assessment of *RPM* on consumer welfare would become much less clear-cut and it is basically an empirical question. As an empirical note, we re-examine an extensive set of survey data published by the Druggist's Research Bureau in view of our theoretical model. On the basis of the model, we share the same feeling expressed by Frankel a long time ago about the inconclusiveness of any empirical evidence regarding the impact of *RPM* on the average price level.

6 PERSISTENCE OF PRICE DIFFERENCES EVEN WHEN CONSUMERS LEARN

In the context of imperfect information, we have thus explored various implications for industry equilibrium in which prices may be charged to different consumers with the practice of price discount as the basis for some sort of discrimination pricing. An immediate implication of the existence of these industry equilibria is that at any given period of time, unit prices of identical products may vary from store to store. As we have analyzed in the previous section, a basic explanation for the existence of such equilibria is rooted in the general framework of economic decisions for agents with incomplete information. In particular, Pratt, Wise and Zeckhauser [1979] showed that price dispersion exists in equilibrium if a potential buyer has to pay a positive search cost every time he secures a price quotation. The customer engages in search activities since he does not know with certainty the distribution of prices across stores. Another model of monopolistically competitive price variation was proposed by Salop and Stiglitz [1977] in which they assumed that potential customers differ in their information-gathering costs. In their model, there exist two groups of stores in equilibrium: high-price stores which sell the product to uninformed customers who are of the higher information-gathering cost type and low-price stores which sell the product to informed customers (lower information-gathering costs) and lucky uninformed customers. This characterization of market equilibrium thus gives rise to the possible price variation even for homogeneous products. In another paper on the subject, Varian [1980] offered another theoretical justification for spatial price dispersions. He showed that in order to price discriminate between informed and uninformed customers, firms would choose a mixed (randomized) strategy of pricing. Basically, in order to sell his product to informed customers, the seller should offer the lowest price among his competitors. However, the seller would get his equal share of uninformed customers no matter how high his price is, given that it does not exceed the customer's reservation price. Thus, in a probability sense, every seller tends to charge either the lowest permissible price (to gain informed customers) or the (higher) reservation price (to get the largest possible unit profit from selling to uninformed customers). From this equilibrium configuration, a cross-section survey of all stores' prices at any given time would yield a dispersion in prices.

We shall argue that the major weakness of the literature on this subject stems from the fact that economists perhaps over-emphasize the crucial role of search costs for the lowest price, and in the process under-estimate the learning capabilities of potential customers. More specifically, we note first of all that the issue under examination is the price dispersion of an identical product. Thus, the only piece of information that the buyer is interested in is the quoted prices. One could hardly think that the buyer has to pay a substantial cost just to find out the price of a product. In many cases, we are overfed with information regarding prices in the form of weekend newspaper advertisements. "Catalog" stores send us catalogs which contain unit prices for all the items they carry. When such price information is not readily available, one can almost surely get a price quotation from a telephone call which can be considered costless. We are not therefore convinced that information-gathering costs would be sufficient to explain the existence of a stable equilibrium in which unit prices of an identical product differ from one store to another.

To further reinforce the preceding argument, let us assume that information-gathering can be *initially* costly. When purchase of a product is subject to repetition, it is likely that, over time, customers form an expectation about certain stores' "average" prices. This in effect would reduce the costs of search because the customer is now faced with a smaller set of alternatives based on which he performs his search activities. To avoid the problem of learning, several work on the subject made the convenient assumption that the product is durable and thus the consumer purchases one and only one unit. However, since durable goods are usually expensive, the search cost, in comparison to the potential gain in getting the product at a lower price, is relatively cheap. It is thus hard to believe that search costs alone could explain the persistence of price dispersion among durable products which are identical.

For the case of repeat purchases, elements of learning on the part of the rational customer would either drive out the high-priced stores or force them to reduce their prices. One result of these processes is the disappearance of price dispersion. Learning, of course, does not come without economic costs to customers. Casual observations, however, appear to indicate that if purchase is repeated, learning is of a passive type and its implicit costs may be negligible. A typical consumer can usually come to realize how (in)expensive a particular store is after a couple of visits to that store and other stores in the area. This is of course one form of learning by doing. A consumer can also gather information regarding a *general* impression on (in)expensiveness of competing stores by means of social gatherings (word-of-mouth), and advertisements. This form of information-gathering is almost costless and we believe that a consumer would typically form his or her expectations about prices using this kind of passive learning in making purchase decisions. We have thus argued against the very basic and crucial assumption of an absence of learning in the works cited earlier. If this argument is valid, why do we still actually observe price variations in reality?

We sketch here an argument to offer an alternative explanation for stable equilibrium of different prices among various stores for identical products. We propose to study the question of price dispersion within the context of a multiple-product purchase with learning through repeated experimentation. One can show that if the average price in each purchase is statistically the same among competing stores, there would not exist a lowest-priced store for the consumers to pick, even when consumers are able to learn through time. Yet when one looks at the price levels of any identical products among stores, it is more than likely that their prices vary; and more importantly, such a price variation can be shown to persist in equilibrium.

A number of assumptions will be needed to advance the argument. Consumers are attracted to certain stores by prices of *some* products which are lower than the general market prices that the consumers *perceive*. The consumers obtain information about the general market prices by past experiences and other forms of information dissemination. The lower prices of *some* products are brought to the potential customers' attention mainly through advertisement (the dominant form of advertising is newspapers). Further, consumers purchase not one single item, but rather a basket of several items. While the low prices of some products brought the customers to the store, the customers do not always end up buying only those products which are offered at the lower prices. A good example of this assumption can be easily found in the real world. Usually, once a week, our newspapers carry a section on food in which virtually all grocery stores in a given area advertise about price discounts for various products. A potential customer can always use some of the coupons offered in those ads but he or she almost surely ends up buying many other items at the "regular" prices. Consumers are typically attracted by a significantly reduced price at a hardware store on an item they plan to buy and end up purchasing other items in the same store. Since one does not originally plan to buy those other items, information regarding their prices in comparison to other stores' is not complete. Also, consumers form expectations about the (in)expensiveness of different stores by past purchase experiences. Basically, every time the consumer shops a particular store, information about that store's prices will be added to the consumer's previous knowledge regarding the store's price level. The revising scheme is of a Bayesian type.

On the side of the sellers, it is assumed that they are aware of the fact that consumers are attracted to the stores by the lower prices of some items, that consumers may purchase many more items than those which originally attract them to the store, and that customers learn to form a general perception about their "average" price level. (See, e. g., Simon [1989]).

In this framework, one could construct a model from which market equilibria can be derived. An equilibrium of particular interest for the present purpose is the one in which for any given product, its unit prices vary from store to store and yet equilibrium is attained since to the customers, all stores are equally (in)expensive. For the sellers, there exists an optimal level of price variance as compared to the general market prices. If price variance is too small, products with prices not sufficiently low would not attract enough customers to the store; and if price variance is too large, customers would eventually learn about the too expensive items to avoid purchasing them. Thus, in this equilibrium, price dispersion for any particular item may arise; the model could thus be used to explain this phenomenon.

In order to formulate the consumer's learning behavior, Bayes' formula in revising expectations about product prices is used. Basically, we view a typical consumer's purchase as an experiment based on which he or she can learn more about certain stores' price levels. Every time the consumer shops at a particular store, new information about that store's prices will add to the consumer's knowledge and would thus help revising his or her expectation about the store's general price level. The learning is more complicated when one notes that stores induce consumer's visits by offering special sales in which many products are offered at a substantially lower price.

For simplicity, we assume two distinct states regarding the average price level for each store: high-price state and low-price state. The information issue confronting the potential customer is that he or she is not certain about which state (high or low average price) a particular store is in. One should carefully note that the kind of information about product prices which are subjects of study in literature is simply the distribution of product prices among various stores. We had earlier argued that if the only piece of information the consumer does not have is that on price, the learning process would, in equilibrium, drive out any dispersion in prices. In the present framework, any store can either be in a state of higher or lower price and since the consumer is not certain about a particular state for a particular store at a given time, the kind of information the consumer lacks is much more difficult to obtain. We can then identify conditions under which even learning will not be able to help the potential customer to find out a precise state before he or she makes a purchase decision. Thus, it can be shown that even in the presence of learning on the part of the consumers, price dispersion may still exist in equilibrium.

The preceding theoretical argument is originally motivated by observing the pricing behavior of many grocery supermarkets. Without any exceptions every supermarket claims that its prices are lowest in town. Some even go so far as to offer to triple or double the price differentials in cash if a buyer can demonstrate that he or she spends less money in other stores to buy the same *basket* of commodities. This is a very strong, challenging statement indeed and one would believe that the only way this particular store can make and keep that commitment is to price its products so that the total cost of each basket of goods for a potential customer would *not* consistently be higher than that offered at competing stores. On the other hand, one is led to believe that the only way for the competing stores to maintain their market shares in equilibrium is to design their pricing policy so that the total cost for each purchase of a basket of goods is at a comparable level with that of the challenging store.

An empirical implication of the theory is that while one may observe different prices in different stores for a particular product, the average price may be the same for all stores. One way to test this result is to calculate the weighted average price for each purchase of a basket of goods for a typical consumer. One would first need to empirically show that for each particular product, there exists a statistically significant degree of price dispersion. One would need then to empirically demonstrate that in spite of this, average prices for random bundles of goods do not statistically differ from one store to another.

The notion of loss-leader implied in the preceding analysis have been, in completely different contexts, formalized for an oligopolistic market structure. Lal and Matutes [1994] consider a special kind of promotional activity used by retailers called "loss-leader pricing". The practice has two major characteristics: first, the price charged may be at or even below the product's marginal cost and second, the items' prices are heavily advertised. Several authors, exemplified by Nagle and Holden [1995], assert that due to economies of scale in shopping, customers tend to buy other items in a store once the loss leaders attract them to the store; typically requiring a pricing strategy on other items so that they compensate for the loss leading pricing. Lal and Matutes then argue that why does not competition lead to lower prices for all goods carried by a given store. We have argued against this particular reasoning in the conceptual model above involving price differences even when consumers learn. Lal and Matutes seek to explore the loss-leader pricing in a context of a duopolistic model for a multi-product environment with an additional assumption that consumers are not generally informed about a store's prices unless advertised. They show an interesting result that loss leaders do attract consumers into the store even though they expect to pay higher prices for unadvertised goods.

We should mention a number of other papers on this literature on loss-leader pricing. Bliss [1988] develops a theory of retail pricing in which buyers have perfect information on prices but in equilibrium, due to asymmetries in cross-price elasticities among goods, some goods may be priced below cost. Feichtinger et al [1988] show that if both price and advertising create a store image which in turn affects sales, certain allocative scheme may be designed to allocate the firm's marketing budget to pricing and advertising. Hess and Gerstner [1987] classify goods into two groups, "impulsive" to be bought on sight and "shopping" to induce informed consumers to visit a particular store. They show that equilibrium may yield the scenario that shopping goods are priced below marginal cost to attract consumers who in turn buy impulsive goods based on which firms make profits. The Lal and Matutes analysis, on the other hand, assumes that customers are uninformed unless advertised so the role of expectations and advertising are spelled out. The interaction between uninformed rational customers and multi-product competition can lead to an equilibrium in which firms use advertising to inform consumers of its low prices of loss-leader items to increase the store traffic. We will touch upon this topic again in Chapter 8 within the context of the competitive framework.

7 CONCLUSIONS

In this chapter, we have explored a number of models which have an economic flavor of the marketing phenomenon of price discount. As we mentioned in the introductory remark to this chapter, there exist excellent surveys on different economic and marketing models which provide rationale for the firm's price discount behavior. These surveys, even though they are more general, contain also work done under the assumption of imperfect information and thus contains elements of uncertainty. Since they are readily available, it is not our purpose to report them here. Instead, we have analyzed a number of models which reflect very strongly our own approach to this important phenomenon of marketing. Further, it has been our effort to provide to the largest extent possible available empirical efforts along this line. The section on price differences even when consumers learn remains informal and yet the empirical implications can clearly be seen; as these implications can be readily tested with reasonable resources for market surveys, etc.

We began the chapter with a particular model to explain a basic mechanism for a monopolistic firm to practice price discrimination. The sorting device is based on the firm's knowledge that consumers differ in their taste or wealth which we assume to be represented by a single-valued parameter. The way the firm is actually implementing this mechanism is to offer the product at a sales price which is lower than the regular price at certain time intervals. The consumers will self-select in the sense that they have certain knowledge on the frequency of sales, thus on expected amount of monetary savings from waiting for the sale. Against this benefit is the cost of waiting which involves the desire to purchase the product immediately when the need arises or to reflect the opportunity cost which is assumed to be higher, the wealthier the consumer. We then consider a stochastic model of cyclic behavior where the arrival time is itself a random variable, following a Poisson process to be more specific. We show that by offering a discount price at certain intervals allows the firm to earn higher profits. The notion of a two-price scheme is used again in our effort to analyze a policy-oriented issue of resale price maintenance on the basis of the difference in the firm's investment in the provision of information. We indicate why the equilibrium two-price configuration offers important insights into the determination of the average price facing a representative consumer. Finally, we explore a potential issue of equilibrium price differences even when the consumers learn. This is analyzed within a context quite similar to the frequently observed phenomena of loss leader. While the model is only a sketch of the basic argument, we believe that it is rich enough to actually test the idea against collected data in actual market settings.

REFERENCES

BLATTBERG, Robert C., T. BUESING, P. PEACOCK and S. K. SEN, 1978, "Identifying the Deal Prone Segment," *Journal of Marketing Research*, Vol. 15, pp. 369-77.

BLATTBERG, Robert C., and Scott A. NESLIN, 1990, *Sales Promotion: Concepts, Methods, and Strategies*, Prentice Hall, Englewood Cliffs, NJ.

BLATTBERG, Robert C., Richard BRIESCH, and Edward J. Fox, 1995, "How Promotions Work," *Marketing Science*, Vol. 14, pp. G122-G132.

BLISS, Christopher, 1988, "A Theory of Retail Pricing," *Journal of Industrial Economics*, Vol. 37 , pp. 375-391.

CONLISK, John, Eitan GERSTNER, and Joel SOBEL, 1984, "Cyclic Pricing by a Durable Goods Monopolist," *The Quarterly Journal of Economics*, pp. 489-505.

FEICHTINGER, Gustav, Afred LUHMER, and Gerhard SORGER, 1988, "Optimal Price and Advertising Policy for A Convenience Good Retailer," *Marketing Science*, Vol. 5, pp. 187-201.

FELLER, William, 1971, *An Introduction to Probability Theory and Its Applications, Volume II*, Second Edition, John Wiley & Sons, Inc., NY.

FRANK, R. E,. and W. F. MASSY, 1965, *Market Segmentation and the Effectiveness of a Brand's Price and Dealing Policies*, Vol. 38, pp. 186-200.

FRANKEL, M., "The Effects of Fair Trade: Fact and Fiction in the Statistical Findings," *Journal of Business*, Vol. 28, 1955, pp. 182-194.

HESS, J., and F. GERSTNER, 1987, "Loss Leader Pricing and Rain Check Policy," *Marketing Science*, Vol. 6, pp. 358-374.

JEULAND, A. P. and C. NARASIMHAN, 1985, "Dealing — Temporary Price Cuts — by Seller as a Buyer Discrimination Mechanism, *Journal of Business*, Vol. 58, pp. 295-308.

KALWANI, M. U., and C. K. YIM, 1992, "Consumer Price and Expectations: An Empirical Study," *Journal of Marketing Research*, Vol. 29, pp. 90-100.

LAL, Rajiv, and Carmen MATUTES, 1994, "Retail Pricing and Advertising Strategies," *Journal of Business*, Vol. 67, No. 3, pp. 345-370.

LILIEN, Gary L., Philip KOTLER, and K. Sridhar MOORTHY, 1992, *Marketing Models,* Prentice-Hall, Englewood Cliffs, NJ.

MATHEWSON, G. F., and R. A. WINTER, 1983, "The Incentives For Resale Price Maintenance under Imperfect Information," *Economic Inquiry,* Vol. 21, No. 3, pp. 337-348.

MIRRLEES, J., 1971, "An Exploration In the Theory of Optimum Income Taxation," *Review of Economic Studies,* Vol. 38, pp. 175-208.

MONROE, K. B., A. BITTA, and J. DELLA, 1978, "Models for Pricing Decisions," *Journal of Marketing Research,* Vol. 15, pp. 413-28.

NAGLE, Thomas T., and Reed K. HOLDEN, 1995, *The Strategy and Tactics of Pricing,* 2nd edition, Prentice-Hall, Englewood Cliffs, NJ.

NATIONAL RETAIL MERCHANTS ASSOCIATION, 1969, 1970, *Merchandising and Operating Results for 1968 and 1969.*

OSTLUND, H. J., and C. R. VICKLAND, 1940, *Fair Trade and The Retail Drug Store,* Druggists' Research Bureau.

PRATT, J. W., David A. WISE, and Richard ZECKHAUSER, 1979, "Price Differences in Almost Competitive Markets," *Quarterly Journal of Economics,* pp. 189-211.

RAO, Vithala R., 1993, "Pricing Models in Marketing," in Jehoshua ELIASHBERG, and Gary L. LILIEN (eds.), *Marketing,* Handbooks in Operations Research and Management Science, Vol. 5, pp. 517-552, Elsevier Science Publishers, Amsterdam, The Netherlands.

SALOP, Steven, 1977, "The Noisy Monopolist: Imperfect Information, Price Dispersion and Price Discrimination," *Review of Economic Studies,* Vol. 44, pp. 393-406.

SALOP, Steven, and Joseph STIGLITZ, 1977, "Bargains and Ripoffs: A Model of Monopolistically Competitive Price Dispersion," *Review of Economic Studies,* pp. 493-510.

SCHERER, F. M., and D. ROSS, 1990, *Industrial Market Structure and Economic Performance,* 3rd edition, Houghton Mifflin Co., Boston, MA.

SIMON, Herman, 1989, *Price Management,* Elsevier, North Holland.

SOBEL, Joel, 1984, "The Timing of Sales," *Review of Economic Studies,* pp. 353-368.

STIGLITZ, Joseph, 1977, "Monopoly, Non-Linear Pricing and Imperfect Information: The Insurance Market," *Review of Economic Studies,* Vol. 44, pp. 407-430.

STOKEY, Nancy, 1979, "Intertemporal Price Discrimination," *Quarterly Journal of Economics,* pp. 355-371.

VARIAN, Hal, 1980, "A Model of Sales," *American Economic Review,* Vol. 70, pp. 651-659.

5

SALESFORCE SIZE, COMPENSATION AND LABOR HETEROGENEITY

1 OVERVIEW

The subject of interest in this chapter falls under the general heading of salesforce management. It has been estimated that in aggregate, expenditures related to the operations of a company's salesforce exceed those for advertising and other marketing activities. In general, salesforce management involves not only administrative aspects such as recruiting, training, assigning, compensating, motivating and controlling the firm's salesforce, but also decisions within the context of its marketing strategy such as the size of the salesforce and sales territory designs. We will in particular be interested in exploring the managerial implications for compensation schemes for the firm's salesforce as well as the firm's decisions regarding the optimal employment of its workers. The large and growing literature on employment contracts and incentive-related pay schemes has been explored in several management fields, marketing included. For our present purposes, we have to be very selective in addressing issues which are most directly relevant to the present work. As such, there is a clear personal bias in the sense that the materials reported below do not simply represent a review of existing literature on the subject. Rather, we will begin with a summary of a number of current results; then quickly address certain issues which, in the author's opinion, are important and yet remain largely unexplored in the current literature. For the purpose of literature review, we are fortunate to have at least two major surveys published within the last couple of years: one is done by Coughlan [1993] in the Eliashberg and Lilien [1993] volume and the other in Chapter

129

8 of the Lilien, Kotler and Moorthy [1992] text; the former being an extensive and more technical-oriented revision of the Coughlan-Sen [1989] review.

We will devote more space to the issue of salesforce size within the context of the firm's maximization problem. Even though it is well known that the rate of salesman turnover is exceedingly high in marketing, it is equally true that certain firm-specific human capital in marketing is normally necessary; hence we can not simply treat salesforce as a pure temporary employment decision. Thus we shall assume that salesforce size should also be determined prior to the realizations of the random demand. This allows us to explore the possibility of the divergence of the firm's labor decisions under uncertainty in comparison to those which are made when the firm's demand is known with certainty.

We shall first concentrate on the size of the salesforce, starting with standard and simple analysis under conditions of certainty in demand. The extensions to the stochastic demand will then be made. We will note there the effort to incorporate all the effects of pricing as well as advertising and selling effort within a unified framework. To facilitate the analysis, we will typically model the problem using the simplest possible formulation. In particular, we shall by and large assume additive random term and we will report on an analysis using the valuation approach popular in finance literature. This has the added advantage that an empirical implementation can actually be carried out. We will then shift our focus to the issue of compensation to the salesforce. Once again, we shall first discuss the case when the sales response function is known to the firm, then analyze the case where the sales response function is not completely known to the firm. We then look at the scenario with heterogeneous salesforce and address certain issues of information asymmetry in the labor market. As mentioned earlier, we are fortunate to have had two recent comprehensive surveys within the marketing literature on this subject. We will therefore be very brief on this topic and instead refer the readers to those surveys. In its place, we will devote some space to develop a simple model involving the potential mobility of salespersons among different industries and then discuss the implications of potential wage differentials. This analysis captures certain aspects of information asymmetry as well as the internal labor market. Decisions on aspects of salesforce are by nature dynamic, subject to both internal and external conditions. This has the implications for the nature of promotion/demotion framework which we will explore in a section in this chapter. Decisions regarding the firm's salesforce tend to involve significant lead time in recruiting and training; thus they represent a gradual process reinforced by the difficulties with which employees can be terminated during short-term economic downturns.

2 STATIC SALESFORCE SIZE

Typically, the decision on size of the salesforce is related to other elements of the marketing mix such as pricing, advertising and sales promotional efforts. In this section, we start out with an extremely simple problem facing the firm in determining its optimal salesforce size, first under conditions of known sales response functions and then under conditions of demand uncertainty. Of particular emphasis here is our presentation and analysis of problems involving a decision-making process in which the salesforce size, product price and advertising spending are jointly determined. In addition, we will address a specific scenario where the salesforce size is chosen under the assumption that important investment in advertising capital, or goodwill, has to be made by the firm in order to assist the salesforce in its selling efforts.

2.1 Salesforce Size Under Certainty

For purpose of comparison, let us formulate the firm's salesforce size under deterministic conditions as follows

$$\text{Max.} \quad \Pi = pq - C(q) - wL \tag{5.1}$$

where we denote salesforce size as L (to reflect Labor) with unit cost w (that is Wage); the production and/or acquisition costs are summarized in the cost function $C(q)$, and the firm's total sales is a function only of the size of its salesforce:

$$q = f(L) \tag{5.2}$$

which we assume to have the usual property of positive but diminishing returns in relation to the marginal productivity conditions.

The preceding model is quite similar to a version of the model considered by Montgomery and Urban [1969]. Clearly, under this simple formulation, and in particular, if we assume that the production cost is $C = cq$ with a known and constant marginal cost of c, the optimal solution to the preceding problem can be shown simply to be that the size is at the point where the marginal salesperson brings to the firm's a monetary value equal to his or her selling cost, from the firm's point of view.

Certainly, actual implementations of the above economic principles are more challenging; depending on the nature of the specification in (5.2). Similar to the ways in which sales responses to advertising, pricing and promotional efforts we analyzed in earlier chapters, sales response to selling efforts captured by the variable L can be very complex. A rather very large literature, theoretical and empirical, have been developed to address this issue. Such attempts have included field experimentation and subjectively calibrated modelling. For our present purposes, let us consider a scenario where the firm also wishes to make a simultaneous decision on its product's price. The sales response function will now become:

$$q = f(p, L). \tag{5.3}$$

Again, the conditions for optimality are now a little more complicated but the economics remains to be the same regarding the salesforce size with the additional condition that the firm's should set its price so that at the optimal price, marginal revenue equals marginal cost. That is, assuming constant marginal cost c, we need:

$$\frac{\partial \Pi}{\partial p} = (p-c)\frac{\partial q}{\partial p} + q = 0 \qquad (5.4)$$

$$\text{and} \quad \frac{\partial \Pi}{\partial L} = (p-c)\frac{\partial q}{\partial L} - w = 0. \qquad (5.5)$$

It is straight-forward to show in the manner similar to the basic Dorfman-Steiner [1954] result that the joint optimal decisions of salesforce and pricing yield:

$$\varepsilon = \frac{pq}{wL}\varepsilon_L \qquad (5.6)$$

where ε and ε_L denote respectively the (absolute values of) demand price elasticity and the sales elasticity of the salesforce.

While the economic interpretation of the preceding relation is well-known and interesting, we would like to note here that since the total bill for the salesforce is represented by wL and the total revenue received by the firm is pq, the condition implies that the sales elasticity of salesforce is necessarily less than the price elasticity in absolute terms. Further, note that except for the case where both sales elasticity of the salesforce and the demand price elasticity are constant, solving for optimal price and salesforce involves solving a simultaneous equations system which may be non-linear. We shall demonstrate the nature of the solution and the economic meaning and managerial/marketing implications in a simplified numerical example below. Finally, we also note that the joint conditions can be expressed in the following sensible way:

$$\frac{p \cdot \dfrac{\partial q}{\partial L}}{w} = \varepsilon \qquad (5.7)$$

which simply implies that the monetary value of the marginal productivity of the salesforce per dollar spent on its compensation should be equal to the price elasticity of demand.

We think that this expression reveals an interesting implication in the context of the marketing salesforce. Typically, one would consider optimal employment in the framework of a firm's least cost combination problem in which the firm would want to employ its workforce until such point where the wage rate is equal to the marginal value product, the latter measures the monetary contributions of the marginal worker to the firm's revenue. On the basis of this expression, we note the explicit consideration of the price elasticity of demand in such a decision.

In order to see clearly the nature of the solution, we provide here a very simple example. Assume that the demand function is:

$$q=10-p+L^{1/2} \qquad (5.3a)$$

and the firm's profit function is:

$$\Pi=(p-c)q-wL \qquad (5.1a)$$

where we assume $c=4$ and $w=1$.

Maximizing profit would yield the following solution:

$$p=8; \quad L=4; \quad q=4; \quad \text{and } \Pi=12. \qquad (5.8)$$

One useful way to see the marketing implication of this salesforce decision is to think of the preceding example in the context of the firm's effort to enhance sales by home visits. Consider L in the example as the in-home visit salesforce. Without this salesforce, the firm can still make sales through regular channels and the demand function would be

$$q=10-p \qquad (5.3b)$$

with the profit function

$$\Pi=(p-c)q \qquad (5.1b)$$

where $c=4$ as before.

The optimal solution is of course:

$$p=7; \quad q=3; \quad \text{and } \Pi=9. \qquad (5.8a)$$

Thus we note that the use of in-home visit marketing force is profit-enhancing, resulting in the process a larger quantity sold and a higher price for the product. We should also note the following interesting economic implication. It is well-known that for a linear demand schedule, as the product's price increases, the price elasticity of demand increases. Here, however, due to the sales-enhancing effect of the in-home marketing efforts, the quantity demanded also increases, resulting in a *decline* in the price elasticity. The demand schedule in fact shifts to the right. An immediate managerial implication of this example is the consistency with the empirical notion that personal marketing efforts tend to reduce the price sensitivity of the product. Now noting the implication expressed in equation (5.7) above that $p(\partial q/\partial L)/w=\varepsilon$ we see that in order to have an interior solution to the optimal salesforce problem, it is necessary that the marginal productivity of the marketing salesforce be decreasing sufficiently.

2.2 Salesforce Size: Random Demand

Consider now a simple stochastic extension of the previous deterministic results. Let us assume the following demand function:

$$q = 10 - p + L^{1/2} + \xi \qquad (5.9)$$

where we assume that ξ takes on two values $+2$ and -2 each with a probability of .50.
    More generally, let us specify:

$$q = f(p,L) + \xi \qquad (5.10)$$

and as before the profit function is

$$\Pi = (p-c)q - wL. \qquad (5.1a)$$

    Upon assuming a quadratic utility function, the first-order condition to maximize the firm's expected utility of profit can be written as:

$$\frac{\partial E(\Pi)}{\partial p} = (1/2)r[\frac{dE(\Pi - E\Pi)^2}{dp}] \qquad (5.4a)$$

$$\text{and} \quad \frac{\partial E(\Pi)}{\partial L} = (1/2)r[\frac{dE(\Pi - E\Pi)^2}{dL}] \qquad (5.5a)$$

where $dE(\Pi - E\Pi)^2/dp = 2(p-c)\sigma_\xi^2$.
    It then follows that the first-order condition with respect to the price variable can be written as:

$$\frac{\partial E(\Pi)}{\partial p} - r(p-c)\sigma_\xi^2 = 0 \qquad (5.11)$$

and the second-order condition is:

$$\frac{\partial^2 E(\Pi)}{\partial p^2} - r\sigma_\xi^2 < 0. \qquad (5.12)$$

    Now one can determine the effect of risk aversion on the firm's optimal price by totally differentiating the equation expressing the first-order condition in (5.11). Assuming that the second-order condition is satisfied, it follows that $\partial p/\partial r < 0$.
    Similarly, one can establish a similar result regarding the effect of risk aversion on the employment level of the in-home salesforce. Further, one can examine the impact of increasing sales uncertainty reflected through the variance of the error terms, on the price level and the salesforce level as well.
    Again, by way of the simple example we have given above with the logarithmic utility function, it can be verified that the optimal solutions are $p = 7.25$ and $L = 2.64$

which are clearly smaller than the optimal levels under deterministic conditions as we summarize in (5.8).

We chose to use an illustrative example to make the point since its more formal development can easily be done, using the same method we have used in the previous chapter. Further, we will analyze immediately below another approach to study similar marketing decisions under random demand.

Theoretical analyses of the impact of uncertainty have been successfully carried out in finance literature using what has been known as the Capital Asset Pricing Model (*CAPM*). Interestingly, one of the earlier studies in marketing literature dealing with the issue of uncertainty has been motivated by this approach (Jagpal and Brick [1982]). Our presentation here follows the Jagpal-Brick analysis. In this framework, the value of the *i*-th firm is defined to be:

$$V_i = \frac{E(\Pi_i) - \lambda cov(\Pi_i, M)}{(1 + r_F)} \tag{5.13}$$

where Π_i represents the cash profits, M the market portfolio's wealth, r_F the risk-free interest rate, $cov(.,.)$ denotes the covariance operator, and λ denotes the market price of risk, defined to be

$$\lambda = \frac{E(r_M) - r_F}{var(r_M)M}$$

where r_M is the random rate of return of the market portfolio, and $var(.)$ denotes the variance operator.

Let us assume here that the random demand function can be specified as:

$$q = f(p, m, L) + \xi \tag{5.14}$$

where m is the marketing expenditure and L represents the number of salespersons employed.

The random profit of the firm is

$$\Pi = (p - c)q - m - wL - FC = (p - c)[f(p, m, L) + \xi] - m - wL - FC \tag{5.15}$$

where again w is the wage rate and FC stands for the firm's fixed cost.

The value of the firm can thus be expressed as:

$$V = \frac{(p - c)[f(p, m, L) + \{E(\xi) - \lambda cov(\xi, r_M)\}] - m - wL - FC}{(1 + r_F)}$$

from which the first-order conditions are:

$$\frac{\partial V}{\partial p}=0 \Rightarrow \overline{q}+(p-c)\frac{\partial \overline{q}}{\partial p}=0 \qquad\qquad (5.16)$$

$$\frac{\partial V}{\partial m}=0 \Rightarrow (p-c)\frac{\partial \overline{q}}{\partial m}=1 \qquad\qquad (5.17)$$

$$\text{and } \quad \frac{\partial V}{\partial L}=0 \Rightarrow (p-c)\frac{\partial \overline{q}}{\partial L}=w \qquad\qquad (5.18)$$

where $\overline{q}=f(p,m,L)+E(\xi)-\lambda cov(\xi,r_M)$, which is defined to be the risk-adjusted demand.

Now if quantity demanded can be expressed in terms of the risk-adjusted sales $\overline{q}$, then the preceding optimal conditions can be analyzed in the same fashion as in the deterministic model of marketing mix (see eq. (1.2) and the ensuing discussion in Chapter 1). Except for the replacement of the $\overline{q}$ in place of q, these conditions can be expressed in terms of various elasticities as in the Dorfman Steiner well-known results. In particular, we note here the results written in terms of elasticities:

$$\varepsilon=\frac{p\overline{q}}{wL}\varepsilon_L=\frac{p\overline{q}}{m}\varepsilon_m \qquad\qquad (5.19)$$

with standard economic interpretations in which the notion of risk-adjusted quantity demanded is used instead of the certain, known quantity demanded q.

We summarize below some comparative-static results of interest:

***Demand shifts*:**   While the impact of a shift in demand on the firm's price is unambiguously positive, its effects on advertising level and personal selling are less clear cut. For the latter, determinate signs can be obtained, for example, if together or independently, both advertising and selling efforts tend to reduce demand's price sensitivity (a reasonable assumption), and in addition, advertising and personal selling are either complementary in the sense that each activity enhances the marginal "productivity" of the other or they are independent; in this case both advertising and salesforce increase as the demand shifts upward.

We have shown in our earlier example of how an increase in personal selling effort can lead to a decline in price sensitivity. While the empirical results remain weak on this account, it is reasonable to speculate that personal selling to some extent help reduce sales loss in an event of a price hike, hence reducing the price elasticity. Similarly, casual observations seem to indicate that advertising campaigns are some-times designed to lessen the negative impact of an imminent price increase. Thus we consider the case of declining price sensitivity in view of both increase in personal selling efforts and advertising a reasonable working scenario for the analysis. In our example above, note that the way the personal selling efforts enter the demand equation dictates that their effects are independent from the price effect on sales. In spite of this fact, it is still the case that an increase in personal selling effort leads to a decline in the price elasticity.

Change in Risk: An increase in additive risk, given that $cov(\xi,R_M)>0$, has an identical effect as a decrease in the demand in terms of a negative shift. For the multiplicative specification, the results are less clear-cut.

Again, using the same scenario described in the previous paragraph, one particular result which is of interest for us here is that related to the effect of increasing risk. It has been established that the impact of an increase in risk in the sense just defined will be identical to the effect of a decline in demand. Thus an increase in risk, which is, in this context, similar to an increase in uncertainty, would lead to a reduction in advertising, in price as well as in personal selling efforts. In essence, this is the main result which we have actually captured in the simple example above.

2.3 Salesforce Size: Random Demand and Supporting Advertising

In this sub-section, we are motivated partly by the current development of the joint decision involving the firm's different marketing activities as well as the potential interactions among the firm's different departmental activities. An example of the latter involves production and marketing decisions the managerial implications of which we will explore in greater details in Chapter 7. Also, the implications for departmental wage differentials will be analyzed in a section below in this chapter. Here, we wish to explore the potential interaction between advertising and personal selling within the context of random demand. We should note too our presentation of the Jagpal-Brick paper involves the joint decision in the Dorfman-Steiner sense the personal selling and advertising activities. For our present purposes, we shall assume that the firm's total sales is characterized by the following implicit random demand function:

$$h(q,p,\xi)=0 \qquad\qquad (5.10a)$$

where ξ represents the random term.

In addition, in order to sell a certain quantity, it is assumed that in addition to the salesforce we also assume a supporting advertising campaign. Let us specify such a relation as:

$$q=Q(G,L) \qquad\qquad (5.20)$$

where G represents the goodwill in the Nerlove-Arrow tradition as a form of capital invested by the firm in support for the salesforce's selling efforts.

It should be immediate that the preceding specification reminds us of the production function in economics. As a matter of fact, it is motivated by such theory. More specifically, we reinterpret a paper by Holthausen [1976] who examine the input choice under uncertainty in his effort to extend the Leland-Baron framework of the firm's decisions under uncertainty which we discussed in earlier chapters. It is also reasonable to follow the neo-classical theory of production in assuming positive but diminishing marginal contribution by both G and salesforce L to sales.

Thus, unlike the discussion we did earlier where the salesforce is decided jointly with a pricing policy, the specification we use here is designed to capture the potential supporting role of an advertising campaign for the selling efforts. We should also note that the notion of advertising as a form of investment has been well accepted in the literature since the publication of the Nerlove-Arrow paper [1962]. We also discussed this particular interaction in the Dehez-Jacquemin paper presented in Chapter 3 in which advertising plays the dynamic role over time. We will simplify the discussion by focusing only on the static aspect of the problem even though, on the basis of our discussion in dynamic advertising in the previous chapter, such an analysis seems readily available.

It turns out that the firm's appropriate mode of decision in terms of pricing vs. producing has important bearing on the optimal decision problem here in a fashion parallel to the different implications of the pricing vs. producing decisions under uncertainty we analyzed in Chapter 2. We will thus discuss both processes. Viewed under this light, the firm's decision on its optimal salesforce is a two-stage process. When production represents the dominant decision variable and if the goods under consideration are perishable, then the firm would need to make decisions on the quantity to produce as well as its advertising budget in order to sell all the goods produced; the price will have to be adjusted as the random term is being realized. If the goods are storable, then the role of inventory would become essential in the firm's decision process. On the other hand, when pricing is a major marketing variable which, together with the firm's advertising effort, affects the firm's total sales, then the salesforce size can be determined once the random sales level is realized in the market. In either case, we shall assume that salesforce size is an *ex post* choice variable in the sense that it is sufficiently flexible to accommodate whatever the quantity of demand realized whereas advertising represents prior capital commitments, thus an *ex ante* decision variable. To capture the notion that the size of the salesforce can be chosen after the realization of the random disturbance ξ in the demand facing the firm has been observed, we shall follow Holthausen to define the following relation:

$$L = \ell(q, G). \tag{5.21}$$

We will first consider the problem for a firm which chooses an optimal output level to produce. As argued earlier, while this type of quantity-setting procedure is not commonly viewed as a traditional marketing activity, it is essential within the framework of the joint marketing-production problem; thus its introduction here may be helpful. Also, our discussion in the competitive chapter will indicate that it may be more commonly used than previously thought. We will then consider the salesforce size issue within the more familiar context of the firm's price-setting decision process.

The maximization problem for the quantity-setting firm is greatly simplified when (5.21) is taken into account. The objective function is:

$$\text{Max.} \quad E[U(\Pi)] \qquad (5.15a)$$
$$\{q,G\}$$

$$\text{subject to} \quad \Pi = (p-c)q - wL - m \qquad (5.22)$$

$$(5.21), \text{ and } \quad p = g(q,\xi) \qquad (5.10b)$$

where c again denotes the constant marginal production or acquisition cost, m the advertising cost, and an explicit random demand function on the basis of (5.10a) is represented as $p = g(q,\xi)$ in eq. (5.10b).

Clearly, in a dynamic framework, the accumulation of goodwill G represents a process of building with additional advertising m and forgetting at a "depreciation" rate δ as we discussed in Chapter 3 on dynamic advertising. For our present static formulation, we will operationalize this notion by defining a "shadow" cost λ so that in order to attain the goodwill level G, the firm has to incur the advertising budget $m = \lambda G$. As our discussion in the previous chapter indicates, such a shadow cost typically involves the firm's time discount rate and the rate of forgetting. Using this relation, let us note that there are only two decision variables in the above problem in (5.15a), namely, output q and capital stock G as the size of the salesforce required, L, can be calculated through (5.21) once q and G are determined. The first-order conditions can be readily derived to be:

$$E\{U'(\Pi)[\frac{\partial[(p-c)q]}{\partial q} - w.\frac{\partial \ell(q,G)}{\partial q}]\} = 0 \qquad (5.23)$$

$$\text{and} \quad E\{U'(\Pi)[-w.\frac{\partial \ell(q,G)}{\partial G} - \lambda]\} = 0. \qquad (5.24)$$

To give an economic interpretation to these conditions, we note that the expression $[\partial \ell(q,G)/\partial G]$ represents the marginal rate of substitution between goodwill and labor, invoking the same notion between capital and labor in production economics. Further, upon noting that the $\ell(q,G)$ function is deterministic, the condition in eq. (5.24) can be written as:

$$\frac{-\partial \ell(q,G)}{\partial G} = \frac{\lambda}{w}. \qquad (5.25)$$

The optimality condition can therefore be interpreted as the equality of the marginal rate of substitution between advertising and salesforce on the one hand and the ratio of their respective unit costs. This would be exactly the deterministic rule for cost minimization for a given sales level. So we note that the presence of a random demand instead of a deterministic one does not in any way affect the firm's optimal decision concerning the optimal choice for the size of the salesforce in conjunction with the supporting advertising campaign.

For the price-setting firm, the relevant choice variables are the goodwill variable G, and the price level p. The problem is:

$$\text{Max. } E[U(\Pi)] \qquad (5.15b)$$
$$\{p,G\}$$

Subject to conditions in (5.21), (5.22), and $q = f(p,\xi)$

where $f(p,\xi)$ is the familiar random sales response function.

One of the necessary conditions for optimality is:

$$E\left[U'(\Pi).\left\{-w\frac{\partial\ell[f(p,\xi),G]}{\partial G}-\lambda\right\}\right]=0. \qquad (5.24a)$$

Since p is an *ex ante* variable and q is a random variable, the $\ell(q,G)$ function is stochastic. The condition in (5.24a) can be expressed as:

$$E\left[\frac{-\partial\ell[f(p,\xi),G]}{\partial G}\right]=\frac{\lambda}{w}-\frac{cov[\frac{-\partial\ell}{\partial G},U'(\Pi)]}{E[U'(\Pi)]} \qquad (5.26)$$

where the term $cov(.,.)$ denotes the appropriate covariance of the two variables.

It is obvious that the deterministic rule for cost minimization which is found applicable for the quantity-setting firm will no longer be valid for the price-setting firm. A comparison between (5.25) and (5.26) reveals the fact that the covariance term on the right-hand side of (5.26) would affect the decision rule for an optimal solution. The preceding discussion once again confirms the asymmetry between the behavior of a price-setting and a quantity-setting firm under conditions of uncertainty as indicated in our discussion in Chapter 2 on pricing.

3 THE SALESFORCE COMPENSATION

The previous sections address the salesforce size problem in a simplest possible fashion in that labor plays a very passive role in the firm's overall profit-maximizing decision process. Thus the issue of a particular salesperson's choice to offer his service, given his opportunity cost, is largely assumed away. Instead, the salesforce supply is summarized by an exogenously determined wage or salary level denoted as w. There are significant research efforts in the existing literature to endogenize this choice behavior regarding labor participation, but we will not develop this particular theoretical development here except for one specific context of inter-departmental wage differentials in Section 4 below. We briefly report in this section some basic structure of the salesforce compensation formulation in which the salesperson's objective function is explicitly expressed and optimized in conjunction with the firm's profit maximization motive. The analysis in the next sub-section on known sales response follows the pioneering work of Farley [1964] and the subsequent sub-section's focus on unknown sales response is based on the work by Basu, Lal, Srinivasan, and Staelin [1985] which was in turn inspired by Holmstrom's [1979] paper. The final sub-section addresses the compensation issue within the context of salesforce heterogeneity and information asymmetry.

3.1 Known Sales Response

The first published work in this area dealing with issues relevant to marketing appears to be that of Farley [1964] who formulates the salesforce compensation problem in terms of the interactions between the firm's objectives of profit maximization and those of the salespersons. One particular notion worth emphasizing here is that the firm is assumed to have multiple products, which we will designate as $1,2,...N$. The salesperson's objective function can be written as:

$$\text{Max. } w_{\{h_i\}} = \sum \beta_i p_i q_i = \sum \beta_i p_i f(h_i) \qquad (5.27)$$

$$\text{subject to } \sum h_i \leq H; \ i=1,2,...N \qquad (5.28)$$

where we denote the salesperson's earnings as w (as in **W**age), the total available time as H (as in **H**our), the total time devoted to selling the i-th product as h_i, and the percentage commission rate as β_i.

Note that we have specified the i-th product's sales as $q_i = f(h_i)$ in (5.27). For our present purposes, the total available hour H is assumed fixed and exogenously given, even though one can actually model this to be part of the salesperson's maximizing behavior (Srinivasan [1981]). On the other hand, the firm's decision problem can be stated as follows:

$$\text{Max. } \Pi_{\{\beta_i\}} = \sum [(1-\beta_i)p_i q_i - C_i(q_i)]$$

$$= \sum [(1-\beta_i)p_i f(h_i) - C_i\{f(h_i)\}]. \qquad (5.29)$$

One interesting variant of the preceding model which has important implications is that the commission is based *not* on gross sales but rather on gross margin, namely, the firm's gross profits before payment to the salesforce. Thus, we write the salesperson's objective function and the firm's objective function, respectively, as:

$$\text{Max. } w_{\{h_i\}} = \sum \beta_i [p_i q_i - C_i(q_i)] = \sum \beta_i \{p_i f(h_i) - C_i[f(h_i)]\} \qquad (5.30)$$

and Max. $\Pi_{\{\beta_i\}} = \sum (1-\beta_i)[p_iq_i - C_i(q_i)]$

$$= \sum (1-\beta_i)\{p_if(h_i) - C_i[f(h_i)]\}.$$

(5.31)

Under the assumption of constant marginal production cost c_i, maximizing (5.30) subject to the time constraint in (5.28) can be shown to yield the following conditions:

$$\frac{\partial f(h_i)/\partial h_i}{\partial f(h_j)/\partial h_j} = \frac{\beta_i(p_i - c_i)}{\beta_j(p_j - c_j)} \quad \text{for all } i,j.$$

On the other hand, Farley shows that maximizing (5.31) subject to the salesperson's time constraint in (5.28) results in the following conditions:

$$\frac{\partial f(h_i)/\partial h_i}{\partial f(h_j)/\partial h_j} = \frac{(1-\beta_i)(p_i - c_i)}{(1-\beta_j)(p_j - c_j)} \quad \text{for all } i,j.$$

From the preceding two sets of conditions, it then follows that in order to simultaneously maximize both the firm's objective and the salesperson's, the commission rates should be set so that:

$$\frac{\beta_i(p_i - c_i)}{\beta_j(p_j - c_j)} = \frac{(1-\beta_i)(p_i - c_i)}{(1-\beta_j)(p_j - c_j)}; \text{ or } \beta_i = \beta_j$$

which represents the central result in the original Farley paper that the commission rates set on gross margins of the firm's different products must be equal in order to obtain optimality for both the firm and the salesperson.

It has been remarked in the literature that if gross sales serve as a basis for setting the commission rates, the preceding procedure would not yield the optimal results except only in extremely special circumstances. In this situation, maximizing (5.27) and (5.29) subject to (5.28) would require:

$$\frac{\beta p_i}{\beta p_j} = \frac{(1-\beta_i)p_i - c_i}{(1-\beta_j)p_j - c_j}.$$

Another major extension, especially in view of our emphasis on interactive marketing decision-making, is the incorporation of pricing as a major and concurrent decision variable (Weinberg [1975]). In these instances, the sales response functions can be written in the following forms:

$$q_i = f_i(DIS_i, h_i)$$

where we once again note that $i = 1,2,...N$ and we have used DIS_i to denote the percentage of discount as we used in the previous chapter on price promotion.

Using the previous notation, $DIS_i=(p_i-s_i)/p_i$ where s_i denotes the i-th product's discount or Sales price, the objective for the firm can now be written as:

$$\text{Max. } \Pi_{\{\beta_i,s_i\}} = \sum (1-\beta_i)[s_i-c_i]q_i$$

$$= \sum (1-\beta_i)[s_i-c_i]f(h_i,s_i)$$

where note that we have explicitly assumed constant marginal costs for all products, and that Weinberg's sales response function can be effectively rewritten as $q_i=f(h_i,s_i)$.

Subject to the salesperson's time constraint, the necessary conditions for maximizing the preceding function can be shown to be:

$$\frac{\partial f(h_i,s_i)/\partial h_i}{\partial f(h_j,s_j)/\partial h_j} = \frac{(1-\beta_i)(s_i-c_i)}{(1-\beta_j)(s_j-c_j)} \quad \text{for all } i,j$$

$$\text{and } (s_i-c_i)\frac{\partial f(h_i,s_i)}{\partial s_i} + f(h_i,s_i)=0. \qquad (5.32)$$

On the other hand, the salesperson's objective in income maximization can be expressed as:

$$\text{Max. } w_{\{h_i,s_i\}} = \sum \beta_i[s_i-c_i]q_i = \sum \beta_i[s_i-c_i]f(h_i,s_i)$$

subject to the time constraint as before.

Again, the first-order conditions are given as:

$$\frac{\partial f(h_i,s_i)/\partial h_i}{\partial f(h_j,s_j)/\partial h_j} = \frac{\beta_i(s_i-c_i)}{\beta_j(s_j-c_j)} \quad \text{for all } i,j$$

$$\text{and } (s_i-c_i)\frac{\partial f(h_i,s_i)}{\partial s_i} + f(h_i,s_i)=0. \qquad (5.33)$$

Due to the fact that the conditions in (5.32) and (5.33) are identical, Weinberg [1975] obtains the result that the salesperson's pricing decision which is to optimize his own income would lead to the firm's optimal profit-maximization objective as well. We shall be able to analyze this particular issue of whether or not pricing decisions should be delegated to the salesforce within the context of information asymmetry below. In the meantime it should be noted once again that the number of hours the salesperson is willing to supply can be endogenized in the compensation framework presented in this section. This issue has been addressed by Srinivasan [1981]. Further, Tapiero and Farley [1975] consider dynamic aspects of the compensation issue using an optimal control approach.

3.2 Unknown Sales Response

The basic theoretical framework used here is the principal-agent problem. We report below a simple version in the context of the firm's salesforce compensation. Assuming that the agent, which in this case is represented by a salesperson, is risk-averse, his utility is well-behaved and separable in monetary income, and (disutility) in Hour of work. We thus write:

$$\text{Max. } V = u(w) - v(h)$$

where the hour of work, or generally the effort of the agent, is not observable to the firm, which is the principal.

The crux of the problem eventually is for the firm to design a compensation contract so that it will ultimately maximize its economic profits, given that the salesperson would choose the hour of work to maximize his own utility. Thus, in the preceding optimization facing the agent, the reward w should represent the firm's choice of the compensation package which is a function of the observable measure of output, i.e., the salesperson's total sales q. In order to construct a solvable problem, it is assumed that the conditional density of q given a certain number of hours of work is known to the firm, which we write as $\varphi(q|h)$. Hence the agent's problem can be written as:

$$\text{Max. } E(V) = \int u[w(q)]\varphi(q|h)dq - v(h) \tag{5.34}$$

which yields the following first-order condition:

$$\int u[w(q)]\frac{\partial\varphi(q|h)}{\partial h}dq - \frac{\partial v(h)}{\partial h} = 0. \tag{5.35}$$

Further, the salesperson is willing to work only if doing so yields net utility at least at certain positive utility level V_0. Thus we have:

$$\int u[w(q)]\varphi(q|h)dq - v(h) \geq V_0. \tag{5.36}$$

Given that the procedure for utility maximization by the agent is known to the firm, as well as the conditional density for observable output given the work hours, the firm's optimization involves searching for optimal solutions to the compensation scheme to offer and hence indirectly decides on the eventual hour of work decided by the agent. Let us therefore write the firm's problem as:

$$\text{Max. } \Pi = \int [(p-c)q - w(q)]\varphi(q|h)dq \tag{5.37}$$

Subject to (5.35) and (5.36).

The standard solution to the preceding constrained problem involves the Lagrangian method which necessitates the definition of the Lagrangian $\mathscr{L}$ as:

$$\mathscr{L} = \int [(p-c)q - w(q)]\varphi(q\,|\,h)dq$$

$$+\lambda\{\int u[w(q)]\varphi(q\,|\,h)dq - v(h) - V_0\} \qquad (5.38)$$

$$+\mu\{\int u[w(q)]\frac{\partial\varphi(q\,|\,h)}{\partial h}dq - \frac{\partial v(h)}{\partial h}\}.$$

The first-order condition of central interest for the present purpose can be expressed in the following form:

$$\frac{1}{u'[w(q)]} = \lambda + \mu\frac{\dfrac{\partial\varphi(q\,|\,h)}{\partial h}}{\varphi(q\,|\,h)}. \qquad (5.39)$$

The interpretation of the preceding condition can be given as follows. For constant and positive values of λ and μ, and noting that marginal utility of income $u'(w)$ is positive but decreasing in w, the expression on the left-hand side is increasing as wages increase, which should correspond to a scenario where the ratio $(\partial\varphi(q\,|\,h)/\partial h)$ to $\varphi(q\,|\,h)$ is increasing with respect to q. Consequently, the optimal compensation should be an increasing function with respect to observed total sales, provided that higher sales indicate that the agents are working longer hours, or putting in more effort.

It has been originally shown by Holmstrom that for all probability distributions which satisfy the condition that the ratio $(\partial\varphi(q\,|\,h)/\partial h)$ to $\varphi(q\,|\,h)$ is non-decreasing in q, the optimal compensation implied by (5.39) above, denoted as $w(q)$, is a non-decreasing function of q. In particular, Basu, Lal, Srinivasan and Staelin [1985] show that for a class of power utility functions of the form $w(q)^\delta/\delta$ where $\delta < 1$ and when $\varphi(q\,|\,h)$ is either gamma or binomial, the optimal compensation can be expressed in general as:

$$w(q) = (a + bq)^{1/(1-\delta)} \quad \text{where } a \geq 0 \text{ and } b \geq 0. \qquad (5.40)$$

Clearly, the positive parameter a reflects the *salary* component of the compensation scheme which is independent of the sales q; and b reflects the rate at which the *commissions* to the salesperson depend on the realized quantity sold.

Of particular interest for our present purposes are results concerning the impact of sales uncertainty on the salesforce's selling efforts and on the compensation plans. While the results we report below are obtained on the basis of additional assumptions which are required to facilitate the derivations of closed-form solutions, the implications seem to be consistent with some of the results we reported earlier in this chapter. Further, under the assumptions made in the model by Basu, Lal, Srinivasan and Staelin, sales uncertainty is characterized by certain parameters in the sales probability distributions (gamma or binomial). It is shown that an increase in sales uncertainty tends to reduce selling effort by the salesforce. This result is quite consistent with a result we reported previously that risk aversion leads to a reduction in quantity sold as uncertainty increases. However, in spite of the similarity in the ultimate implications regarding the salesforce's behavior, the motivating factors differ in a significant fashion. In the principal-agent framework, it can be interpreted that the salesperson's optimal portfolio selection choice dictates that in the face of increasing uncertainty, he tends to allocate less effort on the riskier activities which in this case are related to selling. A consequence of the analysis is that the firm will be prepared to obtain a smaller expected profit as well. Another interesting result we should report here concerns the effect of increased sales uncertainty on the relative proportion of salary vs. the commission. It was shown that the optimal compensation plan in a more uncertain environment tends to consist of a higher salary parameter a and a lower commission rate b. In view of an increase in sales uncertainty, the salesperson expects to have a declined total compensation in which the relative proportion of salary will be higher.

In addressing the interaction between compensation and pricing decisions in a manner similar to Weinberg's paper we cited earlier, Lal [1986] considers the following problem facing the firm:

$$\text{Max.} \int [(p-c)q - w(q)]\varphi(q|p,h)dq \tag{5.37a}$$

$$\text{Subject to:} \int u[w(q)]\varphi(q|p,h)dq - v(h) \geq V_0 \tag{5.36a}$$

$$h \in \text{argmax} \int u[w(q)]\varphi(q|p,h)dq - v(h) \tag{5.41}$$

where the expression "$h \in$ argmax" denotes the fact that h is the decision variable which maximizes the maximand to be followed.

Clearly, the major difference between this formulation and the immediately preceding formulation is the assumption that the firm's product price is not exogenously given; rather it constitutes an integral part of the firm's decision making process. Consequently, the sales response function is obtained conditional on, in addition to the salesperson's hours of work, the optimally chosen price. Note also the significance of the condition in (5.41) which indicates that it is the firm which makes the pricing decision, leaving hours of work to be the only choice variable for the salesperson. This is to be contrast with the following scenario where the agent is allowed to make pricing decisions. Formally, under this situation, the formulation in (5.37a), (5.36a) and (5.41) must be modified to read:

$$\text{Max.} \int [(p-c)q-w(q,p)]\varphi(q\,|p,h)dq \tag{5.37b}$$

$$\text{Subject to:} \int u[w(q,p)]\varphi(q\,|p,h)dq-v(h)\geq V_0 \tag{5.36b}$$

$$h,p \in \text{argmax} \int u[w(q,p)]\varphi(q\,|p,h)dq-v(h). \tag{5.41a}$$

A priori, the optimal decisions regarding the firm's output price, compensation scheme, and hours of work are presumed to be different; for present purposes, the compensation package $w(q)$ should be read to be different even though we still denote them by the same notation.

It can be argued as Lal did that the two problems yield the same solution; hence it does not matter whether the firm makes the pricing decision or delegates that responsibility to the salesperson. This particular result applies when one assumes information symmetry in the sense that the density function representing the sales response is known to both parties. Lal went on to demonstrate that when information regarding demand uncertainty is not symmetrical, in particular the salesforce is more aware of the selling environment and factors which affect sales, it is best to leave pricing decisions to the salespersons. Formally, the firm's optimization problem is:

$$\text{Max.} \sum \pi_i \int [(p_i-c)q-w(p_i,q)]\varphi_i(q\,|p_i,h)dq \tag{5.37c}$$

$$\text{Subject to:} \sum \pi_i \int u[w(q,p_i)]\varphi_i(q\,|p_i,h)dq-v(h)\geq V_0 \tag{5.36c}$$

$$h,p_i's \in \text{argmax} \int u[w(q,p_i)]\varphi_i(q\,|p_i,h)dq-v(h) \tag{5.41b}$$

where π_i represents the probability that the sales response function being $\varphi_i(q\,|p_i,q)$ and the subscript i denotes the i-market segment corresponding to locality, $i=1,2,...R$ (as in **Region**).

On the other hand, the counterpart optimization problem for the scenario where pricing is being made by the firm can be written as:

$$\text{Max.} \sum \pi_i \int [(p-c)q-w(q)]\varphi_i(q\,|p,h)dq \tag{5.37d}$$

$$\text{Subject to:} \sum \pi_i \int u[w(q)]\varphi_i(q\,|p,h)dq-v(h)\geq V_0 \tag{5.36d}$$

$$h \in \text{argmax}\sum \pi_i \int u[w(q)]\varphi_i(q\,|p,h)dq-v(h). \tag{5.41c}$$

The method of analysis involves comparing the resulting solutions to find out if a particular pricing scheme can prove to be superior.

3.3 Heterogeneous Salesforce and Information Asymmetry

In this sub-section, we follow closely the results obtained by Lal and Staelin [1986]. The formulation has both the feature of self-selection and moral hazard within a context of information asymmetry. It is assumed that while each salesperson has complete knowledge of his or her selling effort and the sales response to those efforts, the firm only has a prior over the range of sales response functions. Sales consist of a deterministic response function which is a function of the salesperson's effort and a stochastic error term. In general, the risk-neutral firm is assumed to offer a menu of compensation contracts for each of its risk-averse potential salespersons who in turn would choose a contract and an effort level devoting to selling activities. The firm will pay salespersons on the basis of the chosen contract which depends on realized sales.

Formally, let us rewrite the salesperson's objective function as

$$\text{Max. } V = u(w) - v(h)$$

which implies that the salesforce is homogeneous in terms of its utility function.

However, the salesforce is heterogeneous in its productivity. For simplicity, there exist two types of salespersons, one low performance (indexed b as in **B**ad) and the other high performance (indexed g). Thus, the effort level h by the i-th salesperson affects sales in the following fashion:

$$q_i = \bar{q}_i(h) + \xi_i \quad ; \quad i = b, g \tag{5.42}$$

where, upon denoting the distribution of sales conditional on a given effort level h as $\varphi_i(q_i | h)$; $i = b, g$, it is assumed that $\varphi_g(q | h)$ dominates $\varphi_b(q | h)$ in the sense of first order stochastic dominance.

Let us note that the sales response function consists of two parts, the deterministic function $\bar{q}$ and the random error term ξ. As a result of asymmetry of information, the firm is assumed to have a prior probability density function characterizing the distribution of high-performance salespersons, denoted by $h(G)$, where G represents the number of high-performance salespersons within the total pool of candidates L.

The strategies considered involve on the one hand, single contracts offered so that either low-performance salespersons or high-performance salespersons will choose to work and on the other hand, a set of two contracts so that the different types of salespersons will then self select.

The authors identify a number of strategies: the first involves a single contract designed to get only high-performance salespersons; the second designed to get only low-performance salespersons; and the third involves a set of two contracts which are truth-revealing in the sense that workers with different productivities self select the types of contract considered best by them. Due to the assumption that $\varphi_g(q|h)$ stochastically dominates $\varphi_b(q|h)$, it can be demonstrated that any single contracts offered to low-performance salespersons will also be acceptable to high-performance salespersons. Thus the remaining two feasible strategies are either single contracts to high-performance workers or the set of multiple contracts. The central result involves a comparison of these two strategies and one can summarize the major implications as follows. Out of the total number of candidates L, the expected number of high-performance salespersons, defined by $E(G)$, ranges from zero to L. Defining the (unique) cut off point of $E^*(G)$ at which the two feasible strategies yield identical expected payoffs. Its is then shown that if the firm's prior on the distribution of high-performance salesforce is such that the expected number $E(G)$ is larger than $E^*(G)$, then it is optimal for the firm to offer a single contract to induce only the high-performance salesforce to join the firm. Otherwise, it will be optimal for the firm to offer a multiple contract so that the salesforce will be heterogeneous in equilibrium where both types of workers will be hired.

It should be noted that the Lal and Staelin analysis does not involve the specific design of optimal multiple contracts. For certain specific sales response functions, Rao's paper [1990] seeks to characterize the firm's optimal compensation plan in the environment of a heterogeneous salesforce, using the principal-agent framework. The author begins with a deterministic function of sales in relation to the workers' quality and their efforts. It is assumed that the quality of as well as the efforts by the salesperson are unknown to the manager of the firm. The analysis is then extended to the situation where realized sales are subject to uncertainty. Let us detail the analysis here.

Rao [1990] considers two forms of sales response functions: the first is a normalized Cobb-Douglas and the second a response function used by Lodish [1971]. Consider the normalized Cobb-Douglas:

$$q = \theta^\beta h^\gamma \tag{5.43}$$

where θ represents the quality index, h the effort (hour of work), and coefficients β and γ are elasticities. Normalize further so that $\beta = 1$, the preceding equation becomes:

$$q = \theta h^\gamma. \tag{5.43a}$$

The second sales response form adopted can be written as:

$$q = q_0[1 - \exp(\theta h)] \tag{5.44}$$

where q_0 represents the saturation level of sales and as before, the parameter θ reflects the individual worker's quality index and h represents that worker's efforts.

It should be noted that both of the preceding sales response specifications are deterministic; hence in order to obtain any given specific sales level, an effort level h needed for a salesperson of quality θ can be calculated. One can express these relations by inverse sales functions of the general form:

$$h = g(q;\theta) \tag{5.45}$$

where assumptions are made to reflect the well-known characteristics of positive but declining marginal "sales productivity" for both the quality index and the effort level.

More specifically, a number of conditions on the partial derivatives of h with respect to the two arguments of the inverse function g are specified. Among these assumptions are that (i) for a given skill level, higher sales require higher effort; (ii) to obtain a particular sales level, lesser effort is required of a higher-quality salesperson; (iii) the marginal effort required to obtain an additional unit of sales is non-decreasing in sales; (iv) the marginal effect of the quality index on effort is also decreasing; and (v) the marginal effort to obtain an additional sales unit is less for a higher-quality salesperson.

Under the assumption of uncertainty regarding the realized sales, one can specify the sales response function as follows:

$$q = f(h,\theta,\xi) \tag{5.46}$$

where ξ represents a random error term.

Assuming that the heterogeneous salesforce is distributed with a density function of the form $\varphi(\theta)$, the firm's problem is to determine the optimal compensation scheme in order to:

$$\text{Max. } \Pi = \int [(p-c)q - w(q)]\varphi(\theta)d\theta \tag{5.47}$$

where it is noted that the sales q generated depends on the salesperson's skill level θ, given the compensation scheme of $w(q^0)$ which is dependent on the firm's announced quota q^0.

On the other hand, the agent's optimization problem can be seen as to choose an effort level to:

$$\text{Max. } U(h;\theta) = w(q) - v(h). \tag{5.48}$$

In terms of the observable quota q^0, the preceding problem can be seen as:

$$\text{Max. } U(q^0;\theta) = w[g(q^0;\theta)] - v(q^0) \tag{5.49}$$

which also implies that the salesperson is risk-neutral since his utility is linear in money.

As usual, the Individual Rationality constraint is written as:

$$U(q^0;\theta)\geq V_0. \tag{5.50}$$

The optimal scheme can be described by a mechanism $\{w(\theta), q^0(\theta)\}$ so that the salesperson will self-select to reveal his/her true quality by choosing his/her quota q^0. The agent's problem of choosing a quota can then be expressed as an optimization problem in which the salesperson will announce his skill or quality level, denoted by θ^*. Let us formally write the problem as:

$$\text{Max. } U(\theta^*,\theta)=w(\theta^*)-v[g(q^0(\theta^*));\theta] \tag{5.51}$$

subject to the preceding Individual Rationality constraint.

Defining the premium to be the difference between a salesperson's optimal utility resulting from the preceding optimization problem and his minimum (alternative) utility, it has been found that: the higher the skill of a salesperson, the higher the premium he receives, except for the case of the salesperson with the lowest skill whose premium may be zero. Note that it is the heterogeneity in the salesforce which yields the preceding results.

Another interesting result is that under the optimal scheme, the quota $q^0(\theta)$ and compensation $w(\theta)$ are not lower for higher skill salespersons. Another result is that the highest-skilled salesperson will put in the same effort regardless of whether he is a member of a homogenous or heterogeneous salesforce. On the other hand, all other salespersons will exert less effort if they are members of a heterogeneous salesforce instead of a homogeneous salesforce.

Of particular importance is the analysis involving practical implementation of the optimal compensating scheme by a menu of linear plans. More specifically, the menu of linear plans can be characterized by the following schedule:

$$W(q;q^0)\equiv a.[\theta(q^0)]+b.[\theta(q^0)][q-q^0] \tag{5.52}$$

where a and b are, as before, coefficients and where the skill index is written explicitly as an inverse function of the quota q^0.

Clearly, the interpretation of the preceding linear schedule involves the fixed payment of a to the salesperson for meeting exactly the chosen quota q^0, and either the bonus for exceeding the quota or the penalty for falling short of the quota, both at the commission rate of b.

In terms of implementing the menu of linear plans as specified in the preceding schedule, Rao works with the specific sales response functions we reported previously, namely, the restricted Cobb-Douglas and the Lodish form, and in addition, certain specification regarding the probability density function of skill across the heterogeneous salesforce, and a quadratic (dis)utility function of effort levels. He shows that under these specifications, the optimal compensation scheme can be implemented as a menu of linear plans as specified and further, both the commission rate b and the fixed payment a are increasing in quota q^0.

For our present purposes, an interesting question would be to investigate the impact of random sales on the implementation of the optimal scheme just reported. Note that the optimal compensation which is based on the optimal self-selecting mechanism $\{w(\theta), q^0(\theta)\}$ can be seen to be in general a non-linear function of the realized sale q, which we will denote as $W(q)$. The non-linear schedule $W(q)$ is optimal if the response function is deterministic and hence q can be observed. On the other hand, if a salesperson's realized sale is affected by both his/her skill and effort, and in addition, it is also subject to some random fluctuations as specified previously, then $W(q)$ may no longer be optimal. In contrast, if it can be shown that under certain conditions, a menu of linear plans of the form $W(q,q^0)$ can be found to be equivalent to the non-linear schedule $W(q)$, then the linear plan can be seen to be optimal even under random sales response situation provided that the random sales is an unbiased estimate of the true sales and the error terms ξ's are distributed independently among salespersons. Clearly, this result is obtained on the basis of the assumption of risk neutrality for both the principal, the firm, and the agents, the salespersons.

4 HETEROGENEOUS SALESFORCE: OTHER DEVELOPMENT

We have devoted considerable space to capture some of the main ideas involving the optimal compensation scheme, in particular the notion of scheme under the scenarios of imperfect knowledge on the heterogeneous salesforce. The most significant among recent development of research on this general subject is related to the literature on the theory of agency in incorporating the assumption of unknown sales response to the salesperson's efforts. Perhaps a most important implication of these analyses is the models' ability to formalize the well-observed practice of commission payment scheme where the firm's payment to its salesforce is dependent partially on the realized sales in comparison to the established quotas. In this section we wish to formulate the problem differently to examine situations in which the salesforce is also heterogeneous and more importantly it is the salaries instead of commission rates which play the major role in the payment schemes. This we will depart from the standard literature and thus offer some additional insights towards the complex phenomenon of labor compensation, in particular with a view towards comparisons of compensations across different industries or different departments within a corporation.

We are motivated by the long held observation that marketing salesforce, in comparison to the workforce in other departments such as production, manufacturing, can be compensated in a fashion which reflects more closely each individual's contribution to the firm (see Farley [1964] and citations there). We wish to address one particular implication of this observation in this section. More specifically we would like to find out how such a difference in the ability of the firm to observe each individual salesperson's performance would lead to potential differentials in wages across different departments or line of work.

Thus, we present this model in the context of a firm's operating structure in which the marketing department operates in conjunction with other departments such as production. The empirical observation that a common practice in compensation policy for the salesforce involves elements of a commission-based payment scheme in itself suggests the very idea as to why such a compensation scheme would not typically apply to the firm's other employees who are not salespersons. Clearly, this represents a very complex phenomenon; we will however concentrate on one particular feature which is that it is easier to measure individual performance in the marketing division in contrast to other divisions within the firm. The implications for this observation is that compensation on the basis of commission rate can be interpreted as a form of salary payment except that it is adjusted quickly to reflect each individual salesperson's marginal contribution to the firm's total profits. Let us sketch the basic model in the following.

Suppose that functional departments differ in their abilities to correctly assess their workers' individual productivities; due mainly to the intrinsic nature of different production processes involved in each department. Workers, on the other hand, are identified by their observable qualifications but also possess other qualities which are not measurable and may change over time. All the functional departments possess identical information regarding potential workers' observable qualifications and are equally capable of screening candidates. Departments which can easily verify their workers' productivities are more capable of paying their workers at levels reflecting more closely their marginal contributions through promotion and demotion over time. We should note that promotion/demotion in this framework should be interpreted as changing the payscale which is dependent on the observed output. Departments which cannot do so are faced with a situation where better workers should be promoted, due perhaps to their threat to leave and competing offers from other departments or companies, but worse workers cannot be easily demoted due to potentially high costs of verification for the negative assessment of such employees. Since all departments are equally capable of screening candidates, equilibrium grade distributions of workers with apparently comparable qualifications differ from department to department across all companies. Consequently, even when wages are set competitively in the tradition of classical economics, inter-department wage differentials result. It then follows that departments where demotions are more difficult to carry out would in effect pay higher wages.

It is important to point out that the preceding argument would be subject to objections if all workers are *identical, not only in observable qualifications but also in unobservable qualities*. It can be demonstrated that when workers are homogeneous, wages in the functional departments where it is more difficult to demote workers can be set at levels lower than those offered in other departments where low-performance workers can be demoted more easily. This reasoning follows the same line with that advanced in a model of internal markets by Oswald [1984] and is similar in spirit with earlier papers on implicit contract theory (Azariadis [1975] and Baily [1974]. That is, some workers are willing to accept lower wages in exchange for job security. However, when workers possess some qualities which are unobservable as we assume in this section, we are faced with a problem of adverse selection. Wilson [1980] demonstrated in his analysis of Akerlof's [1970] used car model that characterizations of equilibrium in markets with adverse selection are problematic and sensitive to different conventions in which prices are set. Here we assume the convention that wages are set by an auctioneer to equate demand and supply. In order to make our argument regarding the wage-setting mechanism with heterogeneous labor as transparent as possible, we will work with a simple example in the following sub-section.

To summarize, the idea here is that we are assuming that there are two departments/divisions within the firm; in the production department, salaries are more stable even though it is subject to certain amount of risk of unemployment; and in the marketing department, salaries depend heavily on the sales generated by individual salespersons, in the latter situation, we interpret the compensation mechanism of commission-based scheme as demotion/promotion. We will start with a very simple model in the next sub-section and then offer some generalization of the basic argument.

4.1 A Simple Model

In this sub-section we will advance the argument regarding the market-clearing process in determining compensation under the assumption of heterogeneous labor. In order to simplify the analysis, we consider a two-period dynamic model for companies whose organization structures consist of two major functional departments, sectors, or areas, one is the marketing department where demotion is possible and the other is the production department where it is *not*. We make this particular assumption with some extreme interpretations so that the production processes in the production department are actually based strictly on team work; thus significant problems would arise in assessing individual performance and hence performance-based incentives and compensation. In order to account for heterogeneity of labor, we assume that there are two types of workers, one has *high* productivity which we will term with the G index, the other *low* productivity with the B index. It should be pointed out that the model we described verbally briefly earlier is much richer and more realistic than the example discussed here. The use of the following model, however, simplifies the mathematics considerably while still formalizes the main thrust of the argument we propose in this sub-section.

The supply of total labor L, assumed fixed, consists of G number of high productivity and B of low productivity. The production sector operates under a constant budget constraint of C, an assumption made mainly for mathematical simplicity. The wage paid to a production worker is $\bar{w}$ to be determined endogenously. The marketing department makes compensation decisions on the basis of the individual salesperson's marginal contribution to the department's profits, paying wage or compensation at rate w. It is important in the present context to note that the manner with which the salesforce compensation is calculated for the marketing area amounts to a performance-based commission approach. All workers are *observationally identical*, labor productivity is initially of private information; available to the workers but not to the managers. They live and work for two periods. All workers are hired at the beginning of the first period; at the beginning of the second period, low-productivity workers, if employed in the marketing department will be fired; they become unemployed. Assume further that the nature of uncertain aggregate demand is such that some of the high-productivity workers in the production department will also be laid off, at a *known* rate f. Once laid off, these workers cannot find employment during the remaining time in the second period. On the other hand, low-productivity workers in the production department, once found out by its managers, will not be fired. To sharpen the result, we assume further that high-productivity workers will contribute one unit of effective labor, low-productivity worker will contribute none. In addition, we also assume zero rate of discount for simplicity.

Assuming decentralization to the extent that the marketing department seeks to maximize its own contribution of profits to the firm, the risk-neutral marketing or sales department's objective is to:

$$\text{Max } E(\Pi) = E(Revenue) - Labor\ Cost$$

where E is the expectations operator, reflecting the assumption of uncertain demand.

To do so, the sales/marketing department will offer compensation so that only high-productivity workers will find it attractive to join the salesforce while low-productivity workers will be discouraged, given that $\bar{w}$ is being offered in the production department. In other words the objective function facing the marketing department is:

$$\text{Max.} \quad E(\Pi) = E(Revenue) - wG_1$$
$$\{w, G_1\} \tag{5.53}$$
$$= ER(G_1) - wG_1$$

$$\text{Subject to: } w \leq 2\bar{w} \tag{5.54}$$

$$\text{and} \quad w + (1 - f)w \geq 2\bar{w} \tag{5.55}$$

where G_1 is number of high-productivity workers employed in the sales/marketing department with the index 1, w is the wage rate offered to those workers, and note also that we write explicitly the expected revenue function ER.

Constraint (5.54) is to make the sales/marketing department unattractive to the low-productivity workers since he/she will be fired in the second period and consequently earns zero wage whereas he/she will earn wage $\bar{w}$ in both periods in the production department. Constraint (5.55) allows the sales/marketing department to attract high-productivity workers since, adjusting for the known probability of being laid off f, the total wage earnings should at least equal to the total wage earnings in the production department.

For $0 < f < 1$ and assuming that constraint (5.55) holds with equality in equilibrium, i.e., $w + (1-f)w = 2\bar{w}$, we note that $w < 2\bar{w}$. There could conceivably be corner solutions to the above problem. In what follows we will concentrate on only the following most interesting equilibrium configuration in which the sales/marketing department offers:

$$w = \frac{2}{(2-f)}\bar{w} \qquad (5.56)$$

to attract only high-productivity workers and the production department will employ both high- and low-productivity workers at wage $\bar{w}$.

Note that in equilibrium, low-productivity workers do not want to apply for a job in the sales/marketing department since their total (at zero discount rate) earnings there will be less as the managers will find out their true productivities in the second period; high-productivity workers are indifferent between the two departments because on average the earnings are equalized in both departments.

Hence the demand of the sales/marketing department for high-productivity workers is based on:

$$\partial ER(G_1)/\partial G_1 = w. \qquad (5.57)$$

from which we write $G_1 = h_1(w) = g_1(\bar{w})$ for a given f as can be seen from (5.56).

For the production department with the index 2, the demand for high-productivity workers, denoted as G_2, subject to the budget constraint C, is:

$$\bar{w}B + \bar{w}G_2 = C \qquad (5.58)$$

which says that both types of workers are paid the same wage rate.

Hence:

$$G_2 = \frac{C - \bar{w}B}{\bar{w}} = \frac{C}{\bar{w}} - B \qquad (5.59)$$

which yields $G_2 = g_2(\bar{w})$.

We thus write the total demand function for high-productivity workers as:

$$G=G_1+G_2=h(\overline{w}). \tag{5.60}$$

Due to the fixed supply of high-productivity workers, G^S, the market-clearing wage rate $\overline{w}$ is determined as:

$$h(\overline{w})=G^S. \tag{5.61}$$

We assume that $\overline{w}$ is uniquely determined; hence the equilibrium wage w offered by the sales/marketing department will also be endogenously determined.

It is important to realize that at the first glance, higher wages are paid to workers in the sales/marketing department which employs, on average, the more productive workers. The fact that higher-productivity workers are paid higher wages constitutes essentially the classical economics argument. In contrast, in our model, wages are *in effect* higher in the production department simply because of its inability to fire low-productivity workers who would continue to earn identical positive wages $\overline{w}$ in the second period. It is the larger concentration of low-productivity workers in the production department which yields the effective higher wages in this department.

4.2 The More General Model

The example in the preceding sub-section makes it clear that departmental wage differentials exist as a *passive* outcome of the way equilibrium distributions of workers with different productivities result once true performances are subsequently observed and wages adjusted. In the remaining analysis, we will characterize these equilibrium distributions using more general and realistic assumptions regarding labor quality, the number of departments as well as the dynamic pay scale adjustment process. It is most convenient to specify certain assumptions used in our basic argument.

Functional Departments: Departments differ in their abilities to verify each worker's individual contributions to the organization. The very nature of the production processes which differ from department to department is the basis for this assumption. There are processes in which each worker can individually produce the product; his marginal productivity can be easily measured and thus verified. On the other hand, when workers mainly work as a team to produce a particular product, each worker's marginal productivity can not be easily verified when necessary.

Further, departments are separate entities within the firm, hence each seeks to maximize its profits; each is assumed to be risk-neutral. This reflects our assumption that compensation is a decentralized decision in each department/division. Each will not offer wages higher than that level which can attract workers of certain qualifications. They are identical in their ability to screen applicants. This in effect assumes away certain features of information asymmetry of the type studied by Greenwald [1979] and Kwok and Leland [1982].

Workers: There are different "grades" of workers identified by their qualifications (e.g. education, age, experience, etc., ...). They form common pools from which all departments can consider hiring. Workers choose a functional department solely on the basis of wage offerings. There are unobservable measures regarding a worker's quality. In one particular analysis below, we assume that this quality becomes known to the departments after a time period, a year, say. For the most part, however, we assume that labor quality may itself be changing over time. This represents a clear departure from most of the literature involving labor or product of unknown quality. While the assumption that quality is a constant and can be assessed with certainty after certain periods of use is reasonable in a commodity market, it should be challenged in the labor market. Unlike a product, labor quality and ability is capable of changing.

Wage-setting mechanism: Wages for a given qualification are set at market-clearing levels where demand equals supply. Unlike the search literature, information on job opportunities is equally available to all candidates and information on applicants is equally available to all departments. For comparable workers, working conditions are identical and so are other non-wage compensations such as fringe benefits. Assume further that there are neither turnover costs to the department nor costs of switching jobs for workers.

Ideally, one would like to develop a model incorporating the behavior of heterogeneous workers as well as the behavior of departments with different demotion rates, so that a complete characterization of wage determination in equilibrium can be derived. However, except for the simplified case as we analyzed in the previous sub-section, we found out not only that the mathematics for the general case becomes intractable but also that it would be impossible to obtain sensible economic interpretations. The difficulties associated with the characterization of equilibrium in adverse selection models due to labor heterogeneity are not unique to our problem; they were noted, for instance, by Holmstrom [1983] and Oswald [1984].

On the basis of the preceding observations, coupled with the fact that it is the asymptotic grade distributions of seemingly similar workers which yield the resulting departmental wage differentials, we will first look at the simple case where labor quality becomes known after just one period and then analyze the more important case where quality may change over time.

One-Period Adjustment
Workers of similar observable qualifications are hired into different departments at wages set at market-clearing levels. Since the worker's "true" quality is not perfectly observable to the organizations, some adjustments will take place after one period of employment. Departments such as the marketing/sales department (and we will conveniently call them the lower-verification-cost department, due to our assumption of their higher ability to verify workers' individual contributions) are more capable

of assigning workers at grades more truly reflecting their "revealed" quality. Thus, the majority of workers originally hired into certain grades remains to be there, perhaps by virtue of the department's experience in judging them. However, those workers who make contributions less than what is expected of them in their originally intended grades will be demoted to lower grades compatible to their lower quality. Meanwhile, workers who make larger contributions will be rewarded with promotions. At the extreme case where individual contributions can be perfectly measured, departments can assign exactly the appropriate grade for each worker, each earning a wage equal to his marginal product as specified in the standard competitive theory.

At the other end of the spectrum, higher-verification-cost departments such as production teams will have a more difficult task of verifying individual contributions. Since departments are assumed to have similar ability to judge the common pool of candidates, there is also a similar problem of hiring into a certain grade workers with different true (realized) degrees of quality. After one period, workers who are capable of contributing more than their wages will be promoted in the same manner as their counterparts in lower-verification-cost departments. Since workers' performance is not readily verifiable in these departments, using an argument in the principal-agent literature, a department may have an incentive not to promote these workers. However, as Fama [1980] and subsequently Holmstrom [1982] have pointed out, in different contexts, once a worker's higher ability becomes observable, the manager will be pressured to promote him due to his credible threat to leave the organization coupled with other competing departments' offers for his service. On the other hand, lower quality workers may remain in the original grades to which they were hired. Even though these workers' lower quality becomes observable, demoting them could be too costly in these high-verification-cost departments. It may be useful to think of a scenario where a demoted worker may want to challenge the employer's decision in court. Given that this worker's presumably lower performance is not costlessly verifiable, the department may not want to demote this worker after all.

Thus, regardless of the department in which he is employed, an employee who possesses observable and unobservable quality compatible with a certain grade but was originally hired into a lower grade will be promoted. On the contrary, if such an employee was originally hired into a higher grade, the probability that he will be demoted to a lower grade depends on which department he is currently employed in. The higher the degree of verifiability of his contribution to the firm, the lower the cost of verification, and the higher the probability of him being demoted to a lower, more appropriate grade. An asymmetry of sorts arises, due mainly to the nature of production processes which vary from department to department. For ease of future reference, we will refer to this as *structural asymmetry* as opposed to the more familiar information asymmetry in labor and other markets with elements of uncertainty.

We should point out that the reason why a department cannot hire workers at a lower pay scale and if found productive, then promote them is two-fold: First, departments may not maximize profits if they choose not to hire more productive workers, in their best estimation, at higher pay scales. This can be most clearly seen in the example in the previous sub-section with the dramatic (but commonly used in the related literature) assumption that only good workers are to produce any amount of positive output at all. Secondly, following an earlier argument to be seen more explicitly in the indefinitely-adjustment case below, labor quality may itself be changing over time; thus the preceding strategy would not be optimal.

Let us formalize the argument a bit here. Suppose that there are n "grades" of workers in various departments throughout the firms in the economy. At the end of a period, say a year, a constant fraction a_{ij} of the total workers in the j-th grade is either promoted to an i-th grade for $i > j$, or demoted to an i-th grade for $i < j$. The fraction of the total workers remaining in the same j-th grade is represented by a_{jj}, $j=1,2,...,n$. Clearly $\sum_{i=1}^{n} a_{ij}=1$ for each $j=1,...,n$. Let us denote this transition matrix as $\mathbf{A} \equiv [a_{ij}]$. The matrix $\mathbf{A}$ thus defined is a nonnegative column stochastic matrix.

We now write the resulting grade distribution of workers after a one-period adjustment through promotion and demotion as:

$$\pi_i = \sum_{j=1}^{n} a_{ij}\pi_{j0} \qquad (5.62)$$

where π_{j0} denotes the original grade distribution.

Since functional departments differ in their ability to demote worse employees, only the demotion coefficients in the transition matrix vary, i.e., the a_{ij}'s where $i < j$. Let us now summarize the impact of changes in these demotion coefficients, to be denoted as da_{ij} for $i < j$, on the resulting grade distributions.

From the previous equation, we have:

$$d\pi_i = \pi_{i0}da_{ii} + \sum_{j>i}^{n} \pi_{j0}da_{ij} \ .$$

Noting that $\sum_{i=1}^{n} a_{ij}=1$, the preceding expression becomes

$$d\pi_i = -\pi_{i0}\sum_{z=1}^{i-1} da_{zi} + \sum_{j>i}^{n} \pi_{j0}da_{ij} \ .$$

It can be seen clearly that, for $da_{ij} > 0$, we have $d\pi_1 > 0$; $d\pi_n < 0$; and $d\pi_i \gtrless 0$ for $i=2,...,n-1$. It is of interest to note that for $i=2,3,...,n-1$, $d\pi_i$ may change signs in no particular pattern depending on the relative strengths of opposing forces, one from the extent of the arrivals of workers demoted from higher grades, the other the departures of current workers to be demoted to lower grades. This particular result will be contrasted with that in the dynamic case we study subsequently.

The implication of the preceding analysis for the inter-department wage differentials is straight-forward. We will elaborate this in a sub-section below. We now address the more important case of changing labor quality.

Indefinite Adjustments

We have developed the argument mainly on the basis of a one-period adjustment mechanism. Labor quality is a static notion in the sense that it does not vary over time; it takes just one period for the departments to be able to learn about the true quality of their employees and then make appropriate decisions regarding promotion and demotion.

The way our model is set up, however, allows us to introduce certain dynamic aspects into the labor quality as well as the firm's decision processes in a rather natural fashion. Labor quality, to be realistic, can not simply be represented by a simple index as customarily assumed in the literature. Rather it should be related not only to a worker's observable profile involving factors such as work experience, education, and employment history, etc. but also other unobservable measures such as work ethics and creativity, etc. Now this is an extremely complex issue and we do not pretend to address it in the present framework. However, some of these features can be captured in our model if we were willing to interpret the transition matrix $A = [a_{ij}]$ specified previously as a constant matrix. That is, after the one-period adjustment of the original set of workers of different grades, the resulting grade distribution of workers is subject to another round of adjustment via the constant transition matrix A. This process continues well into the indefinite future. This repetitive process is required since labor quality can not be "revealed" in a one-period adjustment, due to the very possibility that it is changing over time. Thus, a worker who is demoted in a given period may be promoted in a future period through further on-the-job training, improved performance, etc. Likewise, a worker who is promoted in the first period may be demoted in the next because of his changing work habits, etc. These characteristics seem to represent, to a certain extent, the richness in the labor market in reality.

Another important interpretation of the constant transition matrix A and the indefinite adjustment involved is related to external shocks in the economy at large. Thus during the peaks of the business cycles, workers would be hired or promoted to grades higher than those normally accorded certain levels of qualifications such as education and experience. Conversely, during economic troughs, only higher than normal qualifications would enable a worker to enter and remain in the workforce of a certain grade. Clearly, this interpretation follows naturally if one were to view different pay scales as reflecting closely different "grades" of workers: when demand for the firm's product is higher (lower), its demand for labor is higher (lower), the resulting pay scales offered are higher (lower). While one would typically assume that pay is a continuous variable, we have in effect assumed discrete pay scales corresponding to different grades of workers.

Our analysis of the impact of the structural asymmetry defined earlier on the resulting grade distributions of workers across departments and the associated inter-department wage differentials applies equally well to this dynamic version of the model.

Let us recall the transition matrix $A = [a_{ij}]$ which is a nonnegative column stochastic matrix. For mathematical tractability, we make two additional assumptions as follows: First, there are no new arrivals to and no complete departures from the workforce as a whole. One can use the lowest grade ($i = 1$) to represent the low wage home production industry for workers who are unemployed at any time period. However, in the dynamic version of this model, these unemployed workers are capable of being "promoted" back to full-fledged employment: they have not departed completely from the workforce. Second, we assume that workers are promoted or demoted only one grade per period of time. Both of these assumptions are made mainly for mathematical simplicity; they are not crucial for the essence of the theoretical argument advanced here. Let us now write the matrix A as:

$$A = \begin{bmatrix} a_{11} & a_{12} & 0 & 0 & \cdots & & 0 \\ a_{21} & a_{22} & a_{23} & 0 & & & \vdots \\ 0 & a_{32} & a_{33} & \ddots & & & \\ 0 & 0 & \ddots & \ddots & & & 0 \\ \vdots & & & & & & a_{n-1,n} \\ 0 & \cdots & & 0 & a_{n,n-1} & a_{n,n} \end{bmatrix}.$$

It is a well-known application of the Perron-Frobenius theorem that the equilibrium (asymptotic) distribution of workers among different grades is independent of any initial distribution; and it is proportional to the eigenvector associated with the Perron root of A. Since the Perron root of A, a stochastic matrix, is 1, its associated eigenvector X satisfies:

$$(A - I)X = 0.$$

Upon normalizing that $X_1 + X_2 + \dots + X_n = 1$, where X_i denotes the i-th element of vector X and then replacing the normalized X_i's by the π_i's to reflect the resulting grade distribution of workers, we obtain the following result for the effect of the variation of the demotion coefficients among different departments on asymptotic grade distributions:

Theorem 5.1. *For $da_{ij} > 0$ where $i < j$, $d\pi_1 > 0$; $d\pi_n < 0$; $d\pi_j$; $j = 2, \dots n-1 \lessgtr 0$. Further, if $d\pi_j > 0$ then $d\pi_{j-1} > 0$; $j = 2, \dots , n-1$.*

While we will not report the rather long proof of this result here, it can be clearly seen that it parallels the main result given above for the one-period case. It is interesting to note the pattern of the change in the π_j's for $j = 2,3,\dots,n-1$. Like the case of the one-period adjustment analyzed previously, the preceding theorem tells us that for departments where demotions are easier to carry out, because bad performances can be easily assessed and verified, there exists a heavier concentration of workers in the lowest grade and a lighter concentration of them in the highest grade. However, unlike the one-period adjustment case, there exists a particular distribution pattern of workers in the remaining grades. In comparing any two departments such as the marketing department vs. the production department, there is a cut-off grade below which workers from the marketing department are more heavily distributed and above which the reverse is true.

4.3 Departmental Wage Differentials

As the formal results as well as our earlier theoretical arguments indicate, due to the assumption of structural asymmetry, the equilibrium pay scale/grade distributions of workers of comparable qualifications differ across departments. The easier it is to verify workers' individual contributions, the closer the department is able to assign workers to grades more truly reflecting their observable and unobservable quality through promotion and demotion over time. The reverse is true for those firms belonging to departments whose production processes by their very nature make it difficult to measure and thus verify workers' individual productivities. Since departments of all types have similar capability to screen candidates, at any point in time and for any particular grade, the higher-verification-cost departments contain higher fractions of workers who *should* belong to certain lower grades with corresponding lower wages. This would give rise to the scenario of persistent inter-department wage differentials observed in the empirical literature. While we are not able to provide any serious empirical results on wage differentials across different fields or departments within corporations, supporting evidence for this prediction can be casually given here. In one account, there exists a large empirical economics literature on inter-industry wage differentials (Krueger and Summers [1988]) and more casually, one typically sees reports on differential earnings for newly graduated MBA students in different fields of study.

The model we propose in this section thus provides a completely different interpretation of the empirical result. For employees with the same qualifications (human capital variables, etc.), the lower pay scales apply to a larger portion of this group in departments which can more easily verify their contributions and vice versa. It is in this sense that wages differ across departments even for similarly-qualified workers.

In summary, the major purpose of this analysis has been to propose a view towards an understanding of the firm's different departmental compensation structure. A unique characteristic of the model proposed here is the classical assumption that firms offer identical market-clearing wages to workers of the same observable qualifications across departments. This assumption follows Wilson's notion of Walrasian equilibria in analyzing markets where adverse selection is present. Each candidate's observable qualifications such as education are known to all participants; other dimensions of his quality are not observable *ex ante* and may be capable of changing over time. While departments will not be able to identify precisely each worker's true quality, itself a moving target, they all try to assign and reassign their employees, through series of promotion and demotion, to grades/pay scales more compatible with their contributions. Departments differ in their ability to do so even though they are equally capable of screening candidates. For any grade and at any particular period of time, better workers have to be promoted regardless of the departments they are employed in. Worse workers, however, are demoted more easily in some departments but less so in others where, because of the nature of production processes involved, it may be too costly to verify these workers' lower productivity. As a result, asymptotic grade distributions of seemingly similar workers differ from department to department: Inter-department wage differentials thus arise.

5 CONCLUSIONS

This chapter addresses some aspects of the salesforce size and compensation under conditions of uncertain sales response to personal selling as well as asymmetry in information. We started out with a standard treatment of the firm's decision on the size of its salesforce with the introduction of random demand. We then report on the results in the marketing literature regarding compensation with a contrast between the firm's objective and the salesperson's income-maximizing objective. Finally, we consider a particular issue involving inter-departmental wage differentials where different departments across companies may be faced with vastly different production processes and thus the resulting optimal compensations may have very different implications. Our study on this latter aspect of course reflects our own interest in this subject but also in our effort to connect with the growing interest in the joint decisions between the marketing and production activities as exemplified in the recent work by Eliashberg and Steinberg [1993].

Some of the topics and approach we have chosen for this chapter are not conventional. We have benefited from a number of recent comprehensive surveys on the issue of salesforce compensation with unknown response function which would fall under our general notion of marketing decision under uncertainty. Yet since these surveys are readily accessible, we did not find the need to present its full details here. Instead, we concentrate on a number of issues which we believe offer important topics of future research in this general area. The notion of advertising as an investment activity will continue to generate additional research interest, especially when it is jointly considered with the determination of the salesforce size. The issues of interactions among different departments within the firm's organization structure as we explore in Chapter 7 and its implications for wage differentials among departments and the impact of labor inter-departmental mobility appears to present interesting and important research opportunities as well.

Finally, we should also note that we have not covered the general subject of salesforce operations which involves the kind of activities exemplified by the recent survey by Vandenbosch and Weinberg [1993].

REFERENCES

AKERLOF, George A., 1970, "The Market for 'Lemons': Quality Uncertainty and the Market Mechanism," *Quarterly Journal of Economics*, Vol. 84, pp. 488-500.

AZARIADIS, C., 1975, "Implicit Contracts and Underemployment Equilibria," *Journal of Political Economy*, Vol. 83, pp. 1183-1202.

BAILY, Martin N., 1974, "Wages and Employment Under Uncertain Demand." *Review of Economic Studies*, vol. 41, pp. 37-50.

BASU, Amiya K., Rajiv LAL, V. SRINIVASAN, and Richard STAELIN, 1985, "Salesforce Compensation Plans: An Agency Theoretic Perspective," *Marketing Science*, Vol. 4, No. 4, pp. 267-291.

COUGHLAN, Anne T., 1993, "Salesforce Compensation: A Review of MS/OR Advances," in J. ELIASHBERG, and G. LILIEN (eds.), *Marketing*, Handbooks in Operations Research and Management Science, Vol. 5, pp. 611-651, Elsevier Science Publishers, Amsterdam, The Netherlands.

COUGHLAN, Anne T., and Subrata K. S. SEN, 1989, "Salesforce Compensation: Theory and Managerial Implications," *Marketing Science*, Vol. 8, No. 4, pp. 324-342.

DORFMAN, R., and P. O. STEINER, 1954, "Optimal Advertising and Optimal Quality," *American Economic Review*, Vol. 64, pp. 826-836.

ELIASHBERG, Jehoshua, and Gary L. LILIEN (eds.), 1993, *Marketing*, Handbooks in Operations Research and Management Science, Vol. 5, Elsevier Science Publishers, Amsterdam, The Netherlands.

ELIASHBERG, Jehoshua, and Richard STEINBERG, 1993, "Marketing-Production Joint Decision-Making," in Jehoshua ELIASHBERG, and Gary L. LILIEN (eds.), *Marketing*, Handbooks in Operations Research and Management Science, Vol. 5, pp. 827-880, Elsevier Science Publishers, Amsterdam, The Netherlands.

FAMA, E., 1980, "Agency Problems and the Theory of the Firm," *Journal of Political Economy*, Vol. 88, pp. 288-307.

FARLEY, John U, 1964, "An Optimal Plan for Salesmen's Compensation," *Journal of Marketing Research*, 1, 39-43.

GREENWALD, Bruce, 1979, *Adverse Selection in the Labor Market*, London: Garland.

HOLMSTROM, B., 1979, "Moral Hazard and Observability," *Bell Journal of Economics*, Vol. 10, No. 1, pp. 74-91.

HOLMSTROM, B., 1982, "Managerial Incentive Problems: A Dynamic Perspective," in *Essays in Economics and Management in Honor of Lars Wahlbeck*. Helsinki: Swedish School of Economics.

HOLMSTROM, B., 1983, "Equilibrium Long-Term Labor Contracts," *Quarterly Journal of Economics*, Supplement, Vol. 98, pp.23-54.

HOLTHAUSEN, Duncan M., 1976, "Input Choice and Uncertain Demand," *American Economic Review*, Vol. 66, pp. 94-103.

JAGPAL, H. S., and I. E. BRICK, 1982, "The Marketing Mix Decision Under Uncertainty," *Marketing Science*, pp. 79-92.

KRUEGER, A. B., and L. H. SUMMERS, 1988, "Efficiency Wages and Inter-Industry Wage Structure," *Econometrica*, Vol. 56, pp. 259-293.

KWOK, V., and H. LELAND, 1982, "An Economic Model of the Brain Drain," *American Economic Review*, Vol. 72, pp. 91-100.

LAL, Rajiv, 1986, "Delegating Pricing Responsibility to the Salesforce," *Marketing Science*, Vol. 5, No. 2, pp. 159-168.

LAL, Rajiv, and Richard STAELIN, 1986, "Salesforce Compensation Plans in Environments With Asymmetric Information," *Marketing Science,* Vol. 5, No. 3, pp. 179-198.

LILIEN, Gary L., Philip KOTLER, and K. Sridhar MOORTHY, 1992, *Marketing Models,* Prentice-Hall, Englewood Cliffs, NJ.

LODISH, L. M., 1971, "CALLPLAN: An Interactive Salesmen's Call Planning System," *Management Science,* Vol. 18, No. 4, Part II, December, 25-40.

MONTGOMERY D. B., and G. L. URBAN, 1969, *Management Science in Marketing,* Prentice-Hall, Englewood Cliffs, NJ.

NERLOVE, Marc, and Kenneth J. ARROW, 1962, "Optimal Advertising Policy Under Dynamic Conditions," *Economica,* Vol. 39, pp. 129-142.

OSWALD, A. J., 1984, "Wage and Employment Structure in An Economy with Internal Labor Market," *Quarterly Journal of Economics,* Vol. 84, pp. 693-716.

RAO, Ram C., 1990, "Compensating Heterogeneous Salesforces: Some Explicit Solutions," *Marketing Science,* Vol. 9, No. 4, pp. 319-341.

SRINIVASAN, V., 1981, "An Investigation of the Equal Commission Rate Policy for a Multi-product Salesforce," *Management Science,* Vol. 27, No. 7, pp. 731-756.

TAPIERO, Charles S., and John U. FARLEY, 1975, "Optimal Control of Sales Force Effort in Time," *Management Science,* Vol. 21, No. 9, pp. 976-985.

VANDENBOSCH, Mark B., and Charles B. WEINBERG, 1993, "Salesforce Operations," in Jehoshua ELIASHBERG, and Gary L. LILIEN (eds.), *Marketing,* Handbooks in Operations Research and Management Science, Vol. 5, pp. 653-694, Elsevier Science Publishers, Amsterdam, The Netherlands.

WEINBERG, C. B., 1975, "An Optimal Commission Plan for Salesmen's Control over Price," *Management Science,* Vol. 21, No. 8, pp. 937-943.

WILSON, C.A., 1980, "The Nature of Equilibrium in Markets with Adverse Selection," *Bell Journal of Economics,* Vol. 11, pp. 108-30.

Part II

CONTEXTS FOR POSSIBLE INTERACTIVE DECISIONS

6

MARKET SHARE AND
DIFFUSION MODELS

We are now departing from the treatment involving standard topics in research in marketing such as advertising, pricing, promotion and personal selling in order to explore managerial implications of risk-taking behavior and market uncertainty within certain integrative contexts. Our focus in the previous chapters was on each of the marketing decision variables mostly in isolation and to the extent that certain theoretical frameworks were used to allow for minimum marketing interactions, the latter classification is of secondary importance. On the other hand, in this chapter as well as in the remaining chapters of the book, we will concentrate mainly on the contexts and treating the various decision tools as secondary. Thus we will encounter often theoretical structures in which one or two or more decision variables may enter and thus interact among themselves. In Chapter 6, we will be dealing with market share models as well as diffusion models. Specific interactions between production processes and marketing variables will be highlighted and analyzed in Chapter 7. We then turn our attention in Chapter 8 to the issue of competition under uncertainty in oligopolistic markets and Chapter 9 will address adaptive behaviors in marketing together with a number of empirical results.

1 OVERVIEW

This chapter is divided into two major subjects. The first is related to a number of development in market share analysis and the second addresses stochastic versions of the Bass model as well as some of its deterministic extensions. We will see that certain market share specifications represent specific forms of the diffusion process themselves and they are mainly motivated by econometric analysis and simulation exercises. On the other hand, other forms of market share models are intrinsically more theoretical and the market share specifications are not directly related to the diffusion process since it does not involve dynamic specifications. In the latter cases, we will formalize the notion that some specific types of market share models are derived from certain random utility specifications. In particular, the stochastic nature of these models has its root in the development of the random choice of individual consumers. Thus we will analyze them within the choice context where individual consumers will choose certain brands with certain probabilities. In this situation, it should be clear then that analysis of these specific deterministic market share models is in fact analysis of the aggregate market implications of the random choice at the individual level. We will devote a significant number of pages to analyze these models in this chapter with a particular emphasis on equilibrium analysis. The second major objective of this chapter is to report a number of research in dealing with stochastic issues concerning the popular diffusion process associated with Bass [1969] and some versions of its subsequent extensions. While theoretical and empirical studies addressing the Bass diffusion process have developed into a large marketing literature (see Mahajan, Muller, and Bass [1993]), we have not seen a concerted effort to bring together a limited number of diffusion models under uncertainty. We are motivated in this chapter to partially fill this gap. We will proceed by considering the market share models first.

2 SOME MARKET SHARES MODELS

In this section, we examine theoretical structure as well as economic and strategic implications for some market share models. It has been shown in the literature that various market share specifications have proven useful in analyzing competitive behavior as well as in estimating and predicting firm behaviors.

One of the major purposes for us here within the present context of our interest in the effect of uncertainty is to examine how the environment's randomness would impact upon the firm's managerial decision. It turns out that, due to its intrinsic logical consistency, a market share model is basically a competitive model; this is so since by its definition a brand's or a firm's market share is defined in terms of the total market which naturally includes the sales of competitors. Thus, unless one is making a rather strong assumption that every competitor's decisions are assumed fixed or exogenous to the firm under consideration, each firm's action invites the reactions from its competitors as well as the fact that its action is also a reaction to other competing firm's initiatives. With this in mind, the theoretical challenge in addressing the impact of uncertainty on market share analyses is similar to the issue of uncertainty within a competitive framework. This is the subject best left to be treated in Chapter 8 under the heading of "Competitive Marketing Strategies" which we will explore later. Meanwhile, since market share analysis has a special place in marketing literature, as witnessed by a recent book by Cooper and Nakanishi [1988], we will devote a large portion of this chapter to explore various theoretical aspects of these models. A couple of comments are in order to motivate the way in which our approach to this subject is undertaken. Unlike Cooper and Nakanishi, we will exclusively address theoretical implications of certain market share models; thus the econometric studies are not examined in this chapter. Second, several important work have appeared to address certain market share models on the basis of the market attraction formulation. The market attraction hypothesis has served as a workhorse for much of theoretical research in market share models. In particular, various versions of the multiplicative competitive interaction model (MCI) have been estimated as well as being subject to normative analyses based on which economic implications and managerial and strategic implications are advanced. On the other hand, while the multinomial logistic models (MNL) have been used in several empirical studies, equilibrium analyses have not yet been fully developed.

2.1 A Random Linear Market Share Model

In this section we examine a simple version of the linear model of market share. Our motivation is to start with a simplest specification to highlight the role of random sales response. Further, it has been shown that in terms of predictive power, the linear market share version performs at the same level with other more logically consistent model such as the MCI and the MNL and yet it is simple to analyze and estimate. Since the impact of uncertainty and risk behavior plays an important role in predicting the firm's marketing decision, it would be appropriate to study them here. The basic specification can be written as follows:

$$s_i = a_i + b_i^* \frac{m_i}{\sum_{j \neq i} m_j} + \xi_i \qquad (6.1)$$

where a_i and b_i^* denote known parameters, s_i denotes the market share of brand i, m_i denotes brand i's advertising activities, and where we assume that the random variable ξ has zero mean and variance σ_ξ^2.

This specification has been tested extensively and has been strongly supported by econometric work and filed studies. It is also a version of the Pekelman and Tse [1980] model. The i-th brand's sales is defined to be

$$q_i = s_i.S \qquad (6.2)$$

where in the mean time we assume that S represents a fixed total industry sales, i.e., fixed market size which is most applicable for relatively mature consumer products.

If we make an additional assumption that the combined competitors' marketing activities are governed outside of the brand's decision making process and that the cost of marketing activities is linear, then the i-th brand's sales can be rewritten as:

$$q_i = (a_i + b_i m_i + \xi_i)S \tag{6.3}$$

where $b_i \equiv b_i^* / \sum_{j \neq i} m_j$.

Assuming further that the manufacturing cost excluding the marketing expenditure is a convex quadratic function of sales in the following form:

$$C(q_i) = cq_i + \frac{1}{2} dq_i^2$$

the i-th brand's expected utility of profit function is then:

$$EU(\Pi_i) = \int U[p_i q_i - C(q_i) - m_i]\varphi(q_i)dq_i \tag{6.4}$$

where $\varphi(q_i)$ denotes the density function of q_i which amounts to the density function of random variable ξ_i.

Working with a quadratic utility function, the first-order condition for optimality can be written as: (subscript i omitted)

$$\frac{\partial E(\Pi)}{\partial m} = \frac{1}{2}r[\frac{dE(\Pi - E\Pi)^2}{dm}]$$

where $r = -(U''/U')$ represents the Pratt-Arrow index of risk aversion and where, upon setting $S = 1$ without loss of generality, it can be shown that

$$\frac{dE(\Pi - E\Pi)^2}{dm} = 2b^2 d^2 \sigma_\xi^2 m + bd\sigma_\xi^2[2da + (c - p)]$$

which is positive.

Further the second-order condition for an interior solution can be shown to be:

$$\frac{\partial^2 E(\Pi)}{\partial m^2} - rb^2 d^2 \sigma_\xi^2 < 0$$

which is assumed to be satisfied.

The preceding development allows us to examine the impact of uncertainty in the market response and the firm's attitude toward risk. We shall show here that as the firm becomes more risk averse, it tends to reduce marketing activities; and further as uncertainty increases, at any given degree of risk aversion, the firm tends also to reduce its marketing activities. These results conform with much of the literature in this regard and our results are shown formally here as in the following equations:

$$[\frac{\partial^2 E(\Pi)}{\partial m^2} - rb^2 d^2 \sigma_\xi^2]\frac{\partial m}{\partial r} = b^2 d^2 \sigma_\xi^2 m + bd\sigma_\xi^2[da + \frac{1}{2}(c - p)]$$

and $\left[\dfrac{\partial^2 E(\Pi)}{\partial m^2} - rb^2 d^2 \sigma_\xi^2 \right] \dfrac{\partial m}{\partial \sigma_\xi^2} = rb^2 d^2 m + rbd[da + \dfrac{1}{2}(c-p)].$

Some comments on the preceding model should be in order. On the basis of our assumption that the combined competitors' marketing activities are exogenously determined, the i-th brand's sales level is a linear function of the decision variable, namely m. Consequently, the analysis of the impact of risk and uncertainty can be seen in a fairly straight-forward fashion. However, in spite of the fact that there exists significant empirical evidence as well as theoretically sound arguments in favor of the simplifying assumption of exogenous competing advertising and other promotional spending, it is an important feature in a highly competitive framework to explicitly include the competitors' marketing activities in the firm's decision-making. The appropriate method to deal with these competitive issues will be explored further in Chapter 8 and we also address some competitive implications within some other market share specifications later in this chapter. In the next section, however, we will introduce an element of nonlinearity which is intrinsic to the market share specification, following the work by Pekelman and Tse [1980]. While their work is concerned mainly with the issue of experimentation within an adaptive control theoretical structure, their brief analysis of the impact of uncertainty on the firm's promotional spending would be useful here for our present purposes.

2.2 A Random Nonlinear Market Share Model

The first major departure from our earlier formulation in the preceding sub-section is that the impact of one particular brand's advertising activity on its market share is summarized not by the ratio of its advertising budget to all other competitors' advertising budget combined as in eq. (6.1), but rather by its ratio to the industry's total advertising budget (which also includes its own spending on marketing effort). Now, from an estimation and empirical viewpoint, the difference is perhaps negligible especially if the firm under question is relatively small compared to the industry. However, when the firm is a significant part of the industry, the divergence from the previous formulation becomes more important. Further, theoretically, it creates the potential problem of nonlinearity in the decision variable which would make an analysis of uncertainty much more challenging. The second major element in the present formulation is related to the dynamic nature of the market share specification. We shall indicate that a static version is sufficient for us to establish the central result here that uncertainty would play no role for a risk neutral firm. We will address the dynamic dimension of the firm's marketing decision in Chapter 9 with much more detail.

$$s_{t+1} = \alpha_t + \gamma_t s_t + \beta_t \frac{m_t}{m_t + (\sum_{j \neq i} m_j)_t} + \xi_t \qquad (6.5)$$

where it should be noted that the familiar notion of "us/[us+them]" appears here and all the coefficients denoted by Greek letters are unknown but have known distribution functions.

Assuming further that the industry sales follows a first-order autoregressive seasonal time series and that the competitive advertising is generated by another first-order autoregressive process, the firm is assumed to maximize the following objective function of discounted sum of profits over the planning horizon T with a known discount factor ρ:

$$V = E \sum_{t=1}^{T} \rho^t [(p_t - c_t) s_t S_t - m_{t-1}]. \tag{6.6}$$

Now this is an exceedingly difficult stochastic (discrete) problem to deal with mainly due to the nonlinearity in the "control" variable m_t. An analytical solution would not be available. One way to gain insight to this problem is to assume that uncertainty enters linearly only through the random term ξ_t while all other coefficients are assumed known.

It is then shown by Pekelman and Tse that the (non-zero) optimal solution has the following form:

$$m_t = [\frac{1}{\rho_{t+1}} (p_t - c_t) \beta_t (\sum m_j) (\rho^t S_t + \sum_{\tau=2}^{T-t} \prod_{i=t+1}^{t-1+\tau} \gamma_i \rho^{\tau} {}^t S_{\tau+t})]^{1/2} - (\sum m_j)_{t+1}. \tag{6.7}$$

For the problem at hand, it is easier to consider the static version of the model where the combined competitive marketing effort is fixed and known, the lagged market share is s_0, and dropping the time subscript t and firm subscript for brand i, we have:

$$E(V) = (p - c) s S - m \tag{6.8}$$

$$\text{where} \quad s = \alpha + \gamma s_0 + \beta [\frac{m}{m + \sum_{j \neq i} m_j}] + \xi.$$

Maximizing the objective function in (6.8) yields the following solution

$$m^* = [(p - c) \beta (\sum_{j \neq i} m_j) S]^{1/2} - \sum_{j \neq i} m_j$$

which is of course a much simpler form of (6.7).

It should be recognized that uncertainty specified in this fashion, within the dynamic specification above, would not induce the firm to change its decision regarding its marketing effort. Pekelman and Tse note that the optimal solution, even though involving nonlinearly the control variable, is open-loop in that the realized market share in the current period does not affect the firm's advertising budget in the following time period. For our present purpose, it should also be noted that a fundamental assumption in the preceding solution concept is that the combined competitive advertising activities are exogenously determined.

Our understanding of these phenomena will be deepened at least in two major broadly defined directions. First, to what extent the dynamic characterization of the preceding problem can give rise to the issue of the firm learning about some unknown parameters in the sales response function. Second, how would the preceding analysis be modified to take explicit account of the competitors' decision within a common framework. Pekelman and Tse approach the first question on the basis of a simulation on the basis of a dual control formulation; the approach necessitated by complicated and fairly extensive stochastic specifications of the system involved. In order to approach the problem in a more tractable and more analytical fashion, we will address this experimentation and learning problem in a simpler stochastic structure in Chapter 9. On the other hand, the second broad issue of competition, as we mention above, will be given more detailed analysis in Chapter 8. In the remaining part of this chapter, we will concentrate on the competitive issues specifically relevant to what has been called logically consistent market attraction models. Since we will show how simple specification of uncertainty and risk behavior will significantly modify the firm's marketing decisions and equally important, the theoretical development of the strategic implication of these types of models is of a very recent origin, we will first analyze the models under deterministic conditions in the following section.

3 THE *MCI* MODELS

Of particular interest to us here are two major market attraction specifications widely used in the literature, the *MCI* models and the *MNL* models. In this section, we will focus on the *MCI* specification while the *MNL* models will be analyzed in the next section. It should be pointed out that while the two types of models have been equally and extensively analyzed in empirical work, theoretical developments regarding equilibrium analysis have been done exclusively on the *MCI* model. On the other hand, the *MNL* development on this account has only recently been analyzed and we will provide a brief discussion on the basis of an on-going work of Basuroy and Nguyen [1996].

3.1 *MCI* Models: Deterministic Analysis

The Basic MCI Version
In this sub-section we deal with a most basic specification of the *MCI* model to facilitate our discussion involving the impact of uncertainty. We will show below a more elaborate version with richer strategic and managerial implications. Consider a two-firm industry in which the only decision variable is the marketing activity.

Assuming differential effectiveness regarding marketing efforts, the attraction can be written as:

$$A_1 = a_1 m_1^\beta \qquad (6.9)$$

$$\text{and} \quad A_2 = a_2 m_2^\beta \qquad (6.10)$$

which, together, make up the industry's total attraction, to be denoted as D, as in Denominator:

$$D \equiv A_1 + A_2 = a_1 m_1^\beta + a_2 m_2^\beta \qquad (6.11)$$

and for the moment, the industry sales or industry output is fixed at S_0.

The first brand's profit is then written as

$$\Pi_1 = pq_1 - m_1 = ps_1 S_0 - m_1 \qquad (6.12)$$

where as before, we denote its market share as s_1, which is equal (A_1/D), and clearly the brand's sales is $q_1 = s_1 S_0$.

Upon normalizing the fixed market potential at $S_0 = 1$, we can write the first-order condition for an optimal advertising spending as:

$$\frac{\partial \Pi_1}{\partial m_1} = 0 \Rightarrow m_1 = \beta p \frac{A_1 A_2}{D^2} = \beta p s_1 s_2. \qquad (6.13)$$

Similarly, the second brand's optimal marketing expenditure is

$$\frac{\partial \Pi_2}{\partial m_2} = 0 \Rightarrow m_2 = \beta p \frac{A_1 A_2}{D^2} = \beta p s_1 s_2. \qquad (6.14)$$

Upon comparing the preceding conditions, and it can be easily seen that the second-order condition is satisfied, an immediate result is that the Nash solution to this *asymmetric* game implies that both firms' promotional budgets are the same. A number of comments are in order. We emphasize that this is not a result of an assumption on symmetry of the two firms since we specifically specify *a priori* the differences in their advertising effectiveness. Second, we have assumed that the price variable is exogenously determined at a common value as a result of product homogeneity (which runs counter to the very basic assumption that the products are typically differentiated to invoke the need for or because of promotions). Third, it is also assumed that the market share elasticities β's are identical. Fourth, there are only two firms in this industry. Clearly, the preceding three assumptions have been made in various studies in the literature; here we will eventually consider their relaxation one by one in the pages which follow. Finally, we should also note the assumption of a fixed market size, an assumption which we will also re-examine.

Yet, these comments aside, it points to a result which we think is interesting in its own right, that identical advertising budgets could arise in an asymmetric setting of competitive promotions. Further, within this simple framework we will show in a sub-section below how the existence of uncertainty and the firms' attitude toward risk can significantly modify these outcome with their corresponding managerial implications.

The MCI Models: Extensions

Getting back to the model we specify in (6.9) and (6.10), let us now briefly consider three major extensions of this model and consequently, various versions appearing in the literature can be seen as special cases of the present analysis. For our present purpose, we will not detail its development here but the formulation we present below can be readily analyzed to obtain comparative-static results of interest.

We begin by writing the attraction equations in the general setting of n firms with individual firm subscript i as follows:

$$A_i = a_i p_i^{-\gamma} m_i^{\beta} \tag{6.15}$$

and each brand's sales is

$$q_i = s_i S_0 D^{\theta} \tag{6.16}$$

where D is defined, as before, to be the sum of all attraction measures, and the exponent θ reflects the rate of industry expansion; we will continue to find it convenient to normalize S_0 to be unity.

From an analytical point of view, each of the three major extensions implied in the preceding formulation may cause difficulty. The first is related to the number of competitors n which poses no significant issue if one were to treat all firms to be symmetrical. However, if one wishes to maintain asymmetry in the sense of differential advertising effectiveness, we will have to explicitly address the non-symmetric Nash solution for a general n firms. The second extension involves the inclusion of the price variable in the market share equation. While non-price competition is a significant phenomenon in a large and important group of commodities in which we can take comfort in assuming a given constant industry price, it is the marketing mix which forms a rather unique feature of marketing research in relation to other aspects of applied microeconomic theories and industrial organization problems. It can be shown that the mere addition of the price variable will render a particularly simple solution on optimal advertising infeasible. The third is related to the assumption of a dynamic market in the sense that the total industry sales potential is not fixed, rather changing, or more specifically, expanding. We will show that this extension in general has very significant bearing on the firm's strategy, a result which is by and large assumed away in much of the research on this subject and a result which is particularly relevant in the context of our assumption of an uncertain market size.

The i-th firm's profit function is

$$\Pi_i = p_i q_i - m_i = p_i \frac{A_i}{D} D^\theta - m_i = p_i A_i D^{\theta-1} - m_1 \qquad (6.17)$$

where again S^0 is set to unity.

The first-order conditions can be written as

$$\frac{\partial \Pi_i}{\partial p_i} = 0 \Rightarrow (1-\gamma) - \gamma(\theta-1)s_i = 0 \qquad (6.18)$$

and $\quad \dfrac{\partial \Pi_i}{\partial m_i} = 0 \Rightarrow m_i = (\beta/\gamma)D^\theta s_i p_i.$ $\qquad (6.19)$

   The solutions are obtained in principle by solving the preceding $2n$ equations for $2n$ unknowns, involving n price variables and n marketing variables.

   As mentioned above, since we are not interested in analyzing the deterministic results per se, we will not pursue the comparative-static exercise any further. However, we can readily apply standard techniques to conditions in (6.18) and (6.19) to assess the impact of increasing competition and industry expansion on the firm's pricing as well as its marketing activities. For instance, a most useful way to interpret the model and make the solution most transparent is to concentrate on the case where the price is constant and exogenously given, then (6.19) becomes:

$$m_i = (\beta/\gamma)pD^\theta s_i \qquad (6.20)$$

which implies an interesting and important result that for a fixed market, each firm's marketing expenditure in equilibrium is directly proportional to its market share; a result which can be related to empirical observations and subject to further empirical validations. Ultimately, the question is still to determine what are the major factors which affect the firm's market share in equilibrium. Now clearly, the attraction formulation also indicates that the equilibrium market share is determined by each firm's marketing effort. More specifically, in the simple framework of these types of model, it is the effectiveness of advertising campaigns which ultimately determines the equilibrium market shares.

3.2 *MCI* Models: Sales Uncertainty

We now consider a simple stochastic extension of the basic *MCI* model above. For convenience, we assume β to take on the value of unity. While the market share elasticity of promotion can be shown to have important implications for the firm's marketing decisions in general, it will not affect our qualitative analysis on sales uncertainty in this section in any substantive way. Our departure from the deterministic world has a simple form in terms of the total market size. Let us assume that

$$S = \overline{S} + \xi.$$

Suppose now that the firms maximize their respective expected utilities of profits which for clearer results are assumed to be quadratic. Using the familiar approach which we have demonstrated in a number of previous contexts, it is straight-forward to show that the first brand's optimal marketing expenditure is determined by the following condition:

$$\frac{\partial E(\Pi_1)}{\partial m_1} = \frac{1}{2}\frac{r}{D}[2(p-c)^2 s_1 s_2 a_1 \sigma_\xi^2]$$

where as before r is defined to be the Pratt-Arrow measure of risk aversion.

Similarly, the second brand's optimal decision is dictated by

$$\frac{\partial E(\Pi_2)}{\partial m_2} = \frac{1}{2}\frac{r}{D}[2(p-c)^2 s_1 s_2 a_2 \sigma_\xi^2].$$

Noting that the right-hand sides of the preceding equations are not identical and noting further that the expressions on the left-hand side can be written as:

$$\frac{\partial E(\Pi_i)}{\partial m_i} = \frac{[(p-c)\overline{S} s_1 s_2 - m_i]}{m_i}; \quad i = 1,2$$

it follows immediately that for any non-zero index of risk aversion, the two competing firms' optimal marketing efforts are not identical.

The implication of the preceding simple demonstration is that unlike the deterministic scenario we work with in the previous sub-section, the presence of uncertainty alone even with identical risk attitude would induce firms to make different efforts in promoting their respective products.

Clearly, one can also derive further results regarding the potential differential risk-taking behavior among the duopolists. Instead of pursuing this issue here, we are more interested in examining the specific directional impact of uncertainty on each firm's marketing activity in view of their difference in marketing effectiveness. In particular, it can be established that the expected profits function in the preceding equation is a decreasing function with respect to the level of m; that is, we can show specifically here:

$$\frac{\partial^2 E(\Pi)}{\partial m_i^2} = -2(p-c)s_i^2 s_j \overline{S} < 0.$$

That is, as each firm's advertising expenditure grows, its effect on the firm's expected marginal profits from marketing activities should decline. Of course, this result conforms with the sensible assumption of decreasing marginal returns to marketing activities in equilibrium. Consequently, it can be seen that the firm's advertising effort is inversely related to its effectiveness; that is the more effective advertising campaign requires less amount of advertising spending under the assumption of risk aversion when the total market sales is subject to the simple linear form of zero mean uncertainty. This should be contrasted to some earlier findings within the deterministic specification of market share models exemplified in Monahan [1987].

In summary, contrary to the prediction of our simple *MCI* version with asymmetry in advertising effectiveness which suggests identical promotional budgets for both firms, the presence of uncertainty coupled with risk aversion tends to induce the more effective firm to invest less in marketing spending.

A similar analysis can be carried out with respect to the impact of uncertainty itself. In general, as industry sales becomes more uncertain in terms of larger variances, the duopolists' marketing efforts differ in that the more effective firm tends to spend less on advertising.

It would also be interesting to confirm our intuition when we allow for a complete symmetric scenario as follows. Given that each firm has a market share of one-half and that in equilibrium, each firm decides on an identical advertising budget *m*, the optimal level of marketing efforts can be readily calculated to be:

$$m = \frac{(p-c)\bar{S}}{4} - \frac{r(p-c)^2\sigma_\xi^2}{8}$$

from which it immediately follows that

$$\frac{\partial m}{\partial r} < 0 \quad ; \quad \frac{\partial m}{\partial \sigma_\xi^2} < 0.$$

4 RANDOM UTILITY AND *MNL* MODELS

Unlike the *MCI* versions we presented in the previous section, the *MNL* models have a solid theoretical foundation rooted in theories of random utilities. It is in this sense that we consider the *MNL* models an integral part of the treatment of decision under uncertainty. We have noted that the present work does not in general address the micro, individual-based consumer behavior which serves as the foundation for the realized demand in the market place. The presentation of the *MNL* models in this chapter represents a major exception to this orientation. We do so since we believe that this type of equilibrium analysis on the *MNL* models has not been fully developed and yet it represents a particularly constructive, common framework to address several issues of central interest to the academician and the practical manager alike such as the marketing mix, the competitive environment as well as the empirical implementation of its theoretical results.

4.1 Random Utility

The Consumer's Utility Maximization Foundation
We first note that the standard specification of the multinomial market share model represents an aggregate concept and it has been claimed (see, Cooper and Nakanishi [1988], p.51) that the consumer choice-based utility theory developed by McFadden [1974] and others may serve as a foundation for individual rational decision-making in formulating market shares in the aggregate. Since we are not aware of its full development in the literature, we will formalize this notion as follows. Using the insight of Thurstone's [1927] paper, random utility models assume that individual utility is represented by a random variable. In the context of our model, consider an individual who chooses among n brands of a particular product to purchase. Let the utility of alternative j be:

$$V_j = U_j + \xi_j$$

where U_j is the deterministic component of the utility which may be affected by the j-th firm's decisions such as advertising, prices, etc., i.e.:

$$U_j = f(p_j) + g(m_j) \tag{6.21}$$

and where the ξ_j 's are i.i.d. with a common distribution function H.

For simplicity, we consider the complete choice set, $C_N = \{1, 2, \ldots, N\}$ so that each individual is faced with a complete menu of brands. Clearly, we will typically assume for generality that $N > 2$. We assume further that each individual in the buyer population would buy at most one unit of the product and would pick a brand to maximize his/her utility. That is, the choice probabilities are defined so that the probability that an individual picks brand j is given by:

$$\pi(j|C_N) = Prob. \ (U_j + \xi_j \geq U_i + \xi_i \text{ for } j, i \in C_N).$$

It has been shown that (McFadden [1974] and Yellott [1977]; for exposition, see, e.g., Cooper and Nakanishi [1988] and Maddala [1983]) if the common distribution function H is double exponential, i.e.,

$$Prob. \ (\xi \leq \varepsilon) = H(\varepsilon) = \exp[-\exp(-\varepsilon)]$$

$$\text{then} \quad \pi(j|C_N) = \frac{\exp(U_j)}{\sum_{i=1}^{N} \exp(U_i)}$$

where U_j is defined in (6.21) above.

Now consider a homogenous set of individuals from the buyer population of Size S, consisting of S persons whose purchasing decisions are independent from each other. Defining a random variable Y_{tj}, $t=1,2,...,S$ so that $Y_{tj} =1$ if individual t picks brand j, and $Y_{tj} =0$ otherwise, it then follows that

$$Prob. \ (Y_{tj}=1) \equiv \pi(j|C_N) = \frac{\exp(U_j)}{\sum_{i=1}^{N} \exp(U_i)}$$

$$\text{and} \quad Prob. \ (Y_{tj}=0) = 1 - \pi(j|C_N).$$

Due to our assumption of independent buying decisions among buyers, the random variables Y_{tj}'s are mutually stochastically independent. Consider total sales of brand j, denoted by Q_j. For the buying population of size S, we have:

$$Q_j = \sum_{t=1}^{S} Y_{tj}.$$

It follows that the probability that total sales is a particular value q_j is:

$$Prob. \ (Q_j = q_j) = \binom{S}{q_j} \pi(j|C_N)^{q_j} (1 - \pi(j|C_N))^{S-q_j}; \ q_j = 0,1,...S.$$

It is well known that the mean value of sales of brand j from a population of size S, given the probability specified in the preceding expression, is:

$$E(Q_j) = S\pi(j|C_N).$$

Similarly, expected sales of all other brands, $j=1,2,...N$ can be obtained. Consequently, the *MNL* market share specification, which represents an aggregate market notion, is directly related to the individual consumer choice behavior as follows:

$$E(s_j) = \frac{E(Q_j)}{S} = \pi(j|C_N). \tag{6.22}$$

Thus, strictly speaking, the relevant objective function facing each firm is to maximize the *expected* profits due to the fact that the market share is itself a random variable with mean $E(s_j)$. Upon assuming risk neutrality, it is straight forward to show that the resulting solution is identical to a certainty-equivalent solution in which firms behave as if the mean value will be realized with certainty. Consequently, to simplify notation, we will suppress the expectation operators $E(.)$ in the analysis that follows.

The MNL Basic Model

Let us consider a simple version of the MNL model wherein there are two firms in the market the potential size of which, for the moment, is assumed fixed. Consider the attraction for firm i:

$$A_i = a_i e^{\beta m_i} \quad ; \quad i = 1, 2$$

where e denotes the natural log base.

Assume further that the cost function of marketing is nonlinear and convex as in $C(m_i) = m_i^\delta$. Then the first-order conditions, upon normalizing pS_0 to unity, can be shown to yield the result that:

$$m_1 = m_2 = m$$

which indicates that in spite of the fact that the firms are not symmetrical to begin with, they both spend an equivalent amount of marketing expenditure.

The resulting market share is determined solely by the differential marketing effectiveness as follows:

$$s_i = \frac{a_i}{a_1 + a_2}; \quad i = 1, 2.$$

Further, it can be shown that the optimal marketing spending in equilibrium has the form:

$$m^{\delta-1} = (\beta/\delta)\left[\frac{a_1 a_2}{(a_1 + a_2)^2}\right].$$

For clarity, assuming that $\delta = 2$, the resulting optimal marketing expenditure can be immediately seen to be subject to the property that

$$\frac{\partial m}{\partial a_i} = 2\beta a_j(a_1 + a_2)(a_j - a_i); \quad i = 1, 2$$

which says that as a particular firm finds itself in an improving position in terms of its marketing effectiveness, its decision to change its spending depends on the relative effectiveness itself.

4.2 *MNL* Models: Further Development

Industry Expansion Effects: Symmetry
Once the assumption of a fixed industry sales in the basic *MNL* model in the preceding sub-section is relaxed to allow for potential industry expansion, the conditions can be seen to be modified as:

$$\frac{\partial \Pi_i}{\partial m_i} = 0 \Rightarrow m_i = \frac{1}{2} D^{\theta-2} \beta A_i [A_j + \theta A_i] \qquad (6.23)$$

where again for clarity, we continue to set $\delta = 2$.

Clearly, the potential of an expansion of the market size implies that the identical marketing spending solution is no longer an equilibrium solution. One can of course find the specific solution for optimal advertising expenditure for each firm by simultaneously solving the preceding equations; and to the extent that an analytical solution is not generally available due to the non-linearity in those equations, certain numerical methods may be utilized. For our purposes, the numerical approach would not be helpful. One can proceed with certain kind of comparative static exercise but here we choose to try to gain additional managerial insights by parameterizing the coefficients to produce an interpretable analytical solution. The nature of the directional implications should not be inconsistent with the analytical results.

As a first step, the symmetric solution should be recorded; that is for identical a_i, the solution implies $A_1 = A_2$ and advertising budgets are identical; then the optimal value of m can be shown to be:

$$m = \frac{1}{8} \beta (1 + \theta)(2A)^{\theta} \qquad (6.24)$$

based on which it follows immediately that $\partial m / \partial \theta > 0$.

Effect of Competition: Asymmetry
Let us now analyze further the solution involving the common m even when firms are not symmetrical. Working with the scenario of fixed market size, the solution implies that

$$m_1 = m_2 = m = \frac{1}{2} \beta s_1 s_2$$

and consequently each firm's profit is

$$\Pi_i = s_i - m^2.$$

The symmetric solution has already been obtained. Now we are more interested in the solution pertinent to the dominant firm. Let us designate the dominant firm as number 1, or subscript d, the parenthetical number in the subscript denotes the number of competitors in the market. Let us compare the two scenarios, one in which there are two competing firms and another in which a third firm enters the market. First, rewrite the condition for the 2-firm case as:

$$\frac{\partial \Pi_1}{\partial m_{d(2)}} = \beta \frac{A_1}{D} \frac{A_2}{D} - 2m_{d(2)} = 0 \qquad (6.25)$$

and then, that for the 3-firm case as:

$$\frac{\partial \Pi_1}{\partial m_{d(3)}} = \beta \frac{A_1}{D} \frac{(A_2 + A_3)}{D} - 2m_{d(3)} = 0.$$

The preceding two relations allow us to simplify a particularly useful rule of optimal advertising as follows. Consider the function

$$\Phi(s_1) = s_1(1 - s_1)$$

which clearly is maximized at $s_1 = 1/2$.

Now, initially, the market share is determined by the relative effectiveness of marketing spending and by definition, the dominant firm in a two-firm market has more than one-half of the total market to begin with. Within the context of the attraction model, the presence of the third competitor will result in a decline of the dominant firm's share of the fixed market size. Hence, the nature of the optimal marketing efforts can be expressed as

$$m^* \propto \Phi(s_1)$$

where $\propto$ denotes a factor of proportionality.

The preceding rule dictates that as the new entry takes place, the dominant firm will find it necessary to raise its marketing expenditure in a fixed market. This is the essence of the Gruca-Kumar-Sudharshan [1992] solution in its simplest form, and it is demonstrated here in the context of a simple *MNL* model. Now, in a similar demonstration, one can show that in a fixed market, the smaller firm, denoted as firm 2, will find it optimal to reduce its optimal spending; and again it is similar to a central result obtained by Gruca, Kumar, and Sudharshan for the *MCI* model. This particular result for non-dominant firms, which should be compatible to their symmetry equilibrium solution, is consistent with other studies, specifically the Defender model originally published by Hauser and Shugan [1983]. We shall show shortly below that such a response from a non-dominant incumbent to new entry may no longer be optimal for an expanding market. Before doing so, we summarize our preceding analysis in the following diagram.

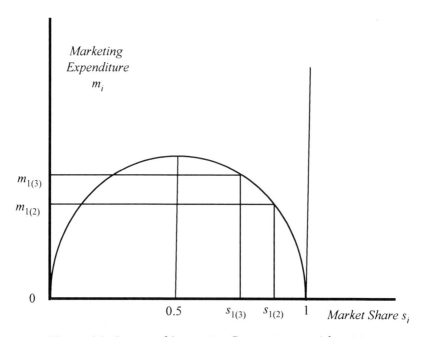

Figure 6.1 *Impact of Increasing Competition on Advertising:*
Fixed Market Size

Industry Expansion: Asymmetry
For the dominant firm, designated as 1, the optimal condition in (6.23) can be written
as follows:

$$m_1 = \frac{1}{2} D^{\theta-2} \beta A_1 [A_2 + \theta A_1]$$

which can be rewritten as:

$$m_1 = \frac{\beta}{2} D^{\theta} s_1 [s_2 + \theta s_1]$$

on the basis of which we obtain:

$$\frac{\partial m_1}{\partial \theta} = \frac{\beta}{2} s_1 [D^{\theta} s_1 + (s_2 + \theta s_1) D^{\theta} \ln D] > 0.$$

Consequently, a small perturbation around the existing equilibrium with respect
to the rate of industry expansion induces the dominant firm to increase its advertising.
A similar result can be obtained for the non-dominant firm as well.

An Alternative Attraction Specification

In the following discussion, we briefly analyze the effect of entry on asymmetric firms' marketing activities in a growing market, using the following specification for attraction by the *i*-th firm:

$$A_i = a_i e^{\log m_i} \quad ; \quad i=1,....n.$$

Assuming further linear cost of marketing and industry expansion rate of θ, upon normalizing pS_0 to be one, the condition for optimality is:

$$D^{\theta} s_i [\sum_{j \neq i} s_j + \theta s_i] = m_i$$

on the basis of which the dominant brand, again designated as d or 1 interchangeably, follows the optimal rule:

$$D^{\theta} s_{d(n)} [\sum_{j \neq i} s_j + \theta s_{d(n)}] = m_{d(n)} \tag{6.25a}$$

which would yield a generalization of a similar result reported earlier in (6.25) for the dominant firm operating within a static, fixed market size as:

$$m_{d(n)} = s_{d(n)} [\sum_{j \neq i} s_j] = s_{d(n)} [1 - s_{d(n)}]. \tag{6.25b}$$

Similarly, for the additional entrant $(n+1)$:

$$m_{d(n+1)} = s_{d(n+1)} [\sum_{j \neq i} s_j] = s_{d(n+1)} [1 - s_{d(n+1)}].$$

Once again, note that it is reasonable to assume that $s_{d(n+1)} < s_{d(n)}$, the cumulatively dominant firm which is defined to be greater than 50% will find it optimal to raise its marketing level in view of the new entry of an additional competitor. On the other hand, the non-cumulatively dominant firm will find it necessary to reduce its marketing activities.

Getting back to the possibility of market expansion, rewrite (6.25a) as

$$m_{d(n)} = D^{\theta} s_{d(n)} (1 - s_{d(n)}) + \theta D^{\theta} s_{d(n)}^2$$

from which we can calculate the effect of increasing competition and market expansion on the dominant firm's marketing efforts.

Specifically, we can then show that, for $\theta > 0$ but $d\theta = 0$; that is, there is a constant, not increasing growth in the industry total sales, the impact on the dominant firm's optimal advertising expenditure can be written as:

$$\frac{\partial m}{\partial s_{d(n)}} = D^{\theta} [1 - 2 s_{d(n)} (1 - \theta)].$$

Again, the maximum value for $m_{d(n)}$ can be found to be at

$$s_{d(n)} = \frac{1}{2(1-\theta)}.$$

This relation would serve as a basis to assess the impact of new entry on the dominant firm's marketing activity given that the industry sales is expanding at a constant rate, that is $\theta > 0$ but $d\theta = 0$. Since it continues to follow that $s_{d(n+1)} < s_{d(n)}$, it can be seen that as the new entrant gets in the market, the sufficiently dominant firm would raise its marketing spending; otherwise it would reduce its advertising efforts. The "sufficiently" dominant firm is now defined to be more than 50%. More specifically, m would go up (down) if

$$s_{d(n)} > (<) \frac{1}{2(1-\theta)}.$$

The combined effect of both new entry and expansion of the industry can be generally seen as in the following expression

$$dm_i = [>0]d\theta + \frac{\partial m_i}{\partial s_i}\frac{\partial s_i}{\partial n}dn$$

where the term in the first square bracket has been demonstrated to be positive and so denoted and we have just shown that the sign in the second square bracket depends on the particular brand's market share.

Except for the case where one particular firm is sufficiently dominant, the two effects summarized in the preceding expression typically involve two opposing forces. Clearly, a most interesting implication of these effects is the real possibility that the incumbents, including dominant as well as non-dominant firms will find it optimal to increase their marketing activities in view of new entry to the market. This represents a much stronger result than those currently available in the literature where this possibility would only occur in the case of a cumulatively dominant firm.

We will find the following diagram useful to capture these effects.

Joint Price-Advertising

Once again, in line with our effort to provide as much as possible interactive decisions among the firm's marketing mix, let us consider the following specification for attraction in which $\theta = 0$

$$A_i = a_i e^{-p_i + \log m_i}; \quad i = 1,2.$$

Then upon maximizing profit for each firm, the optimal conditions are:

$$p_i s_j = 1 \quad ; \quad p_i s_i s_j = m_i$$

which implies the solution to be of the following form:

$$p_i = \frac{1}{s_j} \quad ; \quad m_i = s_i.$$

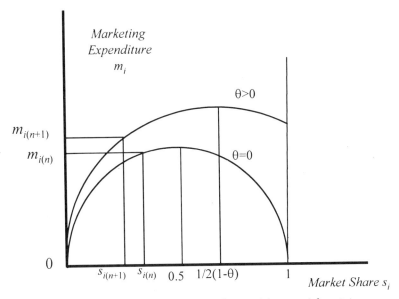

Figure 6.2 *Impact of Increasing Competition on Advertising:*
Market Expansion

Note again that the preceding expressions do not represent closed-form solutions; however, they are in implicit forms which would still permit us to draw useful implications.

It can be easily verified that the market share solution of $s_i = a_i/(\Sigma_i \, a_i)$ would not be possible unless they are symmetric, a case which we wish to rule out. We present below a simple illustration of how to specifically obtain the value of m and p for a simple and workable scenario. Assume that the model is

$$A_i = a_i e^{-p_i + m_i}; \quad i = 1, 2$$

and the nonlinear marketing costs are $(\frac{1}{2})m_i^2$.

It can be shown that the solutions are identical to those reported in the above model. Now our objective is to find a pair of the advertising effectiveness coefficients so that a particular market share outcome is equilibrium with its consistent levels of advertising and prices. Normalizing $a_2 = 1$. What would be the value of a_1 so that

$$s_1 = \frac{A_1}{D} = \frac{a_1 \exp\{[-1/(1-s_1)] + s_1\}}{a_1 \exp\{[-1/(1-s_1)] + s_1\} + \exp[-(1/s_1) + (1-s_1)]}?$$

Routine calculation yields the result to be:

$$a_1 = [\frac{s_1}{s_2}] \exp[\frac{(s_1 - s_2)(1 - s_1 s_2)}{s_1 s_2}].$$

So, in order to attain a market share of $s_1 = .6$ (hence $s_2 = .4$), a_1 must be approximately 2.826; that is, a firm's marketing activities should be almost three times as effective in its marketing activities to gain three fifths of the market.

5 DIFFUSIONS MODELS UNDER UNCERTAINTY

This section reports the results obtained by Tapiero and others in recent years to address the impact of stochasticity and uncertainty on the product diffusion process. We will follow the same approach set out at the beginning of the book by paying particular attention to the economic implications as well as the interpretations of the more formal mathematical and statistical results in view of their relevance to managerial and strategic decision process facing a manager. Thus we will not pay too much attention to some of the formal, theoretical development in what follows.

As we remark earlier, we will not address the important issue of the probabilistic response of the consumers, a subject which is central to a major branch of research in marketing related to the consumer's behavior in general and that under uncertainty in particular. However, we should draw the reader's attention to some of the major surveys in the recent years by Roberts and Lilien, and Corfman and Gupta, both in the Eliashberg and Lilien volume [1993], and relevant chapters in the Lilien, Kotler, and Moorthy text [1992]. Within the scope of this study we will focus more on the firm's decision process instead.

5.1 The Bass Diffusion Process: Deterministics

The Basic Specification
Let us define S to be the fixed potential number of ultimate adopters, which is related to market size potential when appropriately interpreted; f_t to be the density function of time to adoption; and consequently F_t to be the cumulative fraction of adopters at time t. Then at time t, the cumulative number of adopters, denoted as Q_t, will be $Q_t = F_t.S$. The basic equation which describes the Bass [1969] diffusion process is written as:

$$\frac{dQ_t}{dt} \equiv q_{t+1} = (S - Q_t)[a + b^*(\frac{Q_t}{S})] \tag{6.26}$$

where the coefficients a and b^* represent, respectively, the innovation and imitation effects and where we have used the superscript * in b^* and the subscript $(t+1)$ in q_{t+1} for ease of later reference.

Since motivations, descriptions as well as mathematical characterizations and empirical implications of the preceding diffusion process are reasonably well-known and available in several surveys, we will not detail them here. We should, however, record an empirical note that surveys of an extensive literature on the Bass model show an average estimate of $a=.03$ and $b*=.38$ (Sultan, Farley, and Lehmann [1990]). We further note that for a fixed S, the preceding relation can be expressed in terms of the cumulative fraction of adopter F_t as follows:

$$\frac{dF_t}{dt} = (1-F_t)[a+b*F_t].$$

(6.27)

This specification can be written in the following form:

$$\frac{f_t}{1-F_t} = a+b*F_t$$

(6.28)

which is a hazard function, describing the conditional probability of an adoption at time t.

Some Extensions

Other extensions of the preceding model have been summarized in the Mahajan-Muller-Bass [1993] paper as well as elaborated in Mahajan, Muller, and Bass [1995] and Bass, Krishnan, and Jain [1994]. Among the most interesting extension, for our purposes here is the fact that the potential market is not static, rather it is a function of other marketing variables.

Normative implications for the preceding model with its extensions are also summarized in the Mahajan-Muller-Bass [1993] survey; involving isolated effect of pricing, advertising as well as marketing mix within both the monopolistic framework and oligopolistic framework. In general, with the assumed discount rate of r, the objective of the firm is written as:

$$\int \Pi(Q_t, x_t) e^{-rt} dt$$

(6.29)

where x_t denotes the decision variables such as price, advertising, etc. and the firm's dynamic equation is as in (6.26) or some other versions which can written in general as:

$$\frac{dQ_t}{dt} = f(Q_t, x_t).$$

It should be noted that under the assumption that the total market size is fixed at S, eq. (6.26) can be rewritten in the following form which has been used in several studies:

$$q_{t+1} = (S-Q_t)[a+bQ_t]$$

where $b \equiv b*/S$ to establish the connection with the original model.

On the other hand, if one is assuming that the total market potential is a variable function of price as in Mahajan Peterson [1978] and Kalish [1983] as well as Horsky [1990], the preceding equation is modified to be

$$q_{t+1} = [S(p) - Q_t][a + bQ_t].$$

Alternatively, in assuming a multiplicative effect of price on the probability of adoption as in Robinson-Lakhani [1975], the expression becomes:

$$q_{t+1} = (S - Q_t)[a + bQ_t]e^{-vp_t}. \tag{6.30}$$

We record here a number of results of interest: For the Robinson Lakhani model, the total effect being decomposed into two separate effects, one is the saturation effect and the other the word-of-mouth or diffusion effect. A typical optimal price path involves raising the product's price from an initially relatively lower level to stimulate the word-of-mouth effect for market *penetration* and eventually the firm will get to certain demand-saturation point in the time horizon when it begins to lower its price in the same fashion of the price *skimming* practice in order to maximize the discounted profits. It is of interest to note that similar results are found for the Horsky and the Mahajan Peterson model where market potential is a function of price.

5.2 Some Stochastic Diffusion Models

In this sub-section we report a number of papers dealing with stochastic versions of the Bass or Bass-based diffusion models. We have already discussed in Chapter 2 the dynamic, optimal pricing for firms facing stochastic demand function, using optimal control approach. In this sub-section, we will focus on studies which are, in the Eliashberg Chatterjee [1985] classification scheme of stochasticity, structurally stochastic. The parameter uncertainty issues will be discussed in Chapter 9. The results obtained by Tapiero [1990] will be described first, followed by a paper by Monahan [1984], both of whom characterize diffusion as stochastic birth processes. We then present another study by Tapiero [1982] in which the deterministic multi-stage model of Dodson and Muller [1978] is extended into a stochastic version under the assumption that the diffusion follows a birth-and-death process.

Diffusion as a Birth Process
In his book, Tapiero [1990] assumes that the number of new adopters of a product is proportional to innovation and imitation effects, motivated by the Bass diffusion model, according to the following specification

$$\Delta Q = (S - Q)(a + bQ)\Delta t \; ; \; Q(0) = 0 \; ; \; Q = 0, 1, 2 \ldots S \tag{6.31}$$

where a and b capture the innovation and imitation effects; S represents, as before, the fixed market potential; Q represents the cumulative number of adopters at time t; and the growth rate of the cumulative adopters is defined by $\Delta Q = Q(t+1) - Q(t)$.

The number of new adopter as specified in the preceding equation can be interpreted as being generated by a pure birth process $\{Q, t > 0\}$ with birth growth parameter

$$\lambda(Q, t) = (S - Q)(a + bQ)$$

which bears a strong resemblance to the Bass deterministic diffusion process discussed earlier.

The firm's profit function in the small time interval of dt is given as:

$$\Pi dt = (p - c)dQ - mdt \qquad (6.32)$$

where as customary we define m to represents the expenditure of a particular marketing activity, typically advertising; and where we assume c to be the constant marginal cost. It should be noted that dQ is the limit of ΔQ as Δt approaches zero.

The firm's maximization problem can then be defined as:

$$\text{Max. } V = E\left[\int_0^\tau e^{-rt} \, \Pi dt\right]$$

subject to the profit function in (6.32).

Assuming existence of an interior solution, Tapiero indicates that for a given fixed product price p and that $a = \alpha + \ln m$, the first-order condition for an optimal marketing effort is given by:

$$m = Q(S - Q)\{[V(Q + 1) - V(Q)] + (p - c)\}.$$

A numerical solution for optimal advertising expenditure can subsequently be obtained on the basis of the following recursive relations:

$$Q = S - 1; \quad V(Q - 1) = (p - c) - \frac{e^{-(\alpha + r)/(Q - 1)}}{Q - 1}$$

with the terminal condition $Q = S$; $V(Q) = 0$.

It follows from the preceding solution that the firm's optimal promotional activities are characterized as a declining function of the remaining sales potential. This particular result parallels its deterministic counterpart in dynamic pricing models using the Bass diffusion process in generating sales (see the 1993 survey by Mahajan, Muller and Bass, for example).

On the other hand, for the stochastic extension of the Robinson Lakhani model where we concentrate only on the pricing decision, the number of new adopter can be specified as

$$\Delta Q = (S - Q)e^{-vp}(a + bQ)\Delta t$$

which represents a stochastic version of eq. (6.30) above.

If one concentrates on the pricing decision and thus assumes that $m = 0$, the optimal price was shown by Tapiero to follow

$$rV(Q) = e^{-vp(Q)}[S-Q][a+bQ]$$

which yields an approximation for a numerical solution of the optimal price function of the form:

$$p(Q) = [1 - \frac{rV(Q)}{(S-Q)(a+bQ)}]^{\frac{1}{\varepsilon}}$$

on the basis of which the firm's optimal price path can be characterized and analyzed.

To account for the effect of advertising in the diffusion process under the assumption of sales uncertainty, Monahan [1984] specifies that total sales in any period depends additively on both advertising and word of mouth as in the standard literature, except that the effects are modeled as a continuous Markov decision chain, then transformed into a discrete-time version. To this end, consider a firm which is advertising at the rate m and has currently i customers, the rate at which customers are acquired is:

$$\lambda(i,m) = g(m)[S-i+1] + \omega(i)$$

$$= 0 \qquad i \geq S+1$$

$$\text{where} \quad \omega(i) = (S-i+1)(a+bi)$$

for the special case of linear word of mouth function.

Defining the objective function, denoted as $V_\tau(i)$, to represent the optimal expected value when there are i customers and τ periods remaining, the solution in terms of the recursive dynamic programming algorithm is written as:

$$(\Lambda+r)V_\tau(i) = \text{Max.} \ \{\Pi(i,m) + [V_{\tau-1}(i+1) - V_{\tau-1}(i)]\lambda(i,m) + \Lambda V_{\tau-1}(i)\} \qquad (6.33)$$

where $\Pi(i,m)$ represents profits for the firm which has i customers and promotes at rate m; r is the discount rate, $\lambda(i,m)$ as defined above, is the rate at which customers are acquired and Λ is a new, constant rate chosen so that $\Lambda \geq 2\lambda(i,m)$; the process above is a result of the uniformization which transform an originally continuous-time formulation to an equivalent discrete-time counterpart.

On the basis of the solution algorithm in (6.33), and further assumptions regarding the behavior of the advertising function and the profit functions (concavity in the usual sense of positive and diminishing returns of marketing expenditures), and in addition, for our present purposes here, for the case where the word of mouth effect is described as $\omega(i) = (S_0 - i+1)bi$; then Monahan shows that the optimal marketing expenditure with τ periods remaining would be non-increasing as the number of customers increases as the firm has gained at least half of the potential market.

The Stochastic Multistage Diffusion Model

The major feature of Tapiero's model [1982] is to analyze the stochastic version of the Dodson-Muller paper which represents an extension of the Bass model on the basic assumption that the consumer/producer interactions involve different stages. Thus potential consumers basically proceed from being unaware (state 1); then possibly aware (state 2); then possibly purchasing the product (state 3). The probability that one consumer switches from a particular state i (i=1,2,3) to a state j (j=1,2,3) during a small time interval Δt is denoted as π_{ij}. Thus, to allow for a growth in the potential consumers pool, the probability π_{11} is positive; to model the possible effect of "forgetfulness", the probability π_{21} is some positive; to account for the possible effect of word-of-mouth, the probability π_{23} is positive; and to effectively model the possibility of repeat purchase, the probability π_{32} is also positive. The model, in its full generality becomes virtually impossible to interpret. So, in order for us to see a little more clearly the consequence of the stochastic nature of the model structure, it would be useful to simplify the model by assuming that the market size is fixed, that only advertising has an impact on the consumer's probability to be aware of the product (no word-of-mouth effects), that the goods under questions are infinitely durable. These are the major assumptions in the Dodson-Muller model. For our current purposes, let us consider the normative implications for the firm. Using a standard and tractable formulation regarding the firm's risk-taking attitude in the tradition of the Capital Asset Pricing Model in finance, the firm's objective can be written as:

$$V = \int e^{-rt}[E(\Pi) - \lambda \beta \sigma_\Pi] dt$$

where E denotes as usual the expectation operator, λ the market price of risk, and β the correlation coefficient relating the firm's profits to the market's returns.

The firm's profits are then defined as:

$$\Pi = (p-c)Q - m$$

where c is the constant average cost, excluding advertising costs and m represents the firm's marketing activities, Q the firm's (accumulated) sales which is of course a random variable with mean μ_Q and variance σ_Q^2.

The preceding two equations yield:

$$V = \int e^{-rt}\{(p-c)[\mu_Q - \lambda \beta \sigma_Q] - m\} dt.$$

For our present purpose it suffices to note that Tapiero shows that both the mean value of sales $E(Q)$ and its variances are ultimately functions of the variance-covariances of the number of consumers in three states 1, 2, and 3. Consequently, even for a risk-neutral firm, i.e., λ=0, the optimal values for the firm's advertising expenditures will be different under a stochastic environment in comparison to its deterministic counterpart due to the non-zero values of the variance-covariance terms. One can certainly develop the analysis further to specify conditions under which a particular directional impact of uncertainty on the firm's advertising decisions can be established. These will be involving various specifications of the variance-covariance structure which would be hard to specify a priori.

To relate to the deterministic version of Dodson-Muller, note that in view of the "multistage" diffusion model, it would be necessary to identify the total **P**opulation, denoted as P_t, to represent the potential market at large. Thus, the potential market size we defined earlier is modified to be

$$P_t = S_t + U_t$$

where U_t represents the number of **U**naware customers.

We thus decompose the preceding expression as:

$$P_t = U_t + (S_t - Q_t) + Q_t$$

which upon defining $S_t - Q_t \equiv W_t$ to denote the number of a**W**are customers, can be written as:

$$P_t = U_t + W_t + Q_t$$

which upon using the assumption that the population is fixed, i.e., $dP_t/dt = 0$, enables us to describe the system by the following two equations:

$$\frac{dQ_t}{dt} = a(S_t - Q_t) = aW_t$$

which is a special form of the Bass model and

$$\frac{dS_t}{dt} = (a' + b'S_t)(P_t - S_t) = (a' + b'S_t)U_t$$

which is again another form of the Bass diffusion model.

Let us now rewrite Tapiero's stochastic model as follows. The basic assumptions are:

$$\pi_{12}(t) = (a'U_t + b'S_t U_t)\Delta t$$

which represents the probability that one customer switches from being unaware (state 1) to being aware (state 2).

On the other hand, the probability that one customer switches from being simply aware (state 2) to being a purchaser (state 3) is postulated as:

$$\pi_{23}(t) = (aW_t)\Delta t.$$

Specifying the evolutions of the means and the variance-covariance for U_t, $(S_t - Q_t)$ and Q_t can then be done; noting that one would need to look only at two equations since the total population is assumed fixed.

To clearly see the possible impact of uncertainty, it is recorded here the time paths of the means, denoted by μ's, of the random variables W_t and Q_t, again noting that it is redundant to report that for U_t for a fixed population P_t. They are:

$$\frac{d\mu_W}{dt} = a'\mu_U + b'\mu_U(\mu_W + \mu_Q) - a\mu_W + b'(\sigma_{UW} + \sigma_{UQ})$$

$$\text{and} \quad \frac{d\mu_Q}{dt} = a\mu_W$$

where we also denote the relevant covariance terms by σ_{ij}.

Note that the Dodson-Muller deterministic results are simply:

$$\frac{dW}{dt} = a'U + b'U(W + Q) - aW$$

$$\text{and} \quad \frac{dQ}{dt} = aW$$

as seen in Mahajan and Peterson's exposition [1985] of the Dodson-Muller model.

As mentioned previously, the mean value of sales will ultimately depend on the covariance terms whose values do not disappear even when we are dealing with risk-neutral firms.

Other Diffusion Models under Uncertainty

One basic premise behind the original Bass diffusion model and its numerous extensions is that the buying population is homogeneous in its valuation of the product. To certain extent, there have been efforts in the literature to introduce elements of stochasticity to the Bass model by assuming heterogeneity in the buying population. For instance, Jeuland's extension [1981] of the Bass model has the form:

$$\frac{dF_t(\theta)}{dt} = (1 - F_t(\theta))[\theta + k\theta F_t(\theta)]$$

where the parameter θ characterizes an individual, assumed to follow a gamma distribution function, and k denotes a constant parameter.

As noted in Eliashberg and Chatterjee [1985], while the preceding process is stochastic since θ is a random variable, the resulting aggregate model for the population as a whole is deterministic.

Another model which introduces stochastic elements into the Bass model is due to Kalish [1985] who, on the basis of Nelson's [1970] classification of information types, decomposes the diffusion process into two separate steps, one is related to *awareness* and the other is the *adoption* process itself. The model characterizes certain features involving the diffusion of information and subsequently, elements of uncertainty regarding the product's experience attributes are considered. The awareness (information) equation is specified as follows:

$$\frac{d\iota_t}{dt} = (1 - \iota_t)[g(m_t) + \gamma\iota_t + \gamma'(\frac{Q_t}{S_0})]$$

which implies that the rate of awareness depends positively partly on the extent in which consumers are not aware of the product, and partly on the conditional likelihood of becoming aware; the latter being affected both by marketing activities and by word of mouth effects through the transmitters.

On the other hand, the market potential is generated by integrating all individuals, each is characterized by an index v which follows a known cumulative distribution function $F(v)$, who value the product at least at p. That is:

$$S(p_t)=S_0\int_{v\geq p_t}F(v)dv.$$

An interesting device to introduce uncertainty is to allow for a risk-related adjustment such that the larger the number of adopters the less would be the extent of product uncertainty; consequently, the market potential in the preceding equation is rewritten explicitly as

$$S(p_t)=S_0\int_{vu_t\geq p_t}F(v)dv=S(\frac{p_t}{u_t})$$

where u_t represents certain price "discount" due to product uncertainty, which is assumed to be increasing in the ratio of adopters (q_t/S_0).

The aggregate adoption equation is then assumed to be:

$$q_{t+1}=k(\iota_t S_t-Q_t)$$

where it is assumed that k represents a constant coefficient, that sales levels and the number of adopters coincide, and ι_t and S_t are generated in the previous equations.

Normative analysis can then be carried out by assuming profit maximization for a monopolist. Consequently, the results regarding the impact of product uncertainty can be inferred. Further, optimal paths for the monopolist's pricing and marketing activities can also be characterized. We record here some of the main theoretical results: (*i*) For both durables and repeat-purchase products, optimal advertising expenditure is typically declining over time; (*ii*) For durable goods, optimal price is typically decreasing over time. However, if the effect of initial adopters in generating awareness and/or reducing product uncertainty is sufficiently high, then the optimal price path is parallel to that characterized for the standard deterministic dynamic pricing case, i.e., price should be first increasing then declining, as we summarized earlier in the last paragraph of Sub-section 5.1.

More recent efforts in addressing the implications of stochasticity on the basis of the Bass diffusion process include studies by Jain and Raman [1992] and Raman and Chatterjee [1995].

We conclude the discussion in this section by presenting some basic features of a model due to Boker [1987] who uses a counting process approach to address the stochastic diffusion issue. Unlike Tapiero [1982] in which a Markov process approach is used to examine the implications of elements of stochasticity in certain diffusion models, in particular the Dodson-Muller model which involves a three-stage characterization of the diffusion process: uninformed, informed, and purchaser, Boker applies the statistical techniques of counting process which appear to readily enable one to perform estimation and simulation exercises. The key notion here is the *intensity* function, which, in the spirit of the Bass diffusion model, can be defined as:

$$\lambda_t = \frac{f_t}{(1-F_t)}(S_t - Q_{t-})$$
(6.34)

which simply states that the total intensity is the product of the conditional likelihood for a potential customer to purchase a unit of good at time t, that is $[f_t/(1-F_t)]$ or the "hazard function", and the (random) number of all potential customers who have not made the purchase, i.e., $(S_t - Q_{t-})$ where we maintain Boker's notation that Q_{t-} denotes the number of customers prior to but not including t.

Thus, intuitively, the expression in (6.34) is identical to the Bass formulation of the diffusion process, appropriately adjusted for a linear hazard function involving the coefficients a and b we defined earlier. In order to offer an interpretation for a contrast between the deterministic model and the stochastic model, an interpretation which unfortunately could be made more clearly by Boker, let us write down a fundamental result which can be written as:

$$Q_t = \int \lambda_\tau d\tau + \mu_t$$

where μ_t stands for a zero mean square integrable martingale.

One way to look at the preceding expression is that the total sales at t, Q_t, consists of a "deterministic" part, represented by the integrated intensity function and the stochastic part, represented by the random noise characterized by the martingale μ_t. To get a sense of the estimation technique involved, let us examine the standard Bass model.

$$\frac{dQ_t}{dt} = (S-Q_t)[a+bQ_t].$$

It has been shown then that the maximum likelihood estimators for the unknown but constant parameters a and b are

$$\hat{a} = \frac{Q(T)\sum i(\tau_{i+1}-\tau_i)-[\sum i(S-i)(\tau_{i+1}-\tau_i)]\sum[1/(S-i)]}{[\sum(S-i)(\tau_{i+1}-\tau_i)][(\sum i(\tau_{i+1}-\tau_i)]-T\sum i(S-i)(\tau_{i+1}-\tau_i)}$$

and $\hat{b} = \dfrac{[\sum(S-i)(\tau_{i+1}-\tau_i)]\{\sum[1/(S-i)]\}-TQ(T)}{[\sum(S-i)(\tau_{i+1}-\tau_i)][(\sum i(\tau_{i+1}-\tau_i)]-T\sum i(S-i)(\tau_{i+1}-\tau_i)}.$

As any explicit expressions of statistical estimators, the preceding formulae look more complicated than they are actually calculated. They can be obtained on the basis of simple observations.

6 CONCLUDING REMARKS

This chapter reflects our attempt to present some specific contexts within which the firm's marketing mix components can potentially interact. We have addressed in this chapter the two particular contexts in which research in marketing has made substantial advances over the year for deterministic models. The literature on market shares has been summarized in the book by Cooper and Nakanishi [1988] and in the updated survey by Cooper [1993]. We have noted that while much of the equilibrium analysis focuses on the *MCI* version, the *MNL* version seems to escape from equilibrium analysis. We report a number of results of some of our on-going research effort along this line. We also in this framework begin to develop certain implications for random sales using the commonly familiar tools developed in the literature and illustrated in several models in the present work. While we have interpreted the *MNL* within the uncertainty framework because of its uniquely close relation with the random utility models, it should be more satisfactorily analyzed with explicit random sales response models. This represents an interesting area to do additional work. As mentioned, we have made a preliminary approach at the *MCI* model and it seems the results should be readily obtainable.

Regarding the diffusion models, there exists a huge literature on the Bass diffusion process and its various extensions. We have presented certain results by Tapiero and others who provide stochastic extensions to some of these models in this literature. We stated earlier that stochasticity should be an integral part of a satisfactory treatment for diffusion processes due to their intrinsic unpredictability and since this subject has not been fully developed, it should offer an important topic for further research as well.

REFERENCES

BASS, Frank M., 1969, "A New Product Growth Model for Consumer Durables," *Management Science*, Vol. 15, pp. 215-227.

BASS, Frank M., Trichy V. KRISNAN, and Dipak C. JAIN, 1994, "Why the Bass Model Fits Without Decision Variables," *Marketing Science*, Vol. 13, pp. 203-223.

BASUROY, Suman, and Dung NGUYEN, 1996, "Multinomial Logit Market Share Models: Equilibrium Characteristics and Strategic Implications," *manuscript*.

BOKER, Fred, 1987, "A Stochastic First Purchase Diffusion Model: A Counting Process Approach," *Journal of Marketing Research*, Vol. 24, pp. 64-73.

COOPER, Lee G., 1993, "Market Share Analysis," in J. ELIASHBERG, and G. LILIEN (eds.), *Marketing*, Handbooks in Operations Research and Management Science, Vol. 5, pp. 259-314, Elsevier Science Publishers, Amsterdam, The Netherlands.

COOPER, Lee G., and Masso NAKANISHI, 1988, *Market Share Analysis: Evaluating Competitive Effectiveness*, Kluwer Academic Publishers, Boston.

CORFMAN, Kim P., and Sunil GUPTA, 1993, "Mathematical Models of Group Choice and Negotiations," in J. ELIASHBERG, and G. LILIEN (eds.), *Marketing*, Handbooks in Operations Research and Management Science, Vol. 5, pp. 83-142, Elsevier Science Publishers, Amsterdam, The Netherlands.

DODSON, J. A., and Eitan MULLER, 1978, "Models of New Product Diffusion through Advertising and Word-of-Mouth," *Management Science*, Vol. 24, pp. 1568-1578.

ELIASHBERG, Jehoshua, and Rabikar CHATTERJEE, 1985, "Stochastic Issues in Innovation Diffusion Models," in *Models for Innovation Diffusion*, Vijay MAHAJAN and R. A. PETERSON (eds.), Sage, California, pp. 151-199.

ELIASHBERG, Jehoshua, and Gary L. LILIEN (eds.), 1993, *Marketing*, Handbooks in Operations Research and Management Science, Vol. 5, Elsevier Science Publishers, Amsterdam, The Netherlands.

GRUCA, Thomas S., K. Ravi KUMAR, and D. SUDHARSHAN, 1992, "An Equilibrium Analysis of Defensive Response to Entry Using a Coupled Response Function Model," *Marketing Science*, Vol. 11, No. 4, pp. 348-358.

HAUSER, John R., and Steven M. SHUGAN, 1983, "Defensive Marketing Strategies," *Marketing Science*, Vol. 2, 319-360.

HORSKY, Dan, 1990, "A Diffusion Model Incorporating Product Benefits, Price, Income and Information," *Marketing Science*, Vol. 9, pp. 342-365.

JAIN, Dipak C., and Kalyan RAMAN, 1992, "A Stochastic Generalization of the Bass Model," *Journal of Scientific and Industrial Research*, pp. 216-228.

JEULAND, Abel P., 1981, "Parsimonious Models of Diffusion of Innovation: Part A, Derivations and Comparisons," *manuscript*, University of Chicago.

KALISH, Shlomo, 1983, "Monopolist Pricing With Dynamic Demand and Production Cost," *Marketing Science*, Vol. 2 , pp. 135-159.

KALISH, Shlomo, 1985, "A New Product Adoption Model With Price, Advertising and Uncertainty," *Management Science*, Vol. 31, No. 12, pp. 1569-1585.

LILIEN, Gary L., Philip KOTLER, and K. Sridhar MOORTHY, 1992, *Marketing Models*, Prentice-Hall, Englewood Cliffs, NJ.

MADDALA, G. S., 1983, *Limited-Dependent and Qualitative Variables in Econometrics*, New York: Cambridge University Press.

MAHAJAN, Vijay, Eitan MULLER, and Frank M. BASS, 1993, "New-Product Diffusion Models," in Jehoshua ELIASHBERG, and Gary L. LILIEN (eds.), *Marketing*, Handbooks in Operations Research and Management Science, Vol. 5, pp. 349-408, Elsevier Science Publishers, Amsterdam, The Netherlands.

MAHAJAN, Vijay, Eitan MULLER, and Frank M. BASS, 1995, "Diffusion of New Products: Empirical Generalizations and Managerial Uses," *Marketing Science*, Vol. 14, pp. G79-G88.

MAHAJAN, Vijay, and R. A. PETERSON, 1978, "Innovation Diffusion in a Dynamic Potential Adopter Population," *Management Science*, Vol. 24, pp. 1589-1597.

MAHAJAN, Vijay, and R. A. PETERSON (eds.), 1985, *Models for Innovation Diffusions*, Sage, California.

McFADDEN, D., 1974," Conditional Logit Analysis of Qualitative Choice Behavior," in P. Zarembka (ed.), *Frontiers in Econometrics*, Academic Press, NY.

MONAHAN, G. E., 1984, "A Pure Birth Model of Optimal Advertising With Word-Of-Mouth," *Marketing Science*, Vol. 3, No. 2, pp. 169-178.

MONAHAN, G. E., 1987, "The Structure of Equilibria In Market Share Attraction Models," *Management Science*, Vol. 33, No. 2, pp. 228-243.

NELSON, P., 1970, "Information and Consumer Behavior," *Journal of Political Economy*, Vol. 78, pp. 311-329.

PEKELMAN, D., and E. TSE, 1980, "Experimentation and Budgeting in Advertising: An Adaptive Control Approach," *Operations Research*, Vol. 28, No. 2, pp. 321-347.

RAMAN, Kalyan, and Rabikar CHATTERJEE, 1995, "Optimal Monopolist Pricing Under Demand Uncertainty in Dynamic Markets," *Management Science*, Vol. 41, No. 1, pp. 144-162.

ROBERTS, John H., and Gary L. LILIEN, 1993, "Explanatory and Predictive Models of Consumer Behavior," in Jehoshua ELIASHBERG, and Gary L. LILIEN (eds.), *Marketing*, Handbooks in Operations Research and Management Science, Vol. 5, pp. 27-82, Elsevier Science Publishers, Amsterdam, The Netherlands.

ROBINSON, Bruce, and Chet LAKHANI, 1975, "Dynamic Price Models For New-Product Planning," *Management Science*, Vol. 21, No. 10, pp. 1113-1122.

SULTAN, F., John U. FARLEY, and Donald R. LEHMANN, 1990, "Meta-Analysis of Applications of Diffusion Models," *Journal of Marketing Research*, Vol. 27, pp. 70-77.

TAPIERO, Charles S., 1982, "Stochastic Diffusion Models With Advertising and Word-of-Mouth Effects," *European Journal of Operational Research*, No. 12, pp. 348-356.

TAPIERO, Charles S., 1990, *Applied Stochastic Models and Control in Management*, 2nd impression, Elsevier Science Publishers, The Netherlands.

THURSTONE, L. L., 1927, "A Law of Comparative Judgement," *Psychological Review*, Vol. 34, pp. 273-286.

YELLOTT, John I. Jr., 1977, "The relationship between Luce's Choice Axiom, Thurstone's Theory of Comparative Judgement, and the Double Exponential Distribution," *Journal of Mathematical Psychology*, Vol. 15, pp.109-144.

7

MARKETING, INVENTORY AND PRODUCTION DECISIONS

1 OVERVIEW

This chapter explores aspects of the firm's production and inventory activities, with particular emphasis on possible interactions with its marketing efforts within a common framework. We begin by focusing on the short-run analysis of the case of perishable goods where no inventory is possible, hence the problem is purely that of production. While the marketing literature mainly concentrates on marketing mix variables such as pricing, advertising, promotion, and product quality, an important example involves a quantity decision, namely, the Federal marketing orders for agricultural products. To gain insights into this problem with potential applications in public policy, we will devote a section on this issue to see how interactions between quality and quantity control can be analyzed in a simple framework. We then follow with the case of storable goods where inventory plays a very significant role. This is where the important literature on inventory has been and continues to develop in operations research and production management. There, the deterministic models will be presented first and stochastic extensions will then be analyzed. We will pay attention to the integration of the firm's inventory/production with its pricing decisions. Next, we examine the firm's production decisions under random demand both for the single-product case and the multiple-product case. Finally, we consider long-run behavior of the firm, focusing less on inventory but rather on investment which builds the firm's capital stocks to be used in its production processes. Once again, the firm's short-run marketing decisions such as pricing will be considered jointly with investment to maximize its expected discounted economic profits.

We should mention that this chapter is motivated partly by a recent survey by Eliashberg and Steinberg [1993] on the marketing-production side and that by Porteus [1990] on stochastic inventory theories. We believe that efforts to integrate the multi-disciplinary nature of traditionally distinct fields such as economics, production, marketing, and finance represent a very promising and important research agenda in the coming years.

2 PRODUCT QUALITY AND FEDERAL MARKETING ORDERS

Agricultural marketing orders regulating grade and size apply to many noncitrus fruits and vegetables sold on the fresh market. The orders serve to divert from the market produce not meeting established standards which might apply to size and sugar content. The rationale underlying the minimum quality standard concept is to help industry groups "create buyer confidence in (product) quality," with the ultimate intent of increasing returns to farmers (USDA Farmers' Cooperative Service [1975]). Perhaps the first formal treatment of this subject was given in an insightful paper written by Price [1967], followed by an empirical paper published by Shafer [1968], dealing with the effect of a marketing order on winter carrot prices. Both theoretical and empirical implications of the impact of federal marketing orders for fruits and vegetables were further examined in a series of papers by Jesse [1979, 1981] and Jesse and Johnson [1981]. Our analysis is based on Nguyen and Vo [1985].

Price's argument can be summarized as follows. Consider a price elastic demand function for a particular agricultural product, the quality of which varies over a certain range such as different fruit sizes. If a portion of the harvest which contains the lowest quality produce is discarded, then an immediate effect is a reduction in supply, which results in a higher price according to the demand schedule originally facing the industry under consideration. This increase in price is called the *quantity price increase*. Because in his paper Price assumed (the relevant portion of) the demand function to be elastic, such a price increase would give rise to a decline in total producer receipts. However, as Price argued, because the low quality portion of the total harvest is discarded, the demand function for the product (of a relatively higher quality) is shifted upward. Hence, the actual unit price increase might be sufficiently high to make the resulting total receipts for producers higher than the original total receipts, had no discarding taken place. If this is the case, then it is better for producers to discard some optimally chosen portion of the harvest, i.e., an optimal rate of culling. The price increase as a result of a shift in the demand schedule is called the *quality price increase*.

The analysis which follows is, first of all, motivated by noting that Price's analysis as well as subsequent studies assume that the demand function is linear. The assumption of linear demand is an overly restrictive one; for example, welfare implications derived in Jesse's 1979 paper crucially depend on this linearity assumption. Second, many of Price's results were obtained on the basis of some hypothetical numerical values of the model's parameters. Thus, for instance, the role of the price elasticity of demand was not formally discussed. Third, even though the minimum quality issue was analyzed implicitly, its relationship to the industry's culling decisions was not fully demonstrated.

Each of the preceding observations will be treated here. We will first analyze the theoretical model and then derive conditions for optimal culling, optimal minimum quality for the industry.

2.1 The Analysis

Consider an inverse demand function for a particular agricultural product in the following form:

$$p = g(Q) \tag{7.1}$$

where p is unit price, Q the quantity demanded, and

$$g'(Q) = \frac{\partial g}{\partial Q} < 0, \text{ and } g''(Q) = \frac{\partial^2 g}{\partial Q^2} \gtrless 0. \tag{7.2}$$

We have used Q instead our customary notation of q for quantity in order to avoid some possible confusion later. Let us suppose that the original market equilibrium is obtained simply by the industry's total supply of "raw" quantity (i.e., without any consideration of quality of the produce). We denote the equilibrium quantity and price as Q_1 and p_1, respectively. It should be noted here that our specification of a single inverse demand function in (7.1) assumes away the rather complex nature of possible interrelations among different demand functions for different quality groupings. Adopting the single demand specification makes the problem more tractable for our current purposes.

Assume now that the industry considers discarding a portion κ consisting of the produce with the lowest quality from the total harvest. If we denote Q_2 as the new level of the industry's quantity supplied (with a better quality), it then follows by definition that

$$Q_2 = Q_1(1 - \kappa) \tag{7.3}$$

where κ is called the culling rate.

With this new level of Q_2, the corresponding price, according to (7.1), would be $p_2 = g(Q_2)$ and the resulting price increase is $\Delta p_n = p_2 - p_1$ if the quality improvement does not affect the demand function. The change Δp_n thus defines the quantity price increase. However, it is reasonable to assume that as quality of the product increases, the demand function is shifted upward. The next subsection will discuss the shifted demand function. In the meantime, we are interested in deriving what Price calls the break-even quality price change. For a particular level of Q_2, there exists a price p_3 such that the resulting total revenue equals to the original total revenue $TR_1 = p_1 Q_1$. That is, we define

$$p_3 = \frac{p_1 Q_1}{Q_2} = \frac{p_1}{(1-\kappa)} \qquad (7.4)$$

which follows directly from (7.3).

The break-even quality price increase is, therefore, defined to be

$$\Delta p_g = p_3 - p_2 = [\frac{p_1}{(1-\kappa)}] - g(Q_2). \qquad (7.5)$$

To investigate the properties of the curve Δp_g, we have

$$\frac{\partial \Delta p_g}{\partial \kappa} = [\frac{p_1}{(1-\kappa)^2}] + g'(Q_2) \cdot Q_1 \qquad (7.6)$$

and $$\frac{\partial^2 \Delta p_g}{\partial \kappa^2} = [\frac{2 p_1}{(1-\kappa)^3}] - Q_1^2 \cdot g''(Q_2) \qquad (7.7)$$

where $g'(Q_2)$ and $g''(Q_2)$ refer, respectively, to the first and second derivatives of price with respect to quantity evaluated at Q_2.

Consider the slope of the Δp_g curve; we note from (7.6) that

$$[\frac{\partial \Delta p_g}{\partial \kappa}] \gtrless 0 \text{ if } [\frac{p_1}{(1-\kappa)^2}] + g'(Q_2) \cdot Q_1 \gtrless 0 \qquad (7.8)$$

$$\text{or if } (1-\kappa)^2 \lessgtr -\frac{p_1}{Q_1} \cdot [\frac{1}{g'(Q_2)}]. \qquad (7.9)$$

Noting that $0 \le \kappa < 1$, and denoting the point price elasticity at (p_1, Q_1) as $\varepsilon_1 = (\partial Q_1 / \partial p_1) \cdot (p_1 / Q_1)$, the preceding condition can be written as

$$[\frac{\partial \Delta p_g}{\partial \kappa}] \gtrless 0 \text{ if } \kappa \gtrless 1 - \sqrt{\varepsilon_1 \cdot [\frac{g(Q_1)}{g'(Q_2)}]}. \qquad (7.10)$$

Let us note that we have expressed (7.10) in terms of ε_1 simply because we wish to use the premarketing orders price-quantity combination (p_1, Q_1) as our point of reference. It is easy to see that Price's result regarding the characteristics of the break-even quality price change curve Δp_g is a special case of those indicated in (7.6) and (7.7). Consider the sign of $(\partial \Delta p_g / \partial \kappa)$, for instance, in (7.10). If the demand function is linear, $g'(Q_1) = g'(Q_2)$; hence,

$$[\frac{\partial \Delta p_g}{\partial \kappa}] \gtrless 0 \text{ if } \kappa \gtrless 1 - \sqrt{\varepsilon_1}. \qquad (7.10a)$$

If the demand function is elastic, $\varepsilon_1 > 1$; hence, $1 - \varepsilon_1^{\frac{1}{2}} < 0$. Since $\kappa \geq 0$, the condition in (7.10a) that $\kappa > 1 - \varepsilon_1^{\frac{1}{2}}$ is satisfied, which in turn implies that $[\partial \Delta p_g / \partial \kappa] > 0$, i.e., the break-even quality price change curve is an increasing function of κ. For a more general demand function, we note from (7.10) that the sign of $[\Delta p_g / \partial \kappa]$ depends upon the price elasticity ε_1 and on the shape (concavity-convexity) of the demand function itself. One might be faced with a situation in which the demand function is highly convex, i.e., $[g'(Q_1)/g'(Q_2)] \ll 1$, such that even for an elastic demand function $(\varepsilon_1 > 1)$, we obtain $\varepsilon_1 \cdot [g'(Q_1)/g'(Q_2)] < 1$, which would in turn imply that for a sufficiently small level of culling rate κ, we may have from (7.10) that

$$[\frac{\partial \Delta p_g}{\partial \kappa}] < 0 \text{ if } \kappa < 1 - \sqrt{\varepsilon_1 \cdot [\frac{g'(Q_1)}{g'(Q_2)}]}. \tag{7.11}$$

Let us now examine the sign of $\partial^2 \Delta p_g / \partial \kappa^2$ in (7.7), which further characterizes the shape of the break-even quality price change curve. For a linear demand function $g''(Q_2) = 0$; hence from (7.7), $\partial^2 \Delta p_g / \partial \kappa^2 > 0$ which implies that the break-even quality price change is increasing in the culling rate κ at an increasing rate. However, in general, the sign of $[\partial^2 \Delta p_g / \partial \kappa^2]$ depends upon the concavity-convexity of the demand function as we can see from (7.7). If the demand function is concave, $g''(Q_2) < 0$; hence, $\partial^2 \Delta p_g / \partial \kappa^2 > 0$. If the demand function is convex, $g''(Q_2) > 0$; hence,

$$[\frac{\partial^2 \Delta p_g}{\partial \kappa^2}] \gtrless 0 \text{ if } g''(Q_2) \gtrless \frac{2p_1}{(1 - \kappa)^3 Q_1^2}.$$

2.2 Actual Quality Price Change and Optimal Minimum Quality

The break-even quality price increase that results from culling serves as a reference for the industry to decide whether or not culling is more profitable. If discarding a lower quality portion of the harvest results in an actual quality price increase which is larger than the break-even quality price increase, then culling is a better choice as compared to the noculling policy. Otherwise, culling is not more profitable. Once the industry decides that culling is more profitable, the next decision is to determine the optimal rate of culling. Instead of using an optimal rate of culling, we will use some measure of minimum quality of a given agricultural product as a choice variable for the industry under consideration. As will become clear later, only under certain special circumstances will the two choice variables, namely, the rate of culling and some measure of minimum quality, be operationally equivalent in the industry's decision processes. Our preference for using minimum quality as the choice variable can be justified as follows.

(a) The notion of culling can easily be identified with some type of quantity control instead of quality control as we wish to address here. Using the minimum quality variable would clearly distinguish between quantity and quality price effects of discarding. This distinction may be particularly important in view of the controversy over whether or not quality standards have been used for purposes of supply control.

(b) At least in the context of the problem under study, the upward shift in the demand function (as a result of discarding lower quality products) takes place because of an improvement in the quality of the produce, not culling per se. Thus, if the quality is "sufficiently" high, further culling may only affect the quantity price increase but not significantly induce any quality price increases. In other words, the actual quality price increase is a function of the minimum quality rather than the culling rate.

Let us denote the quality, broadly defined, of a given product as γ. This quality parameter γ may refer to size, grade, shape, maturity, etc., of that product. Let $\gamma \in [\gamma^L, \gamma^H]$ where γ^L and γ^H denote the lowest and highest quality, respectively. The industry's problem is to find the optimal minimum quality in order to maximize its total profits to be defined later. From the discussion in the preceding subsection, we know that culling is more profitable (as compared to not culling) if the actual quality price increase is greater than the break-even quality price increase. We had earlier specified the latter in equation (7.5). We now specify the former. As a result of culling, one observes an actual price, to be denoted by p_a. Then, the actual quality price increase is defined to be

$$\Delta p_a = p_a - p_2 \text{ where we recall } p_2 = f(Q_2). \tag{7.12}$$

We now assume the following specification concerning the actual quality price increase:

$$\Delta p_a = \phi(\gamma^*) \tag{7.13}$$

where γ^* denotes the minimum quality, and $\phi'(\gamma^*) > 0$ and $\phi''(\gamma^*) < 0$.

The function $\phi(\gamma^*)$ states that as the minimum quality increases, the actual quality price will increase but at a decreasing rate. The assumption that $\phi''(\gamma^*)$ is negative appears reasonable, and in addition it would not affect the following discussion in any crucial way.

Let us further assume that for a particular harvest the distribution function of the produce according to each value of parameter γ can be specified as $h(\gamma)$. The quantity supplied to the market after discarding those elements of the harvest with a parameter lower than γ^* can be written as

$$Q_2 = \int_{\gamma^*}^{\gamma^H} h(\gamma) d\gamma \tag{7.14}$$

where the notation Q_2 of the previous subsection is used.

It is not necessary for our present purposes to characterize any further details of the function $h(\gamma)$. Presumably, for a particular parameter γ and a particular produce, $h(\gamma)$ can be a uniform distribution function, normal even a monotonically increasing or decreasing function of γ.

To summarize, culling is at least as profitable in comparison to no culling if $\Delta p_a \geq \Delta p_g$. Substituting (7.3), (7.5), (7.13), and (7.14) into this comparison yields

$$\phi(\gamma^*) \geq [\frac{p_1 Q_1}{\int_{\gamma^*}^{\gamma''} h(\gamma)d\gamma}] - g\left[\int_{\gamma^*}^{\gamma''} h(\gamma)d\gamma\right]. \qquad (7.15)$$

The lower and higher bound of the permissible set for γ^* can be directly seen from (7.15) to be, respectively.

$$\phi(\gamma^L) = p_1 - p_1 = 0$$

$$\text{and} \quad \phi(\overline{\gamma}) = \left[\frac{p_1 Q_1}{\int_{\overline{\gamma}}^{\gamma''} h(\gamma)d\gamma}\right] - g\left[\int_{\overline{\gamma}}^{\gamma''} h(\gamma)dy\right] \qquad (7.16)$$

where we note that $\int_{\gamma^L}^{\gamma''} h(\gamma)d\gamma = Q_1$.

We now formally state the optimization problem facing the industry as follows. Find an optimal minimum quality from the permissible set $[\gamma^L, \overline{\gamma}]$ as specified in (7.16) in order to maximize total profits net of costs of culling:

$$\text{Max. } p_a Q_2 - \psi(\kappa)$$

where $\psi(\kappa)$ is the cost function of culling. Or,

$$\text{Max. } \Pi = [g(Q_2) + \phi(\gamma^*)]Q_2 - \psi(\kappa)$$
$$\{\gamma^*\}$$

$$\text{where } Q_2 = \int_{\gamma^*}^{\gamma''} h(\gamma)d\gamma$$

$$\text{and} \quad \kappa = 1 - \left[\frac{\int_{\gamma^*}^{\gamma''} h(\gamma)d\gamma}{Q_1}\right].$$

The first-order and second-order conditions for optimality are:

$$-[g(Q_2) + \phi(\gamma^*)]h(\gamma^*) + Q_2[-g'(Q_2)h(\gamma^*) + \phi'(\gamma^*)]$$
$$= \left[\frac{\psi'(\kappa) \cdot h(\gamma^*)}{Q_1}\right] \qquad (7.17)$$

$$\text{and} \quad \frac{\partial^2 \Pi}{\partial \gamma^{*2}} = \{-[g(Q_2) + Q_2 g'(Q_2)] - \phi(\gamma^*) - \frac{\psi'(\kappa)}{Q_1}\} h'(\gamma^*)$$

$$+ [2g'(Q_2) + g''(Q_2).Q_2 - \frac{1}{Q_1^2} \psi''(\kappa)][h(\gamma^*)]^2 \qquad (7.18)$$

$$-2\phi'(\gamma^*)h(\gamma^*) + Q_2\phi''(\gamma^*) < 0.$$

Let us now offer some economic interpretations for condition (7.17). The right-hand side simply represents the marginal cost of culling, which is clearly positive. The left-hand side represents the marginal revenue of culling and consists of two components: the first, $-[g(Q_2) + \phi(\gamma^*)]h(\gamma^*)$, is negative and shows the loss in marginal revenue due to a reduction in quantity sold as a result of culling; the second, $Q_2[-g'(Q_2)h(\gamma^*) + \phi'(\gamma^*)]$, is positive and indicates the gain in marginal revenue due to both quantity price increase and quality price increase as a result of culling. The optimality condition in (7.17) thus requires that marginal revenue of culling be positive and be equal to marginal cost of culling. One should also note that (7.17) can be rewritten so that it involves the price demand elasticity at (p_2, Q_2). The decision for the industry is that for a given harvest $Q_1 = \int_{\gamma_L}^{\gamma_H} h(\gamma)d\gamma$ and a given function $\phi(\gamma^*)$, a level of γ^* is determined to satisfy (7.17), based on which Q_2 can be calculated, which in turn would imply a corresponding level of culling rate κ.

It can be seen from (7.18) that if the distribution function of the produce under consideration is uniform, then $h'(\gamma^*) = 0$; hence, it would be sufficient (but may not be necessary) for (7.18) to be satisfied if the demand function is concave $[g''(Q_2)<0]$ and the culling cost function is convex $[\psi''(\kappa) > 0]$. If $h'(\gamma^*) > 0$, an additional sufficient condition for (7.18) to be satisfied is a positive marginal cost function.

We have thus presented a simple model of optimal culling in which we show that for a nonlinear demand function, the shape of the break-even quality price change curve depends on both the concavity-convexity of the demand function and the price elasticity. We then formulate a profit-maximization problem facing the industry which considers the minimum quality of its produce as the decision variable. We specify that the actual quality price change is an increasing function of the minimum quality but at a decreasing rate. Conditions are then obtained to ensure that a minimum quality level chosen from a permissible set would yield maximum total profits for the industry.

There are many other interesting and important aspects of quality control of agricultural produce which may present opportunities for possible future research. First, the theoretical model has its limitations in its treatment of the product quality issue in the traditional quantity-price demand framework. A formulation explicitly involving both quality and quantity in the tradition of Lancaster's theory of product characteristics may prove to be more fruitful. Second, for each particular agricultural product, there are secondary markets for its by-products or for its lower quality portion. The secondary markets may or may not be competitive for potential consumers in the primary markets. The growing importance of secondary markets (food processing is an example) would make inappropriate the assumption of zero-value for discarded produce. We believe that the presence of secondary markets will significantly affect the industry's culling decisions as well as its production decisions. Third, another important line of research in this area is to implement empirically the theoretical model we consider in this analysis. Works conducted by Jesse and others at the U.S. Department of Agriculture could serve as a helpful base for further investigations into this important subject of federal marketing orders and the associated issue of agricultural produce quality.

3 MARKETING-INVENTORY-PRODUCTION

3.1 Deterministics

Let us start with a well-known deterministic model designed mainly to address the inventory issues facing the firm; a static model is sufficiently convenient for us here. We take a clue from Porteus [1990] that the dynamic extensions involving more than two-period decision framework are analytically and computationally challenging but present no major conceptual difficulties.

The popular economic lot-size model (to simplify the presentation, we only look at the simple case involving no shortage allowance) is recorded here for purpose of comparison with the stochastic versions in this chapter as well as the integrative marketing-production formulations. The firm's objective is to minimize the total cost which consists of production costs (with average cost c), a fixed setup cost, denoted as c_S, and proportional holding (inventory) cost, denoted as c_H as follows:

$$C(q,Q) = cq + \frac{c_S q}{Q} + \frac{c_H Q}{2} \tag{7.19}$$

where q denotes quantity demanded per unit of time, and Q the lot size.

The well-known square-root formula obtained from solving the preceding problem can be written as:

$$Q^* = \sqrt{\frac{2 c_S q}{c_H}} . \tag{7.20}$$

Now, suppose that instead of assuming a stationary demand q, we postulate that the demand facing the firm is affected by its pricing, in a linear fashion:

$$q = a - bp \tag{7.21}$$

with known intercept a and slope coefficient b and where p denotes unit price.

The firm's objective function is now reformulated to reflect profit maximization as follows:

$$\Pi=R-C=pq-C=(p-c)q-\frac{c_s q}{Q}-\frac{c_H Q}{2} \qquad (7.22)$$

where Π denotes the firm's profits, R represents revenue, and we ignore the firm's other types of fixed costs.

Taking into account the linear demand specification in (7.21), maximizing (7.22) with respect to both decision variables Q and p, then solve the two resulting two equations reflecting the first-order conditions would yield an optimal solution which can be shown to be unique. This formulation was originally done by Whitin [1955] and recently analyzed by Eliashberg and Steinberg [1993] within the context of the decentralized/coordinated marketing-production decision framework.

3.2 Marketing-Production: Stochastics

Pure Production/Inventory

Now, suppose that the quantity demand is a random variable which by convention in the stochastic inventory literature, will be denoted by ζ (we use this symbol, *zeta*, in place of the more conventional ξ, *xi*, to denote random demand so that ξ can be consistently used to denote the random error term throughout this work). Again, the unit production cost or ordering cost is c, the unit shortage cost which represents the cost per unit of unsatisfied demand is c_U (U stands for Unsatisfied), and the unit (inventory) Holding cost is c_H. The quantity sold by the firm is

$$q=\min(\zeta,y) \qquad (7.23)$$

where the quantity sold is denoted by q and y represents the starting stock at the beginning of a period.

Note that in some contexts where no initial inventory is available, y could represent the quantity produced, or the case of retailing, the quantity ordered.

Assume that the random demand ζ has a probability density function, again typically denoted in the stochastic literature as $\varphi(\zeta)$ with mean μ, the expected cost facing the firm, assuming zero setup cost for convenience, which consists of the ordering (production) cost, the holding cost and the shortage (loss of sales) cost, can be written as:

$$E[C(q,y)]=cy+\int_0^y c_H(y-\zeta)\varphi(\zeta)d\zeta+\int_y^\infty c_U(\zeta-y)\varphi(\zeta)d\zeta \qquad (7.24)$$

which upon minimization, yields the formula for the optimal quantity ordered y^* implicitly defined to be

$$\Phi(y^*)=\frac{c_U-c}{c_U+c_H}$$

where $\Phi(.)$ denotes the cumulative distribution function of random demand.

Thus the preceding condition can be interpreted as the decision rule for calculating the optimal probability of *not* stocking out, based on which an optimal stock y^* can typically be found.

One particularly insightful way to spell out the effect of random demand in this model is to rewrite (7.24) as:

$$E[C(q,y)] = c\mu + (c + c_H)(y - \mu) + (c_U + c_H) \int_y^\infty (\zeta - y)\varphi(\zeta)d\zeta$$

where we recall that μ denotes demand mean.

Thus, in the usual way of interpreting the notion of certainty equivalence, one notes that if demand is known to take on the value of its mean μ, the last two terms of the preceding expression would disappear as the optimal stock y^* would be equal to μ. In this case, the expected cost facing the firm would be only the production or ordering cost $c\mu$. Consequently, this term, $c\mu$, represents the firm's expected cost under perfect information. Under random demand, however, the firm's expected cost is of course $E[C(q,y)]$. The difference between the firm's expected cost under perfect information and that under imperfect information would then indicate certain value of perfect information. It may be instructive to relate this notion of value of perfect information to that of learning we defined in Section 5 of Chapter 2 on pricing. Since the value of perfect information in this context arises because of random demand and the firm's effort to satisfy it, it is referred to as buffer cost in the literature.

Inventory-Marketing Decisions

We report under this sub-heading efforts to address possible interactions between production-inventory and marketing decisions. We first analyze the inventory-pricing model due to Young [1979], then briefly discuss a recent model due to Sethi and Zhang [1994] who analyze the production-advertising decision-making using a multilevel hierarchical formulation.

Following Young, let us now assume that the firm's random demand can be postulated as:

$$\zeta = \mu(p) + v(p)\xi \tag{7.26}$$

where the random term ξ, as opposed to ζ, has the density $f(\xi)$ which has zero means and known variance σ_ξ^2. For a chosen price p, the resulting density function of ζ is denoted as $\varphi(\zeta,p)$.

The firm's decision is to choose price and the stock level y to maximize its expected profits which is defined as the difference between its expected revenue and its expected total costs:

$$E(\Pi) = E(TR) - E(C) \tag{7.27}$$

$$\text{where}\quad E(TR)=E(pq)=pE(q) \tag{7.28}$$

$$\text{and}\quad E[C(p,y)]=c(y-x)+c_H\int_0^y(y-\zeta)\varphi(p,\zeta)d\zeta+c_U\int_y^\infty(\zeta-y)\varphi(p,\zeta)d\zeta \tag{7.29}$$

where x denotes the initial inventory.

Noting that

$$E(\zeta)=\mu(p)=\int_0^\infty\zeta\varphi(p,\zeta)d\zeta$$

and that $E(q)=\int_0^y\zeta\varphi(p,\zeta)d\zeta+y\int_y^\infty\varphi(p,\zeta)d\zeta$, one can write

$$E(q)=E(\zeta)-\int_y^\infty(\zeta-y)\varphi(p,\zeta)d\zeta.$$

$$\text{Or}\quad E(q)=y-\int_0^y(y-\zeta)\varphi(p,\zeta)d\zeta.$$

Using the preceding relations and with the discount rate of r, the firm's objective function can then be written as:

$$E(\Pi)=(p-c)E(\zeta)-[c(1-r)+c_H][y-E(\zeta)]$$
$$-(p-cr+c_H+c_U)\int_y^\infty(\zeta-y)\varphi(p,\zeta)d\zeta \tag{7.30}$$

where we note that in order to see the intertemporal implications of the unsold inventory, its present value is

$$x=r\int_0^y(y-\zeta)\varphi(p,\zeta)d\zeta=r[y-E(q)]$$
$$=r[y-E(\zeta)+\int_y^\infty(\zeta-y)\varphi(p,\zeta)d\zeta]. \tag{7.31}$$

The firm's objective in (7.30) enables us to clearly see the impact of random demand on the decision-maker's optimal pricing and inventory policy.

First, economic interpretations can be seen to be parallel to those obtained for the simpler case of optimal stocking with fixed price discussed earlier in this sub-section. Second, let us recall the deterministic pricing rule discussed in Chapter 2. Specifically, we reproduce here the pricing rule recorded in eq. (2.6) as:

$$p^*=[\frac{\varepsilon}{\varepsilon-1}]MC \tag{7.32}$$

where ε represents the price elasticity of demand.

For the present formulation, if the firm is able to observe demand before making an order, then there would be no excess inventory, and the certainty-equivalent solution can be obtained by maximizing the simplified objective of the form:

$$E(\Pi)=(p-c)E(\zeta)=(p-c)\mu(p)$$

which would yield the certainty-equivalent solution of $MC=E(MR)$, or

$$p+\frac{\mu}{\partial\mu/\partial p}=p[\frac{\varepsilon-1}{\varepsilon}]=c \qquad (7.34)$$

which is identical to that in (7.32).

The effects of uncertain demand are captured by the remaining two expressions in (7.30) which reflect the buffer costs which also represent the expected value of information in the sense that it would be eliminated if the information about demand is known to the firm prior to its decisions. Young also obtains certain results to indicate the directions of the impact of uncertain demand on the firm's decisions.

To see the connection between the basic inventory structure with its solution summarized in (7.25) above, let us consider the simple static problem in which pricing is not within the firm's decision framework. The objective function in (7.30) can be maximized by looking for the first-order condition which can be written as:

$$\frac{\partial E(\Pi)}{\partial y}=-[c(1-r)+c_H]+(p+c_H+c_U-cr)\int_y^\infty\varphi(\zeta)d\zeta \qquad (7.35)$$

which upon noting that $\int_y^\infty\varphi(\zeta)d\varphi=1-\Phi(y^*)$, yields the following solution for an optimal order:

$$\Phi(y*)=\frac{p+c_U-c}{p-cr+c_U+c_H}. \qquad (7.36)$$

The nature of the modified solution can be seen by directly comparing (7.36) and (7.25). Consider now the interaction with the firm's pricing decisions. We now have an additional first-order condition in which price represents the decision variable. We thus write:

$$\frac{\partial E(\Pi)}{\partial p}=(p-c)\frac{\partial E(\zeta)}{\partial p}+E(\zeta)+[c(1-r)+c_H]\frac{\partial E(\zeta)}{\partial p}$$

$$-\int_y^\infty(\zeta-y)\varphi(\zeta)d\zeta-(p-cr+c_H+c_U)[1-\phi(y)]\frac{\partial E(\zeta)}{\partial p}=0. \qquad (7.37)$$

Assuming that the second-order conditions are satisfied, the necessary conditions in (7.35) and (7.37) can be used to derive the basic rule for the stochastic demand inventory policy as follows:

$$\frac{d[E(\Pi)]}{dp}=\frac{\partial E(\Pi)}{\partial p}+\frac{\partial E(\Pi)}{\partial y}\frac{\partial E(\zeta)}{\partial p}=0.$$

Or: $(p-c)\frac{\partial E(\zeta)}{\partial p}+E(\zeta)-\int_y^\infty(\zeta-y)\varphi(\zeta)d\zeta=0. \qquad (7.38)$

While the preceding expression does not itself present a closed-form solution, it can immediately shed light on the key difference between the stochastic demand rule and the certainty-equivalent solution summarized in (7.34) above. The preceding equation in (7.38) can be rewritten as :

$$ p + \frac{E(\zeta)}{\frac{\partial E(\zeta)}{\partial p}} = p[\frac{\varepsilon-1}{\varepsilon}] = c + \frac{\int_y^\infty (\zeta-y)\varphi(\zeta)d\zeta}{\frac{\partial E(\zeta)}{\partial p}}. $$

$$ \text{Or} \quad p = [\frac{\varepsilon}{\varepsilon-1}]c + \frac{\int_y^\infty (\zeta-y)\varphi(\zeta)d\zeta}{\frac{\partial E(\zeta)}{\partial p}}[\frac{\varepsilon}{\varepsilon-1}]. \tag{7.39} $$

Again noting that the second-order condition is satisfied, a comparison between the stochastic rule in (7.39) and the certainty-equivalent rule in (7.34) hinges on the sign of the second term in the preceding expression which is clearly negative due to the standard assumption of a downward-slope demand curve. Consequently, the optimal price under uncertainty is seen clearly to be lower than that under deterministic conditions. While this particular result has of course been long ago obtained as we reported in Chapter 2, our presentation and approach in this section clearly indicates the nature and the cause for such a divergence.

We now briefly describe a simplified version of the Sethi-Zhang formulation [1994, Ch. 11] of the firm's production-advertising decision making. Defining the state variable z_t to represent the single-product firm's total "surplus", the dynamic equation is written as:

$$ \frac{dz}{dt} = y_t - \zeta_t; \quad z_{t=0} \equiv z_0 \tag{7.40} $$

where y_t denotes production, ζ_t random demand in period t which follows a finite Markovian process, and surplus can take on a positive value (inventory) or a negative value (shortage).

The firm's objective function is, as usual, to maximize its expected discounted profit defined to be:

$$ \text{Max.} \quad V = E \int_0^\infty = e^{-rt}[\Pi(y_t, m_t, z_t, \kappa_t)]dt $$

subject to (7.40) and the production capacity constraint $0 \le y_t \le \kappa_t$.

where as before m_t denotes advertising efforts and κ_t represents a finite state Markovian stochastic production capacity process, reflecting the possibilities of breakdown and repair.

The profit flows are defined as:

$$\Pi_t = p\zeta_t - cy_t - C(z_t)$$

in which, as before, p and c are unit price and unit production cost, respectively, and $C(z_t)$ denotes costs associated with "surplus" which may involve shortage costs and holding costs (cf eq. (7.29)).

The problem is then approached by decomposing the global decision process into a hierarchical, two-level decision-making procedure in which advertising budgets m_t are determined first by the marketing department on the basis of certain production capacity averages. Then, the production division would make production decisions y_t, taking into consideration the stochastic demand ζ_t, which is in turn influenced partly by the firm's advertising effort. The authors then show that the preceding procedure yields asymptotically optimal results for the optimization problem facing the firm.

4 PRODUCTION DECISIONS

Our discussion in this section concentrates on the firm's pure production decisions, particularly in the case where the firm produces multiple commodities. Before we provide such an analysis, it will be helpful to review some standard results for the single-product case in the following sub-section.

4.1 Single Output

In the previous chapters, we have examined the potential effects of demand uncertainty on the firm's various decisions such as price, advertising and personal selling. We have also, in some contexts, discussed the firm's output decision under random demand. It is well-known that these issues have been examined both in economics as well as operations research literature. For example, Horowitz [1970] surveyed much of the earlier economics literature on economic decisions under uncertainty in general. Levary and Dean [1980] examined the storage and purchasing policies under random demand using a multiperiod linear programming model. Deshmukh and Winston [1977, 1979] considered the firm's pricing decisions under the assumption of stochastically changing demand using Markov decision models. Jucker and Carlson [1976] extended the deterministic plant-location problem to take into account the potential effect of price and/or demand uncertainty. In particular, the economics literature on the monopolist's decisions under random demand concentrated mostly on the static analysis of the one-period decision problem as we analyzed in Chapter 2.

For ease of reference, let us briefly recall the major results for the one-period model of Baron [1971] and Leland [1972]. The objective of the monopolist is to maximize

$$W = E[U(\Pi)|q] = \int U[pq - C(q)]\varphi(p|q)dp \qquad (7.41)$$

where E denotes the expectation operator, Π the profit function, p the unit price, q quantity demanded, $C(q)$ the known cost function which has positive and increasing marginal cost, and $\varphi(p|q)$ the conditional density.

The utility function $U(\Pi)$ is assumed to have positive marginal utility everywhere with increasing (constant, decreasing) marginal utility for the risk-preferred (risk-neutral, risk-averse) firm. The explicit inverse demand function is $p = g(q,\xi)$ where ξ is a random term with known density, and it is further assumed that $(\partial p/\partial q) < 0$ and $(\partial p/\partial \xi) > 0$.

The necessary and sufficient conditions for optimality in the one-period model in (7.41) can be written as

$$E\{U'(\Pi)[MR(q^*,\xi) - MC(q^*)]|q^*\} = 0 \qquad (7.42)$$

$$\text{and} \quad E[U'(\Pi)\frac{\partial^2\Pi}{\partial q^2} + U''(\Pi)\left[\frac{\partial\Pi}{\partial q}\right]^2|q\} < 0 \qquad (7.43)$$

where the primes denote partial derivatives, and MR and MC stand for marginal revenue and marginal cost, respectively. For later reference, we will refer to the output which satisfies (7.42) and (7.43) the one-period optimal output, to be denoted as q^*.

The preceding one-period stochastic model can be compared to a corresponding certainty-equivalent model. To represent such a deterministic model, we adopt the notion of expected price certainty demand defined by Leland as the curve which would result if the firm knew price would equal its conditional expected value with certainty for all levels of q. Using this definition of a certainty-equivalent demand function, coupled with the notion of principle of increasing uncertainty which states that as total expected revenue increases the "riskiness" of total revenue will increase, Leland showed that for a risk-averse monopolistic firm, one obtains

$$E\{U'(\Pi)[MR(\bar{q},\xi) - MC(\bar{q})]|\bar{q}\} < 0 \qquad (7.44)$$

where $\bar{q}$ denotes the output level which would be optimal for the firm facing the certainty-equivalent demand curve.

From (7.42) and (7.44), given that the sufficient condition in (7.43) is satisfied, it follows that $q^* < \bar{q}$, i.e. demand uncertainty induces a smaller output level for the risk-averse firm. This represents the major result in the literature on the theory of the firm under random demand within the one-period static framework.

4.2 Multiple-Production

Introduction

A typical monopolistic firm often produces more than one product. If production and pricing decisions are made independently for each product, then the theory of multi-product firm is identical to that for a single-product firm. In reality, however, decisions about certain choice variables concerning the firm's many related products are jointly made within a single managerial structure. The theory of the monopolistic multi-product firm under deterministic conditions have been long developed. (See, for example, Weldon [1948]). On the other hand, while the theory of the single-product firm under uncertainty has been extensively examined (see Baron [1971], Sandmo [1971], Leland [1972], and Horowitz [1970], among others), we have seen only a couple of papers in the economics literature specifically dealing with the multi-product firm's decisions under demand uncertainty (see Dhrymes [1964] and Blair and Heggestad [1977]).

It appears that little progress has actually been made towards understanding of the multi-product firm under uncertainty. This is mainly due to the difficulty associated with the evaluation of the effects of changes in the firm's risk behavior, uncertainty parameters, and tax rates on output levels of the firm's several products. Working with a quadratic utility function, a general conclusion reached by Dhrymes [1964, p. 256] was that "the response of the multi-product firm to changes in the state of uncertainty, both in terms of its attitude toward risk and changes in the parameters of the relevant distribution, is much more complex than in the case of the uniproduct firm."

In this section, we extend the single-product model of monopolistic firm under uncertainty and in the process, we seek to strengthen some of Dhrymes' results concerning the evaluation of the impact of uncertainty, attitude toward risk, and taxation on the firm's outputs. Our presentation follows Nguyen [1984]. For a good portion of the analysis, our main limitation is that we will be concerned with a monopolistic firm which produces only *two* products. It seems that this assumption is necessary in order to make our results stronger and more specific. In management literature on the multi-product inventory theory (e.g., see Deuermeyer [1980]), we note that several authors adopted the simplified assumption of a two-product firm in their studies (see Nahmias and Pierskalla [1976], and Deuermeyer [1979]). On the more positive side, we believe that the two-product firm represents a sufficiently interesting class to be studied. It is well-known that the peak-load pricing problem can be viewed in the framework of the two-product firm: peak period vs. off-peak period. Products can also be classified into new vs. old products. This distinction is important since under conditions of random demand, it is reasonable to assume that the demand for a new product is subject to a higher degree of uncertainty as compared to an old product. One can further categorize the products produced by a monopolistic firm into those which are subject to regulation and those which are not. Nevertheless, certain results obtained here apply equally well to a larger number of commodities which are produced by the firm. We will indicate whenever this observation is valid.

The Model

Consider a quantity-setting firm which produces N distinct products, $N \geq 2$. The inverse demand function for the i-th product is specified as:

$$p_i = g(q_1, q_2, ..., q_N, \xi_i); \quad i = 1, 2, ..., N \tag{7.45}$$

where p_i is the unit price of the i-th product, q_i is the quantity demanded for the i-th product, and ξ_i represents the random term.

As before, let $E(p_i | q_1, q_2, ..., q_N) = h(q_1, q_2, ..., q_N)$ and let $\Omega \equiv [\sigma_{ij}]$; $i,j = 1, 2, ..., N$ be the conditional variance-covariance matrix of product prices. For the expected profit maximizing firm, the objective is to

$$\text{Max. } E[\sum_{i=1}^{N} p_i q_i - C(q_1, q_2, ..., q_N)] \tag{7.46}$$

where $C(q_1, q_2, ..., q_N)$ denotes the known cost function and E is the expectation operator.

The necessary conditions for (7.46) subject to (7.45) are:

$$E(p_i | \mathbf{q}) + \sum_{j=1}^{N} q_j \left[\frac{\partial E(p_j | \mathbf{q})}{\partial q_i} \right] = \frac{\partial C(q_1, q_2, ..., q_N)}{\partial q_i}$$

for $i = 1, 2, ..., N$ and where we denote $\mathbf{q} \equiv \{q_1, q_2, ..., q_N\}$.

For a non-linear utility function, the objective of the firm is to maximize

$$E[U(\Pi) | \mathbf{q}] = \int \int ... \int \{U[\sum_{i=1}^{N} p_i q_i - C(q_1, q_2, ..., q_N)]\} \varphi(p_1, p_2, ..., p_N | \mathbf{q}) dp_1, dp_2, ..., dp_N$$

where $\varphi(p_1, p_2, ..., p_N | \mathbf{q})$ is the conditional joint density of product prices.

Once again, using a Taylor's series expansion about $E(\Pi)$ as illustrated in Chapter 1, and with a quadratic utility function, the first-order conditions for optimality to the preceding problem can be shown to be:

$$[U'] \frac{\partial E(\Pi)}{\partial q_i} = -(\sum_{j=1}^{N} \sigma_{ij} q_j) U''; \quad i = 1, 2, ..., N$$

which, upon using the Pratt-Arrow index of risk aversion r defined earlier, can be written in matrix notation as:

$$\frac{\partial E(\Pi)}{\partial \mathbf{q}} - r\Omega \mathbf{q} = 0 \tag{7.48}$$

where as before, r is positive for a risk-averse firm and negative for a risk-preferred firm and where $\partial E(\Pi)/\partial \mathbf{q} = \{[\partial E(\Pi)/\partial q_1],[\partial E(\Pi)/\partial q_2],...,[\partial E(\Pi)/\partial q_N]\}^T$ and $\mathbf{q} = \{q_1,q_2,...,q_N\}^T$.

The second-order condition can be shown to be of the same form we derived in Chapter 2 for the multiple-product pricing decisions so we will not repeat it here.

Economic Analysis
In this sub-section, we first analyze the effect of the firm's risk behavior on its output decisions. We then examine the impact of uncertainty in terms of a change in elements of the variance-covariance matrix of the demand equations system on the firm's optimal outputs. Next, we consider the effect of an imposition of a specific tax on the firm's products. We will then study the impact of a profits tax which is imposed on the firm's total profits. Finally, we examine possible effects of an *ad valorem* sales tax on outputs of the firm.

Risk Aversion and Optimal Output
Recalling that r is the Pratt-Arrow index of risk aversion, let us examine the sign of $\partial \mathbf{q}/\partial r$. Differentiating (7.48) with respect to r yields:

$$\frac{\partial^2 E(\Pi)}{\partial \mathbf{q}^2} \frac{\partial \mathbf{q}}{\partial r} - \Omega \mathbf{q} - r\Omega[\frac{\partial \mathbf{q}}{\partial r}] = 0.$$

$$\text{Or} \quad (\mathbf{J} - r\Omega)[\frac{\partial \mathbf{q}}{\partial r}] = \Omega \mathbf{q} \tag{7.49}$$

where $\mathbf{J}$ is the Hessian matrix of the expected profit function with respect to $\mathbf{q}$, $(\mathbf{J}-r\Omega)$ is assumed to be negative definite; i.e., the appropriate second-order condition is satisfied.

From the preceding equation, we have:

$$\frac{\partial \mathbf{q}}{\partial r} = (\mathbf{J} - r\Omega)^{-1}\Omega \mathbf{q}. \tag{7.50}$$

Dhrymes has shown that when the firm's products are such that $\sigma_{ij} > 0$; $i \neq j$, it follows that $(\partial \mathbf{q}/\partial r) \leq 0$ if $\mathbf{J}_{ij} \geq r\sigma_{ij}$; $i \neq j$, where $\mathbf{J}_{ij}$ is the (i,j)-th element of matrix $\mathbf{J}$. On the other hand, when the firm's products are such that $\sigma_{ij} < 0$; $i \neq j$, no comparable results were given by Dhrymes. Originally, Dhrymes defined that two goods q_i and q_j are said to be stochastically complementary if $\sigma_{ij} > 0$ and stochastically competitive if $\sigma_{ij} < 0$. It appears that this designation is incorrect since positive (negative) covariance between p_i and p_j does *not* necessarily imply that quantities q_i and q_j tend to vary in the same (opposite) direction(s) as we would normally define complementarity (competitiveness — substitution). Actually, we shall show later that the sign of the price covariance has little to do with the conventional notion of complementarity and competitiveness.

For the case of a two-product firm, we obtain below a necessary and sufficient condition under which an increase in the index of risk aversion would induce a decline in production levels of both products for both cases of negative and positive conditional covariance of product prices. Let us summarize this result in the following

Theorem 7.1. *Consider a monopolistic firm which produces two products q_1 and q_2, and its risk behavior is represented by the index of risk aversion r where $r > 0$. Then as the firm becomes more risk-averse, both output levels will decline, for any initial output levels, if and only if:*

$$(i) \quad \infty > [\frac{\partial^2 E(\Pi)}{\partial q_1 \partial q_2}] > \beta_L \quad (lower\ bound)\ when\ \sigma_{12} > 0 \qquad (7.51)$$

$$and\ (ii)\quad (upper\ bound)\ \beta_U > [\frac{\partial^2 E(\Pi)}{\partial q_1 \partial q_2}] > \beta_L \quad when\ \sigma_{12} < 0$$

$$where\ \beta_L = \max\ \{\sigma_{12}[\frac{J_{22}}{\sigma_{22}}], \sigma_{12}[\frac{J_{11}}{\sigma_{11}}]\}$$

$$and\ \beta_U = \min\ \{[\frac{(J_{11}\sigma_{22} - r\Delta)}{\sigma_{12}}], [\frac{(J_{22}\sigma_{11} - r\Delta)}{\sigma_{12}}]\}$$

$$where\ \Delta = \sigma_{11} \cdot \sigma_{22} - \sigma_{12}^2.$$

When the two prices are stochastically uncorrelated (zero covariance), the above conditions apply where $\beta_L = 0$ and $\beta_U = \infty$.

Proof. The proof of the above result is tedious but straight-forward. From (7.50), we note that, for arbitrary levels of $\mathbf{q}$, dq/dr is negative if and only if all the elements of the matrix $(\mathbf{J} - r\Omega)^{-1}\Omega$ are negative. We explicitly calculate the inverse of the 2×2 matrix $(\mathbf{J} - r\Omega)$, and then postmultiply the resulting inverse matrix by Ω. In the process of obtaining (i) and (ii) in Theorem 7.1, we impose the conditions that $\mathbf{J}$ be negative definite, Ω be positive definite, and that $(\mathbf{J} - r\Omega)$ be negative definite. Other conditions concerning σ_{12} are imposed depending on whether the two prices are positively or negatively correlated. It is also obvious to see that as $\sigma_{12} = 0$, $\beta_L = 0$ and $\beta_U = \infty$.

                                                                                                    Q.E.D.

It is of interest to note that even though β_2 is similarly defined for both cases of positively and negatively correlated prices, actual values of β_L differ. When $\sigma_{12} > 0$, β_L can be seen to be negative and when $\sigma_{12} < 0$, the lower bound β_L is positive. The fact that the lower bound β_L for the case of positive covariance is negative indicates that, for the two-product firm, the Dhrymes result cited earlier can be strengthened.

Since the Dhrymes (sufficiency) result is that $\mathbf{J}_{12} > r\sigma_{12}$ in order to have $(d\mathbf{q}/dr)<0$, it implies that the lower bound for $\mathbf{J}_{12}$ is positive if $\sigma_{12} > 0$.

We now offer some economic interpretations for the results in Theorem 7.1. Let us first note that for the special case of a single-product firm, the relation in (7.50) reduces to:

$$\frac{\partial q}{\partial r} = \left[\frac{1}{\dfrac{\partial^2 E(\Pi)}{\partial q^2} - r\sigma_q^2} \right] \sigma_q^2 q$$

where the notation is slightly modified as we now refer to the single output as q.

For the risk-averse firm, the preceding expression clearly indicates that $\partial q/\partial r < 0$, a result which has long been obtained. For the two-product case, one can readily verify that:

$$\frac{\partial q_1}{\partial r} \propto A q_1 + B q_2 \tag{7.52}$$

where $A = (\mathbf{J}_{22}\text{-}r\sigma_{22})\sigma_{11}\text{-}(\mathbf{J}_{12}\text{-}r\sigma_{12})\sigma_{12}$ and $B = (\mathbf{J}_{22}\text{-}r\sigma_{22})\sigma_{12}\text{-}(\mathbf{J}_{12}\text{-}r\sigma_{12})\sigma_{22}$ and $\propto$ denotes the proportionality factor.

Since Ω is positive definite, one can show that if $B < 0$, it should follow that $A < 0$. Thus, for arbitrary levels of q_1 and q_2, $\partial q_1/\partial r$ is negative if $B < 0$; or $\mathbf{J}_{12} > \sigma_{12}$ $(\mathbf{J}_{22}/\sigma_{22})$, confirming parts of Theorem 7.1. Our interpretation of the theorem would be simpler for the case in which $\sigma_{12} > 0$. From (7.52), one can see that whether q_1 would decline or increase as a result of an increase in risk aversion would depend on whether the condition $\mathbf{J}_{12} > \sigma_{12}$ $(\mathbf{J}_{22}/\sigma_{22})$ is satisfied or not. Everything else being the same, the higher the level of $\mathbf{J}_{12}$, the easier it is for the said condition to be satisfied which in turn implies the higher tendency for q_1 to decline. Similarly, *ceteris paribus*, the higher the level of σ_{12}, the easier the said condition is to be satisfied (noting that $\mathbf{J}_{22} < 0$); hence the higher the tendency for q_1 to fall. The same arguments can apply to the output level q_2 as well; i.e. higher levels of both $\mathbf{J}_{12}$ and σ_{12} induce a decline in q_2. Thus, if either $\mathbf{J}_{12}$ or σ_{12}, or both, are sufficiently high, an increase in risk aversion would result in a reduction in levels of both products, provided that $\sigma_{12} > 0$. Of some interest is the observation that higher level of σ_{12} promotes *complementarity* between the two products since they are both reduced as a result of an increase in risk aversion. This would appear to lend some support to the Dhrymes original definition that positive σ_{12} corresponds to complementarity between the two products. However, if σ_{12} is sufficiently low even though still positive, it *may* well be the case that while an increase in the index of risk aversion brings about a decline in output of one product, at the same time it may result in an increase in output of the other product. This possibility of *substitution* between the two products can be realized in the presence of a positive correlation of the two prices. The preceding discussion thus indicates that the sign of σ_{12} should *not* be used as a basis for defining product complementarity/substitutability.

The case of negative price correlation ($\sigma_{12}<0$) is exceedingly difficult to interpret. We simply mention here that the effect of a change in the level of $\mathbf{J}_{12}$ as well as that of σ_{12} on ($\partial q_i/\partial r$) are quite unpredictable. Our result in part (*ii*) of Theorem 7.1 defines a bounded range for $\mathbf{J}_{12}$ within which both q_1 and q_2 decline as the monopolistic firm becomes more risk-averse. When $\mathbf{J}_{12}$ falls outside of this range, it may be the case that while an increase in risk aversion results in a decline in one product, it results in an increase in production of the other product.

In spite of its simplicity, the above discussion has an important econometric implication as can be seen as follows: For a single-product firm, it is well-known that the higher the risk aversion, the smaller the level of optimal output as we reported in Chapter 2. In the context of a two-product firm as we just analyzed, the production level of a product could be higher even when the firm is becoming more risk-averse (an increase in the degree of risk aversion). This situation can easily be misinterpreted as the effect of the firm's risk-taking attitude if one applies directly the results obtained from the single-product firm.

Effects of Increased Price Variances
We now examine the possible impact of a change in the elements of the variance-covariance matrix of the product price vector in the demand equations.

Differentiating (7.48) with respect to σ_{ij} yields:

$$(\mathbf{J}-r\Omega)[\frac{\partial \mathbf{q}}{\partial \sigma_{ij}}] = r\mathbf{M}_{ij}\mathbf{q}; \; i,j=1,2$$

where $\mathbf{M}_{ij}$ denotes a 2×2 symmetric matrix whose (i,j)th or (j,i)th elements are unity and the remaining elements are zero. Rewrite the preceding equations as:

$$\frac{\partial \mathbf{q}}{\partial \sigma_{ij}} = r(\mathbf{J}-r\Omega)^{-1}\mathbf{M}_{ij}\mathbf{q} \; ; \; i,j=1,2$$

where we recall that ($\mathbf{J}-r\Omega$) is negative definite.

It is straight-forward to verify that for arbitrary levels of $\mathbf{q}$, an increase in the covariance σ_{12} of the two goods produced by a risk-averse firm would lead to a reduction in production levels of both goods if and only if $\mathbf{J}_{12} > r\sigma_{12}$. This result applies to both cases of positively and negatively correlated product prices. It can also be readily shown that:

$$\frac{\partial q_i}{\partial \sigma_{ii}}<0 \; ; \; i,j=1,2$$

and $\dfrac{\partial q_j}{\partial \sigma_{ii}} \begin{cases} <0 \text{ if } \mathbf{J}_{ij}>r\sigma_{ij} \\ >0 \text{ if } \mathbf{J}_{ij}<r\sigma_{ij} \end{cases} \; ; \; i \neq j.$

The preceding results state that the production level of a good declines if the variance of its own price increases. On the other hand, whether the output of a good declines or increases as a result of an increase in the variance of the price of the other good would depend on whether $\mathbf{J}_{12}$ is greater or smaller than σ_{12}. Finally, it may be of interest to note that if the condition $\mathbf{J}_{12} > r\sigma_{12}$ is satisfied, an increase in either the variance term or the covariance term would lead to a decline in production levels of both products.

Impact of Taxation
We now consider the possible effects of various kinds of taxation on the firm's outputs. We first examine the effect of a specific tax, then that of a profits tax, and finally that of an *ad valorem* sales tax. Each of these modes of taxation gives rise to different and interesting results concerning the optimal output mix to be produced by the firm.

Specific Taxes. Recalling that the firm's utility function of profits is approximated by a quadratic specification, we now define:

$$\Pi = \sum_{i=1}^{2} (p_i - t_i)q_i - C(q_1, q_2)$$

where t_i is the tax imposed on good i.
The first-order condition for optimal $\mathbf{q}$ can be shown to be:

$$[\frac{\partial E(\Pi)}{\partial \mathbf{q}}] - r\Omega\mathbf{q} = \mathbf{I}\mathbf{t} \tag{7.53}$$

where $\mathbf{I}$ is the 2×2 identity matrix and $\mathbf{t} = \{t_1, t_2\}^{\mathrm{T}}$.
Differentiating (7.53) with respect to t_i yields:

$$(\mathbf{J} - r\Omega)[\frac{\partial \mathbf{q}}{\partial t_i}] = \mathbf{e}_i \quad ; i = 1,2 \tag{7.54}$$

where $\mathbf{e}_i$ is a column vector whose elements are all zero except the i-th element which has the value of one.
More specifically, it follows from (7.54) that

$$\frac{\partial \mathbf{q}}{\partial t_i} = (\mathbf{J} - r\Omega)^{-1}\mathbf{e}_i$$

which gives:

$$\frac{\partial q_i}{\partial t_i} = \mathbf{J}_{jj} - r\sigma_{jj} < 0; j \neq i$$

and $$\frac{\partial q_j}{\partial t_i} = -(\mathbf{J}_{ij} - r\sigma_{ij}) \quad ; i \neq j.$$

From the preceding equation, we see that if a specific tax is imposed on a certain product of a risk-averse firm, the output level of that product decreases. On the other hand, the impact of such a tax on the output level of the other good depends once again upon the relative values of J_{ij} and σ_{ij}. If $(J_{ij} - r\sigma_{ij})$ is positive, an imposition of a tax rate t_i on good i reduces the quantity of good j produced. However, if $(J_{ij} - r\sigma_{ij})$ is negative, output level of good j would increase as a result of such a tax on good i.

Profits Tax. We now assume that a profits tax is imposed on the firm. While the objective function remains to be the same, the net profit is now defined to be:

$$\Pi = (1-t)[\textstyle\sum_{i=1}^{2} p_i q_i - C(q_1, q_2)]$$

where t denotes the profits tax rate.

The first-order condition for the resulting maximization can be written as:

$$[\frac{\partial E(\Pi)}{\partial \mathbf{q}}] - r(1-t)\Omega\mathbf{q} = 0. \tag{7.55}$$

Upon differentiating (7.55) with respect to t, we obtain:

$$[\mathbf{J} - r(1-t)\Omega]\frac{\partial \mathbf{q}}{\partial t} = -r\Omega\mathbf{q}.$$

$$\text{Or} \quad \frac{\partial \mathbf{q}}{\partial t} = -r[\mathbf{J} - r(1-t)\Omega]^{-1}\Omega\mathbf{q}. \tag{7.56}$$

To make use of the results obtained earlier in Theorem 7.1, let us rewrite (7.56) as:

$$\frac{\partial \mathbf{q}}{\partial t} = -[\frac{r}{(1-t)}][\mathbf{J} - r(1-t)\Omega]^{-1}(1-t)\Omega\mathbf{q}. \tag{7.56a}$$

On the basis of Theorem 7.1, we see immediately that for the risk-averse firm $(r > 0)$, the column vector $\partial \mathbf{q}/\partial t$ is positive if and only if those conditions (*i*) and (*ii*) in Theorem 7.1 are satisfied with a minor exception to be pointed out shortly. We thus state the following

Theorem 7.2. *For a risk-averse monopolistic firm which produces two products q_1 and q_2, and which is subject to a profits tax of rate t, an increase in the tax rate would result in an* increase *in output levels of* both *products if and only if:*

$$(i) \quad \infty > [\frac{\partial^2 E(\Pi)}{\partial q_1 \partial q_2}] > \beta_L \quad when \, \sigma_{12} > 0$$

$$and \quad (ii) \quad \beta_U > [\frac{\partial^2 E(\Pi)}{\partial q_1 \partial q_2}] > \beta_L \quad when \, \sigma_{12} < 0$$

where β_L and β_U are defined previously in Theorem 7.1 with the following modification in the definition of Δ:

$$\Delta = (1-t)[\sigma_{11}.\sigma_{22}-\sigma_{12}^2].$$

It is of interest to note that the conditions under which output levels of both products decline as the firm becomes more risk-averse are virtually identical to those under which output levels of both products increase as a profits tax is imposed on the firm. An intuitive reason behind this is not difficult to spell out, however. In the presence of a profits tax, the degree of riskiness at the after-tax profit level is less than that at the pre-tax profit level. Hence, an increase in the rate of profits tax has an identical effect on outputs as a decrease in the degree of riskiness. Operationally, this effect can also be realized if the firm becomes *less* risk-averse. The preceding analysis thus indicates that the effect of an increase in the profits tax rate is equivalent to that of a decline in the index of risk aversion.

Ad Valorem Sales Tax. We finally consider the case in which an *ad valorem* sales tax is imposed on the firm. The net profit function is written as:

$$\Pi = (1-t)[\sum_{i=1}^2 p_i q_i] - C(q_1, q_2).$$

To simplify the analysis, let us make an additional assumption that the cost function is linear in both output levels of the firm's products. We now write the necessary conditions as:

$$\frac{\partial E(\Pi)}{\partial q} - r(1-t)\Omega q = [\frac{t}{1-t}]MC \qquad (7.57)$$

where **MC** is the column vector:

$$MC = \{[\frac{\partial C(q_1,q_2)}{\partial q_1}],[\frac{\partial C(q_1,q_2)}{\partial q_2}]\}^T.$$

To consider the effect of a change in the sales tax rate, we differentiate (7.57) with respect to t to obtain:

$$[J - r(1-t)\Omega]\frac{\partial q}{\partial t} + r\Omega q = \frac{MC}{(1-t)^2}.$$

Or $\quad \frac{\partial q}{\partial t} = -[\frac{r}{(1-t)}][J-r(1-t)\Omega]^{-1}(1-t)\Omega q +[\frac{1}{(1-t)^2}][J-r(1-t)\Omega]^{-1}MC. \qquad (7.58)$

It can be seen that the first term on the right-hand side of (7.58) is identical to (7.56a). The sign of that term can be determined via Theorem 7.2 above. Given that the conditions (*i*) and (*ii*) in Theorem 7.2 are satisfied so that the column vector of the first term on the right hand side of (7.58) is positive, it is not certain whether those conditions would tell us something about the sign of the second term. If the column vector of the second term is positive, we can determine unambiguously the impact of an increase in the *ad valorem* sales tax rate on the firm's output levels: $[\partial q/\partial t] > 0$. If it is negative, of course, the sign of $[\partial q/\partial t]$ cannot be obtained unambiguously.

It can be shown that when $J_{ij} > r(1-t)\sigma_{ij}$; $i \neq j$ where $\sigma_{ij} > 0$, the inverse matrix $[J-r(1-t)\Omega]^{-1}$ contains all negative elements. It then follows that for a firm which produces goods whose demand functions are such that $\sigma_{ij} > 0$, and which is subject to an increasing cost function ($MC > 0$), the column vector of the first term is positive whereas that of the second is negative. The relative strengths of these two opposite forces will ultimately determine the possible impact of a change in the sales tax rate on the output mix of the firm.

Summary

In this section, we examine the theory of the monopolistic firm under demand uncertainty when the firm produces more than one product. On the one hand, this analysis can be considered to be an extension of models of single-product monopolistic firms under random demand. It can be clearly seen that a significant divergence exists between the theories of the single-product and the multi-product firm under conditions of uncertainty.

On the other hand, working with a two-product firm, we are able to strengthen a number of results obtained earlier by Dhrymes who considered a more general *N*-product firm. However, not all results contained in this analysis are constrained to the two-product firm since they can readily apply to a general *N*-product firm. For the most part of the analysis concerning the effect of a tax imposition on the firm's output mix, we could have effectively derived those results under the assumption of a *N*-product monopolistic firm.

For the two-product firm, we specify the lower bound β_L for the cross-derivative of the expected profit with respect to output levels of the two products (J_{12}) within which an increase in the degree of risk aversion would result in a decline in quantities produced for both goods. We then show that if J_{12} falls within the bounds $\{\beta_L, \beta_U\}$ similarly defined, then an increase in the profits tax rate would induce an increase in output levels of both outputs for a risk-averse monopolistic firm. We confirm the Dhrymes result that the production level of a good declines if the variance of its own price increases; whereas the effect of a change in the variance of the price of the other good is not clear-cut. In addition, an increase in a specific tax on a certain good unambiguously induces a decrease in production level of that good, while it may lead to an increase or a decrease in production level of the other good. Finally, the effect of a change in the *ad valorem* sales tax rate is examined. We find that it is quite difficult to determine the impact of a change in the sales tax rate on the change in the firm's output levels. Even with a fairly restrictive requirement that $J_{12} > r(1-t)\sigma_{12}$, and under the assumption that the cost function is increasing, the ultimate impact of a tax change depends upon the two forces which operate in opposite directions.

5 LONG-RUN DECISIONS: INVESTMENT

We have examined the firm's short-run decisions regarding its pricing and inventory in view of random demand. As the solution to Young's formulation indicates, once we allow for the valuation of unsold inventory, that is the discounted value of the production/ordering costs, the intertemporal dynamic problem is essentially reduced to a single-period static formulation and its solution algorithm thus follows. However, for a manufacturing industry where production decisions, not ordering decisions are the fundamental variables, one particular aspect in terms of long-term profit maximization for the firm stands out. The firm will need to make investment decisions in its capital equipment to produce in the future. In this framework, the inventory decision regarding starting stock in each period is not as relevant as the decision to invest in its accumulation of capital stock to partially replace its equipment and partially increase its plant and facilities. It is with this feature in mind that we now formulate the dynamic investment problem of the firm facing random demand. Our presentation in this section is based in part on Nguyen [1984].

A typical approach in economic analysis in dealing with the problem of investment under uncertainty for firms with monopoly power would be to treat output as a major decision variable. However, in our effort to examine possible interactions between marketing and other managerial decisions, we will focus our attention in the ensuing analysis on pricing as the dominant marketing component of the marketing mix in the short run. Thus, we will be concerned with the firm which sets a price and then produces whatever quantity is demanded at that price. For a given price, the resulting actual sales level is governed in part by the random disturbances represented by the error terms ξ's. We assume that the product offered by the firm is not storable, and hence there is no inventory in the model as we considered in earlier discussion.

The random sales response function is assumed to be:

$$q_t = f(p_t, \xi_t)$$

where ξ is the random term whose probability density function is subjectively given.

Let us further specify the firm's production function as:

$$q_t = Q(K_t, L_t)$$

which satisfies the usual neo-classical properties of positive and diminishing marginal product of both production factors, capital K_t and labor L_t.

Further, the capital accumulation process is defined to be:

$$K_{t+1} = (1-\delta)K_t + I_t; \quad t=1,2,...,$$

where I_t denotes the firm's investment in period t and δ a constant rate of capital depreciation.

At the beginning of period t, the firm's decision process involves choosing a price level p_t and investment I_t prior to the realization of the random term ξ_t in order to maximize the objective function:

$$\text{Max. } E\{\sum_{\tau=t}^{\infty} \rho^{\tau-t}U[\Pi_\tau(q_\tau)]\,|\,\psi^{t-1},p_t,I_t\}$$
$$\{p_t,I_t\}$$
$$=E\{\sum_{\tau=t}^{\infty} \rho^{\tau-t}U[p_\tau q_\tau - w_\tau L_\tau - rI_\tau]\,|\,\psi^{t-1},p_t,I_t\}$$

where $\tau=t,t+1,t+2,...$, ρ the discount factor, w_t and r_t are respectively the wage rate and the constant rental rate of capital in period t, and where ψ^{t-1} represents a vector of relevant information up to time t-1.

Before presenting the solution to the preceding optimization problem, let us follow Holthausen [1976] in assuming that while both the price level and investment are *ex ante* decision variables, labor is an *ex post* variable. That is, after a price p_t is set by the firm and a realization of q_t is observed, the labor employment level will be determined by a labor-requirement function which contains as its arguments the realized output q_t, and the capital stock K_t. This assumption reflects the fact that labor is considered to be more flexible and it may be adjusted after q_t is known. The reader will recall that a static version of this notion has been advanced in Sub-section 2.3 of Chapter 5 on salesforce size and compensation. Consequently, we write the *labor-requirements function* in the form of:

$$L_t = \ell(q_t,K_t)$$

which is derived directly from the production function $q_t = Q(K_t,L_t)$.

Note that with a known capital stock in the preceding period (t-1), an *ex ante* decision on investment implies an *ex ante* decision on the capital stock in period t. In addition, we assume that the function $\ell(q_t,K_t)$ is well-defined, twice differentiable in its arguments although it will not be necessary for us to completely specify the whole function for our present purposes. We also note that the firm's risk behavior is represented by a von Newmann-Morgenstern utility function which is of an additively separable type. As before, this characteristic of the utility function will enable us to make use of the dynamic programming technique in solving our maximization problem. As usual, we assume positive marginal utility everywhere with decreasing (constant, increasing) marginal utility for the risk-averse (risk-neutral, risk-preferred) firm. Finally, we assume that ξ_t is independent of the price level p_t in the demand function, and that ξ_s is independent of ξ_t for all s and t.

Once again, the following recursive algorithm is obtained by applying the principle of optimality and the principle of iterated expectations the method of which were outlined in the introductory chapter:

$$\text{Max.}_{\{p_t,I_t\}} V_t = \text{Max.}_{\{p_t,I_t\}} E_{t-1}[U(\Pi_t) + \rho V_{t+1}^*] \qquad (7.59)$$

where the asterisk denotes the maximum value and where for notational simplicity, we denote $E_{t-1}(.) \equiv E(.|\psi^{t-1}, p_t, I_t)$.

On the basis of (7.59), let us state without proof the following

Theorem 7.3. *The optimal paths of the inputs employed by the price-setting monopolistic firm facing random demand are characterized by the conditions:*

$$E_{t-1}\{U'(\Pi_t)[q_t + (p_t - w_t \frac{\partial \ell}{\partial q_t}).\frac{\partial q_t}{\partial p_t}]\} = 0$$

$$\text{and } E_{t-1}\{rU'(\Pi_t) - \rho U'(\Pi_{t+1})[(1-\delta)r - w_{t+1}(\frac{\partial \ell}{\partial K_{t+1}})]\} = 0; \ t=1,2,... \quad (7.60)$$

Economic interpretations of the preceding conditions can be briefly given here. The first indicates the condition which can be viewed as a version of the familiar principle of equality between expected marginal revenue and marginal cost, expressed in terms of the price variable and adjusted for the presence of nonlinearity in the firm's utility function. The second requires that the expected marginal contribution of new capital should justify its expected rental cost, expressed in terms of present values and adjusted for non-linear utility as well as capital depreciation. To evaluate the effects of random demand and of the firm's risk behavior, let us further examine the second of the two preceding conditions. Direct calculation of (7.60) yields:

$$\rho w_{t+1} E_{t-1}[U'(\Pi_{t+1}) \frac{\partial \ell}{\partial K_{t+1}}] = -r E_{t-1}\{[U(\Pi_t) - \rho(1-\delta)U'(\Pi_{t+1})]\}. \quad (7.61)$$

Note that the left-hand side of (7.61) can be written as:

$$\rho w_{t+1} E_{t-1}[U'(\Pi_{t+1})].E_{t-1}[\frac{\partial \ell}{\partial K_{t+1}}] + \rho w_{t+1} cov.[U'(\Pi_{t+1}),(\frac{\partial \ell}{\partial K_{t+1}})].$$

Then eq. (7.61) can be shown to give:

$$E_{t-1}[\frac{\partial \ell}{\partial K_{t+1}}] = \frac{-r}{w_{t+1}} \{\frac{1}{\rho} \frac{E_{t-1}[U'(\Pi_t)]}{E_{t-1}[U'(\Pi_{t+1})]} -(1-\delta)\}$$

$$- \frac{cov.[U'(\Pi_{t+1}),(\frac{\partial \ell}{\partial K_{t+1}})]}{E_{t-1}[U'(\Pi_{t+1})]}. \qquad (7.62)$$

The term $[\partial \ell/\partial K_{t+1}]$ represents the marginal rate of technical substitution between capital and labor for a given level of output. On the other hand, the right-hand side of (7.62) consists of two components: the first involves the ratio of input prices, the second the covariance term. For the deterministic model, the covariance term would disappear; thus intuitively, the covariance term represents the only key divergence between the stochastic and the deterministic models. To verify this result as well as to gain additional insights to this issue, we examine the firm's input decision process in which levels of labor and investment represent the firm's two decision variables. With the deterministic production function, choices of the two production inputs amount to setting the output itself. Further, under deterministic demand conditions, we are already aware that price-setting and quantity-setting behavioral modes yield identical results. Thus, our approach should be appropriate for comparing the firm's behavior under conditions of random demand and deterministic demand.

The deterministic solution to the equivalent quantity-setting firm can be obtained in a straight-forward fashion, so we will simply report the first-order conditions here:

$$[p_{t+1} + q_{t+1}(\frac{\partial p_{t+1}}{\partial q_{t+1}})]Q_{L_{t+1}} = w_{t+1}$$

and $$[p_{t+1} + q_{t+1}(\frac{\partial p_{t+1}}{\partial q_{t+1}})]Q_{K_{t+1}} = \frac{r}{\rho}[\frac{U'(\Pi_t)}{U'(\Pi_{t+1})}] -(1-\delta)r$$

where $Q_{L_{t+1}}$ and $Q_{K_{t+1}}$ represent, respectively, the marginal product of labor and of capital at time $t+1$.

Consider now the production of the form:

$$q_{t+1} = Q(K_{t+1}, L_{t+1}).$$

Then for a given level of output q_{t+1}^0, we have

$$\frac{dL_{t+1}}{dK_{t+1}}\Big|_{q_{t+1}=q_{t+1}^0} = \frac{\dfrac{-\partial q_{t+1}}{\partial K_{t+1}}}{\dfrac{\partial q_{t+1}}{\partial L_{t+1}}} = -\frac{Q_{K_{t+1}}}{Q_{L_{t+1}}}.$$

Using the preceding expressions, we obtain:

$$\frac{dL_{t+1}}{dK_{t+1}}\Big|_{q_{i,t}=q_{i,t}^0} = \frac{-r}{w_{t+1}}\{\frac{1}{\rho}[\frac{U'(\Pi_t)}{U'(\Pi_{t+1})}] - (1-\delta)\}. \tag{7.63}$$

One can readily see the correspondence between the optimal conditions under a stochastic environment in eq. (7.62) and that under certainty in (7.63). It can be seen, by a comparison between (7.62) and (7.63), that the decision rule for the stochastic model differs from that for a deterministic model. The divergence between the optimal conditions in (7.62) and (7.63) is mainly due to the existence of a non-zero covariance term on the right-hand side of (7.62).

One cannot in general determine the sign of the covariance term. The impact of uncertainty on the marginal rate of technical substitution between capital and labor thus cannot be assessed. For a risk-neutral monopolistic firm, however, the rule for profit maximization is identical whether the firm operates under certainty or random demand, as can be easily seen. Under the assumption of risk neutrality, the covariance term in (7.62) vanishes. They both become:

$$E_{t-1}[\frac{\partial \ell}{\partial K_{t+1}^*}] = -\frac{r}{w_{t+1}}[\frac{1}{\rho} - (1-\delta)] = \frac{dL_{t+1}}{dK_{t+1}}\Big|_{q_{i,t}=q_{i,t}^0}.$$

6 CONCLUSIONS

We have in this chapter addressed a number of issues related to aspects of production, inventory and product quality under conditions of uncertainty. We started out with the important and practical problem of Federal Marketing Orders in which certain quality standards for agricultural products such as vegetables and fruits have to be maintained. While uncertainty enters only in a weak sense in that the optimal culling rate of a produce has to be determined on the basis of a probability distribution function of its quality, the model offers operational approach to a significant problem with implications for the interaction between restricted output, price and quality in a very simple framework. We are also motivated by an effort to expose marketing phenomena to a larger issue of potential public interest with its consequent public policies. We then examined the interplay between the firm's pricing decision with its inventory and production decisions under stochastic conditions of demand. In doing so, we are mindful of the extent of how little progress research in this field has been made as evidenced by Porteus's survey [1990] and noticed by Eliashberg and Steinberg [1993, p. 873]. We share with the latter authors the sentiment that this topic should be further explored. We then focused our attention to the case of multiple-product where demand is subject to random errors. Even with considerable simplification for the purpose of mathematical tractability, the results concerning the impact of uncertainty on the firm's output decisions are not in general unambiguous as in the case of single product.   In this context, we have also examined the implications of certain types of taxation for the firm's decisions, again with an intended purpose of exposing marketing issues to certain public policy orientations. Finally, we considered the manufacturing firm's long-run problem of investment where we paid attention to the joint decision of pricing and investing for production capacity. As we expect, in general the optimal rules for profit maximization under conditions of certainty and stochastic demand differ for firms which are not risk-neutral. While empirical implications of these types of results remain to be seen, it is still important to recognize and identify elements which eventually affect such a divergence in the decision process for the firm.

REFERENCES

BARON, David P., 1971, "Demand Uncertainty in Imperfect Competition," *International Economic Review*, Vol. 12 , pp. 196-208.
BLAIR, R. D., and A. A. HEGGESTAD, 1977, "Impact of Uncertainty Upon the Multiproduct Firm," *Southern Economic Journal*, Vol. 44, pp. 136-142.
DESHMUKH, S. D., and W. L. WINSTON, 1977, "A Controlled Birth and Death Process Model of Optimal Product Pricing under Stochastically Changing Demand," *Applied Probability*, Vol. 14, pp. 328-339.
DESHMUKH, S. D., and W. L. WINSTON, 1979, "Stochastic Control of Competition Through Prices," *Operations Research*, Vol. 27, pp. 583-594.
DEUERMEYER, Bryan L., 1979, "A Multi-Type Production System for Perishable Inventories," *Operations Research*, Vol. 27, pp. 935-943.
DEUERMEYER, Bryan L., 1980, "A Single Period Model for a Multiproduct Perishable Inventory System With Economic Substitution," *Naval Research Logistics Quarterly*, pp. 177-185.
DHRYMES, Phoebus J., 1964, "On the Theory of the Monopolistic Multi-product Firm under Uncertainty," *International Economic Review*, Vol. 5 , pp. 239-257.
ELIASHBERG, Jehoshua, and Richard STEINBERG, 1993, "Marketing-Production Joint Decision-Making," in Jehoshua ELIASHBERG, and Gary L. LILIEN (eds.), *Marketing*, Handbooks in Operations Research and Management Science, Vol. 5, pp. 827-880, Elsevier Science Publishers, Amsterdam, The Netherlands.
HOLTHAUSEN, Duncan M., 1976, "Input Choice and Uncertain Demand," *American Economic Review*, Vol. 66, pp. 94-103.
HOROWITZ, Ira, 1970, *Decision Making and the Theory of the Firm*, Holt, Rinehart and Winston, Inc.
JESSE, E. V., 1981, *Producer Revenue Effects of Federal Marketing Order Quality Standards*, Washington DC: US Department of Agriculture, Economic and Statistic Services Report No. AGESS 810619.
JESSE, E. V., 1979, *Social Welfare Implications of Federal Marketing Orders for Fruits and Vegetables*, Washington DC: US Department of Agriculture, ESCS Technical Bulletin No. 1608.
JESSE, E. V., and A. C. Johnson, Jr., 1981, *Effectiveness of Federal Marketing Orders for Fruits and Vegetables*, Washington DC: US Department of Agriculture, Economic and Statistic Services Report No. 471.
JUCKER, J. V., and R. C. CARLSON, 1976, "The Simple Plant Location Problem Under Uncertainty," *Operations Research*, Vol. 24, pp. 1045-1055.
LELAND, Hayne, 1972, "Theory of the Firm Facing Uncertain Demand," *American Economic Review*, Vol. 62, pp. 278-291.

LEVARY, R. R., and B. V. DEAN, 1980, "A Natural Gas Flow Model Under Uncertainty in Demand," *Operations Research*, Vol. 28, pp 1360-1374.

NAHMIAS, S., and W. P. PIERSKALLA, 1976, "A Two-Product Perishable/ Nonperishable Inventory Problem," *SIAM Journal of Applied Mathematics*, pp. 438-500.

NGUYEN, Dung, 1984, "Adjustment Costs and Theory of Investment Under Uncertainty," *Journal of Economics and Business*, No. 36, pp. 307-321.

NGUYEN, Dung, 1984, "Product Diversification and Demand Uncertainty," *Southern Economic Journal*, Vol. 51, No. 2, pp 330-340.

NGUYEN, Dung, and Trang T. VO, 1985, "On Discarding Low Quality Produce," *American Journal of Agricultural Economics*, Vol. 67, No. 3, pp. 614-618.

PORTEUS, Evan L, 1990, *Stochastic Inventory Theory*, Chapter 12 in D. P. HEYMAN, and M. J. SOBEL (eds.), *Handbooks in Operations Research & Management Science*, Vol. 2, pp. 605-652.

PRICE, D. W., 1967, "Discarding Low Quality Produce with an Elastic Demand," *Journal of Farm Economics*, Vol. 49, pp. 622-632.

SANDMO, A., 1971, "On the Theory of the Competitive Firm under Price Uncertainty," *American Economic Review*, Vol. 61, pp. 65-73.

SETHI, Suresh P., and Qing ZHANG, 1994, *Hierarchical Decision Making in Stochastic Manufacturing Systems*, Birkhauser, Boston, MA.

SHAFER, C. E., 1968, "The Effects of a Marketing Order on Winter Carrot Prices," *American Journal of Agricultural Economics*, Vol. 50, pp. 879-887.

U.S. DEPARTMENT OF AGRICULTURE, Farmers Cooperative Service, 1975, *Price Impacts of Federal Marketing Order Programs*, Special Report No. 12, Washington DC.

WELDON, J. C., 1948, "The Multi-Product Firm," *Canadian Journal of Economics and Political Science*, pp. 176-190.

WHITIN, T. M., 1955, "Inventory Control and Price Theory," *Management Science*, Vol. 2, pp. 61-68.

YOUNG, Leslie, 1979, "Uncertainty, Market Structure and Resource Allocation," *Oxford Economic Papers*, Vol. 46, pp. 47-59.

8

COMPETITIVE MARKETING STRATEGIES

1 OVERVIEW

In this chapter, our concentration is to analyze the firm's decision making under uncertainty within a competitive framework. It should be pointed out that much of the analytical issues in this broad subject remains open research questions; in particular the stochastic game-theoretic framework has not yet been fully developed. Our approach here is to first present a game theoretic formulation of competition in a deterministic, static framework. In the process, we will also discuss the empirical-ly-motivated formulation of competitive marketing modelling commonly used in the literature. We then report a number of formulation of dynamic games relevant to the marketing literature, pointing out along the way the several recent surveys on the subject.

There exists no singular and unified theoretical framework to examine these issues as the degrees of complexities dictate that simplifying assumptions be made in different contexts to permit tractable formulation and analysis. A useful approach in the literature is to examine the competitive impact by formulating and analyzing the impact of potential entry in a two-stage game subject to various forms of uncertainty. Each of these issues will be taken up in turn in this chapter. One particular dynamic characterization involving learning and experimentation effects will be addressed in the next chapter.

While we could have chosen to present the materials in this chapter on the basis of static vs. dynamic paradigms and then examine various elements of the marketing mix in these two categories, we decided to use the marketing mix as a basis for presentation. In doing so, however, we will not lose sight of our effort to emphasize to the largest extent possible the potential interactions among the marketing mix variables. Thus we will indicate, for instance, how advertising influences the information of the competing firms' prices, how advertising investment during any time period will affect the pricing decision in the next period, and how pricing competition occurs only after firms have already decided upon their production capacities. The chapter is organized as follows. Section 2 highlights formulations of static and dynamic competitive models under deterministic conditions with an emphasis on the presentation of the basic game theoretic framework in which we report certain results which are essentially marketing oriented, and which are subject to stochastic extension in the subsequent sections. We then focus on pricing strategies for competing firms under random demand in Section 3. Section 4 examines mainly advertising strategies subject to uncertainty. The producing strategies will be the subject for Section 5 in which we analyze the effect of the firm's risk-taking behavior and the trade-off between output pre-commitment and production flexibility under uncertain demand. The concluding remarks in Section 6 will complete the chapter.

We should also note that while this chapter essentially sorts out the different categories of some existing literature in marketing and in economics whenever relevant, it is not intended to represent any efforts to survey the literature. Rather, we have chosen a number of formulations in order to facilitate an analysis of the impact of various forms of uncertainty on the elements of marketing strategies. Thus, the reader will clearly notice an apparent lack of a more coherent theme throughout the sections on uncertainty in comparison to the deterministic competitive analysis. As we mentioned, while the application of competitive game theoretic analysis to the marketing literature has been very successful and advanced, development of the game theories under stochastic conditions itself remains at an early stage. The steps to incorporate uncertainty into game theoretic formulation in general and in marketing strategies in particular have only just begun. However, it is our view that this should be a very challenging and yet fruitful area for future research.

2 THE DETERMINISTIC FRAMEWORK

2.1 The Empirically-Motivated, Static Formulation

We start out by reporting a result for optimal *static* pricing for a particular company in a competitive market and under conditions of certainty. It represents a natural extension of the well-known deterministic rule for optimal pricing by a monopolist which we had recorded earlier in eq. (2.6) of Chapter 2. Defining $\bar{p}$ as the average of the prices charged by all the competitors to a particular firm, reflecting the competitive reactions to the firm's price-setting at p, it can be shown that profit maximization yields the following optimal pricing rule under certainty (see, for instance, Simon [1989]):

$$p^* = \frac{\varepsilon + k\eta}{(\varepsilon - 1) + k\eta} MC \qquad (8.1)$$

where k represents the price-reaction elasticity of the average competitive price with respect to the firm's price, i.e., $k = (\partial \bar{p}/\partial p)(p/\bar{p})$, and η denotes the cross-price elasticity of the firm's demand with respect to the average competitive price, that is $\eta = (\partial q/\partial \bar{p})(\bar{p}/q)$.

Clearly, the competitive pricing rule in (8.1) reduces to the optimal pricing rule in (2.6) for the case of a monopolistic firm as the term $k\eta$ is identically zero. It should of course be noted that the preceding rule in (8.1) represents a heuristic approach to the problem of competitive pricing since it assumes that other competitors' reactions to a particular firm's pricing decision can be captured collectively by an average reaction price. This assumption would violate the nature of interdependency among the competing firms' marketing activities, pricing decisions among them. To reflect this sort of behavior, a more satisfactory approach involving game theoretic considerations will have to be used. We have in fact provided a specific application of this approach in our analysis of the market share models in Chapter 6; we will again see an additional formulation in the section on advertising below.

While such a framework may raise important theoretical issues as to what would be the appropriate way to model the interactive behavior of a competitive environment, its simplified reaction functions permit readily feasible econometric exercises. It appears that it is the potential for empirical implementation which motivates this type of formulation for competitive marketing behavior. Such a framework has been used to address the static marketing mix issue in competitive markets. We report here one early study by Lambin, Naert, and Bultez [1975] which shows a flavor of the "best response" approach in static games involving marketing mix. Consider the i-th firm's demand function

$$q_i = f_i(\mathbf{x}_i, \mathbf{x}_{-i}) \qquad (8.2)$$

where $\mathbf{x}_i \equiv \{x_{1i}, x_{2i}, ..., x_{ki}\}$ represent the i-th firm's vector of decision marketing variables such as price, advertising, distribution, quality, etc., and $\mathbf{x}_{-i}$ refers to the appropriate vector of the like for the competing firms. For more focused interpretation, let us assume that $\mathbf{x}_i \equiv \{p_i, m_i, \gamma_i\}$ where γ_i defines certain index of product quality. Then, the firm's profit function is:

$$\Pi_i = [p_i - c_i(q_i, \gamma_i)]q_i - m_i \qquad (8.3)$$

where we note the dependence of the firm's average cost on quantity and product quality.

The nature of the i-th firm's optimal solution can be captured by the following conditions:

$$\epsilon_{q_i,\mathbf{x}} = [\mathbf{I} \mid \mathbf{R}][\boldsymbol{\eta}_{Q,\mathbf{x}} + \boldsymbol{\eta}_{s_i}]^{\mathrm{T}} \tag{8.4}$$

where $\mathbf{I}$ is an identity matrix, $\mathbf{R}$ represents the matrix of reaction elasticities, defined to be

$$\mathbf{R} = [\rho_{ij}]; \quad \text{where } \rho_{ij} = \frac{\partial \bar{x}_j}{\partial x_i} \frac{x_i}{\bar{x}_j},$$

and where $\epsilon_{q_i,\mathbf{x}}$ denotes the vector of the firm's sales elasticities with respect to its various decision variables, $\boldsymbol{\eta}_{Q,\mathbf{x}}$ that of the industry's sales elasticities, and $\boldsymbol{\eta}_{s_i}$ that of the firm's market share elasticities.

Once again, it is the empirical implementation of the approach which makes such a formulation attractive. The decomposition of the sales elasticities into primary demand component and the market shares component enables us to understand how certain real markets conduct its marketing strategies regarding the various decisions.

Hanssens [1980] has extended the preceding framework to take into account the intrafirm effects as well as reactions of individual competing firms instead of the one firm vs. the rest of the industry framework.

So even though the competitive responses are taken into account in a particular firm's decision process, it is not representing equilibrium in the Nash sense. It is also interesting to relate this particular form to the original Dorfman-Steiner marketing mix problem reported in Chapter 1 with the additional impact of competition.

2.2 The Game-Theoretic Formulation

In this sub-section, we will first consider static models and then address the dynamic formulation. In each of these treatments, we will start by addressing the pricing decision, followed by the advertising and then the marketing mix scenario.

Static Models
Let us begin by considering a simple, deterministic formulation of the competitive pricing model. For ease of illustration, we will mostly work with a duopolistic market structure and indicate whenever relevant the extent the increase in the number of competitors would affect the decision variables of interest. This approach would allow us to focus more clearly on the role of competition in a simplest possible environment so that a comparison between the deterministic model and stochastic versions can be later seen. For this purpose, consider a price-setting duopoly, firm 1 and 2 where firm 1's demand is

$$q_1 = f_1(p_1, p_2).$$ (8.5)

The profit maximization problem facing firm 1 is to find price p_1 to

$$\text{Max. } \Pi_1(p_1, p_2) = (p_1 - c_1) f_1(p_1, p_2).$$ (8.6)

The first-order condition can be written as:

$$\frac{d\Pi_1}{dp_1} = \frac{\partial \Pi_1}{\partial p_1} + \frac{\partial \Pi_1}{\partial p_2} \cdot \frac{\partial p_2}{\partial p_1} = 0$$ (8.7)

where the nature of the strategic reactions is indicated by the second term of the middle expression. The conjectural variation approach specifically considers how a firm would assume the reaction of the competing firm as a result of its own price setting. Thus we can write the condition as:

$$(p_1 - c_1) \frac{dq_1}{dp_1} + f_1(p_1, p_2) = 0$$

$$\text{where} \quad \frac{dq_1}{dp_1} = \frac{\partial q_1}{\partial p_1} + \frac{\partial q_1}{\partial p_2} \cdot \frac{\partial p_2}{\partial p_1}.$$

The conjectural variation, denoted as $R_{21} \equiv \partial p_2 / \partial p_1$, reflects the mode with which firms compete; that is whether they compete on price in the Bertrand fashion or the Cournot quantity competition or monopolistic, perfect collusion.

This notion of conjectural variation can be seen more clearly when one considers the quantity version where products are perfect substitutes. Thus the demand is written as:

$$p = g(Q) \quad \text{where } Q = q_1 + q_2$$

and the firm's profit maximization problem, using the quantity version yields the following first-order condition:

$$\frac{\partial \Pi_1}{\partial q_1} = (p - c_1) + q_1 \frac{\partial p}{\partial q_1}$$

$$= (p - c_1) + q_1 \frac{\partial p}{\partial Q} [1 + R_{21}] = 0$$ (8.8)

where the conjectural variation $R_{21} \equiv \partial q_2 / \partial q_1$. Note that Cournot competition is when $R_{21} = 0$ since q_2 is fixed, Bertrand is when $R_{21} = -1$ since this would yield $p = c_1$, and perfect collusion when $R_{21} = 1$ since the resulting necessary condition would become

$$(p-c)+2q_1\frac{\partial p}{\partial Q}=(p-c)+Q\frac{\partial p}{\partial Q}=0$$

which is the condition for a monopolist's optimal price.

Thus the preceding condition in (8.8) would immediately yield the various well-known solutions such as Bertrand, Cournot and perfect collusion.

Regarding the static advertising game, we will postpone such a formulation until the section on competitive advertising below in order to facilitate a comparison of optimal advertising policies under deterministic conditions and those of uncertainty.

We now address a basic game structure to examine the marketing mix problem. Once again, to simplify the presentation, we assume that there will be only one brand to be produced by each firm. Thus we shall speak of a brand i or a firm i, which produces brand i, interchangeably. Further, the assumption of a duopoly will be maintained here.

Let us consider the following sales response function for brand 1:

$$q_1 = f_1(p_1, p_2, m_1, m_2) \tag{8.9}$$

where p_i represents brand i's unit price, q_1 sales level of brand 1, and m_i marketing efforts; $i=1,2$.

Assuming constant average (marginal) cost c, excluding only costs related to marketing activities, the profit function facing firm 1 is:

$$\Pi_1 = (p_1 - c_1)q_1 - m_1.$$

Maximizing economic profits involves setting the price and marketing efforts so that the following first-order conditions are satisfied:

$$\frac{\partial \Pi_1}{\partial p_1} = 0 = \frac{\partial \Pi_1}{\partial m_1}. \tag{8.10}$$

In principle, to the extent where an analytical solution exists and assuming that the second-order conditions are met for an interior solution, one can solve the preceding two first-order conditions to yield the following reduced-formed price and marketing variables:

$$p_1 = p_1(p_2, m_2) \tag{8.11}$$

$$\text{and} \quad m_1 = m_1(p_2, m_2). \tag{8.12}$$

Now, upon assuming further brand symmetry, the preceding two solutions will also be obtained for brand 2, with the consequence that the symmetric Nash-Cournot outcome can be obtained which will be denoted as usual as p^* and m^*.

We need to make a couple of important comments regarding the preceding general method of solution. First, the extension to more than two competing brands in this context is straight-forward. Second, to the extent that the issue of the potential impact of increasing competition is essential in some marketing environment, we can clearly modify the model to take account explicitly of such an impact; an example of it was given in Chapter 6, involving the specific form of the multinomial logit model. Third, for all practical purposes, analytical or closed-form solutions are typically not available; analyses can however be carried out by applying standard comparative-static exercises in order to derive relevant managerial implications.

Dynamic Game-Theoretic Formulations
In different contexts, there exist several surveys on the subject of competitive marketing strategies under deterministic conditions. A general survey which includes various marketing mix variables is that by Moorthy [1993] in the recent volume by Eliashberg and Lilien [1993] which contains other surveys on different components of the marketing mix, many of them include discussions on the impact of competition. Due to the availability of these surveys and more importantly, due to the fact that we want to address some of the potential extension to random demand, we will choose to discuss certain simple formulations of dynamic pricing and advertising to facilitate a comparison with those under uncertainty in the remainder of the chapter.

As before, we begin with a pricing formulation. Eliashberg and Jeuland [1986] considers the impact of the entry of a competitor in the second period on a first-period monopoly. In the first period, which ends at t^* when the entrant enters the market, the monopolistic firm's demand is specified as:

$$\frac{dQ_1(t)}{dt} \equiv q_1(t) = [S - Q_1(t)]\alpha_1[1 - kp_1(t)] \tag{8.13}$$

where the notation is familiar with $Q_1(t)$ indicating the monopolist's *cumulative* sales at time t, and the coefficients α and k denote, respectively the diffusion parameter and the price-sensitivity parameter.

Starting from time t^*, the sales response function facing each of the two firms is as follows:

$$\frac{dQ_i(t)}{dt} \equiv q_i(t) = [S - Q_1(t) - Q_2(t)]\{\alpha_i[1 - kp_i(t)] + \gamma[p_j(t) - p_i(t)]\}; \tag{8.14}$$

$$i,j = 1,2; \; j \neq i$$

where γ denotes the effect of the products' price differential.

Facing with constant marginal costs c_i, and assuming no discounting for mathematical convenience, the firm's objective functions are

$$\Pi_1(t) = \int_0^T [p_1(t) - c_1(t)] q_1(t) dt$$

$$\text{and} \quad \Pi_2(t) = \int_{t_*}^T [p_2(t) - c_2(t)] q_2(t) dt.$$

Maximizing the objective functions subject to the sales response equations yield a number of theoretical results with interesting managerial implications. A major result of the analysis is that for a given t^*, the nonmyopic firm, which perfectly foresees the competitor's entry, sets an optimum cumulative sales target at a level *lower* than that chosen by the myopic firm. Consequently, the nonmyopic firm charges a price higher than that by the myopic firm and in addition, it does not reduce its price as rapidly as the myopic firm.

We should also mention that there are other studies which address various aspects of dynamic competitive pricing, including Rao and Bass [1985] who consider how competition affects the dynamic pricing of new products. In particular, Dockner and Jorgensen [1988] examine optimal dynamic pricing in oligopolistic markets as an extension of the Kalish monopolistic model we presented in Chapter 2 on pricing. With a similar notation, the results and their corresponding interpretations parallel with those in eq. (2.41) with appropriate modifications for the presence of many competitive firms in the industry. On the basis of an open-loop solution to the optimal control problem facing the firm, the optimal price path can be expressed as:

$$p_i^* = \frac{\varepsilon_i}{\varepsilon_i - 1} [c_i - \lambda_i] + \frac{\sum_{j=1, j \neq i}^n \lambda_{ij} \varepsilon_{ji} [\frac{q_j}{q_i}]}{\varepsilon_i - 1} \qquad (8.15)$$

where ε_i denotes the absolute value of firm i's own price elasticity, ε_{ji} the cross price elasticity of the j-th firm's sales with respect to firm i's price change.

The interpretation for λ_i is similar to the monopolistic firm case to reflect the impact of the firm's own pricing on its future profits, represented by the product's own shadow price, and λ_{ij} denotes the shadow price associated with the effect of firm j's pricing on the profits of firm i.

It is clear how the preceding equation represents a modification of the optimal pricing rule of (2.41) to take into account the impact of competition. It is also interesting to observe the time dimension impact on the preceding problem by comparing the result with the static, heuristic result in eq. (8.1).

We should also note an early model of dynamic pricing using the repeated game formulation by Friedman [1971] who argues that in implicitly colluding oligopolies, the threat of punishment of the deviant firm from the jointly optimal price would be sufficient to induce firms not to cheat by cutting price. As a result, in equilibrium, there would be no cheaters and the (subgame-perfect) equilibrium can reinforce the implicit collusion. Consequently, there would not be any price wars. We will note in the next section several efforts to show several different contexts, stochastic demand among them, within which price wars among competing firms may occur.

We now look at a representative approach to competitive advertising under dynamic conditions. Once again, there are several works on this subject, among them we must include Sethi [1977] who concentrates on the optimal control approach in which dynamic characterizations involve mainly the accumulated goodwill effect of advertising activities in the tradition of Nerlove-Arrow model; and Erickson [1991] who examines the dynamic oligopolies on the basis of the Lanchester model of warfare. We illustrate here the study by Fershtman, Mahajan, and Muller [1990] who address the entry game of advertising in a fashion very similar to the pricing entry formulation of Eliashberg and Jeuland presented above. Following the Nerlove-Arrow model of goodwill accumulation, assume that the specification for firm i is:

$$\frac{dG_i(t)}{dt} = m_i(t) - \delta_i G_i(t); \quad i=1,2 \tag{8.16}$$

where $G_i(t)$ denotes accumulated goodwill, δ_i the rate of depreciation of goodwill.

Assume further that sales response function is of the following form:

$$q_i = G_i^{\eta_i} G_j^{-\eta_j} f_i(p_i, p_j); \quad i,j=1,2; \quad i \neq j \tag{8.17}$$

where η_i and η_j denotes, respectively, the own sales elasticity and the cross sales elasticity with respect to goodwill.

Of particular interest for our present purposes is the comparison between a "surprised" monopolist and a far-sighted monopolist in the sense that the latter anticipates entry at time t^*, say. This formulation bears some similarity with that of Eliashberg and Jeuland who examine the pricing decision with the same motivation regarding entry. The objective function facing the short-sighted monopolist is to:

$$\text{Max.} \quad \int_0^\infty [(p_1 - c_1) G_m^{\eta_1} f_1(p_1) - g_1(m_1)] e^{-rt} dt$$

which is the present value of the monopolist's stream of profits, using the discount rate r; the monetary cost of advertising effort m_1 is specified as $g_1(m_1)$; and the subscript m denotes the surprised monopolist.

On the other hand, the far-sighted monopolist is seeking to

$$\text{Max.} \quad \int_0^{t^*} [(p_1 - c_1) G_1^{\eta_1} f_1(p_1) - g_1(m_1)] e^{-rt} dt$$

from present to time t^* and then, from time t^* on,

$$\text{Max.} \quad \int_{t^*}^\infty [(p_1 - c_1) G_1^{\eta_1} G_2^{-\eta_k} f_1(p_1, p_2) - g_1(m_1)] e^{-rt} dt$$

where the monopolist is now designated firm 1.

A result of interest to us here is that the surprised monopolist tends to advertise at a level higher than the far-sighted monopolist during the period leading to t^*, the entry time of the new firm.

Unlike the case of pricing and advertising, the general dynamic game of marketing mix has not been at all addressed, to our knowledge. Consistent with our effort to incorporate a company's other functions outside of marketing such as production and investment, one can interpret a repeated game due to Kreps and Scheinkman [1983] who consider the pricing game under production capacity constraint. It is well-known that under constant unit cost (hence constant marginal cost), Bertrand price competition would lead to an unreasonable result that even within a duopolistic market, competition yields an industry equilibrium characterized by pricing the product at marginal cost c and each duopolist earns zero economic profits. Within marketing contexts, it would be hard to justify this type of price-setting formulation as we know pricing is a most important marketing activity in reality. However, it can be seen that the Bertrand equilibrium as described above will not be realized due to a number of realistic conditions. Tirole [1989] indicates at least three major scenarios which would prevent such an equilibrium in a more realistic setting: the capacity constraints signified by an increasing marginal cost instead of constant marginal cost; the notion of timing pricing decisions which lead to possible collusive behavior; and product differentiation which would enable firms to charge different prices in equilibrium. In our current context, especially in the context of a marketing mix framework , it can be seen that the zero-profit, constant marginal cost pricing Bertrand equilibrium would not be realized.

Regarding the capacity constraint scenario, Kreps and Scheinkman consider a model where pricing simultaneously takes place in the second of a two-stage game once the competing firms simultaneously determine the capacities in the first stage. Thus the conventional Cournot approach of quantity-setting, which is related to the capacity competition in the first stage of this game, is not as unreasonable as it suggests; in fact it allows the firms to compete on prices, once the capacities have been determined, as a marketing practitioner would concur. This is the reason why Kreps and Scheinkman concluded that quantity precommitment and Bertrand competition (in the second stage) yield Cournot outcomes; consequently, "price competition and quantity competition should not be interpreted as the choice of decision variables in the second period, but rather two different reduced forms for determining prices and outputs." (Fudenberg and Tirole [1984, p.365]). It is of particular interest for us to note that this interpretation makes sense in terms of marketing applications. Typically firms do compete on price but in conjunction with other marketing expenditures such as advertising and distribution, capacity competition has already set in and thus the two stage game would lead to the Cournot equilibrium result even though firms compete in the Bertrand fashion in the second stage of the game.

3 COMPETITIVE PRICING DECISIONS

In this section, we shall focus on pricing as the dominant decision variable. As the previous work on the subject indicated, even in the dynamic setting, the basic Bertrand result seems to prevail. For example, the price equal marginal cost result in the entry game of Eliashberg and Jeuland generalizes the Cournot result even for a dynamic context. However, we have also just indicated in the previous section that other dynamic considerations would not yield the Cournot results. Of particular interest for us here is the analysis of what has become to be known as price wars, with an emphasis on the role of uncertain demand in this framework. We should also point out that it is the two-stage decision in the sense of Kreps Scheinkman that we have the marketing mix in the broader context of capacity investment in the first stage and then price competition in the second stage. We shall also address in this section the issue of interaction of advertising in the role of communication to the consumers about the firm's product prices. These issues will be addressed in turn.

3.1 Price Wars

Collusive Behavior Under Stochastic Demand
Recall the deterministic model by Friedman [1971] in the previous section that within an infinitely repeated game context, implicitly colluding behavior may result if there is a threat of reverting to competitive pricing whenever a single firm does not cooperate; thus price wars would not occur. Casual observations as well as empirical studies tend to indicate that price wars do happen. More specifically, the standard empirical observation is that during periods of economic downturn, tacit collusion in pricing tends to break down (Scherer and Ross [1990]) due to the incentives to cut prices; leading to price wars. A formalization of this observation is given in Green and Porter [1984]. Assuming that observability of demand is not perfect, a price reduction by a competitor could be due to a depressing market demand or to a competitor's price-cutting. Hence, the collusive equilibrium is characterized by a price-triggering mechanism such that punishment in the form of price reduction would occur only after certain level of (low) price had been obtained. Consequently, price wars would occur in economic recession. So note that the notion of capacity constraint is absent in this framework, rather it is the imperfect observability of demand which drives the result.

Strategic Pricing
In contrast to the preceding model, with perfect observability in demand, Rotemberg and Saloner [1986] consider a dynamic pricing in the following model. Assume that the inverse demand is $p(Q_t, \xi_t)$ where Q_t denotes industry output at time t and it is assumed further that p is increasing in ξ_t which has the distribution function of $\Phi(\xi_t)$. There are n symmetric firms producing a homogeneous good in an infinite-horizon

setting. In addition, assume that both marginal costs and average costs are constant, denoted as usual as c. Note that the assumption of a constant marginal cost in effect assumes away the notion of capacity competition in the two stage game of Kreps and Scheinkman we discussed earlier. From the preceding setting, there always exists an equilibrium in which all firms set $p=c$ in all periods. Consider, however, a different equilibrium scenario where, at time t, each symmetric firm obtains profit of $\Pi^*(\xi_t)$ by producing q_t^* which is equal Q_t^*/n where Q_t^* denotes the optimal joint profit-maximizing industry output. The authors argue that at time t, firm i would deviate from the joint profit-maximizing output if

$$\Pi^*(\xi_t) > \frac{K}{(n-1)} \qquad (8.18)$$

where K refers to the monetary punishment inflicted upon the firm in such an event.

The equilibrium has the following interesting feature: For $\xi_t > \xi_t^*$ where ξ_t^* is defined as $(n-1)\Pi^*(\xi_t^*)=K$ so that (8.18) holds with equality, the higher is the demand, i.e., the higher is ξ_t, the higher is the equilibrium output and hence, the lower is the equilibrium price.

Consequently, a major finding is that implicitly colluding oligopolies are likely to behave more competitively in periods in which demand is high. That is, it is harder to maintain implicit collusion when the economy is booming. A higher value of ξ tends to satisfy the condition in (8.18), thus encourages the firm's reduction of its price from the implicitly collusive price. Stated differently, at any period of time, each firm has to weigh between the benefit of deviating from the collusion to the costs in the form of certain punishment. During periods of high demand (booming), the benefit of charging a price lower than the industry's current price is higher than the consequent punishment; thus price wars may result.

Staiger and Wolak [1992] consider a model with stochastic demand as in the Rotemberg and Saloner model, subject to the capacity constraint in the sense of Kreps and Scheinkman. Thus, at any time period, demand is realized only after the firm's capacity has been determined. The authors then found that industry equilibrium exhibits features which tend to support the conventional line of argument that during periods of declining economic activities, excess capacity arises, which in turn leads to breakdown of price collusion, hence price wars. While within the context of an infinitely repeated game the role of capacity has been analyzed in the literature, this study introduces the additional element of demand stochasticity. The result of this analysis is that mild price wars result in situations where excess capacity exists but not sufficiently severe; firms reduce their prices below the joint monopoly levels with a resulting stable market shares. When the excess capacity is sufficiently high, price cutting becomes more severe, leading to market share instability.

3.2 A Linear Control Approach

While we will provide in the next chapter a little more technical detail of this formulation, due to Roy, Hanssens, and Raju [1994], it may be useful to introduce its general approach here within the context of dynamic competitive pricing under random demand. The major divergence of this particular formulation is that the objective function facing the firm involves some criteria in seeking to minimize discounted sum of squares of deviations from certain sales targets. Further, the effort there is to formulate a competitive model with potential empirical applications.

The state equations involve a brand's sales equation relating current period sales to its one-year lagged values, its current price as well as the competitor's sales and price. Clearly, the linear assumption facilitates a closed-loop solution as is well-known in this literature. One particular feature is that the sales equation is subject to a random error term and the uncertainty feature involves the firm's forecast of this error term. Optimal pricing rules can be derived as linear functions of state variables as well as the forecast errors; rules for both competing firms are consequently obtained. A major contribution of this approach is the econometric and empirical implications of the resulting optimal pricing. In this regard, both the Stackelberg and Nash versions of competition are estimated using real data together with certain tests for the optimizing assumption.

3.3 Price-Setting vs. Output-Setting

In this sub-section we report a model due to Klemperer and Meyer [1986] who pay particular attention to the price vs. quantity setting under uncertainty. Recall our discussion in Chapter 2 that unlike the scenarios under deterministic conditions in which it does not matter whether one is looking at the firm's pricing or output as the decision variable, the behavioral mode of the choice variable does matter when firms are faced with random demand. It is not surprising, therefore, that within a competitive environment, such an asymmetry continues to exist. Let us examine the Klemperer-Meyer model in some detail here. Allowing for product differentiation in the sense that each brand's sales depends on its own price and the competing brand's price not necessarily in an identical fashion, the inverse sales equations are:

$$p_1 = \alpha - \beta q_1 - \gamma q_2$$

$$\text{and} \quad p_2 = \alpha - \beta q_2 - \gamma q_1$$

where note that products are not perfect substitutes.

It is easy to establish that whether the firm sets its price or its sales would be irrelevant as these two strategies would lead to identical solutions. Now, suppose that the demand functions are subject to an error term ξ. The sales response function for firm i is:

$$p_i = \alpha - \beta q_i - \gamma q_j + \xi; \quad i,j=1,2 \quad j \neq i \tag{8.19}$$

where ξ has zero mean and constant variance.

The solution method can be seen by noting that given its conjecture about firm 2's choice of strategic variable $(\bar{q}_2)$ or $(\bar{p}_2)$, firm 1's position is that of a monopolist facing the uncertain (residual) demand of

$$p_1 = \alpha - \beta q_1 - \gamma \bar{q}_2 + \xi$$

$$\text{or} \quad p_1 = \alpha[\frac{(\beta - \gamma)}{\beta}] + [\frac{\gamma}{\beta}]\bar{p}_2 - [\frac{(\beta^2 - \gamma^2)}{\beta}]q_1 + [\frac{(\beta - \gamma)}{\beta}]\xi.$$

Along the same line with the analysis for the case of a monopolist's pricing and output decision under demand uncertainty which we presented in Chapter 2, we note the following results obtained by Klemperer and Meyer. Given the monopolist's linear demand function with additive random term with zero mean and constant variance and quadratic cost function, the monopolist strictly prefers to set quantity when marginal costs slope upward; price setting is preferred when the marginal costs slope downward; and indifferent only when marginal costs are flat.

Further, for the case of *differentiated* products in which the duopolists are faced with random demand as specified above (linear and additive error term) as well as quadratic cost functions, it is shown that Nash equilibrium involves both firms setting quantities if *MC* slopes upward and setting price if *MC* slopes downward. If the marginal costs are constant, then all the four possible combinations representing both price-setting and quantity-setting chosen by both firms may qualify as Nash equilibria. In contrast, for perfect substitutes, there exist only two equilibria involving either quantity-setting or price-setting by both firms.

Now, the way in which the random term enters the demand function has direct bearing on the firm's decision. First consider the monopoly case in which the slope of the linear response function is random

$$p = a - (\frac{b}{\xi})q \tag{8.20}$$

where ξ is a random variable with mean equal to unity and constant variance.

It is then shown that whether the firm prefers the quantity-setting or price-setting depends on the slope of the *MC* curve, again along the line developed in more detail in Chapter 2 on monopolistic pricing. For the differentiated products duopolistic market, price-setting Nash equilibrium is shown to exist for certain range of *MC*. The analysis can then be extended to a more general demand formulation and the assumed curvature of the demand schedules.

In summary, as demonstrated by Klemperer and Meyer, the role of the firm's production costs characteristics will be crucial in determining the difference between these two strategies. They further show that the nature of uncertainty in the sense that whether firms have better information on the demand schedule's intercept or its slope would have significant bearing on such a comparison. Finally, in general, the demand curvature has also interesting implications within this particular context.

3.4 Interactive Decisions

In this sub-section, we note a number of possible interactions among the firm's pricing policy and its advertising. We first look at a monopolistically competitive model formulated by Butter [1977] in which advertising plays the role of communicating the information on the firm's price and thus differentiating the competing firms' products. We then touch on the recent issue of loss-leader pricing in a competitive framework, exemplified in the work of Lal and Matutes [1994].

Informational Differentiation
Butter [1977] considers a monopolistically competitive market structure in which there exists a large number of firms each facing a downward-sloping demand function, their effects are negligible on the other firms. Differentiation resulted since consumers may not be aware of certain brands. Another model is Grossman and Shapiro [1984] which formulates oligopolistic reactions and introduces product differentiation along another dimension due to location. We will discuss the Grossman-Shapiro model in a sub-section below.

Butter assumes in his model that each consumer has unit demand dictated by his utility of $U = \bar{s} - p$ if he buys one unit at p and zero otherwise. If all consumers are completely informed, it is clear that Bertrand competition takes place, driving price to marginal cost with each consumer's utility of $\bar{s} - c$. Now suppose that information, through advertising activities, on the price is costly, measured by unit cost of advertising and denoted as c_m. Since there are S potential consumers in the market, recalling our notation in Chapter 6 where S refers to Size, each of those consumers has a probability of $1/S$ of receiving a given ad. On this basis, the author notes that the social cost of getting at least one ad to the (cumulative) fraction F is $c_m S \ln[1/(1-F)]$ which yields the advertising cost per consumer of $c_m \ln[1/(1-F)]$. It is then shown that the monopolistically competitive level of informative advertising is socially optimal. To show this result, note that upon denoting $\pi(p)$ as the probability that an ad indicating price p is accepted, zero profit condition of a monopolistically competitive equilibrium can be characterized as

$$(p-c)\pi(p)-c_m=0$$

which can be shown to yield

$$(1-F^*)=\frac{c_m}{\bar{s}-c}.$$

On the other hand, a social planner would choose an optimal cumulative fraction F^{**} in order to

$$\text{Max. } \{F(\bar{s}-c)-c_m\ln[\frac{1}{1-F}]\}$$

which yields the first-order condition identical to the previous equation.

Loss-Leader Pricing

In their paper, Lal and Matutes [1994] consider a duopolistic scenario in which two firms situated at the ends of a segment of unit length, competing in prices for the demand of two products. Consumers are assumed to be uniformly distributed, incurring a transportation cost $.5d$; otherwise they have identical willingness to pay p_H for one unit of each good. Unlike the multi-product oligopolistic model of Lal and Matutes [1989] where, with perfect information on prices, stores seek to discriminate two types of consumers in a noncooperative equilibrium, in this model there exists only one type of consumer and yet it is the price *uncertainty* in its interaction with economies of scale in shopping which drives the results of loss-leader pricing.

Assume that there are two firms A and B in the market, selling two goods: 1 and 2 with advertising cost m. The expected price of good i at store j is $E(p_{ij})$; $i=1,2$ and $j=A,B$. Consider the case where a consumer plans to buy both goods, it was shown that in equilibrium, all consumers buy both goods at a single store; that is an equilibrium in which some customers shop at both stores is shown not to exist. This particular result is driven by the argument that in order to induce the potential consumers to shop at both stores, sufficient discounts should be made to compensate for the transportation costs, a strategy competing firms will not find optimal. Given that in equilibrium, consumers shop only at one store; they rationally form the expectations on prices to include the fact that the store will charge the reservation price p_H to the unadvertised product. Consequently, in equilibrium, each store charges monopoly prices to unadvertised goods in order to extract all consumer surplus since reservation prices are assumed known. In this context, the authors have highlighted the role of advertising, not as an information device just discussed and elaborated below on a basis of a model by Grossman and Shapiro for oligopolistic firms, but rather as a commitment device to guarantee potential consumers certain surplus so as to induce them to shop at a particular store.

4 COMPETITIVE ADVERTISING

In this section we will discuss a number of specific models dealing with specific subjects which, in our view, constitute important aspects of advertising issues. The first model involves what has been known as informative notion of advertising, the second with a market share type of formulation in which we will explicitly analyze the effect of uncertainty, and the third with strategic elements in designing an advertising policy for competing firms.

4.1 Informative Advertisement

We concentrate here only on the informative role of advertising, leaving aside the strategic role of advertising in a later context. The model below is that of Grossman and Shapiro [1984] who consider a duopolistic situation in which the two firms situated at the ends of a line of unit length wherein consumers are uniformly distributed. The consumer is informed of the product through marketing efforts of the competing firms; the monetary cost of the j-th firm's effort is characterized by the following:

$$m(F_j) = \frac{\alpha F_j^2}{2} \tag{8.21}$$

where F_j represents the fraction of the buying population, again recalling our use of the notation F in the analysis of the Bass diffusion process in Chapter 6, and α is a parameter to reflect advertising effectiveness.

Note that this quadratic cost function exhibits increasing at an increasing rate cost of advertising. Denoting the transportation cost as d, an application of the well-known Hotelling spatial model yields the following demand function for firm j:

$$q_j = \frac{(p_i - p_j + d)}{2d}; \ j=1,2; \ i \neq j \tag{8.22}$$

provided that the advertising messages from both sellers reach the entire buying population.

On the other hand, when advertising costs are sufficiently high so that reaching the entire market would not constitute an optimal policy, the demand function facing the j-th firm becomes:

$$q_j = F_j[(1 - F_i) + F_i(\frac{p_i - p_j + d}{2d})]; \ j=1,2; \ i \neq j.$$

Note that if for both firms, $F_j = 1$; $j=1,2$, the preceding demand becomes the previous one in (8.22). The optimization problem facing firm j is to choose price p_j and marketing expenditure m_j in order to maximize:

$$\Pi_j = (p_j - c_j)q_j - m_j - FC_j; \ j=1,2.$$

The first-order conditions can be shown to yield:

$$p_j = \frac{(p_i + d + c_j)}{2} + \frac{(1 - F_i)}{F_i} d$$

and $F_j = \frac{p_j - c_j}{\alpha}[(1 - F_i) + F_i(\frac{p_i - p_j + d}{2d})]; \ j = 1,2; \ i \neq j.$

The symmetric equilibrium solution can be seen to be:

$$p^* = c + (2\alpha d)^{\frac{1}{2}} \quad \text{and} \quad F^* = \frac{2}{1 + (2\alpha/d)^{\frac{1}{2}}}.$$

4.2 Advertising in Market Share Models

We shall first consider a deterministic model of competitive advertising, to be followed by a brief discussion on the possible impact of sales uncertainty.

Deterministic Formulation

The discussion in this sub-section on the deterministic version is based on a model analyzed by Schmalensee [1974]. Let us assume that there are two competitors in the market and each engages only in non-price competition, specifically promotional activities. Certain aspects of this type of model have been discussed in Chapter 6 on market share and diffusion where interactions between pricing and advertising were analyzed. Here, we simplify the presentation by using the Schmalensee model where promotional activities represent the sole decision variable. Suppose that the demand function facing firm j is:

$$q_j(m_1, m_2) \equiv s_j(m_1, m_2) S(m_1, m_2); \ j = 1,2 \qquad (8.23)$$

where s_j denotes the j-th firm's market share and S denotes the market size, that is the industry demand.

Assume that the market share for firm j is specified, following Mills [1961], by:

$$s_j(m_1, m_2) = \frac{m_j^\beta}{m_1^\beta + m_2^\beta}$$

and industry demand is assumed to be

$$S(m_1, m_2) = S_0(m_1 + m_2)^\theta \equiv S_0 M^\theta$$

where S_0 denotes the primary industry sales, $M = m_1 + m_2$ denotes industry advertising, and β and θ are known coefficients with the same interpretations as before.

The demand function facing the j-th firm is thus:

$$q_j \equiv s_j S = \frac{m_j^\beta}{m_i^\beta + m_j^\beta} S_0 M^\theta.$$

The profit function for the firm can then be defined as:

$$\Pi_j = (p-c)s_j S_0 M^\theta - m_j - FC$$

where it is assumed that the product price p, the constant average cost c, and the fixed costs FC are identical among the firms.

It can be shown that the first-order condition for optimality is:

$$\frac{\partial \Pi_j}{\partial m_j} = 0 \Rightarrow (p-c)s_j S_0 M^{\theta-1}[\theta + \beta(1-s_j)\frac{M}{m_j}] = 1. \qquad (8.24)$$

Under the symmetry assumption, the preceding condition becomes:

$$m = \frac{1}{2}[(p-c)S_0(\beta + \theta)/2]^{1/(1-\theta)} \qquad (8.25)$$

For a specific special case where $\theta=0$ (static market), $\beta=1$ as in the Mills model, the preceding solution becomes:

$$m^* = \frac{1}{4}(p-c)S_0$$

and the optimal profit for each of the duopolists is

$$\Pi^* = \frac{1}{4}(p-c)S_0 - FC.$$

A Random Sales Version
Suppose now that the industry sale is not known with certainty but rather it is subject to the following simple additive stochastic specification

$$S = S_0(m_1 + m_2)^\theta + \xi.$$

For the j-th firm, the profit function is:

$$\Pi_j = (p-c)s_j[S_0 M^\theta + \xi] - m_j$$

from which the expected profit is

$$E(\Pi_j) = (p-c)s_j S_0 M^\theta - m_j.$$

To account for risk-taking behavior, assuming quadratic utility function, the first-order condition for optimality is

$$\frac{\partial E(\Pi_j)}{\partial m_j} = \frac{1}{2}r[\frac{dE(\Pi_j - E\Pi_j)^2}{dm_j}]$$

where
$$\frac{dE(\Pi_j - E\Pi_j)^2}{dm_j} = 2(p-c)^2\sigma_\xi^2 s_j^2 s_j \beta m_j^{-1}.$$

Consequently, noting that $\partial E(\Pi_j)/\partial m_j = (p-c)s_j S_0 \theta M^{\theta-1} + M^\theta(p-c)S_0\beta m_j^{-1}s_j(1-s_j)-1$, the first-order condition can then be expressed for the symmetry case as:

$$(p-c)S_0(2m)^\theta(\theta+\beta)-4m = \frac{1}{2}r(p-c)^2\sigma_\xi^2\beta.$$

For ease of interpretation, consider once again the case where $\theta=0$ and $\beta=1$, the preceding relation yields:

$$m = \frac{(p-c)S_0}{4} - \frac{r(p-c)^2\sigma_\xi^2}{8}$$

which is of course identical to the result obtained and reported earlier in Sub-section 3.2 of Chapter 6.

As before, the preceding expression yields the following

$$\frac{\partial m}{\partial r}<0 \quad ; \quad \frac{\partial m}{\partial\sigma_\xi^2}<0.$$

4.3 Strategic Advertising

We will consider in some detail two particular models which have significant bearing in terms of using advertising as a strategic decision variable. The first is due to Fudenberg and Tirole [1984] who examine the strategic role of advertising when the firm is faced with possible entry. The second represents an interpretation of a model formulated by Smets, cited and analyzed by Dixit and Pindyck [1994] who address a more general problem of investment under uncertainty. We start with the Fudenberg-Tirole formulation.

The Fudenberg and Tirole Model
The basic idea for this model is the notion that in some situations, an incumbent may find it strategically advantageous to underinvest in order to increase the incentive to aggressively respond to potential entry by competitors (lean and hungry look). The

authors consider the following two separate scenarios: entry-deterring and entry accommodating.   It was demonstrated that an incumbent may underinvest in advertising in order to deter entry since by lowering its stock of goodwill it establishes a credible threat to cut prices in the event of entry. If accommodating is chosen, the incumbent may overinvest (fat-cat) to soften the entrant's pricing. The driving force behind these results are due to the strategic effect of a firm's advertising decision. Let us sketch the basic argument here.

For the accommodating scenario, there would be two firms in the second stage. If a consumer is aware of both firms, his or her demand is $q_1=q_1(p_1,p_2)$ and $q_2=q_2(p_1,p_2)$; if aware only of firm 1, it is $q_1=q_1(p_1,\infty)$; if only of firm 2, it is $q_2=q_2(\infty,p_2)$. The only relevant cost here is advertising which is used to inform consumers of the brand's existence with price information. The solution is the standard Nash-Cournot game, determining the prices to be charged. The dynamic characterization involved in this framework is due to the fact that the incumbent's (the first mover in this context) advertising level in period 1 creates goodwill which carries over to period 2. Consequently, the incumbent's optimizing decision regarding its advertising should take into account the fact that its decision influences the entrant's pricing behavior. An important theoretical result is based on the sign of the response of the (equilibrium) price to period 1's advertising which could be positive.   That is, by increasing the first period advertising, the incumbent's equilibrium price tends to go up. In comparing that optimal policy with the open loop/precommitment solution, it can be shown that perfect equilibrium solution (where strategic effect is included) exceeds its counterpart in the non-strategic case. Consequently, the incumbent will have an incentive to advertise heavily in the first period to soften the entrant's pricing behavior.

On the other hand, in order to deter entry, the incumbent may want to under-advertise so that in the process it establishes a credible threat that it will cut prices in the event of the entry in the second period; this is what has been termed as playing the lean and hungry look. This is seen by analyzing the entrant's profit maximization objective function; its decision (to entry) depends on the incumbent's period 1's advertising. The incumbent's advertising level has a direct effect on the market which is negative from the entrant point if view: increasing in m_1 leads to smaller sales for the entrant with reducing potential profits. However m_1 also has the indirect (strategic effect) which is positive since increasing m_1 induces an increase in the firm equilibrium price which enhances the entrant's potential profits. So if the indirect effect is dominant, by increasing m_1, the incumbent may trigger the entrant's decision to enter.

The Smets and Dixit-Pindyck Model
In a particular section in their recent book, Dixit and Pindyck [1994] use a formulation by Smets to demonstrate a model involving oligopolistic industries within a stochastic and dynamic setting. From a marketing viewpoint, one can set up the

background for our present interpretation as follows. Think of advertising as a form of investment; an approach which has long been used in the economics and marketing literature. As in any form of investment, the outcomes of such activities will not be known with certainty. Further, part or all of the cost involving in this marketing activity are irreversible in the sense that it may not be recovered. Finally, the timing of such an activity constitutes an integral part of the firm's investment decision. In the context of a competitive market with a few number of firms, the interaction of irreversible marketing spending with the timing option and the uncertainty of the outcomes represents the framework based on which the firm's advertising decision will be made. Such a decision will be balanced between the need for the firm to speed up its marketing efforts under the (potential) pressure of the competition and the hesitation to undertake those projects due to the irreversibility of the investment, which, coupled with the inherent uncertainty in the sales response, induces the firm to postpone its marketing activities in order to gain additional information. The model is set up as follows.

Consider a duopolistic market in which each of the two firms, upon investing an advertising budget in the amount of m, will produce *one* unit of sales forever. To simplify the analysis, suppose further that advertising spending m is the only cost involved in yielding the one unit sales, thus implying zero production cost. Because of these simplifying assumptions, the profit gained by each firm is given by p, as $\Pi = pq = p$. Denoting Q as the industry quantity demanded, the market inverse demand function is specified as:

$$p = yD(Q) \tag{8.26}$$

where y represents a multiplicative shock which is assumed to follow the geometric Brownian motion of the form

$$dy = \alpha y dt + \sigma y dz \tag{8.27}$$

where α and σ are known constants, reflecting respectively the drift parameter and the variance parameter; and dz is the increment of a Wiener process.

The nature of the uncertainty in the firm's profit flow can be seen by noting that due to the randomness in the shock y, for any given industry output, the profit Π also follows a stochastic process identical to that which characterizes y. Assuming risk neutrality and the discount rate of r, the problem facing the competing firms is when, if at all, to engage in investing m. The solution involves characterizations of the firm's decision under different scenarios, the more technical details of which are given in Dixit and Pindyck. We report here some main results regarding the decision by the follower in a leader-follower paradigm of the dynamic duopoly game to gain additional insights into this line of research.

The Follower's Decision

Since each firm produces one unit of output, the industry output can take the values of 0, 1, or 2 depending on the number of firms (zero, one or two, respectively); the follower's profit flow, if it decided to invest m, is $\Pi^f = yD(2)$, given of course the fact that the other firm, the leader, has already made the investment. The decision rule for the follower is that it should advertise once certain threshold level of y, denoted by y^*, is reached. Such a threshold level is determined by:

$$y^*D(2) = \frac{\beta}{\beta - 1}(r - \alpha)m \tag{8.28}$$

where we recall the definitions of the discount rate r and the drift parameter α; and where β is the positive root of the following quadratic equation

$$\frac{1}{2}\sigma^2\beta(\beta - 1) + \alpha\beta - r = 0. \tag{8.29}$$

More significantly, the positive root β is found to exceed unity, i.e., $\beta > 1$. This fact yields a powerful implication for the firm's investment decision-making process as we will show heuristically as follows. First, the expected present value of the follower's stream of future profits Π^f_t, with the initial value Π^f, can be expressed as:

$$\int_0^\infty \Pi^f e^{-(r-\alpha)t}dt = \frac{\Pi^f}{(r-\alpha)} \equiv V(\Pi^f).$$

Then, corresponding to the threshold y^*, the threshold profit $\Pi^{*f} = y^*D(2)$, yields the expected present value $\Pi^{*f}/(r-\alpha) \equiv V^*(\Pi^f)$ as indicated in the preceding expression. Thus, equation (8.28) which determines y^*, can be expressed simply as

$$V^*(\Pi^f) = \frac{\beta}{\beta - 1}m. \tag{8.30}$$

Now, with $\beta > 1$, the preceding relation implies that $V^*(\Pi^f) > m$. The effect of uncertainty can now be seen clearly. As one interprets advertising as a form of investment as we do here, the conventional deterministic rule in project evaluation is that the project is approved as long as $V > V^* = m$; that is as long as the net present value of the project is positive. Here, under the conditions of uncertain profits and irreversibility of investment, the critical value V^* is itself greater than advertising investment m as indicated in (8.30), leading to the decision rule quite different from the conventional net present value criterion. The extent of such a difference depends on the parameter β which, through (8.29), depends on other parameters α, r, and σ.

5 PRODUCT COMPETITION

5.1 Production Competition and Risk Attitude

We next examine the implications of the competitive firm's attitude towards risk on the firm's output decisions. The first model we look at, by Palfrey [1982], explores the impact of asymmetry in the firms' risk behavior on the resulting Nash equilibrium for a random linear demand function. We then report some results obtained by Tessitore [1994] regarding the effects of non-linear utility on a basis of a comparative exercise of an oligopolistic firm which has a quadratic utility function. The crucial role of risk-taking behavior is explored further in a paper by Hviid [1989] who examines its implication for oligopolistic firms to share information on the unknown market demand facing them.

Palfrey's paper examines the issue of how competing firms' risk behaviors may have implications regarding the use and assessment of information on demand. The model assumes a linear demand function where the intercept is not known with certainty. Maximizing expected utility of profits would then yield optimal solutions as usual. More specifically, within a static model of duopoly with uncertain demand, the two firms are supposed to independently and simultaneously make output decisions to maximize their expected utility of profits. The linear demand is:

$$q(p) = \frac{\alpha}{b} - \frac{1}{b}p$$

where it is assumed that while b is known by both firms, α is not known but has the distribution $\Phi(\alpha)$.

For the symmetric information game in the sense that each firm would have to make an output decision before the realization of the random variable α, the i-th firm's maximization problem is :

$$\int U_i[\Pi_i]\varphi(\alpha)d\alpha; \quad i=1,2$$

where we note the firm-specific utility function and as usual, $\varphi(.)$ denotes the density function.

The Cournot-Nash equilibrium can then be determined, being characterized as dependent on the expected values of unknown parameter α.

On the other hand, consider an asymmetric information game scenario in which one firm is now assumed to be able to observe a realization of α, namely a, before making its production decision; firm 1, say. Thus firm 1's strategy involves choosing an output function which is a function of a, while firm 2 chooses an output level to maximize its expected utility of profit.

On the basis of these analyses, the following results are obtained: *i*) in the symmetric game, a particular firm is better off if it is less risk-averse and its opponent is more risk-averse (this is so since risk aversion tends to reduce a firm output, leading to an increase in the other firm's output and expected utility); *ii*) against a risk-averse opponent, a firm is better off in equilibrium when his opponent must face higher risk; *iii*) in the asymmetric game, the equilibrium solution is a function only of the risk attitude of the uninformed player, thus the informed firm's risk behavior bears no beneficial strategic effects as indicated in *i*); and *iv*) the informed firm's output is positively correlated with demand, hence reducing the risk faced by its opponent, a fact which is detrimental to itself. Consequently, for a risk-averse firm, the loss in risk advantage may more than offset the informational advantage; that is being more informed may not be beneficial. Thus, in certain competitive frameworks under uncertainty and risk-taking attitude, information may not be valuable if it changes the risk faced by its opponent in some fashion.

Tessitore [1994], in his paper, assumes that a duopolistic firm has a quadratic utility function, thus expresses the objective function for the *i*-th firm as:

$$V_i = E(\Pi_i) - r_i \sigma_{\Pi_i}$$

where *r* indicates the well-known Pratt-Arrow index for risk aversion.

Assuming the random inverse demand of the form $p = a - bQ + \xi$ in which, as before Q denotes industry output, the value of firm *i* can be written as

$$V_i = (1 - bQ)q_i - r_i q_i^2 \sigma^2$$

which leads to firm *i*'s reaction function as

$$q_i = \frac{1 - bq_j}{2(b + r_i \sigma^2)}; \; j \neq i.$$

Standard analysis leads to the following Cournot-Nash equilibrium output:

$$q_i^* = \frac{b + 2r_j \sigma^2}{\Delta}; \; j \neq i$$

where $\Delta = 4(b + r_1\sigma^2)(b + r_2\sigma^2) - b^2 > 0$.

On the basis of the preceding solution, a number of comparative-static results are obtained. In particular, we note here an interesting result that in strongly segmented duopolistic markets in the sense that firms have sufficiently different degrees of risk aversion, the less risk-averse firm may raise output in the face of increasing demand uncertainty. On the other hand, if the firms' attitudes towards risk are sufficiently similar, then the conventional result that increasing demand uncertainty induces the firms to reduce output will be obtained.

Within the context of output competition games, we thus note that the firm's attitude towards risk coupled with randomness in the demand yield optimal rules which are typically different from deterministic scenarios. It is therefore natural to presume that knowledge about the market demand is valuable and thus would it be beneficial for the competing firms to share those information? The issue of information transmission in the context of competing brands has been analyzed in the literature under the assumption of risk neutrality. Hviid [1989] considers the issue of duopolistic firms' incentives to share information about a random demand under the more realistic condition of risk aversion. It should be noted that standard literature indicates that Cournot duopolists producing a homogeneous good have no incentives to share their information on an unknown parameter of the demand equation. Hviid shows that this conclusion depends on the assumption that firms are risk neutral. The introduction of risk aversion may yield completely different results. It is further shown that Cournot duopolists's output is increasing in their information's quality and decreasing in their perception of risk.

It may be useful to outline the basic structure of the model here. The linear demand function is assumed to have a random intercept. Further, assume that the firms' utility exhibits constant absolute risk aversion and that the decision whether to share information is made prior to observing the signal concerning the random demand. The equilibrium solution is characterized by rational expectations (Bayesian-Nash). The notion is that firms make output decision on the basis of their observing the realization of the random term. Since the other firm is also making its output decision on the basis of its own observations, each firm of a duopoly has to form an expectation on the other firm's reaction.

More specifically, the demand function for a homogeneous good is

$$p = \alpha - Q = \alpha - q_1 - q_2; \quad \alpha \sim N(\alpha_0, \sigma_\alpha^2)$$

where signals concerning the random demand are unbiased estimators of α and N designates the normal density function.

That is, for firm i, before producing at a certain level, it observes a signal $a_i = \alpha + \xi_i$ where ξ has zero mean and constant variance σ_ξ^2. It then can be shown that:

$$\alpha \mid a_i \sim N\{ta_i + (1-t)\alpha_0, (1-t)\sigma_\alpha^2\}$$

$$\text{where} \quad t = \frac{\sigma_\alpha^2}{[\sigma_\alpha^2 + \sigma_\xi^2]}$$

which is a measure of the quality of the private information.

The analysis is then carried out on the basis of an assumed utility function exhibiting constant absolute risk aversion, involving both the scenario where no information sharing takes place and those in which firms are engaged in information sharing. A number of interesting results and their economic interpretations can be reported here: i) the risk-averse duopolistic firm's equilibrium output is increasing in the precision of the private information; ii) the more risk-averse or the higher the variance, the lower the equilibrium output. Further, on the basis of some numerical calculations, it was shown that under risk aversion, duopolists may want to share information with each contributes to the pool.

To conclude this sub-section, we present some basic features of a recent model by Chang and Lee [1994] who also address the related issue of value of information on an unknown demand within a competitive framework. Suppose that the inverse industry demand function for a particular manufacturing good is of the following form:

$$p = a - bQ + \xi$$

where ξ is distributed as normal with zero mean and variance σ.

For simplicity, suppose there are only two manufacturing firms which, prior to making production decisions to compete against each other in a standard Cournot game, may want to purchase an information contract from a monopolistic consulting or marketing firm which provides, at certain price, the information purchaser(s) a signal on the unknown demand. On the basis of either the signal it purchases or on its own private signal, each firm then seeks an output level to maximize its objective function of expected profit.

The i-th firm's private noisy signal about ξ is y_i which is assumed to be unbiased and subject to a measure of precision $t_i = 1/\sigma^2(y_i | \xi)$ where $\sigma^2(.)$ represents the conditional variance. Both firms have a common prior with the precision of $t_0 = 1/\sigma(\xi)$. Assuming stochastic independence between the firms' private signals and linearity in the information-signaling process, it can be shown that

$$E(\xi | y_i) = \frac{t_i y_i}{(t_1 + t_0)}; \quad i = 1, 2$$

which reflects firm i-th's posterior belief about ξ, conditional on the signal y_i .

On the other hand, the monopolistic marketing consulting firm is assumed to make a decision as to how much the fee to charge and what kind of firm it is dealing with so that its profit function is maximized. Thus, conceptually, the decision processes can be described as a three-stage game; in the first stage, the consulting firm offers the two manufacturing firms its signal on the random market demand at a certain fee, in the second stage the manufacturing firms must decide whether they want to purchases the signal, and in the third stage, on the basis of the signal obtained, the two manufacturing firms compete in a Cournot game. As usual, one can solve this type of problem by backward induction. We outline the steps as follows.

In stage 3, the optimal equilibrium production strategy for firm i is :

$$q_i = \frac{a}{3b} + \frac{\lambda_i}{(1 + \sum_{j=1}^{2} \lambda_j) b} . Y_i; \quad i = 1, 2$$

where $Y_i = y_i$ and $\lambda_i = t_i/(t_i + 2t_0)$ if the signal was not purchased; or $Y_i = \xi$ and $\lambda = 1$ if the signal from the consulting firm was purchased.

In stage 2, the value of information to a particular firm is then characterized with the following results: *i*) it is decreasing with the firm's internal information precision and *ii*) it is decreasing with the competitor's information precision. The information purchasing strategy is a pure strategy which is simply that the manufacturing firm would purchase the information if its value exceeds its cost.

Finally, at stage 1, the monopolistic consulting firm identifies the manufacturing firm, then sets the appropriate fee to maximize its profit.

On the basis of the solution to the preceding problem, one can derive important implications regarding the role of information acquisition in dealing with demand uncertainty on the one hand and the competition on the other hand.

5.2 Output Pre-Commitment and Flexibility

We include in this sub-section a description of two particular economic models which offer ways to address the general issue of strategic decision making under uncertainty in the sense we have earlier defined. We have chosen these models mainly because they specifically identify the presence of elements of uncertainty and consequently analyze the effects of those elements. Further, the models consider issues which are potentially applicable directly to marketing problems or if not so, may be interacted with the firm's marketing activities along the line of the production, investment and marketing joint decisions which we explored earlier in the previous chapter. Finally, the solution approaches advanced in these research are by themselves innovative and sufficiently general for applications to competitive marketing issues under stochastic conditions. We first consider a model due to Appelbaum and Lim [1985] who study implications of potential entry and uncertainty in demand in a contestable market where firms make production commitments prior to observing the true demand. We then describe a model by Spencer and Brander [1992] in which oligopolistic firms need to make trade-off decisions regarding output commitment and flexibility.

Contestable Markets under Uncertainty
In order to see the impact of competition, Appelbaum and Lim consider first the problem of a monopolist facing an inverse demand function of the form $p(q,\xi)$ where ξ is a random variable with the assumption that $\partial p/\partial \xi > 0$. A basic assumption here is a partial production commitment process in which the monopolistic firm makes some output commitment $x \geq 0$ *ex ante*, then following the realization of the random demand, the firm *ex post* adjusts its output by $z \geq 0$; thus we have $q = x + z$. The tradeoff between the postponed production and the early production precommitments can be seen by noting that while *ex post* production typically involves higher costs, delaying production gives the firm additional time and opportunity to gain valuable information regarding the uncertain demand. The problem facing the firm is to find an optimal mix of precommitted output x and adjusted output z.

Assume that the cost function is of the following linear form

$$C = c_x x + c_z z$$

where c_x and c_z denote, respectively, the unit cost of precommitted production and that of adjusted, *ex post* production; and naturally, $c_x < c_z$.

The objective of the risk-neutral monopolist is

$$\text{Max. } E[TR(x+z,\xi) - c_x x - c_z z].$$

The solution to this problem can be obtained by first determining the optimal level of *ex post* production z upon applying the *MR=MC* condition, to be followed then by looking for the optimal *ex ante* production level itself. That is, for a given level of precommitted output x and a realized value ξ, an optimal *ex post* production level z solves the problem

$$\Pi^0(x,\xi) \equiv \text{Max. } [TR(x+z,\xi) - c_x x - c_z z]$$

on the basis of which, the risk-neutral firm will then determine the precommitted output level x to maximize the objective function $E[\Pi^0(x,\xi)]$.

We summarize here a number of comparative-static results of interest. The authors find that, everything else being the same, an increase in c_x reduces the advantage of early production and will thus lower the level of output precommitment. On the other hand, an increase in *ex post* average costs will tend to increase the level of output precommitment. Further, an increase in uncertainty in a mean-preserving sense (Rothschild and Stiglitz [1970]) tends to reduce optimal precommitted output, denoted as x^*. Other results on the probability of *ex post* production and on the expected value of *ex post* production are obtained by the authors.

Against the preceding monopolistic analysis, within an *ex post* contestable market, let us now consider the effect of potential entry on the behavior of the incumbent. The reader will notice the familiarity of the sequential decision-making approach we have encountered in a number of previous occasions. As usual, a strategic implication is that the incumbent will take potential entry into account in its choice of the pre-committed output, and in doing so will affect the probability of entry.

Due to the assumption of the existence of the *ex post* contestable market as defined in Baumol, Panzar and Willig [1982], the *ex post* equilibrium implies that all *ex post* production yields nonpositive profit. Subject to this zero economic profit constraint, the incumbent's optimal output precommitment in the *ex post* contestable market, denoted as x^{**}, can then be obtained.

On the basis of the preceding analysis, we report here a number of interesting results obtained by the authors. The presence of an *ex post* contestable market tends to induce the monopolistic incumbent to raise its output commitment, thus behave more competitively. This particular result is driven by the fact that while no economic profits would be earned from *ex post* production due to competition, *ex ante* production may benefit the firm. Also, an increase in the efficiency of *ex ante* production, reflected by a decline in its unit cost of production, will raise the incumbent's output precommitment; hence reducing the probability of entry and the level of expected *ex post* production. Clearly, an increase in the efficiency of *ex post* production in the sense just defined would have the opposite effect. Further, increasing demand uncertainty induces the incumbent to lower its precommitment, thus encourages potential entry with increased level of expected *ex post* production.

The potential tradeoff between cost efficiency associated with early production and the firm's flexibility in adjusting its output in view of uncertain demand can therefore be seen. The next sub-section explores the same concept of trade-off possibilities in oligopolistic markets under conditions of demand uncertainty.

Pre-commitment and Flexibility under Oligopoly
We conclude this sub-section by presenting the model by Spencer and Brander who consider a number of scenarios in which demand uncertainty gives rise to a potential trade-off between flexibility and the incentives to pre-commit early. This is so since delaying production until after actual demand is observed should provide additional flexibility for the firm which may prove beneficial. The authors consider three specific duopolistic settings to illustrate such a trade-off. We will show below the essential feature of the Stackelberg leadership version to get the main message.

Consider a two-firm competitive scenario in which the leader will be exogenously designated firm 1. The random industry inverse demand is specified to be

$$p = a - (q_1 + q_2) + \xi$$

where q_1 represents the potential leader's output, q_2 that of the follower, ξ a random variable with zero mean and variance σ^2 with density $\varphi(\xi)$.

To simplify the analysis, suppose that, in contrast to the Appelbaum and Lim model we just discussed where production commitment may be partial, the leader must either pre-commit *all* output in the first stage of a two-stage game, or remain fully flexible; producing all output in the second stage. Further, assume that the firms are risk-neutral. Consider first the leader's expected profit maximization procedure. As usual for the solution to the Stackelberg type of model, let us examine the follower's objective, which is to maximize

$$\Pi_2 = [a - c + \xi - Q] q_2$$

where $Q = q_1 + q_2$, and c is the constant marginal cost.

The follower's reaction function is then

$$q_2 \equiv q_2(q_1, \xi) = \frac{a - c + \xi}{2} - \frac{q_1}{2}.$$

Consequently, with risk neutrality, the leader wishes to maximize

$$E[\Pi_1^{committed}]=E[a-c+\xi-q_1-q_2(q_1,\xi)]q_1$$

which in turn yields the solution

$$q_1^*=\frac{(a-c)}{2} \text{ and } q_2^*=\frac{(a-c+2\xi)}{4}.$$

It is interesting to note that demand uncertainty of the nature characterized in this illustration has no effect on the level of the leader's production commitment, if this is the chosen strategy. As a result, the leader's expected profits are not affected by demand uncertainty either.

On the other hand, consider the alternative where the "leader" decided to remain completely flexible until the actual demand is realized after the first stage. This scenario of course represents the standard Cournot competition which yields the following equilibrium

$$q_1^{flexible}=q_2^{flexible}=\frac{(a-c+\xi)}{3}.$$

The expected profits for each duopolist is therefore

$$E[\Pi_1^{flexible}]=E[\Pi_2^{flexible}]=\frac{(a-c+\xi)^2+\sigma^2}{9}$$

which indicates that the expected profit is increasing in the variance of demand.

Presented with these two possible choices, fully committed or fully flexible, the leader's decision rule can be written as: fully committed production is a better strategy if and only if

$$\sigma^2<\frac{(a-c)^2}{8}.$$

Clearly, under deterministic demand, the preceding inequality is generally satisfied: commitment is the better choice. Under random demand, high enough degree of uncertainty may induce the leader to wait for the realization of the random term in the sales response function; thus it would choose to compete on an equal basis with the competitor in the second stage of the game. In spite of its simplicity, the illustration demonstrates the trade-off between pre-commitment and production flexibility under conditions of demand uncertainty.

6 CONCLUSIONS

Unlike the cases we have analyzed in earlier chapters where the impact of demand uncertainty on the firm's marketing efforts is largely confined to the monopolistic market structure, whether it is dynamic or static, single-product or multiple-product, this chapter examines the explicit role of competition under stochastic conditions. It should be noted that the research on this general topic is very much under way with a very limited published results currently available. Nevertheless, we have reported in this chapter some basic formulations which should be useful in analyzing these complex phenomena. We have tried, to the largest possible extent, to establish the direct connections between the deterministic versions with various stochastic counterparts. The most ideal theoretical framework for us to address these issues is to have a model which is dynamic, stochastic, and game-theoretic in nature, with ready empirical implementabilities. Clearly, this is a very challenging framework especially as we seek to allow for potential interactions among the firms' marketing mix. Consequently, the approaches taken in much of the literature have been to address these issues from a perspective of accommodating certain objectives while maintaining the tractability of the problems at hand. In this regard, we should note that the market share framework we detailed in Chapter 6 offers an analytically tractable formulation which is quite promising.

In summary, the presence of market competition has been shown in this chapter to have important implications for assessing the impact of uncertainty on the firm's decision-making. For the optimal pricing rules, we analyze how competition modifies the firm's pricing decision both in the static and the dynamic framework. For the advertising activities, we consider the role of this particular marketing activity both as a vehicle of valuable information to the consumers and as the firm's strategic investment in view of competition. The issue of potential entry which is at the heart of the competitive framework can be addressed not only from the perspective of the firm's pricing behavior, but also from that of its advertising and producing decisions. We have also tried to point out the possibility of interactions among the firm's components of the marketing mix. While the presence of competition under random demand and other forms of uncertainty in this general framework adds considerable complexities to the firm's decision-making, we hope that the several problem formulations reported in this chapter provide a useful starting point for further research in this area.

REFERENCES

APPELBAUM, Elie, and Chin LIM, 1985, "Contestable Markets Under Uncertainty," *Rand Journal of Economics*, Vol. 16, pp. 28-40.

BAUMOL, William J., J. C. PANZAR, and Robert D. WILLIG, 1982, *Contestable Markets and the Theory of Industry Structure*, San Diego, CA: Harcourt Brace Jovanovich.

BUTTERS, Gerald, 1977, "Equilibrium Distribution of Prices and Advertising," *Review of Economic Studies*, Vol. 44, pp. 465-492.

CHANG, Chun-Hao, and Chi-Wen J. Lee, 1994, "Optimal Pricing Strategy in Marketing Research Consulting," *International Economic Review*, Vol. 35, No. 2, pp. 463-478.

DIXIT, Avinash K., and Robert S. PINDYCK, 1994, *Investment Under Uncertainty*, Princeton University Press, Princeton, NJ.

DOCKNER, E., and S. JORGENSEN, 1988, "Optimal Pricing Strategies for New Products in a Dynamic Oligopoly," *Marketing Science*, Vol. 7, No. 4, pp. 315-334.

ELIASHBERG, Jehoshua, and Abel P. JEULAND, 1986, "The Impact of Competitive Entry in a Developing Market upon Dynamic Pricing Strategies," *Marketing Science*, Vol. 5, pp. 20-36.

ELIASHBERG, Jehoshua, and Gary L. LILIEN (eds.), 1993, *Marketing*, Handbooks in Operations Research and Management Science, Vol. 5, Elsevier Science Publishers, Amsterdam, The Netherlands.

ERICKSON, Gary M., 1991, *Dynamic Models of Advertising Competition*, Kluwer Academic Publishers, MA.

FERSHTMAN, Chaim, Vijay MAHAJAN, and Eitan MULLER, 1990, "Market Share Pioneering Advantage: A Theoretical Approach," *Management Science,* Vol. 36, pp. 900-918.

FRIEDMAN, J. W., 1971, "A Non-Cooperative Equilibrium for Supergames," *Review of Economic Studies*, Vol. 38, pp. 1-12.

FUDENBERG, Drew, and Jean TIROLE, 1984, "The Fat-Cat Effect, The Puppy-Dog Ploy, and the Lean and Hungry Look," *AEA Papers and Proceedings*, Vol. 74, pp. 361-366.

GREEN, E., and R. PORTER, 1984, "Non-Cooperative Collusion Under Imperfect Price Information," *Econometrica*, Vol. 52, pp. 87-100.

GROSSMAN, G., and C. SHAPIRO, 1984, "Informative Advertising with Differentiated Products," *Review of Economic Studies*, Vol. 51, pp. 63-82.

HANSSENS, Dominique M., 1980, "Market Response, Competitive Behavior, and Time Series Analysis," *Journal of Marketing Research*, Vol. 17, pp. 470-485.

HVIID, Morten, 1989, "Risk-Averse Duopolists and Voluntary Information Transmission," *Journal of Industrial Economics*, Vol. 38, No. 1, pp. 49-64.

KLEMPERER, P., and M. MEYER, 1986, *Rand Journal of Economics*, Vol. 17, No. 4, pp. 618-638.

KREPS, D. M., and J. A. SCHEINKMAN, 1983, "Cournot Pre-Commitment and Bertrand Competition Yield Cournot Outcomes," *Bell Journal of economics*, Vol. 14, pp 326-337.

LAL, Rajiv, and Carmen MATUTES, 1989, "Price Competition in Multimarket Duopolies, *Rand Journal of Economics*, Vol. 20, pp 516-537.

LAL, Rajiv, and Carmen MATUTES, 1994, "Retail Pricing and Advertising Strategies," *Journal of Business*, Vol. 67, No. 3, pp. 345-370.

LAMBIN, Jean-Jacques, Philippe A NAERT, and Alain BULTEZ, 1975, "Optimal Marketing Behavior in Oligopoly," *European Economic Review*, Vol. 6, pp. 105-128.

MILLS, H. D., 1961,"A Study of Promotional Competition," in *Mathematical Models and Methods in Marketing*, F. M. BASS et al. (eds.) , R. D. Irwin, pp. 245-301.

MOORTHY, K. Sridhar, 1993, "Competitive Marketing Strategies: Game-Theoretic Models," in Jehoshua ELIASHBERG, and Gary L. LILIEN (eds.), *Marketing*, Handbooks in Operations Research and Management Science, Vol. 5, pp. 143-190, Elsevier Science Publishers, Amsterdam, The Netherlands.

PALFREY, Thomas R., 1982, "Risk Advantages and Information Acquisition," *Bell Journal of Economics*, pp. 219-224.

RAO, Ram, C., and Frank BASS, 1985, "Competition, Strategy and Price Dynamics: A Theoretical and Empirical Investigation," *Journal of Marketing Research*, Vol. 22, pp 283-296.

ROTEMBERG, J. J., and G. SALONER, 1986, "A Supergame-Theoretic Model of Price Wars During Booms," *American Economic Review*, Vol. 76, pp. 390-407.

ROTHSCHILD, Michael, and Joseph STIGLITZ, 1970, "Increasing Risk: I. A Definition," *Journal of Economic Theory*, Vol. 18, pp. 225-243.

ROY, Abhik, Dominique M. HANSSENS, and Jagmohan S. RAJU, 1994, "Competitive Pricing by a Price Leader," *Management Science*, Vol. 40, pp. 809-823.

SCHERER, F. M., and D. ROSS, 1990, *Industrial Market Structure and Economic Performance*, 3rd edition, Houghton Mifflin Co., Boston, MA.

SCHMALENSEE, Richard A., 1974, "A Model of Promotional Competition in Oligopoly," *Review of Economic Studies*.

SETHI, Suresh P., 1977, "Dynamic Optimal Control Models in Advertising: A Survey," *Siam Review*, Vol. 19, pp. 685-725.

SIMON, Herman, 1989, *Price Management*, Elsevier, North Holland.

SPENCER, Barbara J., and James A. BRANDER, 1992, "Pre-commitment and Flexibility Applications to Oligopoly Theory," *European Economic Review*, Vol. 36, pp. 1601-1626.

STAIGER, Robert W., and Frank A. WOLAK, 1992, "Collusive Pricing With Capacity Constraints In the Presence of Demand Uncertainty," *Rand Journal of Economics*, Vol. 23, No. 2, pp. 203-220.

TESSITORE, Anthony, 1994, "Market Segmentation and Oligopoly Under Uncertainty," *Journal of Economics and Business*, Vol. 46, pp. 65-75.

TIROLE, Jean, 1989, *The Theory of Industrial Organization*, MIT Press, Cambridge, MA.

9

ADAPTIVE BEHAVIOR, EXPERIMENTATION AND SOME EMPIRICAL RESULTS

1 OVERVIEW

This chapter reports some of the efforts in the literature to address a number of issues with an eye towards the implementation of certain theoretical models. It should be clearly pointed out at the outset that while the general marketing literature on the empirical results, some with solid theoretical foundations, is very large — just a glance of the recent work by Hanssens, Parsons and Schultz [1990] would quickly confirm this — the empirical literature on the decisions under uncertainty barely exists. However, as we search for ways to assist managers with advanced techniques in marketing and other managerial decisions, it is imperative that implementabilities of theoretical models be addressed. Consequently, we report here a number of empirical approaches to the various issues we have considered in the previous chapters. We should mention that the general econometric literature on random coefficient models will *not* be included in our discussion in this chapter even though the issue of parameter uncertainty constitutes an integral part of theoretical approach to the firm's decisions under uncertainty. The interested reader will find the Hanssens Parsons Schultz book cited above most comprehensive for those aspects particularly relevant to empirical analysis in research in marketing.

In this chapter, we start out with the issue of experimentation and the pioneering work by Little [1966] on adaptive control within the context of the sales response to advertising. We then examine a number of other studies in the literature on this subject. In Section 3, we will report a number of results concerning the firm's production decision as part of its experimentation plan in order to gain additional knowledge on its uncertain demand. Section 4 specifically analyzes a model of "learning by doing" on the part of the firm to infer the true specification of a linear sales response to advertising. A recent effort to address the empirical implications of stochasticity in a Bass-based diffusion model will be the subject for Section 5. Section 6 will address certain empirical approaches to a couple of theoretical models analyzed in prior chapters, with an emphasis on a particular theoretical result regarding the multi-brand advertising under conditions of uncertainty. The presentation hopefully offers a flavor as to how theoretical analysis can be subjected to certain empirical verifications. Section 6 concludes the chapter.

2 PARAMETER UNCERTAINTY

Following a classification scheme suggested by Eliashberg and Chatterjee [1985], one may categorize aggregate stochastic models into those which are structurally stochastic and those which are parametrically stochastic. In this chapter, we are mostly concerned with various aspects of parameter uncertainty whereas in a section in Chapter 6, we have already dealt with a number of diffusion models in which structural stochasticity plays the central role.

2.1 An Experimentation Plan

We report here a first approach to examine the parameter uncertainty from a marketing point of view. Little's model [1966] of adaptive control of promotional spending represents an effort in formulating the important problem of experimentation regarding the sales response to advertising campaigns which contains an unknown parameter. Let us summarize the basic structure of the model with its analyses and marketing implications. Consider an environment in which the major form of marketing activities is the non-price promotional effort. Denoting, as usual, the unit product price as p, the quantity demanded as q, and the constant unit cost as c, the firm's objective is to find an optimal level of advertising spending m in order to maximize its profits

$$\Pi = (p-c)q - m - FC \qquad (9.1)$$

where FC is the fixed cost, and the sales response function to advertising is quadratic of the following form:

$$q = a + \beta m - \gamma m^2 \qquad (9.2)$$

where a and γ are known parameters and β is a parameter whose value is unknown to the firm.

The resulting optimal advertising level is

$$m^* = \frac{[\beta(p-c)-1]}{2\gamma(p-c)}.$$

Regarding the parameter β, it is assumed that it is generated by a first-order autoregressive process as follows:

$$\beta_t = k\beta_{t-1} + (1-k)\beta^0 + \xi_{\beta,t}$$

where k is bounded within the closed interval $[0,1]$, β^0 denotes the long run average of β, and $\xi_{\beta,t}$ is a random error term with a normal distribution with zero mean and constant variance σ_β^2.

In order to gain information on the unknown parameter β, a sales experiment can be designed so that for a given (presumably optimal) national average of advertising rate $m_{0,t}$, a lower promotion rate m_1 will be given in R markets (recalling our notation of R as in **R**egional markets) and a higher promotion rate m_2 will be given in another R markets. On the basis of these different experimental promotion levels, the resulting sales can then be observed from which the experimental mean for β, denoted by $\hat{\beta}$, can be calculated. It can be shown that $\hat{\beta}$ has a normal distribution with mean β and time-invariant variance denoted by v. It then follows that the Bayesian updating scheme in revising the distribution of the experimental mean can be written as:

$$\beta'_{t+1} = k[\frac{v}{v+v'}]\beta'_t + k[\frac{v'}{v+v'}]\hat{\beta}_t + (1-k)\beta^0 \qquad (9.3)$$

where $\beta_t{}'$ and v' denote, respectively the prior mean and variance of the experimental mean $\hat{\beta}$.

On this basis, the promotion rate can be optimally chosen to be:

$$m_{0,t} = \frac{[(p-c)\beta'_t-1]}{2(p-c)\gamma}.$$

The preceding expressions constitute the central rules in revising the firm's estimates on response parameter β as well as setting the optimal promotion rate. For our present purposes, it is of interest to note that the preceding solution for optimal promotion is essentially that of a single-period optimization problem. The updating mechanism for the response parameter is set within the context of an experiment design involving different number of markets and is independent of the promotion level itself. Thus, promotion rates chosen in each period would not in any way affect the firm's ability to know more about the response parameter. Consequently, optimal promotion rates can be obtained for each separate period of the planning horizon.

This particular feature is to be contrasted with the nature of the learning process in the model considered in a section below where the updating rule and the optimal promotion rate setting are integrated so that in fact as the firm makes decisions on advertising, the resulting sales will provide information valuable for the firm to revise its knowledge on the response parameter of the sale function.

In this context, we should also mention the work by Pekelman and Tse [1980] which we have presented earlier in Chapter 6 on market share and diffusion models. There we noted that due to the nonlinearity in the control variable, which in their model is the firm's advertising budget, analytical solutions are typically not available; thus requiring simulation exercises.

2.2 Normative Implications of Parameter Uncertainty

The paper by Aykac, Corstjens, Gautschi and Horowitz [1989] is motivated mainly by the general issue of parameter uncertainty addressed above. They argue that the regression coefficients which represent estimates of the true values of population parameters, are themselves a source of uncertainty. The implications of this sort of *estimation* uncertainty are explored specifically within the context of the sales response to advertisement. Two particular features of their model stand out in comparison to the previous studies on this issue. First is the role of the firm's attitude towards risk, a subject we have devoted considerable space in this work; and the second is the normative implications for the firm's managerial decision, advertising being the example considered. We report here their model and results.

Using our familiar notation, the firm's objective is to find an optimal level m in order to maximize its expected utility of net profits $E[U(\Pi)]$ in which net profit is defined to be:

$$\Pi = (1-t)[(p-c)q - m - FC]$$

where t is the specific tax rate, and the random sales response function is of the form

$$q = f(m, \beta, \xi) \tag{9.4}$$

where β is a vector of the response function's parameters, and ξ the random term with variance σ_ξ^2.

Assuming further the appropriate concavity in the response function to assure an interior solution and concentrating on the case of risk aversion, the second-order Taylor approximation of the objective function can be written as:

$$E[U(\Pi)] = U[E(\Pi)] + \frac{\sigma_\Pi^2}{2} U''$$

where σ_Π^2 denotes the profit variance.

The first-order condition for an optimal advertising solution can be written as:

$$\frac{\partial E(\Pi)}{\partial m} = \frac{r\dfrac{\partial \sigma_\Pi^2}{\partial m}}{2 + \dfrac{U'''}{U'}\sigma_\Pi^2} \tag{9.5}$$

where r denote the Pratt-Arrow measure of absolute risk aversion and where it can be shown that the denominator of the right-hand side ratio is positive.

The case of risk neutrality can be seen for $r=0$ where the certainty-equivalent results are obtained and of course this is similar to the deterministic rules which we have analyzed in the previous chapters. In terms of the preceding expression, the certainty-equivalent optimal marketing effort is optimally chosen to be at the point at which the expected profit function is maximized. Let us denote such an optimal advertising level (deterministic) as m_d.

For risk-averse firms, $r>0$; hence the sign of $\partial E(\Pi)/\partial m$ depends on the sign of $\partial \sigma_\Pi^2/\partial m$. Thus under the scenario that the profit variance is a strictly convex function of advertising spending where the level of advertising which minimizes the resulting profit variance is uniquely determined — denoting such an advertising level as m_v — then whether risk aversion induces the firm to raise its advertising effort or to reduce it depends on the relative positions of m_d and m_v. This is so since in comparison to the risk-neutral advertising level m_d, if the profit variance is increasing in advertising (i.e. $m_v < m_d$), then $\partial E(\Pi)/\partial m >0$ which immediately implies that, given that the second-order conditions for optimality are satisfied, risk-averse firm will find it optimal to reduce its marketing efforts. This particular result conforms very much with the standard result in the literature which we have also summarized in earlier chapters. Of particular interest, however, is the result where $m_v > m_d$ in which case by using the same argument one would arrive at the conclusion that risk aversion encourages the firm to increase its advertising activities; in doing so, the firm seeks to reduce the variability in its net profits.

Within the framework of their paper and concentrating on the case where sales variance is increasing in advertising, a number of results of particular interest can be summarized here as follows: as the estimation uncertainty increases (decreases), firms will find it optimal to reduce (raise) advertising activities. Thus, everything being the same, as firms gain more and more knowledge on the sales response function to advertisement, they will typically engage in larger marketing efforts. This particular result should be viewed in contrast with the results on experimentation to improve the firm's information on the consumers' response to advertising campaigns. For our current purposes, this is perhaps the most important implication of the analysis. Other interesting results are that: higher (lower) fixed costs will induce risk-averse firms to reduce (raise) marketing activities in the face of estimation uncertainty; and that the impact of price variations on the risk-averse firm's advertising decisions under estimation uncertainty is ambiguous.

3 OUTPUT DECISIONS AS AN EXPERIMENT

We now examine two particular contexts within which the firm's motivations to gain additional information on the random demand facing it can be seen. The first represents an effort to explore the impact of the firm's desire to experiment on its production and investment decisions, using a valuation approach commonly seen in the finance literature. The second investigates the possibility that, facing uncertain demand, firms may want to place a relatively larger order so that they will have a better chance of knowing exactly what the realized demand is, if actual demand turns out to be less than the size of the order.

3.1 A Valuation Approach

Harpaz and Thomadakis [1982] consider the firm's optimization problem involving both the production decision and investment when it is faced with a demand function and a cost function both of which contain unknown parameters. In particular, assume the following linear demand function:

$$p_t = a - \beta q_t + \xi_t. \tag{9.6}$$

On the other hand, the average cost function is:

$$c_t = \gamma q_t + \upsilon_t$$

where both β and γ are unknown parameters, and ξ and υ are random terms.

The time horizon is $1, 2, ..., T$. Following the *CAPM* model, upon denoting the cash flow of the aggregate market portfolio as M_t, and denoting the covariances between the firm's cash flows and M_t as $cov(\xi_t, M_t)$ and $cov(\upsilon_t, M_t)$, the firm's value V at the start of the period t is:

$$V_{t-1} = \frac{E_{t-1}[\Pi_t + V_t - I_{t+1}] - \lambda cov(\Pi_t + V_t - I_{t+1}, M_t)}{1 + r_F} \tag{9.7}$$

where the notation is similar to the *CAPM* model we use previously in Chapter 5 with λ denotes the market price of risk, r_F the risk-free interest rate, I_t the firm's new investment, and where

$$\Pi_t = p_t q_t - c_t q_t - FC$$
$$= (a - \beta q_t + \xi_t) q_t - [(\gamma q_t + \upsilon_t] - FC \tag{9.8}$$

$$\text{and} \quad I_{t+1} = k(q_{t+1} - q_t). \tag{9.9}$$

Note that the latter equation reflects the assumption that investment of I_{t+1} is needed to raise the production from q_t to q_{t+1}, with a constant production coefficient k and assuming no depreciation for simplicity. Further, the numerator in the valuation formula indicates the certainty-equivalent value of $[\Pi_t + V_t - I_{t+1}]$, adjusted for the risk factor reflected by the covariance term, which is denoted by $CE_{t-1}[\Pi_t + V_t - I_{t+1}]$ in order to simplify the presentation.

The intertemporal optimization facing the firm can then be solved by the method of stochastic dynamic programming approach as we summarized in Chapter 1 with the terminal condition $V_T = 0$. The recursive solution can be shown to have the following form:

$$\text{Max. } NV_{t-2} = \frac{CE_{t-2}[\Pi_{t-1} + NV_{t-1}^*]}{1 + r_F} - k(q_{t-1} - q_{t-2}) \qquad (9.10)$$

$$\{q_{t-1}\}$$

where

$$NV_{t-1} = V_{t-1} - I_t = \frac{CE_{t-1}\{[a - \beta q_t + \xi_t] q_t - [(\gamma q_t + \upsilon_t) q_t - FC] + kq_t\}}{1 + r_F} - [k(q_t - q_{t-1})]$$

with NV_{t-1}^* denoting the optimal value of NV_{t-1} which is obtained from the *myopic* output q_t^* which in turn can be shown be:

$$q_t^* = \frac{a - \lambda[cov(\xi_t, M_t) - cov(\upsilon_t, M_t)] - kr_F}{2(\bar{\beta}_{t-1} + \bar{\gamma}_{t-1})} \qquad (9.11)$$

where the bars denote respective mean values of the coefficients.

On the other hand, the experimenting firm would choose an intertemporal optimal output, denoted by q_t^{**} which maximizes eq. (9.10) with appropriate adjustment in the time notation. The necessary condition for such a problem can be seen as

$$\frac{\partial CE_{t-1}(\Pi_t)}{\partial q_t} + \frac{\partial CE_{t-1}(NV_t^*)}{\partial q_t} = k(1 + r_F) \qquad (9.12)$$

which yields an optimal q_t^{**} different from q_t^* defined above. This represents once again the nature of the effect of learning we have explained in other contexts.

We now note some of the interesting results in its comparison to the certainty cases. First, assuming that $cov(\xi_t, M_t) - cov(\upsilon_t, M_t) > 0$, everything else being the same, the myopic firm would choose an output under demand and cost uncertainty smaller than that under certainty. This result has long been obtained and we have summarized some of them in Chapter 2. Secondly, the experimenting firm typically chooses a higher output than that by a myopic firm. Again, this result is known in the literature as we will shortly indicate in the next section. Thirdly, the market value of an experimenting firm is typically higher than that of the myopic firm. This is related to our non-negative value of learning which we discussed in Chapter 2.

3.2 Implications of an Output Experiment

In a recent study, Thompson and Horowitz [1993] are motivated by the observation that uncertainty regarding demand poses the following problem of acquisition of a perishable good. When the seller takes into account the potential learning effect of a present level of purchase, there may be incentives for ordering a quantity larger than an otherwise optimal level in the non-learning case. This is so since larger stock increases the chance that it exceeds demand, hence the exact demand may be known at the end of the period once the realization of the random demand is available. Otherwise, if demand is larger than the available stock, its true demand level may not be known, thus the acquisition contains less valuable information on the true demand. The basic theoretical development can be seen as follows.

Consider a two-period model as we did earlier in Chapter 2, the first period random demand q_1 follows a normal distribution function $\varphi(q_1|\beta)$ with unknown mean μ and a known variance σ^2 where the mean μ has a normal prior with mean m_0 and variance v_0. A decision on q_1, say $q_1{}^*$, is made to maximize the firm objective on the basis of the prior density. The myopic, non-experimenting risk-neutral firm's objective is

$$E(\Pi_1) = p\int_0^{q_1{}^*} q_1\varphi(q_1)dq_1 + pq_1{}^* \int_{q_1{}^*}^{\infty}\varphi(q_1)dq_1 - C(q_1{}^*).\qquad(9.13)$$

On the other hand, the experimenting firm seeks to maximize the discounted sum of profits:

$$\text{Max. } E(\Pi_1) + \frac{1}{1+r}E_1[E(\Pi_2|q_1)]\qquad(9.14)$$

where $E_1[E(\Pi_2|q_1)] = E_1[E(\Pi_2|q_1 < q_1{}^*)] + E_1[E(\Pi_2|q_1 > q_1{}^*)]$

with $E_1(.)$ indicating that the expectation is taken with the information available up to period 1.

On the basis of these two cases, the authors then work with some numerical example and obtain a result that the gain from experimentation is negligible with a rather large range of parameters used. It should be recognized, however, that this learning process is motivated by a very different mechanism in comparison to the unknown random coefficient models usually treated in the literature.

4 AN ADAPTIVE ADVERTISING MODEL

We now develop in some detail an adaptive model for the firm with a motivation very similar to the Little framework presented in Sub-section 2.1 above. Our analysis in this section is based on Nguyen [1985] and is related to our earlier discussion on the issue of optimal advertising analyzed in Chapter 3.

4.1 Theoretical Analysis

We have shown in Chapter 3 that the firm's advertising behavior may be different under random demand in comparison to that under deterministic conditions. Another important aspect of uncertainty involves a particular parameter contained in the response function which is not known but whose true value the firm can learn about through experimentation. Since knowledge about the value of the unknown parameter should help the firm make better decisions in allocating advertising budgets over time, it is important for the firms to design an optimal experimentation plan, taking into account both present profits and future profits. This is the subject which we will be dealing with in this section.

Consider an advertising response function in period t of the form:

$$q_t = f(m_t, \beta, \xi_t) \quad ; \quad t = 1, 2, \ldots, T \tag{9.15}$$

where ξ_t is a random disturbance term whose density is known, and β is a time-invariant unknown parameter which has a given prior density $\varphi_0(\beta)$.

A number of comments on (9.15) are in order. First, the random term ξ_t introduces elements of uncertainty in a manner similar to that analyzed in the various models we have presented. Second, the value of the parameter β appearing explicitly in (9.15) is unknown, and the firm wishes to learn more about it through experimentation. Third, we did not explicitly include the lagged value of sales, which is operationally used to account for the carry-over effect of advertising in the response function. We have chosen to do this in order to emphasize the nature of the intertemporality due solely to experimentation. That is, intertemporality does arise in our model even when there is no (carry-over) effect of lagged sales on current sales. It turns out that our analysis in this section would not be changed in any significant way even when the one-period lagged sales q_{t-1} is introduced into the response function, provided that the coefficient reflecting the effect of q_{t-1} on q_t is known with certainty.

To obtain more specific results later, we will assume the following quadratic response function

$$q_t = a + \beta m_t - \gamma m_t^2 + u(m_t).\xi_t \tag{9.16}$$

where a and γ are assumed known with certainty, β is the unknown parameter, $u(m_t)$ is a known continuously differentiable function of m_t, and the ξ_t's are normally and independently distributed, each with mean zero and known variance σ^2.

Basically, the quadratic response function (9.16) is a slight modification of the response function used by Little in his important paper on adaptive control of promotional spending we reported earlier (cf eq. (9.2)). Little indicates that the quadratic specification would represent a good approximation even if the true response function is not quadratic. The assumption of a known constant curvature parameter γ is taken from Little's paper in which he argues that such an assumption, while it appears unrealistic, may not be serious. Our empirical evidence in a sub-section below offers further support to the quadratic sales response function.

The specification of the disturbance term in (9.16) implies the presence of heteroskedasticity. We know from the econometrics literature that it is not uncommon that the problem of heteroskedasticity arises in many actual applications. The specification in (9.16) is thus more general and it includes the conventional model with homoskedastic disturbance terms as a special case. Once again, we will report some empirical evidence for the assumption of heteroskedasticity in our econometric exercise below. We should also point out that theoretical results regarding the firm's optimal advertising will be shown to depend crucially on the specification of the disturbance term.

On the basis of the preceding discussion we believe that our response function in (9.16) is sufficiently justified. We will henceforth work mainly with this more general specification. For later reference, we note that if the firm estimates the value of β by an estimator b_t defined to be $b_t = (q_t - a + \gamma m_t^2)/m_t$, it follows from (9.16) that:

$$b_t = \beta + \frac{u(m_t)}{m_t} \cdot \xi_t \qquad (9.17)$$

which would imply that $E(b_t) = \beta$ and $var(b_t) = [z(m_t)]^2 \sigma^2$ where we define $z(m_t) = u(m_t)/m_t$.

Assuming a known discount factor ρ, the firm's objective is to maximize the expected value of the discounted sum of utilities $U(\Pi_t)$ over the planning horizon T, conditional on the initial information vector ψ^0:

$$\text{Max. } E[\sum_{t=1}^{T} \rho^{t-1} U(\Pi_t) | \psi^0] \qquad (9.18)$$
$$\{m_t\}_{t=1}^{T}$$

where the profit function Π_t is defined as:

$$\Pi_t = p_t q_t - C(q_t) - m_t \qquad (9.19)$$

where the prices p_t's are known and $C(q_t)$ is the manufacturing cost function with the properties that $C'(q) > 0$ and $C''(q) \leq 0$.

For our present purposes, the vector of information consists of information on past advertisement levels and corresponding sales levels which are used to generate estimations about β. For a new brand, the initial information vector ψ^0 may be based either on the firm's own experience on other established brands or on results of separate market testings.

Thus, the optimization problem facing the firm is to maximize the objective function (9.18), subject to the constraints in (9.16) and (9.19). In any period t within the planning horizon, the firm is assumed to make a decision about the advertising level m_t before the realization of the disturbance term ξ_t. Then, after a level m_t is determined, the firm will be able to observe the corresponding sales level which is ultimately realized depending upon the behavior of the random term ξ_t. The determined advertising and its corresponding observed sales level will then become new elements in the firm's vector of information which will be used for the next period's decision problem.

Applying the technique of discrete stochastic dynamic programming as we outlined in Chapter 1 for the problem in (9.18) yields the following solution:

$$\text{Max. } V_t = E\{[U\{\Pi_t(q_t)\} + \rho V_{t+1}^*(q_t)]|\psi^{t-1}, m_t\} \qquad (9.20)$$
$$\{m_t\}$$

with the terminal condition $V_{t+1}^*(q_t) = 0$, where the information vector ψ^{t-1} summarizes past values of sales and advertising levels, V_{t+1}^* denotes the optimum value of V_{t+1}, and Bayes' formula is used in calculating various expectations in (9.20).

We will now address economic aspects of our solution algorithm. At the beginning of the first period, the firm wishes to find an advertising level to maximize:

$$V_1 = E[U(\Pi_1)|\psi^0, m_1] + \rho E[V_2^*|\psi^0, m_1]. \qquad (9.21)$$

The first-order and second-order conditions for optimality can be readily derived. For later reference, we will term the advertising level which maximizes the objective function in (9.21) for the dynamic model as the *optimal* level, denoted by $m_1{}^{**}$, and that which maximizes the single-period objective function $E[U(\Pi_1)|\psi^0, m_1]$ for the static model as the *myopic* level, denoted by $m_1{}^*$. Clearly, the difference between advertising levels for the one-period model and the multi-period model would depend on the term $E[(\partial V_2^*/\partial m_1)|\psi^0, m_1]$. Our next task involves determining the sign of this term. In the process, we will generalize a result obtained by Prescott [1972] and Grossman, Kihlstrom, and Mirman [1977] who, in different contexts, address the question regarding the effect of learning about an unknown parameter in a linear equation on some general decision problems. In addition, we will offer a method of solution which is much simpler than those proposed by these authors.

Following Grossman, Kihlstrom, and Mirman, we will apply certain results in Blackwell's theory of sufficiency in the context of comparison of experiments to our present problem. See Blackwell [1951], [1953], and DeGroot [1970]. In our framework, the firm experiments by setting various advertising levels in order to gain more information on the true value of β. Thus, let us consider two experiments, one involving advertising level $\hat{m}_t$, another involving $\breve{m}_t$. Corresponding to $\hat{m}_t$, an estimated value $\hat{b}_t$ of β is obtained, using (9.17). Similarly, one can obtain another estimated value $\breve{b}_t$ of β as a result of the experiment involving $\breve{m}_t$. The experiment involving $\breve{m}_t$ is said to be sufficient for the experiment involving $\hat{m}_t$ if the random variable $\breve{b}_t$ can be used to generate the random variable $\hat{b}_t$. That is, once the experiment involving $\breve{m}_t$ is adopted (i.e., $\breve{b}_t$ can be obtained), it is *not* necessary for the firm to carry out the experiment involving $\hat{m}_t$ since $\hat{b}_t$ can be generated from $\breve{b}_t$. Thus, loosely speaking, the experiment involving $\breve{m}_t$ yields more information than the experiment involving $\hat{m}_t$. An economic implication of this is that the experiment involving $\breve{m}_t$ is more valuable than that involving $\hat{m}_t$.

The results contained in the following theorem would enable us to make some comparisons between the myopic advertising level and the optimal advertising level under a random response function.

Theorem 9.1. *For the quadratic advertising response function as specified in* (9.16), *the optimal advertising level* $m_t{}^{**}$ *is greater* (*equal, smaller*) *than the myopic advertising level* $m_t{}^*$ *if the absolute value of* $[z(m_t)]$ *is a decreasing* (*a constant, increasing*) *function of* m_t.

To prove this result, we first need the following lemmas:

Lemma 9.1. *Assume the advertising response specification is given by eq.*(9.16) *where we further define* $z(m_t) = u(m_t)/m_t$; *assume also that* $\hat{m}_t > \breve{m}_t$ *where* $\hat{m}_t$ *and* $\breve{m}_t$ *are two different levels of the firm's advertising budget. Then it can be shown that:*
(*i*) *The experiment involving* $\breve{m}_t$ *is sufficient for the experiment involving* $\hat{m}_t$ *if* $[\partial|z(m_t)|/\partial m_t] > 0$.
(*ii*) *The experiment involving* $\hat{m}_t$ *is sufficient for the experiment involving* $\breve{m}_t$ *if* $[[\partial|z(m_t)|/\partial m_t] < 0$.
(*iii*) *Neither one is sufficient for the other if* $[\partial|z(m_t)|/\partial m_t] = 0$.

Proof. Only a heuristic proof is given here for part (*i*) of the lemma. The basic idea of this proof is to show that if $[\partial|z(m_t)|/\partial m_t] > 0$, it is possible to completely specify the density of $\hat{b}_t$ once the density of $\breve{b}_t$ is obtained.

Corresponding to $\breve{m}_t$ we observe $\breve{b}_t$. Let X be a random variable which is normally distributed with mean zero and variance $[(\hat{z}_t)^2 - (\breve{z}_t)^2]\sigma^2$ where $\breve{z}_t = z(\breve{m}_t)$ and $\hat{z}_t = z(\hat{m}_t)$. Also, let X be independent of the random variable $\breve{b}_t$. Then, from (9.17), the mean and the variance of the newly defined random variable $(\breve{b}_t + X)$ are, respectively, β and $(\hat{z}_t)^2\sigma^2$ which is identical to that of the random variable $\hat{b}_t$. One can thus generate $\hat{b}_t$ by adding a new variable X defined above to $\breve{b}_t$. This process is formally called auxiliary randomization involving X. Using the definition of sufficient experiments given earlier, the experiment involving $\breve{m}_t$ is said to be sufficient for the experiment involving $\hat{m}_t$. In other words, part (*i*) of the lemma is proved.

Similar proofs can be given for part (*ii*) and part (*iii*).   *Q.E.D.*

Lemma 9.2. (Blackwell) *If the experiment involving* $\hat{m}_t$ *is sufficient for the experiment involving* $\breve{m}_t$, *then:*

$$E[V_{t+1}^*|\psi^{t-1},\hat{m}_t] \geq E[V_{t+1}^*|\psi^{t-1},\check{m}_t] \qquad (9.22)$$

where the expectations are calculated in the framework of the algorithm in (9.20).

Proof. See DeGroot [1970], chapter 14.

Proof of Theorem 9.1. We will prove this result by contradiction. For the case in which $[\partial|z(m_t)|/\partial m_t] < 0$, suppose initially that $m_t^* > m_t^{**}$. Then by Lemma 9.1, the experiment involving m_t^* is sufficient for the experiment involving m_t^{**}. Following Lemma 9.2, we have:

$$E[V_{t+1}^*|\psi^{t-1},m_t^*] \geq E[V_{t+1}^*|\psi^{t-1},m_t^{**}]$$

which, on the basis of (9.21), would yield:

$$E\{U'(\Pi_t)[pf'(m_t^{**}) - C'(q_t)f'(m_t^{**}) - 1]|\psi^{t-1},m_t^{**}\} \leq 0.$$

Further, the necessary condition for the static, one-period problem is:

$$E\{U'(\Pi_t)[pf'(m_t^*) - C'(q_t)f'(m_t^*) - 1]|\psi^{t-1},m_t^*\} = 0$$

Given that the second-order condition to the problem in (9.21) is satisfied, it follows immediately from the preceding two expressions that $m_t^{**} > m_t^*$. This, however, would contradict our assumption that $m_t^* > m_t^{**}$. Note also that the solution $m_t^{**} = m_t^*$ cannot be optimal. Hence, it should be the case that $m_t^{**} > m_t^*$. Similar proofs can be given for other cases. $\qquad Q.E.D.$

Note that the theorem depends on the implicit assumption that $|z(m_t)|$ is a monotonic function of m_t. One could theoretically construct examples in which this particular assumption may not be satisfied. The results contained in Theorem 9.1 yield some interesting and important implications regarding the firm's experimentation plan. If the firm is concerned only with the t-th period's expected profits, no experimentation scheme would be designed and the firm would find m_t^* (the myopic level) to be the optimal advertising level. However, when the firm is interested not only in the current period's expected profits but also future periods' expected profits, it would be optimal for the firm to adopt an experimentation scheme to learn more about the true value of the unknown parameter in the sales response function. The optimal advertising level for the experimenting firm has been denoted by m_t^{**}. The experimenting firm's decision to advertise at a level generally different from the myopic level is motivated by its attempt to gain more information about the unknown parameter. Since this parameter is the linear coefficient β in our quadratic response function, it would appear that an experiment at either a higher or a lower level than the myopic advertising level would yield equally valuable information regarding β.

This particular feature was implied in Little's adaptive model of promotional spending in which a higher advertising rate is used in R markets while, at the same time, a lower rate is used in another R markets. On the other hand, Theorem 9.1 suggests that whether it is optimal for the firm to experiment at a higher or lower level than the myopic level crucially depends on the structure of the estimator for the unknown parameter and on the specification of the disturbance term in the sales response function. While both the Little model and our present model share the same notion that the firm revises its expectation about β through experimentation, the nature of the experiments as well as the way the experimentation plan is incorporated in the firm's general decision process in the two models differ significantly. Little's adaptive scheme can be best summarized in his own words: "Based on the company's model of sales response, a calculation is made that sets the promotion rate to maximize expected profit in the next time period. An experiment is designed to monitor the effectiveness of the promotion. The results are then implemented, the market responds, and some sales rate is produced. The data thereby generated represents new information, which is then combined with old information to update the sales model. The cycle is repeated." (Little [1966, p. 1076]). One should first note that the promotion rate is set independently in each period since the Little model implies that the decisions of one period do not affect those of the next period. One should further note that in Little's model, the problem of optimal experimental design is considered separately from the problem of optimal promotion in each time period. On the contrary, in our present model, the issue of experimentation is integrated into the firm's dynamic optimization problem in which the expected value of the discounted sum of utilities of profits over the whole planning horizon is maximized. This process is quite similar to the well-known notion of "learning by doing".

4.2 Some Empirical Evidence

In this sub-section, we first offer some empirical evidence to support the quadratic sales response function, and then empirically investigate the specification of its error term for a particular product. While the quadratic response function has been empirically supported in several studies (Little [1979]), it is necessary for us to examine the specification of the error term in view of its importance in determining the firm's experimentation plan as indicated in Theorem 9.1.

Our empirical results are obtained by estimating the following response specification for twelve major brands of cigarettes:

$$q_t = a + \beta m_t + \gamma m_t^2 + u_t \qquad (9.23)$$

where u_t is the error term, using the *OLS* method.

The brands used in our estimation are: Pall Mall, Camel, Winston, Kent, Salem, L & M, Viceroy, Marlboro, Kool, Tareyton, Parliament, and Raleigh. Annual data on sales (in million units) and advertising (in million dollars) for each of the twelve brands are published in various issues of *Advertising Age*, covering the period from 1956 to 1979. There are, therefore, 24 observations available for our estimation purposes.

The results of estimation for the quadratic response function are reported on the left panel of Table 9.1. Overall, the empirical results are satisfactory; about two-thirds of the twelve regression equations for the twelve brands fitted very well with the specified function. On the basis of their t-statistics, the estimates for the linear coefficient are statistically positive while those for the curvature parameter are statistically negative in most cases as expected. In these cases, the R^2 are reasonably high as can be seen from *Table* 9.1. We thus believe that the quadratic response function in our theoretical analysis is empirically supported.

The next issue we examine is related to the structure of the error term. In particular, we are interested in finding out to what extent the standard assumption of homoskedasticity may be violated on the basis of our empirical exercise. To test for heteroskedasticity we use the Glejser [1969] test by running simple regressions of the absolute values of the residuals $|e_t|$ on some functions of m_t. We report the results for three of those functions on the right panel of *Table* 9.1. One would reject the null hypothesis that no heteroskedasticity exists if the estimate $\hat{\eta}$ of the parameter η is statistically different from zero in some probability sense. Otherwise, one would not reject such a null hypothesis. Our results for the twelve brands of cigarettes indicate that in about two-thirds of all cases, the assumption of homoskedasticity is empirically supported as indicated by low levels of absolute t-ratios associated with $\hat{\eta}$. Heteroskedasticity is found to exist in the remaining cases in one form or another. Since the number of cases in which the assumption of homoskedasticity is seen violated is by no means negligible, we tend to view that our unconventional use of the term $u(m_t)$ in the response function (9.16) is empirically justified.

4.3 Summary

On the basis of a multi-period dynamic model with a quadratic response function to advertising which contains an unknown parameter, we show that whether it is optimal for the firm to experiment at an advertising rate higher or lower than the myopic (one-period) level would depend on the very specification of the response function. This result follows regardless of the nature of the firm's attitude toward risk. Empirical results based on time-series data of twelve major brands of cigarettes lend satisfactory support to our assumption of a quadratic response function together with its general error term specification.

Managerial implications of the above theoretical conclusions are important. In Chapter 3, we noted that within the static, one-period planning horizon, the behavior of the firm concerning risk may give rise to the potential divergence between advertising decisions under conditions of uncertainty and of certainty. The ultimate impact of uncertainty on advertising is further complicated when the response function contains an unknown parameter, and the firm is willing to gain more

Table 9.1. *OLS Estimations of the Sales Response Function*

Brand Codes *	Specification for response function: $q_t = \alpha + \beta m_t + \gamma m_t^2 + error$				Tests for Heteroskedasticity — Specifications:					
					$|e_t| = \alpha_o + \gamma m_t + error$		$|e_t| = \alpha_o + \gamma m_t^2 + error$		$|e_t| = \alpha_o + \gamma m_t^{-1} + error$	
	$\hat{\alpha}$	$\hat{\beta}$	$\hat{\gamma}$	R^2	$\hat{\alpha}_o$	$\hat{\gamma}$	$\hat{\alpha}_o$	$\hat{\gamma}$	$\hat{\alpha}_o$	$\hat{\gamma}$
1	15506.8 (.79)**	5059.1 (1.84)	-119.3 (-1.34)	.31	13793.9 (4.28)	-433.1 (-1.78)	10863.5 (6.38)	-14.37 (-1.84)	3344.2 (.93)	57321.1 (1.45)
2	55169.7 (2.46)	-928.6 (-.31)	4.5 (.07)	.13	18796.8 (7.64)	-495.4 (-2.86)	15017.5 (9.06)	-9.69 (-2.56)	-1936.9 (-.42)	141293 (3.37)
3	5702.0 (.95)	4127.5 (9.47)	-49.7 (-7.0)	.88	7493.0 (4.66)	-83.50 (-1.45)	6228.1 (6.06)	-1.07 (-1.12)	3270.8 (2.26)	41393.4 (1.67)
4	3687.9 (.54)	2653.6 (3.79)	-59.8 (-3.79)	.41	8200.4 (5.48)	-190.6 (-2.24)	6193.9 (7.04)	-3.42 (-1.71)	3407.2 (3.19)	22229.0 (1.99)
5	-4591.9 (-1.25)	3374.2 (11.11)	-45.9 (-8.11)	.90	4569.9 (4.02)	-56.8 (-1.16)	4000.4 (5.80)	-1.15 (-1.27)	3320.1 (4.34)	844.2 (-.1)
6	2456.6 (.15)	1939.0 (.60)	-43.9 (-.28)	.17	5094.7 (1.85)	-55.1 (-.21)	4886.2 (3.18)	-3.24 (-.25)	2126.5 (2.19)	-1132.3 (-.06)
7	3962.2 (.41)	2660.8 (1.58)	-113.5 (-1.59)	.11	318.1 (.15)	214.1 (1.09)	1476.8 (1.37)	9.32 (1.11)	4517.6 (2.17)	-19391.4 (-.98)
8	-12974.7 (-1.49)	4258.6 (5.08)	-37.2 (-2.30)	.88	6299.3 (2.06)	68.7 (.51)	7995.6 (3.85)	-.76 (-.29)	13333.8 (4.28)	-77965.3 (-2.08)
9	-1943.0 (-.47)	3671.5 (6.65)	-53.4 (-3.51)	.87	4424.9 (2.75)	59.7 (.61)	5441.1 (4.70)	-.71 (-.26)	7706.9 (5.41)	-20593.3 (-2.10)
10	7544.8 (2.30)	1121.5 (1.72)	-24.4 (-.81)	.43	2723.9 (2.73)	-29.7 (-.33)	2666.1 (4.20)	-2.01 (-.48)	2578.8 (4.23)	-1259.0 (-.34)
11	-557.9 (-.21)	2853.7 (3.22)	-197.0 (-2.75)	.38	2798.3 (3.57)	-311.5 (-2.21)	1726.0 (3.88)	-18.65 (-1.56)	-700.9 (-1.13)	8770.4 (3.18)
12	1438.33 (.57)	3834.3 (4.38)	-250.8 (-3.79)	.52	2455.3 (3.75)	-77.2 (-.68)	2322.0 (5.83)	-8.07 (-.95)	2048.7 (3.21)	22.0 (.01)

Notes: * They are: Pall Mall (1), Camel (2), Winston (3), Kent (4), Salem (5), L & M (6), Viceroy (7), Marlboro (8), Kool (9), Tareyton (10), Parliament (11), and Raleigh (12).

** *t*-ratios are reported in parentheses below their respective coefficients.

Sources of Basic Data: Advertising Age, various issues.

information about it through experimentation. When this effect of experimentation is combined with the effect of the firm's attitude toward risk, the total effect of uncertainty becomes less predictable. Since the firm rarely makes advertising decisions — and for that matter any managerial decisions — with perfect knowledge, it is important that we explore the possible impact of uncertainty on the firm's advertising behavior.

5 SIMULATIONS

We are now departing the subject of experimentation to look at a number of empirical approaches in dealing with stochastic marketing models. We will first look at some simulation studies and then at a couple of econometric estimation results on pricing and advertising under random sales response functions.

5.1 Stochastic Diffusion Models

We report first a paper by Eliashberg, Morwitz, Tapiero, and Wind [1993] in addressing certain assessment of uncertainty on the firm's decisions. Let us recall some notations used in Bass-based diffusion models analyzed in Chapter 6. Let S be the fixed potential number of ultimate adopters (related to market size potential, appropriately interpreted); $f(t)$ be the density function of time to adoption; and consequently $F(t)$ be the cumulative fraction of adopters at t. Then at time t, the cumulative number of adopters, denoted as $Q(t)$, will be $Q(t)=F(t).S$. The basic equation which describes the Bass diffusion process is reproduced here as:

$$\frac{dQ_t}{dt} \equiv q_{t+1} = (S-Q_t)[a+b(\frac{Q_t}{S})] \qquad (9.24)$$

where the coefficients a and b represent, respectively, the innovation and imitation effects.

In the framework of regression models, Wittink [1977] and Gatignon [1984] characterize uncertainty in terms of stochastic parameters in an effort to incorporate various elements such as changing consumer tastes, uncertain technology and unpredictable competition. On the other hand, Eliashberg, Morwitz, Tapiero, and Wind [1993] explore the impact of uncertainty, characterized by stochastic parameters in the diffusion models, by comparing their forecasts to those obtained by deterministic models.

Eliashberg, Morwitz, Tapiero, and Wind consider the following stochastic specification:

$$\frac{dQ_t}{dt} \equiv q_{t+1} = (S-Q_t+\zeta_t)[a+b(\frac{Q_t}{S})] \qquad (9.25)$$

where ζ_t has a normal distribution with zero mean and constant variance.

Clearly, the preceding specification represents a stochastic extension of the Bass deterministic model above. Equivalently, in terms of the cumulative fraction of adopter F_t, the stochastic version can be written as:

$$\frac{dF_t}{dt} = (1 - F_t + \xi_t)[a + bF_t] \qquad (9.26)$$

where recall that $F_t = Q_t/S$ and the random error term ξ_t, appropriately defined, is also assumed to be normally distributed with zero mean and constant variance σ_ξ^2.

The authors then consider a further extension of the preceding stochastic model by investigating the impact of parametric stochasticity upon assuming that both the innovation parameter a and the imitation parameter b are random parameters. Various assumptions are made regarding the characterizations of these two parameters. In particular, for the fixed-coefficient model, the parameters a and b are assumed to be unknown but constant. For the random-coefficient model, the parameters are assumed to be time-varying and uncorrelated over time each with zero mean and constant variances with the cross-parameter correlation r. That is, $a_t - a = \xi_a(t); b_t - b = \xi_b(t)$ where $E[\xi_a(t)] = E[\xi_b(t)] = 0; E[\xi_a(t)\xi_a(s)] = 0$ for $s \neq t; E[\xi_a^2(t)] = \sigma_a^2$ for all $t; E[\xi_b(t)\xi_b(s)] = 0$ for $s \neq t; E[\xi_b^2(t)] = \sigma_b^2$, and with the correlation between $\xi_a(t)$ and $\xi_b(t)$ be denoted by r. Finally, the authors consider the First-Order Auto-regressive Model which can be characterized with: $a_t - a = \rho_a(a_{t-1} - a) + \xi_a(t); b_t - b = \rho_b(b_{t-1} - b) + \xi_b(t)$ where ρ_a and ρ_b denote the autoregressive coefficients whose values in absolute terms are less than unity to assure convergence.

By making further approximation assumptions in characterizing the stochastic specification of F_t, the authors then conduct extensive numerical simulations to enable them to contrast their stochastic models with the Bass deterministic specification. It is found that the discrepancies in predicting cumulative market penetrating curves between the deterministic and the stochastic models are (i) increasing as σ_a, σ_b, and r increases; (ii) the largest toward the mid-point of the forecasting horizon; and (iii) increasing as b and the ratio b/a increases.

We should note also the current research by Kurawarwala and Matsuo [1992] which represents another extension of the Bass model with important stochastic implications. In particular, their model is characterized with an explicit account for seasonal elements. The Bass model incorporating seasonal influences can be rewritten as follows:

$$\frac{dQ_t}{dt} = [a + (\frac{b}{S})Q_t](S - Q_t)\gamma_t \quad ; \quad Q_0 = 0$$

where γ_t represents the seasonal influence parameter at time t.

From the preceding specification, the authors account for demand uncertainty by incorporating the seasonal influences into the parameters themselves. As a result, the diffusion equation is modified to read:

$$\frac{dQ_t}{dt} = (\alpha + \frac{\beta}{\varphi}Q_t)(\varphi - Q_t)$$

where the Greek letter notation signifies that the time variable is rescaled to reflect the seasonal influence and where the parameters are written to designate that they are random variables which are assumed to have well-defined means and variances.

Initializing sales so that at time zero, accumulated sales is zero, it is further assumed that all the random parameters have independent probability distribution functions. On the basis of such a specification for the product's forecasting model, the authors indicate that data from a PC manufacturer fit well with the model.

5.2 An Efficient Frontier

We now report on another interesting application of a well-known approach in finance to address the practical issue of making managerial decisions under uncertainty. In their paper, Holthausen and Assmus [1982] examine the issue of how to allocate an advertising budget among different market segments (we once again denote regions with notation R). Uncertainty enters the decision process due to the assumption that for each market segment or region, the sales response to marketing efforts is characterized by certain probability functions. Applying the technique which describes the trade-off between expected returns and its variance popular in the finance literature, the allocating mechanism involves establishing an efficient frontier specifying those tradeoff based on which a manager with different attitude towards risk will make an allocation decision.

Consider the following sales response functions:

$$q_i = f_i(m_i, \xi_i); \quad i = 1, 2, ..., R. \tag{9.27}$$

For a given advertising budget M, the firm's objective is to maximize its expected profits defined to be

$$\text{Max. } E(\Pi) = E[\sum_{i=1}^{R} (p_i - c_i)q_i - M] \tag{9.28}$$

in which it can be seen that

$$E(\Pi) = \sum_{i=1}^{R} (p_i - c_i)E(q_i) - M$$

and $\quad var(\Pi) \equiv \sigma_{\Pi} = \sum_{i=1}^{R} \sum_{j=1}^{R} (p_i - c_i)(p_j - c_j)cov(q_i, q_j)$

where $cov(q_i, q_j)$ denotes the variance-covariance between sales in segments i and j.

The approach used is to generate the efficient frontier by selecting certain risk level measured by a given variance σ_0, say, so that the resulting expected profit is maximized, subject to the advertising budget constraint. To illustrate the procedures, Holthausen and Assmus consider the following specification for the sales response function:

$$\ln q_i = \ln S_i + \ln[1 - e^{-v_i/m_i}] + u_i; \quad i=1,2,...,R$$

which implies $q_i = S_i[1 - e^{-v_i/m_i}]\xi_i$ with $u_i = \ln \xi_i$ and based on which one can calculate the necessary expected values in terms of the assumed mean, variances, and covariances of the ξ_i's in order to solve for the preceding maximization problem. The authors then perform the calculation using some hypothetical figures for the market parameters.

6 ECONOMETRIC APPROACHES

As we mentioned earlier, while the rather large literature on random-coefficient models in econometrics can be reasonably viewed as falling within our domain of parameter stochasticity, we have resisted the temptation to include them here in this chapter. Instead, we will present a recent but promising application of the linear control theory with quadratic objective function commonly used in engineering literature and in certain economic stabilization models. We then report an econometric exercise on multi-brand advertising on the basis of the theoretical analysis we examined in an earlier chapter.

6.1 A Linear Control Formulation

In a recent work, Roy, Hanssens, and Raju [1994] offer a practical application of the linear optimal control and estimation problem to marketing decision-making. Even though it has been long applied to studies of stability problems in macroeconomics and in engineering literature, this approach appears to find its applications in management literature until only recently. Its empirical implementability is attractive and it has a reasonably good foundation in terms of the firm's objective of maintaining stable market shares (Saghafi [1988]). The fact that forecasts of certain stochastic variables such as future demand are to be used in the firm's decision process introduces important elements of demand uncertainty with which we are presently concerned in this work. Also, the notion of competition enables one to incorporate certain theoretical implications viewed in game theoretic contexts as well. Let us present the general features of the model as follows. Consider a two-brand scenario of market competition in which the first firm's objective is

$$\text{Min.} \quad \sum_{t=1}^{T} \rho^{t-1}[(q_{1,t}-q_1{}^*)^2 + (q_{2,t}-q_2{}^*)^2] \qquad (9.29)$$
$$\{p_1,p_2,...,p_T\}$$

where $q_{i,t}$ is the i-th firm's sales level in period t, q_i^* the firm's valuation of the i-th firm's constant sales target, assuming for empirical purposes further that the firm's expectation of the competitor's sales target coincides with the competitor's own sales target, ρ the discount factor, and the decision variables are the output prices.

The linear state equations are characterized as:

$$q_{i,t}=a_{ii}q_{i,t-1}+a_{ij}q_{j,t-1}-b_{ii}p_{i,t}+b_{ij}p_{j,t}+\xi_{i,t}; \quad i,j=1,2; \quad i\neq j \tag{9.30}$$

where we note the presence of the carryover effect and the nature of competition is marked by the positive sign of the coefficients b_{ij}; all coefficients are presumably positive; and $\xi_{i,t}$ represents the random term.

Note that intertemporality arises in this context mainly through the existence of the lagged variables in the same fashion which we discussed in Chapter 1. Applying the dynamic programming approach with the quadratic objective function yields the following optimal price rule, which is a feedback equation:

$$p_{i,t}^*=g_i+G_i q_{t-1}+S_i(u_{i,t}-\bar{u}_i) \tag{9.31}$$

where $q_{t-1} = (q_{1,t-1}\ q_{2,t-1})^T$, $u_{i,t} = (u_{ii,t}\ u_{ij,t})^T$, $\bar{u}_i = (\bar{u}_{ii,t-1}\ \bar{u}_{ij,t-1})^T$ in which $u_{ij,t}$ denotes firm i's forecasts of the random term $\xi_{j,t}$; $i,j=1,2$; and $\bar{u}_{ij,t-1}$ denotes the average forecasts by firm i of the ξ_j's over the time period $1,2,...,t-1$; and where

$$g_i=(b_i^T b_i)^{-1}b_i^T(q_i^*-b_j g_j)$$

$$G_i=-(b_i^T b_i)^{-1}b_i^T(A+b_j G_j)$$

$$S_i=-G_i(A+G_i^T b_i^T)+G_j^T b_j^T)\Omega\Gamma_i^{-1}$$

in which $A = [a_{ij}]$, $b_j = (b_{1j}\ b_{2j})^T$, Ω denotes the sales variance-covariance matrix, and Γ_i denotes the covariance matrix between the i-th firm's forecasts and actual sales by both firms.

The authors then illustrate the procedure of this control problem with the automobile industry, specifically the pricing behavior of the two car models, Ford Thunderbird and Chrysler New Yorker. This particular approach seems especially promising within the empirical effort to address the uncertainty issue. We find the notion that firms take into account the sales forecasts, and then through feedback rules, revise their pricing strategies in seeking to attain their objectives of market share stability quite appealing.

6.2 An Econometric Model

Theoretical results obtained earlier in Section 4 of Chapter 3 on multibrand advertising motivate us to estimate various sales-advertising relationships for the cigarette industry, and, in the process, a number of theoretical implications derived from the theoretical model are evaluated from an empirical perspective. Empirical studies on the subject of advertising include estimations of sales responses to advertising in management literature (see Weiss, Houston, and Windal [1978]; Little [1979]; and Windal and Weiss [1980]) as well as industrial organization implications of advertising in economics literature (see e.g., Brown [1978]; and Mueller and Rogers [1980]). Like the theoretical studies, empirical work on sales-advertising relations consists mostly of single-equation/single-brand models. However, the role of advertising is most crucial in a non-pricing-competitive environment in which many brands are produced to promote product differentiation.

One promising approach to capturing the competitive nature of advertising among various brands is to adopt the warfare model originally proposed by Lanchester (see Kimball [1957] for some early industrial applications of this model). Basically, the Lanchester model in the current context of competitive advertising can be spelled out as follows. The change in sales of a certain brand in a given time period consists of the sales gained from the competing brands due to its own advertising and the sales lost from its lagged value due to advertising in the competing brands. It has been shown in the Little survey [1979] that the Lanchester model yields empirically observed phenomena regarding sales responses to advertising, the shape of the steady-state response function, as well as the role of competitive advertising in generating sales. In particular, the Lanchester model yields the interesting result that one company's steady-state response function depends on its competitors' advertising. Previous models that have certain features of the Lanchester model include those considered by Horsky [1977] and Schmalensee [1978]. Little's survey paper provides earlier references on studies that are related to the Lanchester model. In spite of some important theoretical properties implied in it, as indicated in the Little survey, the Lanchester model of competitive advertising has not been seriously tested in the literature until recently. An earlier empirical work that has a flavor of interactive competition in the spirit of the Lanchester-type model is that by Horsky [1977], who considers the simpler case of a two-competitor world in which one competitor is the brand under consideration and the other is the rest of the industry. Although the two-competitor Lanchester model can be shown to be a generalization of the popular Vidale-Wolfe model [1957] with all the nice theoretical properties associated with it, it does not fully take into account interactions among various brands. In this section, econometric specifications are based on a more general version of the Lanchester competitive marketing model, which generally involves more than two brands. In this connection, we should note with particular interest the recent work by Erickson [1991 and 1991] who considers difficult theoretical issues as well as empirical implications of advertising in the Lanchester tradition using the differential game approach. The analysis in this sub-section is based on material reported in Nguyen [1987].

For our purposes here of focusing on the uncertainty aspect of the problem, the model that we empirically test is basically of the Lanchester type, which has been theoretically applied — not without success — to the marketing literature on competitive advertising. As stated before, the Lanchester warfare model seems particularly promising due to the nature of the competition among various cigarette brands. Further, this model readily enables us to perform tests on some of the theoretical specifications considered earlier in Chapter 3. Let us consider the following system of equations in the Lanchester tradition (see Little [1979]):

$$q_{i,t} - q_{i,t-1} = \beta_{ii} m_{i,t} \sum_{\substack{j=1 \\ j \neq i}}^{N} q_{j,t-1} + \left[\sum_{\substack{j=1 \\ j \neq i}}^{N} \beta_{ij} m_{j,t} \right] q_{i,t-1} ; \qquad (9.32)$$

$$i,j = 1,2,...,N; \quad t = 1,2,..., T$$

where there are N brands of a particular type of product, $q_{i,t}$ is the quantity of brand i sold in period t, $m_{i,t}$ is the advertising expenditure of brand i, and β_{ii} and β_{ij} refer to unknown coefficients to be estimated.

Let us note that the dependent variable represents the change in sales levels of brand i and that all sales variables on the right-hand side are of one-period lagged values. We also attempt to estimate a variant of the system in (9.32) in the following form:

$$q_{i,t} = \alpha_i q_{i,t-1} + \beta_{ii} m_{i,t} \sum_{\substack{j=1 \\ j \neq i}}^{N} q_{j,t-1} + \left[\sum_{\substack{j=1 \\ j \neq i}}^{N} \beta_{ij} m_{j,t} \right] q_{i,t-1} \qquad (9.33)$$

which reduces to (9.32) if the restriction that $\alpha_i = 1$ is imposed. It should be noted that (9.33) represents a linear specification of the theoretical sales response function. Estimating (9.33) allows us to test not only a linear version of the model but also the restriction that $\alpha_i = 1$ for all i implied in the Lanchester model.

Before reporting and interpreting the empirical results of our estimations of systems of equations in (9.32) and (9.33), we would like to make some remarks regarding the data to be used, the choice of brands to be included in the samples, and the econometric technique. First, we have chosen the cigarette industry for our empirical work not only because advertising represents a major determinant of cigarette sales but also because of the relative availability of data needed. Annual data on sales (in millions of units) and advertising (in billions of dollars at current prices) for various brands are published in various issues of *Advertising Age*, covering the period 1956-79. Figures on sales and advertising for the whole industry are given in the *Survey of Current Business* (various issues) and in publications by the *Leading*

National Advertisers(various issues). Since we have to deal with a relatively large number of parameters, we cannot afford to disregard a number of years in which data for some variables are not available. In these instances, we apply some simple interpolations in order to maintain a sufficient number of observations for estimation purposes.

Second, if the Lanchester models in (9.32) and (9.33) were to be estimated, all brands in the industry could be included in the analysis. However, one notes that, if the number of brands is N, the number of equations in system (9.32) is N with the total number of parameters to be estimated equal to N^2, which is quite large for a fairly small N, say, $N = 3$ or $N = 4$. This problem is particularly severe for the current empirical exercise due to the lack of time-series observations on sales and advertising (in particular, total number of observations is $T = 23$). Thus we are constrained not to exceed $N = 4$ for estimation purposes. More important, we are presently most interested in examining the effect of risk behavior and uncertainty in sales response functions on advertising decisions of various brands *produced by the same company*. Due to the preceding reasons, for each of the four major cigarette companies (namely, Reynolds, American Tobacco, Philip Morris, and Brown and Williamson), we construct a system of N equations as follows. The first $(N-1)$ equations correspond to the major brands produced by a particular company, and the N-th equation represents the rest of the industry. Third, since we wish to take into account as much as possible the interactions among various brands, we estimate the econometric model using the seemingly unrelated regressions (SUR) technique.

Empirical results are reported in *Table* 9.2. The coding scheme for the 12 brands is given in the note to the table. For each company, the "rest of industry" is coded by the subscript zero. Thus one notes that American Tobacco consists of brands 1 and 10; Philip Morris 8 and 11; Reynolds 2, 3, and 5; and Brown and Williamson 7, 9, and 12. The t-statistics are reported in the parentheses below the estimates of the system's parameters. In each panel, the first column reports the empirical results corresponding to the specification in equation (9.33), and the second column corresponds to equation (9.32).

This empirical exercise yields some interesting results. First, in estimating (9.33), let us note that all alpha coefficients are significantly positive. The t-statistics reported in parentheses under the estimates for these coefficients were calculated on the basis of the null hypothesis that $\alpha_i = 0$. On the other hand, since the Lanchester-type model implicitly imposes the constraints that $\alpha_i's$ are all equal to unity, it is of interest to test the null hypothesis that $\alpha_i = 1$ against the alternative hypothesis that $\alpha_i \neq 1$. Formally, the corresponding t-statistics were calculated as $t_i = (\hat{\alpha}_i - 1)/s_{\alpha_i}$, where s_{α_i} is the estimated standard error of $\hat{\alpha}_i$. The t-values under the null hypothesis that $\alpha_i = 1$ are reported in square brackets corresponding to each $\hat{\alpha}_i$. It follows that the evidence rejects the null hypothesis that $\alpha_i = 1$ in favor of the alternative hypothesis that α_i is different from unity for eight alpha coefficients out of a total of 14 coefficients for all four companies. As a result, estimates for the beta coefficients in (9.33) generally differ from those in (9.32) . In the interest of completeness, we have chosen to report the results for both cases when that constraint is imposed as well as when it is not.

Second, for each company, consider our estimates of the coefficient $\beta'_{ii}s$. Depending on the specifications of the sales-advertising relations, the coefficient β_{ii} represents the effect of advertising of brand i either on its own sales level or on the *change* of its own sales level. To simplify the verbal presentation, we will, however, refer to the dependent variable in both specifications as sales even when it actually represents the *change* of sales in specification (9.32). Since we expect that advertising of a particular brand induces a change in its sales level in the same direction, the null hypothesis is that $\beta_{ii} = 0$ with the alternative hypothesis that $\beta_{ii} > 0$. With the rule-of-thumb critical level of t-statistics at 2.00, one notes from *Table 9.2*, panel *A*, for American Tobacco that the null hypothesis $\beta_{00} = 0$ is rejected in favor of $\beta_{00} > 0$ for specification (9.32) reported in column 2. On the other hand, all the remaining $\hat{\beta}_{ii}$'s are found not to be statistically significantly different from zero (namely, $\hat{\beta}_{11}$ and $\hat{\beta}_{1010}$). For Philip Morris, as can be seen from panel B, it is found that both $\hat{\beta}_{88}$ and $\hat{\beta}_{1111}$ are significantly greater than zero in both specifications (9.32) and (9.33), whereas $\hat{\beta}_{00}$ is not significantly different from zero. Panel C for Reynolds indicates that only $\hat{\beta}_{55}$ in both specifications is significantly positive (perhaps with the exception that $\hat{\beta}_{33}$ is statistically positive at a slightly lower confidence level), while the remaining $\hat{\beta}'_{ii}s$ are found to be statistically zero. For Brown and Williamson in panel D, both $\hat{\beta}_{77}$ and $\hat{\beta}_{1212}$ in both specifications (9.32) and (9.33) are statistically positive while the remaining $\hat{\beta}'_{ii}s$ are zero in the statistical sense. All in all, about half of the 14 $\beta'_{ii}s$ coefficients are statistically positive, indicating that advertising of a particular brand increases its own sales level.

Third, let us now analyze the effects of advertising on other brands (within each company and the rest of the industry) on a particular brand's sales level. Once again, in the following discussion, we will refer to the dependent variable as sales for both specifications (9.32) and (9.33), For American Tobacco, the evidence appears to suggest that advertising on each of the company's two brands (brands 1 and 10) does not have any significant impact on the sales level of the company's other brand. However, advertising on the "non-American Tobacco" brand induces a negative effect on the sales levels of both brands of American Tobacco. On the other hand, while brand 1's (Pall Mall) advertising has no significant effect on the non-American Tobacco brand's sales, an increase in brand 10's (Tareyton) advertising results in a reduction in the sales level of the non-American Tobacco brand. For Philip Morris, the empirical results do not suggest any significant statistical relationships between advertising on various other brands on sales of any particular brand with the exception that advertising on the "non-Philip Morris" brand is negatively related to brand 8's (Marlboro) sales level. In panel C, the effect of the "non-Reynolds" brand's advertising on the sales level of *each* of the three brands of Reynolds is found to be negative. The evidence suggests that advertising on brand 5 (Salem) would induce a change in brand 2's (Camel) sales in the same direction. On the contrary, an increase in advertising on brand 2 would result in a decline in brand 5's

Table 9.2 *SUR Estimation*

	A. American Tobacco			B. Philip Morris			C. Reynolds			D. Brown & Williamson	
Est. Coef.	(1)	(2)	Est. Coef.	(1)	(2)	Est. Coef.	(1)	(2)	Est. Coef.	(1)	(2)
α_1	1.108		α_8	1.117		α_2	.877		α_7	1.089	
	(34.79)[3.40]			(19.58)[2.06]			(15.05)[-2.11]			(16.72)[1.37]	
β_{11}	-.213	.330	β_{88}	.659	1.027	β_{22}	.118	.180	β_{77}	.533	.548
	(-.49)	(.70)		(1.88)	(3.38)		(.70)	(1.33)		(2.73)	(3.15)
β_{110}	.229	.403	β_{811}	-1.139	5.404	β_{23}	-5.937	-2.415	β_{79}	6.419	1.871
	(.09)	(.13)		(-.21)	(.99)		(-1.68)	(-.80)		(1.27)	(.57)
β_{10}	-.424	-.238	β_{80}	-.498	-.491	β_{25}	12.176	12.710	β_{712}	-17.696	-12.020
	(-2.81)	(-1.42)		(-3.66)	(-3.29)		(3.72)	(4.59)		(-1.51)	(-1.26)
α_{10}	1.136		α_{11}	.905		β_{20}	-.310	-1.319	β_{70}	-1.055	-.612
	(14.42)[1.73]			(8.09)[-.85]			(-.44)	(-3.57)		(-2.57)	(-2.59)
β_{101}	2.845	5.313	β_{118}	-6.355	-2.050	α_3	1.128		α_9	1.153	
	(.74)	(1.75)		(-1.28)	(-.57)		(41.48)[4.71]			(15.47)[2.05]	
β_{1010}	.062	.081	β_{1111}	.708	.687	β_{32}	.421	-4.022	β_{97}	7.933	12.616
	(.32)	(.41)		(3.56)	(4.21)		(.21)	(-1.42)		(1.49)	(2.83)
β_{100}	-.688	-.352	β_{110}	.030	-.606	β_{33}	.619	.715	β_{99}	-.062	.158
	(-2.54)	(-1.62)		(.05)	(-1.82)		(1.78)	(1.50)		(-.18)	(.45)
α_0	1.042		α_0	1.048		β_{35}	-3.942	4.395	β_{912}	3.193	6.639
	(37.24)[1.50]			(45.50)[2.07]			(-1.23)	(1.02)		(.45)	(.98)

Coefficient	(1)	(2)
β_{01}	.168 (.10)	.420 (.25)
β_{010}	-7.724 (-3.43)	-8.748 (-3.89)
β_{00}	1.408 (1.48)	2.491 (3.72)
β_{08}	-1.437 (-.69)	.418 (.20)
β_{011}	-4.034 (-1.10)	1.938 (.73)
β_{00}	.370 (.43)	-.314 (-3.61)
β_{30}	-.483 (-1.49)	-.688 (-1.60)
α_{5}	.975 (24.29)[-.62]	
β_{52}	-4.625 (-2.72)	-5.177 (-2.72)
β_{53}	4.907 (-1.79)	-2.569 (-.94)
β_{55}	1.517 (5.02)	1.728 (6.28)
β_{50}	-.598 (-1.52)	-1.165 (-3.52)
α_{0}	1.039 (35.36)[1.34]	
β_{02}	.305 (.20)	-.715 (-.45)
β_{03}	-1.888 (-1.16)	-1.783 (-1.11)
β_{05}	2.002 (.77)	3.867 (1.44)
β_{00}	-.174 (-.31)	-.183 (-.47)
β_{90}	-.619 (-2.94)	-.550 (-2.65)
α_{12}	1.059 (13.84)[.77]	
β_{127}	-4.575 (-.75)	-1.483 (-.33)
β_{129}	-16.535 (-4.57)	-16.620 (-4.94)
β_{1212}	.611 (3.50)	.637 (3.87)
β_{120}	.453 (1.46)	.518 (1.93)
α_{0}	1.084 (36.74)[2.84]	
β_{07}	-3.463 (-1.44)	.625 (.28)
β_{09}	3.397 (1.24)	-1.252 (-.42)
β_{012}	-6.205 (-1.31)	1.920 (.41)
β_{00}	-1.174 (-1.16)	.370 (.32)

Notes: The coding scheme used is as follows:(1) Pall Mall, (2) Camel, (3) Winston, (4) Kent, (5) Salem, (6) L & M, (7) Viceroy, (8) Marlboro, (9) Kool, (10) Tareyton, (11) Parliament, and (12) Raleigh. Columns 1 and 2 correspond, respectively, to specifications in eqs. (9.33) and (9.32) defined in the text. The t-statistics reported in parentheses below each coefficient were calculated on the basis of the null hypothesis that the corresponding coefficient is zero. The t-statistics reported in square brackets below each alpha coefficient were calculated on the basis of the null hypothesis that the corresponding coefficient is equal to one.

sales level. In addition, there is some evidence of a negative impact of advertising on brand 3 (Winston) on the sales levels of both brand 2 and brand 5 at a lower level of statistical confidence. For Brown and Williamson, the empirical results suggest that while advertising on the non-Brown and Williamson brand is negatively related to the sales levels of both brand 7 (Viceroy) and brand 9 (Kool), it is positively related to the sales level of brand 12 (Raleigh). Within the company, sales of brand 9 (Kool) appear to benefit from advertising on brand 7 (Viceroy). However, an increase in advertising of brand 9 (Kool) would induce a decline in brand 12's (Raleigh) sales, and, at a lower statistical confidence level, a change in advertising of brand 12 would lead to a change in brand 7's sales in the opposite direction.

For our current purposes, the empirical evidence that advertising on a company's brand has a (statistically significant) negative impact on sales of the same company's other brand(s) — this being the case for both Reynolds, and Brown and Williamson — is of particular interest. Let us recall from the theoretical analysis in Chapter 3 that the "structural complementarity" condition specifies that the impact of advertising on brand j on the sales level of brand i produced by the same company be nonnegative. Empirical tests thus reveal that this condition of structural complementarity is violated for the industry under consideration.

Fourth, empirical work also allows us to test the "stochastic complementarity" condition postulated in the theoretical model. This condition states that all off-diagonal elements of the variance-covariance matrix of sales should be nonnegative. It is perhaps most useful to calculate and interpret the resulting correlation matrix. *Table* 9.3 reports $(N-1) \times (N-1)$ correlation submatrices which involve only $(N-1)$ brands produced by the same company (note that the N-th brand refers to the rest of the industry). Note also that results are presented for both specifications in (9.32) and (9.33). While we do not report the estimated variance-covariance matrices in the interest of space conservation, all the covariance terms contained in the corresponding $(N-1) \times (N-1)$ submatrices are positive. With the exception of the Philip Morris case, *Table* 9.3 indicates that sales among different brands in each company are positively correlated with each other. Thus it would appear that the condition of stochastic complementarity is supported on the basis of the empirical investigation of the cigarette industry.

Overall, the empirical results reveal some interesting facts regarding the interactions among various brands within a particular company and the remaining brands in the whole industry in terms of sales level and advertising budgets. The sign patterns of those interactions appear to vary from company to company and from brand to brand within each company. For the cigarette industry, these findings offer empirical tests on a number of assumed theoretical conditions and, consequently, enable us to evaluate certain theoretical results obtained earlier. We should emphasize that the econometric exercise reported here is intended to offer some empirical perspectives in assessing the potential effect of risk and uncertainty on the firm's advertising decisions, using the cigarette industry data set as an illustration. Further formal statistical tests need to be developed in future empirical research in order to evaluate fully the validity of the theoretical model. Also, data from other industries such as beer and soft drinks, to the extent that they are available, should yield additional empirical evidence to the issues considered here.

Table 9.3 *Correlation Submatrices*

A. American Tobacco					
1	.713		1	.678	
.713	1		.678	1	
B. Philip Morris					
1	.122		1	.050	
.122	1		.050	1	
C. Reynolds					
1	.388	.829	1	.206	.892
.388	1	.577	.206	1	.253
.829	.577	1	.892	.253	1
D. Brown & Williamson					
1	.648	.551	1	.642	.523
.648	1	.645	.642	1	.687
.551	.645	1	.523	.687	1

Notes: In each company, the left panel corresponds to specification in eq. (9.32) and the right panel corresponds to specification in eq. (9.33).

6.3 Summary

In order to assess certain theoretical implications of the multi-brand model of advertising presented earlier in Chapter 3, we estimate an econometric model in the Lanchester warfare tradition using the *SUR* technique. This estimation method has been used in several marketing studies in different theoretical contexts (see, e.g., Wildt [1974]). However, previous empirical works in the spirit of the Lanchester model of competitive advertising concentrate mainly on single-equation formulations (see, e.g., Horsky [1977]). The empirical exercise reported here generally indicates that the type of competitive advertising model for the cigarette industry considered has reasonable econometric support. The empirical findings show some interesting features regarding potential interactions among various brands produced by a single company. We found that, within a given cigarette company, advertising of its other brands and advertising in the remaining industry may affect favorably or unfavorably the sales level of a particular brand. The nature of the interactions varies from brand to brand within a given company, and it also varies from company to company. Of particular interest is the finding that, for both Reynolds and Brown and Williamson, an increase in advertising of one brand of the company may result in a decline in the sales level of the company's other brand. Consequently, for the cigarette industry under consideration, the empirical evidence indicates that the "structural complementarity" condition is clearly violated. Thus, our earlier theoretical analysis suggests that we would not be able to determine the precise impact of the company's risk behavior on the advertising budgets of its various brands. For this industry, it is quite possible that, as a company becomes more risk averse, it may reduce its advertising on certain brand(s) while it may increase its advertising budgets on the remaining brand(s). An important managerial implication of this outcome is the following. One may interpret an increase in advertising on a brand (and a corresponding increase in its sales level) as a result of the firm's risk-taking attitude —following the conventional result for single-product firms —while in fact the firm becomes more risk averse. Similarly, the impact of uncertainty in the sales response to advertising on the firm's advertising decisions becomes less predictable. The conventional result in the single-brand literature that the firm's advertising declines as uncertainty in the sales response function increases may no longer hold in a multibrand environment.

In short, one cannot be so certain about the potential impact on advertising policy of uncertainty in the sales response function and of the firm's attitude toward risk. It is entirely plausible that, as a change in the firm's risk-taking behavior or a change in the system's randomness takes place, a firm may decide to change advertising levels of some brands in one direction and those of the rest in the other direction. We believe that this type of unpredictable behavior further adds to the already complex sales-advertising relationships among the various brands. We speculate here that this behavior may be one of the explanations for the empirical finding that advertising on a brand may favorably or unfavorably affect its own sales level or the sales levels of other brands produced by the same company. This phenomenon has the important managerial implication that a company's advertising policy could conceivably lead to certain ultimate outcomes that the company does not intend to achieve. Our analysis also implies that it may not be easy to design a corrective strategy to counter this undesirable result in an optimal fashion, as has been suggested in numerous papers on optimal advertising for the single-brand firm (see, e.g., Sasieni [1971]; Horsky [1977]; Sethi [1977]; Horsky and Simon [1983]). This rather pessimistic conclusion should, however, point out the need for further research on optimal advertising in a multibrand competitive environment as opposed to continuing the extensive research on the single-brand firm.

7 CONCLUDING REMARKS

In this chapter, we consider various approaches to empirically assess some of the theoretical implications we have examined in the previous chapters. We first explore issues concerning experimentation plans on the part of the firm as it is faced with unknown parameters in sales response functions. We present a number of scenarios in which a firm may choose its production level in ways which help it learn more about the true market demand or experiment with its different advertising budgets in its effort to infer about the true parameter reflecting the sales response function. While the actual gain from these adaptive behaviors remain to be empirically validated and evaluated, the idea of giving up certain short-term benefits in order to induce a larger benefits through the additional gain in information seems appealing to any manager who has to deal on a daily basis with market uncertainty. On the other major subject in the chapter concerning econometric and simulation exercises in assessing the impact of uncertainty, it is unfortunate that the issues have not been extensively explored. We should mention that the large and important econometric literature on the specification and estimation of general random-coefficient models, while related to the topic of uncertainty in general, is not included in our discussion in this work. On the other hand, for marketing-relevant scenarios under uncertainty, much more econometric work and other statistical studies will be needed if we are to offer practical insights to the manager in dealing with market uncertainty.

REFERENCES

Advertising Age, Chicago: Crain Communications, Various issues.

ADVERTISING PUBLICATIONS, INC., "Cost of Cigarette Advertising," *Advertising Age*, various issues.

AYKAC, A., M. CORSTJENS, D. GAUTSCHI, and I. HOROWITZ, 1989, "Estimation, Uncertainty and Optimal Advertising Decisions," *Management Science*, Vol. 35, No. 1, pp. 42-50.

BLACKWELL, David, 1951, "The Comparison of Experiments," *in Proceedings of the Second Berkeley Symposium on Mathematical Statistics and Probability*, University of California Press, Berkeley, pp. 93-102.

BLACKWELL, David, 1953, "Equivalent Comparisons of Experiments," *Annals of Mathematical Statistics*, Vol. 24, pp. 265-272.

BROWN, R. S., 1978, "Estimating Advantages to Large-Scale Advertising," *Review of Economic Statistics*, Vol. 60, pp. 428-437.

DEGROOT, Morris H., 1970, *Optimal Statistical Decisions*, McGraw-Hill, Inc., New York.

ELIASHBERG, Jehoshua, and Rabikar CHATTERJEE, 1985, "Stochastic Issues in Innovation Diffusion Models," in *Models for Innovation Diffusion*, Vijay MAHAJAN, and R. A. PETERSON (eds.), Sage, California, pp. 151-199.

ELIASHBERG, J., V. G. MORWITZ, C. S. TAPIERO, and C. WIND, 1993, Innovation Diffusion Models with Stochastic Parameters, *manuscript*.

ERICKSON, Gary M., 1991, "Empirical Analysis of Closed-loop Duopoly Advertising Strategies," *Management Science*, Vol. 38, No. 12, pp. 1732-1749.

ERICKSON, Gary M., 1991, *Dynamic Models of Advertising Competition*, Kluwer Academic Publishers, MA.

GATIGNON, H., 1984, "Competition as a Moderator of the Effect of Advertising on Sales," *Journal of Marketing Research*, Vol. 21, pp. 387-398.

GLEJSER, H., 1969, "A New Test for Heteroscedasticity," *Journal of American Statistical Association*, Vol. 64, pp. 316-323.

GROSSMAN, S., R. KIHLSTROM, and L. MIRMAN, 1977, "A Bayesian Approach to the Production of Information and Learning by Doing," *Review of Economic Studies*, Vol. 44, pp. 533-547.

HANSSENS, Dominique M., Leonard J. PARSONS, and Randall L. SCHULTZ, 1990, *Market Response Models: Econometric and Time Series Analysis*, Kluwer Academic Publishers, Boston, MA.

HARPAZ, G., and S. B. THOMADAKIS, 1982, "Systematic Risk and the Firm's Experimental Strategy," *Journal of Financial and Quantitative Analysis*, Vol. 17, pp. 362-389.

HOLTHAUSEN, Duncan M., JR., and Gert ASSMUS, 1982, "Advertising Budget Allocation Under Uncertainty," *Management Science*, Vol. 28, No.5, pp 487-499.

HORSKY, Dan, 1977, "An Empirical Analysis of the Optimal Advertising Policy," *Management Science, Vol. 23*, pp. 1037-49.

HORSKY, Dan, and Leonard S. SIMON, 1983, "Advertising and the Diffusion of New Products," *Marketing Science,* Vol. 2, No. 1, pp. 1-17.

KIMBALL, G. E., 1957, "Some Industrial Applications of Military Operations Research Methods," *Operations Research*, Vol. 5, pp. 201-204.

KURAWARWALA, Abbas A., and Hirofumi MATSUO, 1992, "Forecasting and Inventory Management of Short Life Cycle Products," University of Texas at Austin, Austin, *manuscript.*

LEADING NATIONAL ADVERTISERS, various issues.

LITTLE, John D. C., 1966, "A Model of Adaptive Control of Promotional Spending," *Operation Research*, Vol. 14, pp. 1075-1097.

LITTLE, John D. C., 1979, "Aggregate Advertising Models: The State of the Art," *Operations Research*, Vol. 27, pp. 629-667.

MUELLER, W. F., and R. T. ROGERS, 1980, "The Role of Advertising in Changing Concentration of Manufacturing Industries," *Review of Economics and Statistics*, Vol. 62, pp. 89-96.

NGUYEN, Dung, 1985, "An Analysis of Optimal Advertising Under Uncertainty," *Management Science*, Vol. 31, pp. 622-633.

NGUYEN, Dung, 1987, "Advertising, Random Sales Response and Brand Competition: Some Theoretical and Econometric Implications," *Journal of Business*, Vol. 60, No. 2, pp. 259-279.

PEKELMAN, D., and E. TSE, 1980, "Experimentation and Budgeting in Advertising: An Adaptive Control Approach," *Operations Research*, Vol. 28, No. 2, pp. 321-347.

PRESCOTT, E., 1972, "The Multi-Period Control Problem under Uncertainty," *Econometrica*, Vol. 40, pp. 1043-1058.

ROY, Abhik, Dominique M. HANSSENS, and Jagmohan S. RAJU, 1994, "Competitive Pricing by a Price Leader," *Management Science*, Vol. 40, pp. 809-823.

SAGHAFI, Massoud M., 1988, "Optimal Pricing to Maximize Profits and Achieve Market-Share Targets for Single-Product and Multiproduct Companies," in T. DEVINNEY (ed.), *Issues in Pricing: Theory and Research,* pp. 239-253, Lexington Books, Lexington, MA.

SASIENI, M. W., 1971, "Optimal Advertising Expenditures," *Management Science*, Vol. 18, pp. 64-72.

SCHMALENSEE, Richard A., 1978, "A Model of Advertising and Product Quality," *Journal of Political Economy*, Vol. 86, pp. 485-503.

SETHI, Suresh P., 1977, "Dynamic Optimal Control Models in Advertising: A Survey," *Siam Review*, Vol. 19, pp. 685-725.

THOMPSON, Pattrick, and Ira HOROWITZ, 1993, "Experimentation and Optimal Output Decisions: the Cooperative Versus the Entrepreneurial Firm," *Management Science*, Vol. 39, No. 1, pp. 46-53.

U. S. DEPARTMENT OF COMMERCE, Various issues, *Survey of Current Business.*

VIDALE, M. L., and WOLFE, H. B., 1957, "An Operations Research Study of Sales Response to Advertising," *Operations Research*, Vol. 5, pp. 370-381.

WEISS, D. L., F. S. HOUSTON, and P. M. WINDAL, 1978, "The Periodic Pain of Lydia E. Pinham," *Journal of Business*, Vol. 51, pp. 91-101.

WILDT, A. R., 1974, "Multi-firm Analysis of Competitive Decision Variables," *Journal of Marketing Research*, Vol. 11, pp. 50-62.

WINDAL, P. M., and D. L. WEISS, 1980, "An Iterative GLS Procedure for Estimating the Parameters of Models With Autocorrelated Errors Using Data Aggregated Over Time," *Journal of Business*, Vol. 53, pp. 415-424.

WITTINK, DICK R., 1977, "Exploring Territorial Differences in the Relationship Between Marketing Variables," *Journal of Marketing Research*, Vol. 14, pp 145-155.

10

CONCLUDING NOTES

I have attempted in preceding chapters to analyze various aspects of the firm's decisions under conditions of uncertainty. My focus has been first on analysis in isolation of different components of the marketing mix such as pricing, advertising, price promotion, personal selling and production, then on potential interactions among them in a number of contexts. Important literature on consumer behavior with its intrinsic nature of random choice in the tradition of Thurstone [1927] and Luce [1959] as documented in Lilien, Kotler and Moorthy [1992] was, for the most part, *not* considered in this work. Rather, my emphasis has been on frameworks in which the firm's marketing and other managerial decisions may have to be modified under the presence of market uncertainty.

Uncertainty in a realistic business setting can of course come from different sources and can arise in different contexts. From the point of view of a firm's manager, I have, to a large extent, considered random demand to be the major form of market uncertainty. Actual demand or sales are determined not only by various marketing efforts and activities, but in addition, is subject to random disturbances outside the control of the firm. Thus sales response to a new product, promotional campaigns or pricing strategies can never be known with any great degree of accuracy. A major reason for such an uncertain response is due to the fact that consumers are not homogeneous, each with his or her own preferences and tastes and demographic, economic as well social identity. Even for each consumer, his or her utility is itself a random variable and may naturally be subject to dynamic changes. Yet, a useful approach to address this difficulty is to specify certain tractable statistical forms of random demand based on which the firm can design marketing activities in an effort to maximize its defined objective. The issue becomes even more complex as we consider the realistic assumption that the firm's marginal utility of money is not constant; hence it is the expected utility of profit rather than the profit itself which constitutes the firm's objective. The nonlinearity in utility which reflects the firm's generally non-neutral attitude towards risk, coupled with an effort to incorporate interactive marketing activities within a dynamic, competitive framework would represent a most satisfactory approach to deal with demand uncertainty. However, such an integrated, comprehensive approach, while very attractive, poses almost unsurmountable challenges. Consequently, one has to begin from basic static, stochastic formulations involving separate, individual components of the marketing mix for single-product monopolistic firms; then slowly address the extensions one by one to dynamic, interactive marketing decisions for multiple-product, competitive firms. This represents the approach I have taken in the development and organization of the book.

Even though I have provided a few paragraphs in each chapter's concluding sections to summarize certain major points therein, it may still be useful to recapitulate a number of general features and approaches in which uncertainty can have an effect on the firm's decisions. For the more specific results, the reader will have to refer to the relevant chapters.

Regarding the monopolistic firm's pricing decisions under conditions of random demand, it was shown how uncertainty in demand and the risk-taking behavior affect the well-known deterministic single-product pricing rules. Under similar conditions of a static, stochastic demand, the interaction between pricing and producing was explored. In addition, I examined implications for pricing multiple products as well as stochastic dynamic pricing. Finally, issues such as price wars, strategic pricing, informational differentiation, and loss-leader pricing under demand uncertainty were addressed.

A similar approach was undertaken in studying the firm's advertising effort under random sales response. I attempted to look at not only the way in which the static, deterministic optimal advertising has to be modified, but also how the joint decisions involving production-advertising and pricing-advertising can be made under uncertainty. In addition, the effects of risk aversion and random response were assessed for the multiple-product firms and the dynamic model of goodwill. Managerial implications of competitive advertising were also examined in market share attraction models and game-theoretic frameworks where notions of informative advertising as well as strategic advertising under uncertainty were analyzed.

I then proposed a number of models which have an economic flavor of the important marketing phenomenon of price promotion. The firm's commonly observed practice of offering a product at a discount (sales) price at certain frequency was viewed as a form of price discrimination which seeks to sort out the heterogeneous buying population. Along this line, I also developed an argument for the stochastic cyclic pricing practice in which sales events take place in a random fashion. Further, equilibrium and policy implications of heterogeneity in firms in terms of provision of information on their products were analyzed in connection with the issue of Resale Price Maintenance. I suggested also that even when consumers learn, price differences among stores can be maintained in equilibrium.

On the issue of salesforce and compensation, a number of recent developments on the basis of known and uncertain sales response to personal selling as well as asymmetry in information were briefly reviewed. In the context of principal agent formulations which have both features of self-selection and moral hazard, optimal designs of compensation schemes for the salesforce were obtained and interpreted. Of particular interest is the ability of these types of models in explaining the observed practice involving commission-based compensation schemes for the salesforce. I then formulated a different theoretical structure in dealing with the issue of labor heterogeneity and information asymmetry. An implication of this analysis is that wages for observationally equivalent workers among different functional departments within a firms may differ in equilibrium.

While the isolated treatment involving standard topics in research in marketing such as advertising, pricing, promotion and selling facilitated our basic understanding on each of these marketing decisions, my intention in this work has been geared towards a concerted effort to explore the managerial implications of risk-taking behavior and uncertainty within certain integrative contexts. Thus, I paid particular attention to theoretical structures in which one or two or more decision variables may enter and interact among themselves. In this regard, substantial space was devoted to study a variety of market share models, linear and non-linear, and of the *MCI* and *MNL* types of attraction models. I examined not only the impact of market uncertainty on the firm's marketing effort but also equilibrium analysis involving the effects of increasing competition and industry expansion for the attraction models. A number of stochastic extensions of the Bass-based deterministic diffusion processes were then reported. It was noted that stochasticity should play an essential role in dealing with diffusion processes due to their intrinsic unpredictability as they can easily be subject to random shocks.

In addition to searching for possible integration of different components of the marketing mix, I also considered possibilities for interactions between traditional marketing activities and other decision variables such as product quality, production, inventory and investment. Implications of stochasticity for the firm's joint decisions on production-inventory, inventory-pricing as well as production-advertising and pricing-investment strategies were reported. I devoted considerable space for an analysis on multiple-product production decisions under random demand with detailed discussion on the impact of various forms of taxation, given market uncertainty and the firm's risk-taking attitude. Within the competitive market structure, I also highlighted the role of asymmetry in the firm's risk-taking behaviors as well as the potential trade-off between production commitment and flexibility.

Finally, I recorded a number of empirical approaches in an effort to bring the theoretical development of this subject a little closer to its practicality in the regular conduct of a marketing manager. Among them was the notion concerning the adaptive behavior of the firm in experimenting with different levels of advertising or output in order to learn more about a particular unknown parameter of the sales response function facing the firm. This process of learning was shown to be intimately related to the issue of value of information as the firm seeks to deal with market uncertainty. Other empirically-motivated exercises included a number of approaches to simulation, econometric estimation and linear optimal control formulation.

Overall, I have attempted to include a number of important themes throughout the book. Some of the themes have been developed more extensively, others only at the beginning or in exploring states of research. I have organized these themes not only on the basis of what has already been accomplished in the literature but also on what remains to be done. Consequently, some of the general themes listed below also identify what I believe to be promising areas of possible future research on this subject. Let me list and comment selectively on them here, not necessarily in any order of importance:

1. Interactive marketing activities under random sales response: while significant progress has been made for static analysis, much more work is needed for dynamic characterizations of the firm's optimal marketing mix under uncertainty; further, implications for integrative efforts such as those of advertising and price promotion should be explored.

2. Cross-functional field interactions among marketing and the firm's other decision variables: a variety of models were advanced to address the joint decisions of pricing and production and inventory, of pricing and investment, of advertising and production, and of personal selling and supporting advertising; however, these models are essentially suggestive and preliminary and thus are in need of further refinements.

3. Multi-product marketing decision making: the existing literature has almost exclusively focused on single-product firms whereas reality dictates otherwise; certain analyses of the impact of random demand on multiple-product firms' various marketing strategies were given in the book but not nearly enough, especially in view of competition and dynamic considerations.

4. Empirical and econometric studies: aside form the large econometric literature on general random-coefficient models which is of limited interest in this work, empirical exercises in assessing the impact of uncertainty have not been extensively developed; much more econometric work will be needed to test and evaluate normative implications of the firm's behavior under stochastic conditions.

5. Public policy issues: it is most difficult to sort out public policy implications of various marketing programs and campaigns when their impact is not known with certainty; the notions of false advertisement, price collusion, unfair competition, etc. are intimately related to information and uncertainty issues.

In conclusion, it is my view that deeper understanding of marketing activities and their impact on the firm's profitability under conditions of uncertainty requires not only further theoretical developments but also empirical implementabilities of existing and newly-formulated theories. To accomplish these dual purposes, it appears that normative marketing models should be sufficiently integrative and yet analytically tractable so that simpler decision rules can be derived and empirically evaluated in such a way that the theoretical challenge facing academicians will be transformed into valuable tools readily accessible to practical marketing managers and other decision makers. Hopefully, the background I have gathered in this work may provide a spring board for further theoretical and empirical research towards this objective in the area of marketing decision-making under uncertainty.

REFERENCES

THURSTONE, L. L., 1927, "A Law of Comparative Judgement," *Psychological Review*, Vol. 34, pp. 273-286.

LILIEN, Gary L., Philip KOTLER, and K. Sridhar MOORTHY, 1992, *Marketing Models,* Prentice-Hall, Englewood Cliffs, NJ.

LUCE, Duncan R., 1959, *Individual Choice Behavior*, John Wiley, NY.

SUBJECT INDEX

A

Adaptive behavior. *See* Experimentation
Advertisement, informative, 253-254
Advertising, 64, 67, 76, 275
    adaptive model, 278-284
    and variance of sales, 77-79
    and entry, 245
    budget constraint, 289-290
    capital stock of goodwill, 80. *See also*
        Goodwill models
    competitive, 252-259
    dynamic, 79-86
    in market share models, 254-256
    multi-brand, 70-79
    production-advertising, 216-217
    quadratic response function, 272, 279
    single-product, 60-65
    strategic, 256-259
    supporting, 137-140
Attraction Specification, 187. *See also* Market
    share models

B

Bass diffusion process, 79, 190-197, 199. *See*
    also Diffusion models
Bayesian approach, 52, 54-55
Bellman equation, 44, 82
Bismut's stochastic maximum principle, 83
Brownian motion, 43, 81

C

Capacity constraint, 246, 248
Capital accumulation process, 80, 230
Capital Asset Pricing Model, 135-137, 195,
    276-277
Certainty-equivalent solution, 26-27, 63, 215-
    216, 218, 277. *See also* Determin-
    istic models
Collusion, perfect, 241
Collusive behavior, 247

Commission rates, 142, 145

Compensation. *See* Salesforce compensation,
    Heterogeneous salesforce
Competitive marketing strategies. *See also*
    Pricing, Advertising, Production
    deterministic, 238-246
    game-theoretic, 240-246
Complementarity, product, 223
Complementarity, stochastic, 76, 298
Complementarity, structural, 75, 298
Conjectural variation, 241
Consumer heterogeneity and diffusion pro-
    cesses, 197-198
Consumer's learning behavior, 120-125
Consumer's utility maximization, 181-182
Contestable markets under uncertainty, 264-
    266
Control approach, continuous, 41-45, 81-85
Control formulation, linear, 249, 290-291
Control problem, non-randomized, 16
Control variable, open-loop, 174
Cost functions, 7, 36, 37, 72, 75, 94, 172,
    212, 220, 265, 280
Cost minimization, 140, 212-213
Cost of advertising, 7, 80
Couponing. *See* Price promotions
Culling rate, 205*ff*

D

Deals. *See* Price promotions
Demand, unsatisfied 29-31, 212-213, 278
Deterministic models
    Bass diffusion processes, 190-192
    competitive framework, 238-246
    dynamic advertising, 80-81
    dynamic pricing, 41-43
    economic lot-size model, 211-212
    market share models, 254-255
    MCI models, 175-178
    pricing rule, 27, 80
    salesforce size, 131-133
    Vidale-Wolfe model, 84

M

Market share models, 170-190. *See also, MCI*
    models, *MNL* model
    advertising in, 254-256
    random linear, 171-173
    random nonlinear, 173-175
Market shares, stable, 290
Marketing and production, 155-157
Marketing mix models
    deterministic, 6-8, 136
    dynamic, 246
    price and marketing variables, 242
    static games, 239-240
Marketing strategies. *See* Competitive
    marketing strategies
Marketing-production, stochastics, 212-217
    MCI Models
    basic version, 175
    deterministic, 175-178
    extensions, 177
    sales uncertainty, 178
Minimum quality, optimal, 207*ff*
MNL models
    and random utility, 180-183
    asymmetric competition, 184-186, 187-
        188
    basic, 183
    industry expansion, 184, 186-188
Multi-brand advertising, 70-79, 292-299
Multiple products
    pricing, 36-41, 120-125
    production, 219-229
    salesforce allocative efforts, 141-143

N

Nerlove-Arrow model of goodwill accumula-
    tion, 79*ff*, 137, 245

O

One-period models. *See* Static models
Optimality, Bellman principle of, 17

P

Parameter uncertainty, 272, 274-275
Parameters, stochastic, 287

Perron-Frobenius theorem, 76, 162
Pontryagin's deterministic maximum princi-
    ple, 83
Potential market
    expanding, 184, 186-188
    variable, 46, 191-192
Pratt-Arrow index for risk aversion, 10, 172,
        179, 220, 261, 275
Price differences, 120-125
Price model, administered, 112-115
Price, optimal intertemporal, 49-50, 194, 244
Price promotions, 90, 94
    demand at regular price, 93, 98
    industry equilibrium, 99-101
    single-price solution, 95-96
    two-price solution, 96-98, 106*ff*, 115-118
Price, reference, 92*ff*
Price wars, 247
Price-setting vs. output-setting
    monopolistic, 31-35
    oligopolistic, 249-251
Price-setting,14-19, 24-29, 34, 48*ff*, 139-140,
        231, 240
Price-timing model, 46
Pricing
    competitive, static, 238-240
    competitive, stochastic, 247-248
    dynamic and deterministic, 41-43
    dynamic and stochastics, 43-46
    dynamic with entry, 243-244
    multiple-product, 36-41
    single-product, static 24-35
    stochastic cyclic, 103-111
    strategic, 247-248
Pricing rule
    competitive, 238-239
    monopolistic, 27, 84, 214-215
Principle of increasing uncertainty, 33
Product competition, 260
Production decisions, 33, 217-218
    as an experiment, 278
    fully committed production, 267
    output pre-commitment and flexibility,
        264, 266
    partial production commitment, 266
Production function, 229
Production strategy, 263, optimal equilibrium
Production-advertising decision-making, 216
Production-inventory, 212